The Wars of Justinian

The Wars of
Justinian

Michael Whitby

Pen & Sword
MILITARY

First published in Great Britain in 2021 by
Pen & Sword Military
An imprint of
Pen & Sword Books Ltd
Yorkshire – Philadelphia

ISBN 978 1 52676 088 3

Printed and bound in the UK by CPI Group (UK) Ltd, Croydon, CR0 4YY

Pen & Sword Books Limited incorporates the imprints of Atlas, Archaeology,
Aviation, Discovery, Family History, Fiction, History, Maritime, Military, Military
Classics, Politics, Select, Transport, True Crime, Air World, Frontline Publishing,
Leo Cooper, Remember When, Seaforth Publishing, The Praetorian Press,
Wharncliffe Local History, Wharncliffe Transport, Wharncliffe True Crime and
White Owl.

For a complete list of Pen & Sword titles please contact

PEN & SWORD BOOKS LIMITED
47 Church Street, Barnsley, South Yorkshire, S70 2AS, England
E-mail: enquiries@pen-and-sword.co.uk
Website: www.pen-and-sword.co.uk

Or
PEN AND SWORD BOOKS
1950 Lawrence Rd, Havertown, PA 19083, USA
E-mail: Uspen-and-sword@casematepublishers.com
Website: www.penandswordbooks.com

For Lynne

Contents

Preface

This book originated in an approach from Philip Sidnell in 2010 asking whether I might be interested in contributing a volume on Justinian to his Pen and Sword collection. At the time, though the proposal was interesting, the move to a new job and then the challenges of university affairs and defending the Humanities meant there was no opportunity for anything other than desultory thoughts until my retirement in autumn 2019, so that I could not pretend that the following pages have benefitted from years of reflection and refinement. The delay has, however, enabled me to learn from the numerous recent publications relevant to Late Antiquity that demonstrate the continuing vitality of the subject. Selection of individual items is inevitably invidious, but David Potter's *Theodora* places a much-maligned individual in a proper context and the volumes of Liverpool University Press's *Translated Texts for Historians* series constantly extend the range of material that is readily available in modern versions with good annotation. That said, the arrival of the Covid pandemic in early 2020, while offering some insights into how contemporaries might react to an unfamiliar disease sweeping across frontiers with lethal impact, has prevented me from reading everything that I might otherwise have done in spite of the considerable resources available on-line.

Procopius is inevitably integral to any treatment of Justinian's wars, since his selection and presentation of information dominate our perceptions of events. While many traditional Procopian 'problems' were laid to rest a generation ago by Averil Cameron, the literary study of Procopius as a writer remains in its infancy, although there are encouraging signs in the work of Elodie Turquois on the *Buildings* and Conor Whately on the *Wars*. Although Procopius is our most important source for military events in the first two-thirds of Justinian's reign, I have aimed to avoid my account becoming a mere paraphrase of his version of events by presenting alternative versions wherever possible.

* * *

My main debts are to my family. My three sons, Max, Brodie, and Archie, have all dutifully enquired about progress over the years and, having repeatedly received parental admonitions to submit school and university work on time, have repaid the compliment. My wife Lynne has tolerated my occupation of our dining room for much of the past ten months and has also kept me supplied with all necessities while I was confined during the lock-down as one being 'shielded'. This volume does not represent what she might like me to have written (as she has often made clear!), but then I am a historian rather than a novelist and in any case, it would be a rash individual who attempted to surpass Robert Graves' *Count Belisarius*. It is dedicated to her with love and gratitude for everything, all her love and support over the years as well as the toleration of exile in the West Midlands.

Special thanks are due to Irene Moore for the excellence of her copy-editing and assistance with the images, and to my son Max for his patient tuition and support in the creation of Inkscape maps.

About the author

Michael Whitby is an ancient historian whose main interests lie in the late Roman period, specifically in the eastern empire during the sixth and early seventh centuries with a particular focus on warfare, religion and ancient texts. He studied as an undergraduate and postgraduate at the University of Oxford, where he also held a number of short-term positions, before moving to the University of St Andrews and then the University of Warwick. In 2010 he was appointed to the University of Birmingham as Head of the College of Arts & Law with responsibility for education and research across these broad disciplines. Since retiring in 2019 he has returned to academic research and writing.

The Mediterranean World in the Sixth Century

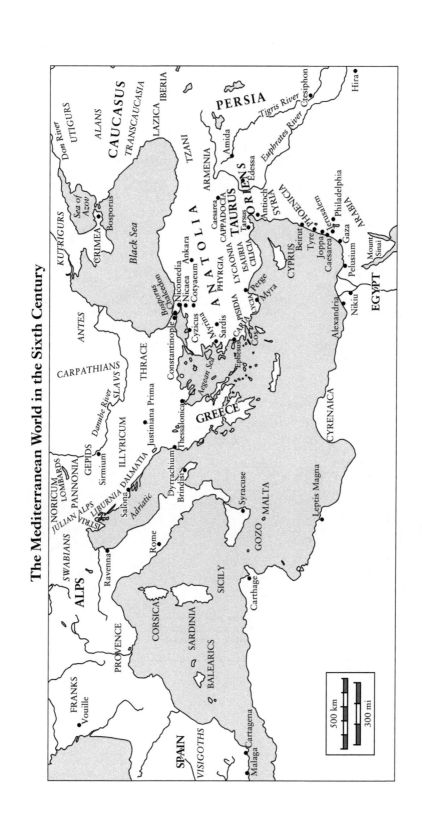

The Roman Near East

North Africa

Italy

The Balkans

NORICUM

PANNONIA

River Drava

Danube

River Sava

CARPATHIANS

SCYTHIA

Turris

BLACK SEA

River Danube

Singidunum

Sirmium

Viminacium

DALMATIA

UPPER MOESIA

DACIA

ILLYRICUM

Horreum
Margi

River Morava

Naissus

Novae

LOWER MOESIA

Asemus

Nicopolis

Odessus

Scardona

Salona

Spalato

Lesina

Dichin

HAEMUS MOUNTAINS

THRACE

Serdica

DARDANIA

Justiniana
Prima

Ulpiana

Epidaurus

Pautalia

Philippopolis

Adrianople

Arcadiopolis

Heracleia

Constantinople

River Hebrus

Selymbria

Drizipera

Dyrrachium

Via Egnatia

Topirus

Anastasiopolis

Apri

Tzurullon

SEA of MARMARA

Melantias

Pylae

Brindisi

Dryus

EPIRUS

Thessalonica

Cassandreia

Pallene

Chersoneese

Panium
Hellespont

Abydus

CORFU

Sybotae islands

ACARNANIA

Thermopylae

AETOLIA

AEGEAN SEA

Athens

CARIA

ZACYNTHUS

PELOPONNESE

CYCLADES

Methone

Cape Malea

Cape Taenarum

150 km

100 mi

Constantinople in the Sixth Century

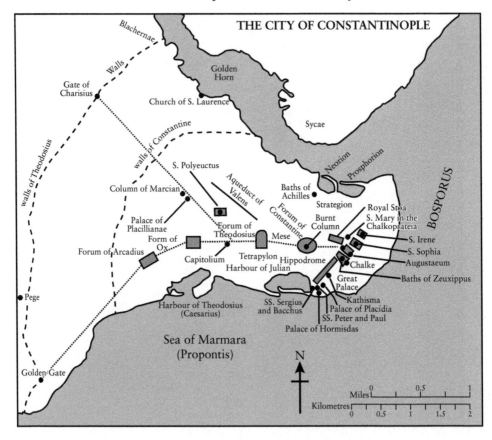

THE CITY OF CONSTANTINOPLE

Blachernae

Walls

Golden
Horn

Gate of
Charisius

Church of S. Laurence

Sycae

walls of Theodosius

walls of Constantine

Neorion

Prosphorion

S. Polyeuctus

BOSPORUS

Column of Marcian

Aqueduct of Valens

Baths of Achilles

Strategion

Royal Stoa

Palace of Placillianae

Forum of Theodosius

Forum of Constantine

Burnt Column

S. Mary in the Chalkoprateia

Form of Ox

Mese

S. Irene

Capitolium

Tetrapylon

Hippodrome

Chalke

S. Sophia

Forum of Arcadius

Harbour of Julian

Augustaeum

Baths of Zeuxippus

Pege

Great Palace

Harbour of Theodosius
(Caesarius)

SS. Sergius
and Bacchus

Kathisma
Palace of Placidia

Sea of Marmara
(Propontis)

SS. Peter and Paul

Palace of Hormisdas

N

Golden Gate

Miles
0   0.5   1

Kilometres
0   0.5   1   1.5   2

Chapter 1

Justinian, Man and Ruler

J ustinian had been born Flavius Petrus Sabbatius, probably in the early 480s, at the small settlement of Tauresium near Scupi (modern Skopje in Northern Macedonia). Nothing more is known about his father Sabbatius, but his mother, whose name might have been Biglenzia,[1] was sister to Justin, a Balkan peasant from Bederiana near Scupi, who had travelled to Constantinople in the 460s or 470s to escape rural poverty through military service. Justin and two companions, Zimarchus and Ditubistus, were promptly enrolled in the imperial guards, perhaps the main units of the *scholae palatinae*, or possibly in the *excubitores*, the new personal bodyguard that Emperor Leo happened to be creating in order to counteract the influence of Gothic federate troops and their leaders in the capital. Whichever unit it was, the ability to enter an elite regiment suggests that one or more of the trio had powerful contacts. Granted the numbers of recruits from the Balkans in imperial armies, it is very likely that they had friends or acquaintances from the region of Scupi who were already pursuing successful careers in Constantinople.

Although he lacked a formal education, Justin clearly established a reputation as a competent soldier, since he had reached the rank of *comes* (count) by the 490s, when he served as a senior officer under the *magister officiorum* Celer in the Isaurian and Persian wars of Emperor Anastasius.[2] He must also have been seen as reliable, perhaps in part because a lack of learning appeared to exclude him from higher things,[3] and by 515 he had become *comes excubitorum*, commander of the most important unit

---

1. Vasiliev, *Justin* 59, acknowledging that the only source for this name, the *Vita Theophili*, is of dubious value.
2. Full details of his pre-imperial career in *PLRE* II 648–51, Iustinus 4.
3. This is not to accept at face value the assertion in Procopius (*SH* 6.11–16) that he was totally illiterate because he had to use a stencil to subscribe documents: the imperial monogram was complex and a stencil would have ensured consistency. But for this accusation to have credence it is likely that Justin's education was limited, as Malalas (17.1) reports.

of imperial bodyguards, when he contributed to defeating the revolt of Vitalian. At some point in his rise Justin adopted his nephew, who hence acquired the additional name Justinianus,[4] quite possibly early in the 500s since the young Justinian benefitted from the sort of expensive education that his uncle lacked. As was common, Justin also secured an imperial position for his adopted son, who was enrolled in the *scholae*, the larger body of imperial guards. There is no evidence that Justinian ever saw active service, but by 518 he had also joined the elite *candidati*, the forty white-clad guards in personal attendance on the emperor. Here was a young man who was already being marked out for rapid advancement.

In 518 the elderly Anastasius died without making arrangements for the succession; although he had three nephews, each of whom had held the consulship and other high offices, none had been identified as the preferred heir. Justin and Justinian were involved in the ensuing machinations, details of which are preserved in a contemporary account by Peter the Patrician.[5] At dawn on 10 July the senators and Patriarch assembled inside the Great Palace to argue over possible successors. The *magister officiorum* Celer urged that a rapid decision was needed if matters were not to be taken out of their hands, but the senators continued to debate. Meanwhile in the adjacent Hippodrome the populace initially chanted respectfully about the Senate, but before long they and the imperial guards began to identify specific candidates. First the *excubitores* chanted for the tribune John, a relative of Justin, but the Blues objected, then the *scholae* moved to crown Flavius Patricius, one of the two *magistri militum praesentales*; Patricius, however, was fiercely opposed by the *excubitores*, to the extent that his life was in danger until Justinian intervened to protect him.

The *excubitores* now tried to proclaim Justinian himself, another indication that he was already a person of some influence, but he demurred. Peter's account now slides from this unregulated confusion to the eventual decision by the senators to select Justin, despite his protestations to the contrary and the opposition of some *scholarii*, one of whom even punched Justin in the face. This decision secured the support of the populace, soldiers and the Blue and Green factions, who led universal chanting:

---

4. The full name is evident at the top of Justinian's consular diptych of 521 (Plate 2).
5. Constantine Porphyrogenitus, *de Caerimoniis* 1.93; Vasiliev, *Justin* 69–73, provides a detailed summary.

Prosperity for the *oikoumene*; as you have lived, so may you reign; prosperity for the state; heavenly father, save the world. Justin Augustus, you are victorious; many years for the new Constantine. We are the slaves of the emperor.

It was subsequently alleged that Justin had received money from the imperial chamberlain, the eunuch Amantius, to distribute among the *excubitores* to support the candidacy of a member of his own household, Theocritus, but instead deployed it in his own interest. Such machinations cannot be corroborated, but are plausible: Amantius shared the anti-Chalcedonian religious preferences of Anastasius and would have feared the consequences of the rise of an orthodox rival such as Celer or Justin, while Peter the Patrician, writing during Justinian's reign, would naturally gloss over such subterfuges in his account of the formal ceremonial process that gave the throne to his imperial master's family.

Justinian was an important person in 518 but his adopted father's accession did not immediately make him the second most powerful person in the empire, as the example of Anastasius' nephews demonstrated. That, however, has not stopped many scholars over the past century from treating Justin as a virtual puppet, ignorant, illiterate, and senile, whose strings were pulled from the outset by Justinian in what was a virtual preface to his own reign. Although this view can be traced back to Procopius, this interpretation reflects Procopius' desire in the *Secret History* to blacken Justinian's reputation by ascribing to him unfavourable events from his uncle's reign.[6] Initially, for the first two years of the new reign it would have appeared that Vitalian, who had rebelled three times against Anastasius on religious grounds, was Justin's right-hand man: he was appointed *magister militum praesentalis* and possibly patrician in 518, and then had the signal honour of being the eastern consul in 520, the first after the new emperor himself in 519. In doctrinal synods at Tyre and Apamea Vitalian, with his reputation as a champion of Chalcedon, was acclaimed alongside the emperor and empress; in Pseudo-Zachariah he is even said to have 'presided over the course of affairs'.[7] As for Justinian, although Justin removed many of Anastasius' senior appointees, it does not appear that he promoted his

6. Proc., *SH* 6.19. Stein, *Bas-Empire* 2.222, 273; Vasiliev, *Justin* 82–5; Evans, *Age* 97; Bury, *HLRE* 2.23.
7. Ps.-Zach., *HE* 8.2.a. Vasiliev, *Justin* 145–60, for translations of the chants that are preserved in the *Acta Conciliorum Oecumenicorum* III. 31–2, 33–7.

nephew into any of the vacant posts, and his name was not included in the bishops' chanting at these synods in 519.

Most of our evidence for Justinian's actions in the first two years of the new reign is preserved in the record of papal correspondence and so naturally relates to his contributions to religious diplomacy. He played a prominent part in re-establishing relations with the Pope in Rome: these had been ruptured in the 480s by the Acacian Schism over Emperor Zeno's initiative to downplay the Council of Chalcedon, and had then been intensified by Anastasius' support for opponents of the Council. Justinian wrote numerous letters to Pope Hormisdas, receiving several replies, accompanied Vitalian and Pompeius as the imperial representatives to welcome Hormisdas' envoys outside Constantinople on 25 March 519, and requested relics of Peter, Paul and Lawrence to sanctify the church he was constructing next to his residence in Constantinople.[8] Justinian is located among a group of the new emperor's inner circle to whom the Pope wrote to advance his interests. If Justinian stands out in any way, it is in his engagement with specific issues, the doctrinal challenge posed by the Theopaschite initiative associated with a group of Scythian monks, and the procedural question of ending the condemnation of the patriarchal contemporaries of Acacius, obstacles which threatened to derail the desired rapprochement of East and West.[9]

Things changed in July 520, when Vitalian and two of his household were summoned by Justin from the baths – probably the adjacent Baths of Zeuxippus – to join Justinian at a banquet in the palace.[10] The three were murdered in the Delphax, the first major courtyard inside the palace entrance. There were accusations that Vitalian was scheming against Justin;[11] Justinian, however, was inevitably held responsible by Procopius, although he is not named in earlier sources.[12] Both accusations are unprovable but not implausible: Vitalian might have been scheming in fear for his prospects

---

8. *Collectio Avellana* 147–8, 154, 162, 176; the three envoys: 223.1; relics: 218. Discussion of the exchanges in Vasiliev, *Justin* 160–83.

9. The Theopaschite formula stressed that it was God who suffered on the Cross, an idea originally advanced by opponents of Chalcedon. It was gradually accepted as orthodox, since it closed a loophole that Nestorians could exploit by arguing that it was only the human person in Christ that had suffered crucifixion, not the divine. *Collectio Avellana* 187–91, 196. See Vasiliev, *Justin* 190–7, for discussion.

10. Ps.-Zach., *HE* 8.2.

11. John of Nikiu 90.11–12.

12. Proc., *SH* 6.28; Marc.Com. *s.a.* 520; Malalas 17.8, Thurn p. 339.

in the medium term, whereas Justinian might have begrudged Vitalian the eminence he believed to be his own by right. Justinian would not have committed the murder in person, but an indication of the culprits may be preserved in the *Chronicle* of Victor of Tunnuna, in which the *factio* of Justinian is blamed.[13] This might mean no more than the party, or partisans, of Justinian, but the information could be linked with the accusation in Procopius that Justinian used members of the Blue Hippodrome faction, of which he was a patron, to terrorize other aristocrats.[14] Vitalian might have been one of their victims, although Procopius would in that case have missed an opportunity to attach a specific incident to his general accusation. At any rate Justinian was the clear beneficiary, since he now succeeded Vitalian as *magister militum praesentalis* and held the eastern consulship in 521. The celebrations in the Hippodrome on 1 January for the start of his consulship were more magnificent and spectacular than anyone could recall, with a massive 288,000 gold *solidi* (4,000 pounds) distributed to the people or spent on entertainments.[15]

The example of Anastasius' reign demonstrated that, even so, Justinian's future elevation was not automatic and he did not yet immediately secure his own way in everything. Apart from Anastasius' nephews, who remained prominent, Anicia Juliana, daughter of the western emperor Olybrius (472) also lived in Constantinople. Her husband, Areobindus, had briefly been acclaimed as emperor in 512 during religious rioting against Anastasius, and she may now have entertained imperial hopes for her son, the patrician Olybrius.[16] At some point early in Justin's reign and in unknown circumstances, Justinian met and fell in love with Theodora,[17] a former mime actress who had previously been the mistress of Hecebolus, provincial governor of Pentapolis (eastern Libya), by whom she had a daughter. It was illegal for a person of Justinian's elevated status to marry a former stage performer or prostitute, and fierce opposition from the empress Euphemia (Lupicina before her elevation) to the liaison prevented anything being done

---

13. Victor, *Chronicle* 107.
14. Cf. Whitby, 'Violence' 242–3. For Justinian and the circus factions, see Ch.9.
15. Marc.Com. *s.a.* 521.
16. Harrison, *Temple* ch.1. The epigram commemorating the dedication in the 520s of her grand church to S. Polyeuctus referred to the past and continuing royal eminence of her family.
17. That Justinian loved Theodora is speculation, but is plausible in view of the lengths to which he had to go in order to marry her. For an image, possibly posthumous, of Theodora and her entourage, see Plate 4.

to change the situation during her lifetime.[18] At some point in 521–2, however, Justin addressed a law to the praetorian prefect Demosthenes,[19] which forgave women the errors of their ways.[20] It is likely that Justinian married Theodora shortly after promulgation of the law.

Even this was not the end of Justinian's difficulties. In 523 he contracted a serious illness, which removed him from public affairs and led to fears for his life; it also provided an opportunity for opponents to act. The major cities of the empire, especially Constantinople, were seriously afflicted by the rioting of the Hippodrome factions until Justin appointed the former *comes Orientis*, Theodotus Colocynthius (the pumpkin), as city prefect. Theodotus acted decisively, arresting and executing a rich *illustris* Theodosius, pursuing many others, and receiving accusations against Justinian. At this point Justinian made a remarkable recovery, with the result that Theodotus, after being accused of killing Theodosius without imperial permission, was relegated to Jerusalem; there, in fear of assassination, he took refuge in a church for the remainder of his life.[21]

Perhaps as a consequence of surmounting this threat Justinian received the exalted title of patrician, hence placing him on the same level as the nephews of Anastasius and probably also Olybrius, with Theodora enjoying the parallel honour of *patricia*. At some point before 527 Justinian was granted the even less common title of *nobilissimus*, which did distinguish him from other senior figures, and he may also have been elevated as Caesar in 525 at the senate's request.[22] In the latter part of Justin's reign, Justinian could be regarded as the virtual ruler of the empire under his uncle, but still Justin resisted a petition from the Senate to make Justinian co-emperor.[23]

---

18. Proc., *SH* 9.47.
19. Accepting the dates for Demosthenes' tenure of office in *PLRE* II.354–5, *s.v.* Demosthenes 4; the earliest attestation, however, for the next praetorian prefect, Archelaus 5, is August 524 so that the law might be slightly later, possibly even after the crisis covered in the next paragraph. The year of Euphemia's death is not known, so does not help clarify matters.
20. For discussion of the law, see Potter, *Theodora* 91–3, but also more generally for his intelligent analysis of Theodora in the broader context of imperial women and Roman social relations.
21. John of Nikiu 90.16–23; Malalas 17.12; Proc., *SH* 9.35–42. John says that Justinian fell ill after his arrest and this triggered his release, but the sequence in Procopius of the serious illness preceding Theodotus' actions against the factions seems more plausible.
22. Marc.Com. *s.a.* 527, indicating that he had held the title for some time but without giving the exact date. Victor of Tunnuna, *s.a.*, is the only evidence for the position of Caesar, but it might have been conferred at the same time as the title of *nobilissimus*, which was reserved for the children of emperors.
23. Cyril, *Life of Saba* 68; Zonaras 14.5.35.

In 525, during discussion of the request from the Persian king, Kavadh, that his third son, Khusro, should be adopted by Justin to strengthen his claim to succeed to the Persian throne, the *quaestor* Proculus opposed the move and urged Justinian to do the same for fear that it might endanger his own chances of succeeding Justin.[24]

Justinian's trajectory was clear in 525, but it was not until April 527 that his place in the succession was eventually confirmed. Justin had fallen seriously ill and, responding to yet another request from the Senate, in a ceremony held inside the palace in the Delphax rather than in the Hippodrome, with the *magister officiorum* Tatianus arranging matters and the Patriarch blessing the result, he appointed Justinian as co-emperor. Four months later Justin died on 1 August, to be succeeded by his nephew who was now probably aged 45.[25]

The contemporary chronicler, John Malalas, presented Justinian as follows:

> In appearance he was short, with a good chest, a good nose, fair-skinned, curly-haired, round-faced, handsome, with receding hair, a florid complexion, with his hair and beard greying; he was magnanimous and Christian.[26]

This description was written in about 530 by someone, who, even though they are most unlikely to have been in close proximity to the new emperor, would have known or worked with people who had seen him or would have seen the images of the new emperor that were routinely distributed throughout the empire's cities. It is compatible both with the hostile account in Procopius and with the most famous representation of Justinian, the mosaic on the apse wall of San Vitale in Ravenna that was created in the mid-540s by craftsmen who must have been working from an image.[27] In terms of nose, skin, curly hair and face there is nothing in the mosaic to contradict Malalas, although the bejeweled crown means that the hairline is not visible and the emperor is beardless. The last bearded emperor had been Julian the Apostate, for whom the beard had philosophical associations, so this was not a good model for a devout Christian; with regard to Anastasius,

---

24. Proc., *Wars* 1.11.11–18.
25. Const.Porph. *de Caer.* 95; Zonaras 14.5.40.
26. Malalas 18.2. This description is compatible with the image of Justinian and his entourage in San Vitale, Ravenna (Plate 3; Plate 1 for detail of the head).
27. Proc., *SH* 8.12.

Malalas had noted that he frequently shaved his greying beard,[28] and Justinian probably did the same.

Unlike his uncle, Justinian could not be accused of illiteracy, although close analysis of Latin texts that may well have been composed by him suggests that he could not achieve the mellifluous style of the professional legal authors in the office of the *quaestor*.[29] His correspondence with Pope Hormisdas reveals that he could cite doctrinal texts by Augustine,[30] while his later doctrinal initiatives, such as the Theopaschite formula and the Three Chapters, demonstrate that he was well-versed in Greek theological literature. He was, indeed, probably one of the very few people in the empire who was equally competent in Latin and Greek patristic argument. Amidst the numerous criticisms of his character and actions in the *Secret History* there may be some elements of truth: the assertion that he could never remain seated for long chimes with the restless energy that characterizes his manifold actions, while the observation that he had little sleep was the inevitable lot of a leader determined to effect change through personal engagement with the intensity of government.[31] In the *Wars* Procopius reported that the plotter, Artabanes, claimed Justinian could be attacked without fear since he sat late into the night unrolling Christian scriptures with old priests.[32]

A ruler can only succeed with a loyal entourage and Justinian was no exception.[33] Family provided a necessary foundation and here Theodora was the key individual from before her marriage in the early 520s to her death on 28 June 548.[34] In the *Secret History* Procopius presented her as Justinian's ideal partner in a joint project to destroy mankind through the exploitation of Christian divisions, the rivalry of the Hippodrome factions, and jealousy of established wealth.[35] There is substantial evidence that

---

28. Malalas 16.1.
29. Honoré, 'Some Constitutions'.
30. *Collectio Avellana* 196.6.
31. Proc., *SH* 12.21; 13.28–33; also 12.20. John Lydus described him as 'the most sleepless of all emperors' (*de Mag.* 3.55), and Justinian himself referred to his wakefulness every day and night to provide for his subjects what was useful and pleasing to God (*Nov.* 8 *pref.*).
32. Proc., 7.23.9. Emperor Julian had complained to his uncle about having to write his own letters when no scribes were available late at night, and commented to the orator Libanius about the weight of business he had to transact each day (*Ep. 3*, 382B; 58, 402B).
33. The San Vitale mosaic (Plate 3) depicts some of the entourage. The base of the Obelisk of Theodosius in the Constantinople Hippodrome shows the emperor in the Kathisma surrounded by those closest to him (Plate 5).
34. See Plate 4 for the depiction of Theodora, possibly posthumously, in San Vitale.
35. Proc., 10.13–18; 11.40–1.

Theodora supported and protected Miaphysite Christians opposed to the Council of Chalcedon whereas Justinian was doing his best to achieve a compromise settlement that, on occasions, extended to applying pressure on the synod's opponents. Her role at court is presented in a favourable light in Procopius' account of the Nika Riot, when, on the final day of unrest Justinian was supposedly contemplating flight from the Great Palace until Theodora spoke up to exhort him to remain, concluding with the aphorism that 'Monarchy is a good shroud'.[36] The intervention may not have occurred quite as reported by Procopius (see chapter 9), but the depiction of Theodora's attachment to her imperial purple is plausible.

Three of Justinian's cousins, the brothers Germanus, Boraides and Justus, contributed significantly to his reign. The latter two were responsible on the final day of the Nika Riot for grabbing Hypatius, the nephew of Anastasius, from his seat in the imperial box and delivering him, together with his brother Pompeius, to Justinian for punishment; Justus was also a general in the Persian campaigns of the early 540s. Germanus was even more prominent, having been appointed *MM per Thracias* by Justin and then given more senior rank as *MM praesentalis* and patrician by Justinian in the 530s. After Theodora's death he was regarded as the most powerful member of Justinian's family, being married to the Ostrogothic princess Matasuentha and entrusted in 550 with command of the major expedition to end the war in Italy, before his sudden death.[37]

Germanus' eldest son, Justin, also had a distinguished career, holding the consulship in 540 and commanding in the Balkans in 551–2, Lazica and Armenia in the late 550s, and then returning to the Balkans in the 560s.[38] Another Justin, son of Justinian's sister Vigilantia and married to Theodora's niece Sophia, appeared to pursue a less prominent career, serving as *curopalatus* for thirteen years until Justinian's death, participating in various missions and suppressing factional rioting in Constantinople; he was, however, on hand in the capital to claim the succession in 565 whereas his cousin was absent on the Danube frontier.[39] Justin's brother, Marcellus, held military command against the Persians in 544 and was a patrician at some time before 565; his sister, Praeiecta, was first married to Areobindus, presumably a descendant of Anicia Juliana, who briefly

---

36. Proc., *Wars* 1.24.33–7.
37. *PLRE* II Germanus 4; *PLRE* III Boraides; Iustus 2.
38. *PLRE* III Iustinus 4.
39. *PLRE* III Iustinus 5.

governed Africa until being murdered during a mutiny, and then John, grandson of Anastasius' nephew, Hypatius.[40] Justin son of Germanus did not survive long after his cousin's accession, an indication that he had been a serious rival to succeed Justinian.

Outside the family, pride of place inevitably goes to Belisarius, his most famous and loyal general, who first appears as an officer in Justinian's bodyguard before he ascended the throne; his marriage to Antonina, a close friend of Theodora, cemented the relationship. For two decades Belisarius held high military office and delivered many of Justinian's greatest successes. Even after he had fallen under suspicion and disappeared from public life, he was the person to whom Justinian turned during the crisis of the Kutrigurs' approach to Constantinople in 559, being brought out of retirement to defend the capital with a scratch force. Another officer in Justinian's guard in the 520s, Sittas, enjoyed a similarly successful military career, becoming *MM per Armeniam* one year before Belisarius achieved this rank, and fighting successfully in the Balkans in the 530s before his untimely death in Armenia in 539. He too was attached to the imperial family, being married to Theodora's eldest sister Comito. A daughter of Antonina was married to Ildiger, one of Belisarius' senior officers in Africa and Italy.[41]

A shared Thracian background may have helped to elevate the likes of Bessas and Buzes, who held military command for long periods even if not always with success, while Germanus, who defended the Chersonese against the Kutrigurs in 559, came from Bederiana, Emperor Justin's home town. The Persarmenian eunuch Narses was a member of the imperial bedchamber by 530 and contributed decisively to suppressing the Nika rioters. He undertook delicate religious diplomacy for Theodora and had risen to be chief eunuch, *praepositus sacri cubiculi*, by 537/8 when he was sent to Italy to support the war against the Goths but with authority independent of Belisarius. In 551 he inherited command of the Italian expedition from Germanus and, after defeating both Goths and Franks, remained in charge of the peninsula until Justinian's death. Another Persarmenian called Narses – but this one a nobleman who deserted the Persians in 530 – served Justinian as commander in Italy and the East until

---

40. *PLRE* III Marcellus 5; Praeiecta 1; Areobindus 2; Ioannes 63. On the continuing importance through the sixth century of the family of Anastasius, see Alan Cameron, 'House'.
41. *PLRE* III Belisarius; Antonia 1; Sittas 1; Comito; Ildiger.

his death at Anglon in 543; his brothers Aratius and Isaac also held senior commands. Another prominent eunuch was Solomon from near Solachon in Mesopotamia, whose career began as secretary to successive *duces Mesopotamiae*, culminating with Belisarius, whom he then accompanied to Africa, where he subsequently combined the roles of military and civil governor; his success furthered the careers of his nephews, Sergius, Cyril, and Solomon.[42]

On the civilian front, Justinian's administration was dominated by three men. Peter the Patrician, another native of Solachon, trained as a lawyer before being used by Justinian in the 530s for delicate negotiations in Italy, where the Ostrogoths kept him captive for several years. On his return in 539 he was appointed *magister officiorum*, serving in this role until his death in 565. On the financial side, John the Cappadocian and Peter Barsymes held the office of praetorian prefect for the majority of the reign, both achieving patrician status; Peter was also twice *comes sacrarum largitionum*, the officer responsible for the emperor's personal finances. Both men were provincial outsiders, from Cappadocia and Syria respectively, and had reputations for financial acumen rather than traditional literary learning; that earned them the hostility of Procopius, who saw them as the agents for Justinian's mission to despoil the whole world.[43] A fourth prominent official was the lawyer Tribonian, who held office as *quaestor sacri palatii* or *magister officiorum* throughout the 530s until his death in the early 540s. Legal expertise clearly brought him to Justinian's attention, as well as the ability to drive forward the emperor's massive project of legal codification.[44] The removal of John and Tribonian was among the demands of the Nika rioters at the start of their insurrection; Justinian obliged, without calming the disturbances, and soon reinstated them.[45]

Loyalty to the emperor was what linked these people, and this was rewarded by Justinian who tended to give the benefit of the doubt to those whom he trusted even when they were unsuccessful. However, mutual rivalry for the emperor's ear divided them and could subvert imperial initiatives. This is most evident in the Italian campaigns of 538–9,

---

42. *PLRE* II Bessas; *PLRE* III Buzes; Germanus 4; Narses 1 & 2; Aratius; Isaacius 1; Solomon 1; Sergius 4; Cyrus 3; Solomon2.
43. E.g. Proc., *SH* 23.24.
44. Tribonian's successor, Junillus, was another outsider who inspired Procopius' contempt because he had never practised as a lawyer and could not pronounce Greek properly (*SH* 20.17).
45. *PLRE* III Petrus 6; Ioannes 11; Petrus 9; Tribonian.

when the independent authority of Narses thwarted Belisarius' efforts to co-ordinate actions, not least in emboldening other commanders to insubordination with results that included the devastating loss of Milan.[46] Theodora was said to be hostile to Justinian's cousin Germanus, and was so fiercely opposed to John the Cappadocian that in 541 she engineered his downfall through her confidante Antonina, being supported in this by the eunuch Narses and Justinian's nephew Marcellus; her enmity continued to pursue John even after his disgrace.[47]

Although such competition was, on occasions, very damaging, overall it served to reinforce the emperor's control of his domain. Particularly on the military side, Justinian was vulnerable since he was not involved personally in any of the campaigns of his reign and indeed may never have experienced active military service. Victory was central to the imperial image, which explains the importance of the Hippodrome and its chariot races: there the emperor presented prizes to the victors in a setting whose monuments celebrated distant and recent victories.[48] Thus Justinian could easily be roused to jealousy against anyone, Belisarius in particular, who achieved signal victories and the popularity that naturally accompanied them.[49] Emperors needed victories to sustain their position, but in the past those who won victories had sometimes aspired to the throne or been pushed in that direction by their troops: failure might result in dismissal, but victory certainly aroused suspicion, so successful generals needed to be cautious.

Justinian's reign can, at risk of considerable simplification, be split into three phases.[50] An initial thirteen years (527–40) witnessed achievements on all fronts that almost surpassed belief. It was a time of hope when possibilities opened out: an 'endless' peace was established in the east,

---

46. Proc., *Wars* 6.19.8–10; 22.4–5.

47. Proc., *SH* 5.8 (Germanus) *Wars* 1.25; *SH* 17.35–44 (John).

48. See Plate 4 for the emperor presenting prizes. The central spina, around which the chariots raced, was decorated with monuments such as the bronze tripod from Delphi commemorating the Greek victory over Xerxes in 480–79 BC (see Plate 17 for this and the Obelisk of Theodosius) and several statues of Porphyrius, the most successful charioteer of the early sixth century.

49. Proc., *Wars* 7.1.2–7. Justinian energetically publicized his claim to victories through artefacts like the Barberini Ivory (Plate 6) or the recycled equestrian statue in the Augustaeum and the mosaics that decorated the reconstructed Chalke entrance to the Great Palace (Proc., *Buildings* 1.2.1–12; 10.15–19).

50. See Honoré, *Tribonian* 20–1.

North Africa and Italy were reconquered with the Vandal and Ostrogothic kingdoms eliminated, Roman Law was systematized for eternity, the new Great Church, S. Sophia, was constructed, and there were even hopes of a resolution to doctrinal disputes between Chalcedonians and Miaphysites. Then followed a dark decade (540–50), which began when Khusro invaded Syria to sack Antioch and extort ransoms from other cities, witnessed the devastating onset of bubonic plague in 542 that Justinian himself contracted, and was then consumed by draining campaigns in the East and the resurgence of Gothic power in Italy, where Totila came close to wresting back control of the whole peninsula. In the religious sphere a separate Miaphysite church hierarchy was created in the East, while in the West Justinian's doctrinal initiatives roused fierce opposition. In 548 Justinian lost two of his closest supporters, when Theodora died and Belisarius withdrew into private life after failures in Italy and under suspicion of conspiring against the emperor.

Finally Justinian oversaw fifteen years (550–65) of gradual and hesitant recovery, as the battered empire eventually concluded open conflict in Italy, Africa remained largely free from damaging Berber inroads, some territory in Spain was secured, and in the East operations were first restricted to Lazica and then peace was established with Persia for fifty years. An ecumenical council at Constantinople endorsed Justinian's current doctrinal project, the Three Chapters initiative, and S. Sophia was rebuilt after earthquake damage. Of course, there are events that run contrary to this scheme, for example the Nika Riot of 532 that came close to toppling Justinian, or the Slav and Hun invasions of the Balkans in the 550s that reached the Aegean and almost the capital, but as a generalization the tripartite scheme holds true.

This book is about campaigns and conflict, but before turning to these activities that consumed so much of Justinian's attention and imperial resources, I will touch on three areas of action that had even more enduring significance, namely Law, Buildings, and Religion; these are too important to overlook completely in any treatment of Justinian and each is indeed connected to warfare. For Justinian, Law and military success went together, as he proclaimed in November 533 in the preface to the law announcing the completion of the *Institutes*:

> The imperial majesty should not only be adorned with arms but
> also be armed with laws, so that there may be good government
> in times both of war and of peace, and the ruler of Rome may not

only be victorious over enemies in war, but also be as devoted to law as triumphant over defeated enemies.[51]

Justinian's codification of Roman Law has been hailed as 'the great lasting achievement' of his reign, a verdict that can be traced back at least to Gibbon's praise for his immortal works.[52] His achievement ultimately is of fundamental importance to the legal systems of many European countries, including Scotland, though much less so for England.[53] On 13 February 528 Justinian informed the Senate that he was establishing a commission to undertake a task that previous emperors had contemplated but never tackled, namely a systematic collection of imperial laws that would now be achieved through the assistance of God Almighty.[54]

The intention was to create a single authoritative source of law, one that would reduce legal wrangling over obscurities and inconsistencies. Ten commissioners, with the praetorian prefect John the Cappadocian in the lead, were to assemble and revise imperial constitutions contained in the Diocletianic *Codex Gregorianus* and *Codex Hermogenianus*, the *Codex Theodosianus* of 438, and subsequent legislation. The legal rulings had to be identified, arranged by subject and ordered chronologically to take their place under the appropriate titles, with contradictions and obscurities removed. All this was to be presented in a new *Codex* that bore Justinian's fortunate name, *sub felici nostri nominis vocabulo*. The resulting collection was issued on 7 April 529,[55] to come into force at Easter (16 April), a remarkable feat considering that a century earlier the Theodosian compilers had taken a decade to complete their smaller task. In its twelve books the *Codex* moved from ecclesiastical law in Book 1 through seven books of civil procedure and private law, to single books on crime and criminal procedure, taxation and local government, corporations, and finally offices and ranks.

Justinian's next legal project was even more ambitious, the codification of the opinions of Roman jurists from Republican times through to the fourth century, a task that had been contemplated by Theodosius a century

---

51. *Inst., Const. Imp.* pr., cf. *CJ Const. Summa* pr. for the security of the state depending on 'the force of arms and the observance of the law'.
52. Evans, *Age* 207; opening paragraph to Gibbon, *Decline* ch. 44. For more detailed discussion of Justinian's actions, see, amongst many others, Liebs, 'Roman Law' 247–52; Humfress, 'Law' 162–6.
53. See, for example, the brief survey in Birks and McLeod, *Institutes* 18–26.
54. *Cod.Iust., Const. Haec.*
55. *Cod.Iust., Const. Summa.*

before but then abandoned. This project, however, was essential, since the promulgation of the *Codex* had stated that its provisions were to be used to determine cases alongside 'the opinions of the ancient interpreters of the law'.[56] This approach was problematic because the long sequence of Roman jurists did not always agree with each other and their arguments also might not be compatible with the definitive imperial view contained in the *Codex*, so that it was vital that discrepancies be removed and uncertainties clarified. On 15 December 530 a second legal commission was established, this time of sixteen experts under Tribonian, who had been a member of the previous commission but as *quaestor* was now Justinian's top legal official. The task was to overcome the challenges in a demonstration of God's power and to the glory of Justinian; it was probably Tribonian who argued for the project against those who thought it unachievable.[57]

Tribonian organized his team into three groups, whose progress he monitored closely, with the result that after only three years, on 16 December 533, the compendium known as the *Digest* or *Pandects* was issued.[58] This work ordered the opinions of centuries of jurists, now harmonized, into fifty books, which constituted the only version of juristic authority that could be cited in court. Although the *Digest* is very large, with over 140,000 lines of text, it at least reduced over 1,500 extant scrolls of jurisprudence into a manageable scope through selection of about 5 per cent of their contents. Promulgation by Justinian transformed the opinions of the jurists into imperial law and, further, by prohibiting citations from outside its contents, prevented clever lawyers from complicating and prolonging court cases by the sudden production of an obscure ruling. In addition to simplifying legal process, the *Digest* also defined what law students needed to master in order to be competent practitioners. Justinian prohibited the production of commentaries on his *Digest* to prevent the clarity of his work from being muddied, but practical needs ensured that before the end of his reign expert lawyers were disregarding his instruction.

The third element of Justinian's legal project, the *Institutes*, provided pedagogic support to the *Digest* by creating an introductory handbook for students of law. This was produced, towards the end of the process

---

56. *Cod.Iust., Const. Summa* 3.
57. *Digest, Const. Deo Auctore* 14. See Honoré, *Tribonian*, for a detailed study of the man, his methods, and contribution to Justinian's legal project.
58. *Digest, Const. Tanta*, which boasts that the project had initially been deemed impossible and then been estimated to require ten years of work.

of compiling the *Digest*, by Tribonian and one professor from each of the two main law schools of Beirut and Constantinople, mainly on the basis of the second-century jurist Gaius; it was ready shortly before the *Digest* on 21 November 533. In the edict that promulgated it, those proposing to study law were exhorted to start from the four books of *Institutes* in their first year, to progress to the *Digest* and finally in their fifth year to study the imperial constitutions in the *Codex*.[59] First-year students were honoured with the emperor's name, *Iustiniani novi*, 'new Justinians'.

A combination of early experience of working with the *Codex* and the massive compilation of the *Digest* necessitated further attention to the former; Tribonian was tasked with producing a second edition of the *Codex*, which was published on 16 November 534 to come into force replacing the first edition on 29 December.[60] The success of this Herculean task, undertaken with the inspiration of heaven, served to glorify God, but also to demonstrate divine favour on Justinian's reign and to constitute an eternal memorial to his name. It was not, however, the end of his legal activities and the remaining three decades of his reign witnessed a series of *Novels* or new laws that were issued, especially in the 530s, on a range of administrative and social issues as well as in response to the inevitable legal uncertainties that survived to defy even his labours. Justinian had envisaged producing an official collection of his *Novels*, but never did;[61] instead this task was left to unknown lawyers, quite possibly attached to the capital's law school, to undertake in the early 540s and then to redo on several occasions throughout the rest of the reign. This legal whirlwind did not please everyone: Procopius criticized the emperor's desire to change everything, including laws, to ensure that everything new might be called after himself.[62] Even Justinian had to acknowledge in the preamble to *Novel* 60, issued in 537, that there were complaints about the mass of laws that were being issued every day.

Buildings rival the Law as the most enduring of Justinian's actions, even though in this case only a small fraction of what he commissioned survives intact. Visitors to Istanbul will see on the skyline, even if they do not visit, the solid dome of his Great Church, S. Sophia, while those interested in antiquities will seek out the palace church of SS. Sergius

---

59. *Inst. Const. Imp.*
60. *Cod.Iust. Const. Cordi.*
61. *Novels App.* 7.11 for a project in the mid-550s.
62. Proc., *SH* 11.1–2.

and Bacchus. The relatively intact survival of two out of the thirty-three churches that Justinian built or repaired in the capital might not seem an impressive rate, but 1,500 years of natural disasters, wear and tear, and religious change have inevitably taken their toll. Outside the capital, the remote monastery of St Catherine on Mount Sinai survives, but other works are largely archaeological ruins. We do, however, have an account of Justinian's constructions that was written towards the end of his reign by the historian Procopius. This work, *The Buildings*, is explicitly panegyrical, being composed to elevate the reputation of Justinian possibly in response to an official commission, so that its claims have to be treated with caution, but attempts to traduce its basic accuracy have foundered.[63]

The greatest of Justinian's constructions was undoubtedly S. Sophia, the capital's Great Church, with whose construction Procopius opens the *Buildings*. This was the third church to be built on the site, its immediate predecessor from the early fifth century having perished in the conflagrations of the Nika Riot in 532. Justinian seized the opportunity to remodel the centre of the capital by creating a distinctive and inspiring edifice.[64] Whereas the previous S. Sophia had been a standard basilica, Justinian instructed his architects, Anthemius of Tralles and Isidore of Miletus, to create a dome, 140 feet in diameter, supported on four massive arches; to east and west these arches opened into further spaces covered by half domes, while to north and south the windowed tympana that occupy the semi-circular portion of the arches sit above two tiers of arcades, five arches at ground level separated by four massive columns and seven at gallery level. The dome is divided by 430 ribs that are separated at their base by arched windows, which flooded the building with daylight and made the dome to appear to be floating over the church's central space. Although elements of the building may have been presaged in SS. Sergius and Bacchus, a church attached to Justinian's residence in the Palace of Hormisdas that was begun before his accession in 527, the scale was completely different and presented its own problems, while there were innovations such as the decision not to align the columns in the north and south walls.[65]

---

63. See Whitby, 'Procopius and the Development' and 'Notes'.
64. For full discussion, see Mainstone, *Hagia Sophia*.
65. Croke, Justinian', but for a different view, see Bardill, 'Date', who dates Sergius and Bacchus to the 530s and argues that its dome was originally seated on an octagonal drum, hence similar to S. Vitale in Ravenna rather than S. Sophia.

Notwithstanding its radical character, the building was ready to be dedicated on 27 December 537, less than six years after the destruction of its predecessor. The building visible today is not quite the one that Justinian commissioned, since the dome, which was originally shallower, was rebuilt at greater height following its collapse in May 558 as a result of damage sustained in the major earthquake of December 557. [66] This was to reduce the problems posed by lateral thrust, which also occasioned the addition over the centuries of the bulky external buttresses that mask the delicacy of the initial design.

S. Sophia remains, as it was intended to be, an awe-inspiring structure, a demonstration after the crisis of the Nika Riot that Justinian's power and ambition far outshone potential rivals. Granted that the Great Church was one of the venues for emperor and people to participate in a shared activity, Justinian had ensured that these regular events proceeded in a fabulous space that was recognizably his own. It has been suggested that Justinian was specifically targeting the church of S. Polyeuctus, previously the largest in the city, which had been built in the 520s for Anicia Iuliana in a style and on a scale to rival Solomon's Temple in Jerusalem. [67] One source claims that, on entering his new church, Justinian exclaimed, 'Solomon, I have surpassed thee'; although from a late and not totally reliable witness, the story has plausibility. [68]

Justinian also completely rebuilt the second most important church in the capital, the Holy Apostles, the site of imperial burials, providing it with a new mausoleum whose first occupant would be his wife Theodora. [69] This church was demolished in the fifteenth century to permit the construction of the Fatih Çami by Mehmet II to commemorate his capture of Constantinople, but an idea of its impressive appearance can be gleaned from its replica, San Marco in Venice. Other major churches to be rebuilt or enhanced by Justinian included S. Irene, the oldest church in the city, and the extramural church to the Virgin

---

66. See Plate 7; the substantial buttresses that partially conceal the building's elegance and the minarets are obviously later additions. Also Plate 17 for a 17th century watercolour that shows S. Sophia with the monuments from the Hippodrome spina in the foreground.
67. Harrison, *Temple* 36–41; Croke, 'Justinian' 53–62, suggested that SS. Sergius and Bacchus had also been built as Justinian's first attempt, in the 520s, to compete against S. Polyeuctus, being distinctive in design albeit smaller in scale and with an inscribed epigram that stressed the current imperial credentials of its patrons.
68. *Narratio de Aedificatione Templi S. Sophiae* 27.
69. Proc., *Buildings* 1.4.9–24.

at the shrine of Pege.[70] These churches were prominent in the annual calendar of processions that paced the life of Constantinople and the Justinianic influence on these public events was reinforced by the fact that the Nika Riot had made it necessary for the emperor to reconstruct the Chalke, the main entrance to the Palace, and the Augustaeum, the central starting point for most processions. The Augustaeum was now dominated by a bronze equestrian imperial statue, which Procopius interpreted as a demonstration of his universal supremacy over all nations through the favour of Christ, whose cross is 'the emblem by which alone he had obtained both his empire and his success in war'.[71]

Outside the capital Justinian was especially active in the threatened frontier regions of the Balkans and the East, in each case continuing and extending the labours of Anastasius while also responding to natural disasters. Relatively little of the archaeological remains can be securely dated to his reign, although the ruins of Caricin Grad in Serbia attest the investment that he devoted to his family's origin, with his birthplace now renamed Justiniana Prima and elevated from obscurity to the status of metropolitan bishopric. The ground plan of the Church of St John at Ephesus reveals another replica of Holy Apostles at a monumental site of devotion and pilgrimage, and the imposing five-arched bridge, over 400 metres long and almost 10 metres wide, that once spanned the Sangarius (Sakarya) near Adapazari survives, as evidence for his attention to efficient communications along the empire's key arteries.[72]

Building works were the occasion for one of Justinian's very rare excursions from the capital. Following the Kutrigur invasion of 559 he spent several months outside the capital in Thrace, clearly supervising the on-going repairs to the Long Walls that Zabergan had overrun with ease. A brief account survives of his ceremonial return to the city on the morning of Monday 11 August, when he entered by the Gate of Charisius rather than the standard Golden Gate, possibly because the Mese was still

---

70. Proc., *Buildings* 1.3.1–9; Justin I had constructed the large basilica to the Virgin at the other major extramural shrine, at Blachernae.

71. *Buildings* 1.2.1–11, quotation from 11. The fact that the statue had originally been erected in honour of Theodosius, as is clear from an inscription visible on sixteenth-century drawings of the lost monument, does not diminish its power in transmitting Justinian's image to his contemporaries.

72. Procopius, *Buildings* 4.1.19–27 with Alchermes, 'Art' 355–7; *Buildings* 5.1.4–6, with Foss, *Ephesus* 88; *Buildings* 5.3.8–11 with Whitby, 'Bridge'. See Plate 8 for the remains of the bridge (the Sangarius has shifted to a new course).

cluttered by rubble from the recent earthquakes.[73] Whether by coincidence or not, Justinian's only other attested trip outside the city also occurred at the end of his reign: in October 563 he travelled to Germia in Galatia to visit the shrine of the Myriangeloi in fulfillment of a vow.[74] En route he would have crossed his new bridge over the Sangarius and it is possible that the vow related to the completion of that major project, though the emperor might just have wanted to visit the substantial cathedral to the Archangel Michael. The reputation of its relic of Christ's tunic was known to Gregory of Tours in Gaul and curative properties were attributed to its fish pond, located at the eastern end of the cathedral, by the pilgrims who flocked to the site.[75] Whether Justinian left the city on other occasions is not known, but, for example, he does not appear to have accompanied Theodora on her visit in summer 533 to the hot springs of Pythia in Bithynia (near modern Yalova), when her substantial retinue of 4,000 included several patricians, the *comes largitionum*, and *cubicularii*.[76]

Religion

If Justinian had been asked what he regarded as his top priority, the goal that he most longed to achieve, he would undoubtedly have answered the restoration of harmony in the Church, elevating this far above achievements such as the overhaul of Roman law or mundane victories in military campaigns.[77] Indeed the latter could not be achieved without divine favour, as Justinian explained in 535 in the preface to *Novel* 6:

> Therefore we have the greatest concern for the true doctrines relating to God and for the honour of his priests; since, if these pertain, we are confident that through it many benefits will be granted us by God, that we shall not only possess firmly what we have but further obtain what we have not yet achieved.

---

73. Const. Porph. *De Caer.* 1. App, pp. 497.13–498.13 (Reiske); also in id. *Three Treatises* 707–23, with Haldon's commentary, citing McCormick, *Victory* 209, on the route.
74. Theophanes 240.11–13.
75. Mitchell, *Anatolia* II 117, 128–9. For the remains of the five-aisled basilica at the modern village of Yürme, near Sivrihisar, see Crowfoot, 'Notes' 86–92.
76. Theophanes 186.8–13; Malalas 18.25.
77. Millar, 'Rome' 62, suggested that Justinian had three major objectives at the start of his reign, first reconquest of the West, second the establishment of Roman Law, and third religious reunification. To my mind, the order is wrong: religion far outweighed the other two and the West could not be seriously considered as an objective until peace had been established in the East.

Religion played a direct part in Justinian's wars and international dealings. The persecution of Catholics by the anti-Nicene Vandals was a factor – even if only a convenient one – in the decision to attack Geiseric, and this aspect was trumpeted in the law that re-established Roman administration.[78] The attractions of controlling Rome, the centre of western Christianity and, again, the question of orthodoxy contributed to the attack on the Ostrogoths. In 539, looking back on the apparent success of the war in Italy as well as the Vandal triumph, Justinian asserted that the wars had been driven by his concern for orthodoxy and the liberty of his subjects.[79]

In the East Khusro clearly enjoyed demonstrating his superiority to bishops, as for example after the capture of Antioch,[80] while refuting Christian belief in the inviolability of Edessa was a factor in his attacks on that city. For their part the Romans embroidered secular narratives with stories of miraculous escape when Sergiopolis and then Edessa managed to survive assaults.[81] Religion furthered Roman interests in the Black Sea area through the baptisms of the Hunnic leader Grod and the Laz king Tzath, with the latter event confirming the Laz switch of allegiance from Persia to Rome. Justinian also exploited religion, less successfully, at the southern end of his confrontation with Persia when he urged the Axumites in Ethiopia as fellow Christians to circumvent the Persian stranglehold on the lucrative silk trade.

Religion had practical benefits in warfare and diplomacy, but the key issue for Justinian was doctrine: heresy was an insult to God and so had to be eliminated to enable the orthodox Church to praise God with a single voice. Justinian had to grapple with the Trinitarian consequences of the conversion of Vandals and Goths in the fourth century by anti-Nicene missionaries,[82] but the most pressing issue for emperors in the fifth and sixth centuries related to Christology: Christ needed to be perfect man in order to guarantee the salvation of mankind through his death and resurrection, while he must also be perfect God to be equal

---

78. *Cod.Iust.* 1.27.1.10.
79. Justinian, *Novel* 78.4.1.
80. Proc., *Wars* 2.9.1–6.
81. Evagrius 4.27–8.
82. Constantius II and Valens espoused the Homoean position that God the Son was 'like' (*homoios*) God the Father, rather than the Nicene doctrine that he was 'of the same substance' (*homoousios*).

to God the Father and capable of performing the Gospel miracles. Nestorius, an Antiochene monk who was patriarch of Constantinople until his deposition after the Council of Ephesus in 431,[83] had emphasized the former position, whereas Cyril of Alexandria and his successors in Egypt privileged the latter, in some cases, as with the monk Eutyches, lapsing into heresy in their disregard for Christ's human aspect. At the Council of Chalcedon in 451 Emperor Marcian had attempted to resolve two decades of dispute: as directed by the secular presidents,[84] the assembled bishops endorsed a compromise Christological formulation contained in a letter from Pope Leo, known as the Tome of Leo.[85]

Thereafter, regional rivalries between the sees of Alexandria, Antioch and Constantinople, the importance to Rome of defending Chalcedon in its entirety as a demonstration of papal authority, and the barrier to perfect comprehension created by translation of doctrinal niceties between Greek, Latin, Syriac, and Coptic compounded the dispute in which the rival sides are known as Chalcedonians and Miaphysites (or the more pejorative Monophysites). The former held that Christ was a single person and *hypostasis* in two natures, while the latter insisted on the one nature (*mia physis*) of Christ as God the Word incarnate, who was one *hypostasis* from two natures.[86] Miaphysites dominated Egypt, Armenia, and parts of Syria, hence much of the frontier with Persia, but could also be found more widely across the East. In 482 Emperor Zeno had attempted to restore unity in the East by endorsing the disciplinary decisions of Chalcedon, upholding the orthodoxy of Cyril of Alexandria's writings, which Miaphysites felt had been impugned at Chalcedon, and evading the doctrinal contributions of Chalcedon by emphasizing accord with Nicaea. With robust imperial direction, this compromise achieved a certain peace in the east but at the cost of schism with Rome.

Justinian's involvement in the rapprochement with Rome at the start of Justin's reign has been noted above. He was determined to find ways

---

83. For the proceedings, which were controlled by Cyril of Alexandria and his supporters, see Price, *Ephesus* 18–56.

84. For this aspect of the council, see de Ste. Croix, 'Council'.

85. For the main events, see Price and Gaddis, *Acts* 37–51.

86. For discussion of *hypostasis*, see Price and Gaddis, *Acts* 60–2. Miaphysites regarded *hypostasis* and nature as virtually identical, whereas Pope Leo intended a distinction to be drawn between generic *hypostasis* and the specific 'nature'. As Evagrius pointed out (2.5) the difference between the two sides could be presented as being a single letter, the difference between *ek* (from) and *en* (in).

around, or through, obstacles, for example the Theophaschite formula ('God-suffering'), which dealt with a Miaphysite concern that the Chalcedonian creed did not clearly affirm that God the Word, namely Christ as one of the Trinity, had suffered on the Cross, so that the miracles and sufferings belonged to the same person. Justinian initially opposed this, but then changed his mind, a *volte face* that has been taken to show that he was no more than a pragmatist with little interest in theological niceties.[87] That verdict is unconvincing in view of Justinian's concern for theological detail over the next forty-five years;[88] it is more plausible to see this as the first example of the dilemma that was to face Justinian until his death, namely how to balance his desire to maintain relations with the Pope and the western churches on the one hand and, on the other, the need to make adjustments to Chalcedon to reduce the intensity of disagreement in the East.

Once on the throne and personally responsible for doctrinal orthodoxy and ecclesiastical unity, Justinian could chart his own course. His marriage to the anti-Chalcedonian Theodora had already indicated that his views on Christology were nuanced. When ousted Miaphysites appealed to her in 523, she intervened with Justin to give some relief to exiles in Alexandria.[89] Justinian's first actions on the religious front related to heresies, pagans, and immorality rather than the divisions caused by Chalcedon. While co-emperor with Justin in 527, legislation was issued against heretics, Manichees, and Samaritans, a reaffirmation or extension of provisions against heresy that Justin had issued six or seven years earlier.[90] As sole ruler this was soon followed by the imposition of penalties on a range of heretics, including Nestorians and Eutychians among others, as well as on Samaritans.[91] In 531 legal and financial restrictions were extended to Jews and in 532 Justinian even stipulated that in synagogues the Bible must be read in Latin or Greek rather than Hebrew.[92] Pagans were very much in his sights, with existing legislation being endorsed, restrictions placed on their rights to inherit, the death penalty proclaimed

87. Gray, 'Legacy' 228.
88. Ashbrook Harvey, *Asceticism* 23, insists, rightly to my mind, that Justinian had a persisting concern for 'a genuine theological resolution' to the doctrinal challenges of his reign.
89. John of Ephesus, *Lives* 13, pp. 189–90.
90. *Cod.Iust.* 1.5.12; 1.4.20.
91. *Cod.Iust.* 1.5.18–19.
92. Justinian, *Novels* 45; 146.

for anyone caught sacrificing, the requirement that all teachers be baptized and public salaries removed from non-Christians.[93] One consequence of this raft of actions was the closure of the Academy at Athens.[94] Homosexuality was severely punished, with two bishops, Isaiah of Rhodes and Alexander of Diosopolis, being interrogated by Victor, the prefect of Constantinople; Isaiah was tortured and exiled, while Alexander's genitals were cut off before he was paraded through the city on a litter.[95]

As soon as military conditions permitted, namely with progress towards a peace agreement with Persia firmly in place, Justinian embarked on discussions to re-establish communion of belief in the East. In 532 doctrinal discussions between supporters and opponents of Chalcedon were held in Justinian's former residence, the Palace of Hormisdas.[96] In terms of theology there was virtually no difference between the sides, but practical issues supervened. Miaphysites had been accustomed for the past eighty years to condemning both the Council and the Tome of Leo as heretical, and had created a dossier of miracles that confirmed this view: on these issues a U-turn was not possible. Justinian also failed to persuade the Miaphysites to renounce the new ordinations that would lead to the creation of a separate ecclesiastical hierarchy, but he did identify some key issues that might make the Miaphysites more amenable to reconciliation.

The breakdown of talks did not lead Justinian to give up, and in 533 he resurrected the Theopaschite approach and issued an edict in which acknowledged heretics were condemned, Mary's status as Theotokos (Mother of God) upheld, and the Theopaschite position articulated; there was no mention of the Tome of Leo.[97] At this point the independence of the papacy constrained Justinian's options, but the recovery of Rome in 537 changed this. In late 544, or early 545, Justinian embarked on another initiative, issuing an edict against three fifth-century theologians, commonly referred to as the 'Three Chapters': the person and works of Theodore of Mopsuestia, the writings of Theodoret of Cyrrhus against

---

93. *Cod.Iust.* 1.11.10.
94. See chapter 2, pp.XX.
95. Malalas 18.18.
96. For discussion, see Brock, 'Orthodox-Oriental' and 'Conversations', the latter with a translation of the Miaphysite records of proceedings; also Frend, *Monophysite* 264–7. A Chalcedonian account is preserved in a Latin translation of a letter from Innocentius of Maronea, one of the participants, to Thomas of Thessalonica; text in *ACO* IV.2. 169–84.
97. *Cod.Iust.* 1.1.6.

Cyril of Alexandria, and the letter to Mari the Persian attributed to Ibas of Edessa.[98] This responded to concerns that Miaphysites had raised with Justinian in 532. There was predictable opposition in the West, since both Theodoret and Ibas had been vindicated at Chalcedon so that their condemnation was seen an attack on that council. In November 545 Pope Vigilius was arrested in Rome and brought to Constantinople, which he reached in January 547, where he remained for eight years. Vigilius came under strong pressure to sign up to this initiative, ultimately with an ecumenical council being held, after long delays, in 553 to ratify Justinian's views.[99] The deliberations of 152 bishops concluded on 2 June, when fourteen canons were approved, and in February 554 these were eventually endorsed by Vigilius, who had refused to attend the Council but now reissued the decisions as if they were those of the Pope. There was fierce opposition in Africa and northern Italy, and Justinian exiled African and Illyrian bishops in the capital who rejected the council. Sustained pressure did pay off in the end, but at the end of the century, in spite of papal support for the Three Chapters initiative, the sees of Milan and Aquileia in northern Italy were still separated from Pope Gregory by this issue.

The Three Chapters controversy demonstrated the pressure that Justinian was prepared to apply to secure support for his doctrinal wishes, but the targets had to be accessible if this was to be effective. The majority of Chalcedonians in the East acquiesced in the results of the council, but Miaphysites saw no benefit in approving the council: it lacked a formal condemnation of Chalcedon, and their leaders were out of reach in Egypt or the borderlands of Syria, where the Jafnid phylarch Harith offered protection and Jacob Baradaeus had consecrated a new generation of leaders. Justinian kept trying and in 564 issued an edict that proclaimed the Aphthartodocetist doctrine espoused by some Miaphysites that Christ's body did not suffer corruption, to which bishops were required to assent on pain of dismissal. Eutychius of Constantinople was immediately removed and only the emperor's death, which was seen as a just reward for this attempt to pervert the faith,[100] prevented extensive disruption.

Justinian was nothing if not persistent in striving to achieve his goal of a united Church, but it is clear that he failed. In 527 he had inherited a

98. For discussion of the complexities of this issue, see the contributions to Chazelle & Cubitt, *Crisis*.
99. The twists and turns of his stay are clearly analyzed by Price, *Acts* 45–58.
100. Evagrius 5.1.

church in which Greek East and Latin West were in communion, even if popes had not recently been in correspondence with Constantinople. In the East there was a single Church, even if a number of sees had two bishops, a Chalcedonian one supported by the state and a Miaphysite who might be in exile or under arrest, and Egypt was effectively a separate entity. In 565 East and West were still in communion, but only as a result of considerable pressure on successive popes and at the expense of local schisms. In the East, Egypt outside Alexandria remained beyond the religious authority of the emperor, a separate Miaphysite church hierarchy had taken root in Syria, and the Miaphysites themselves were divided. Justinian had tried his hardest, combining his considerable powers of theological argument with imperial force. Theological differences within the empire, however, were not amenable to reason and pressure could not be applied to remove all obstacles. Justinian's fiercest opponent in the Three Chapters controversy, Facundus, unfairly accused him of 'trying inappropriately to appear learned, he disturbs the church by inventing problems'.[101] He had inherited the fifth century's Christological problems and, as an accomplished and intellectual theologian, used all means at his disposal to resolve them.

Succession

Justinian died on 14 November 565, at some point during the night when the only witness to his last moments was the patrician Callinicius, who speedily informed the *curopalatus* Justin and his wife Sophia in their palace. Information on the stages of Justin's accession and Justinian's funeral is provided by Corippus in his panegyric of the new emperor.[102] In what is clearly pure invention, Corippus composed some dying words for the emperor in which he named Justin as his successor;[103] in reality, like Anastasius before him, Justinian had avoided showing clear preference to any of his relatives. Although this Justin, as son of Justinian's sister Vigilantia and with the niece of Theodora as his wife, was more closely related to the deceased emperor than the other Justin, son of Justinian's cousin Germanus, the latter had enjoyed a more successful public career as a commander over the previous fifteen years. However, he was currently

---

101. Facundus, *Pro defensione trium capitulorum liber* (*PL* 67, 844C).
102. For discussion of this text, see the introduction and commentary of Averil Cameron.
103. Corippus *In Laudem Iustini* 4.337–63.

active on the Danube as *quaestor exercitus*, and so the *curopalatus* had the opportunity to present the succession as a *fait accompli*. The new emperor may even have made some advance preparations, since Sophia was able to produce an elaborate robe for the funeral in which Justinian's achievements were intricately depicted with gold thread and gem stones: the subjugation of barbarians, defeat of the Vandals, and rescue of Old Rome.[104] These images recall the mosaics that adorned the Chalke, the formal entrance to the Great Palace.[105] Although Corippus refers to gloomy lamentations, the truth was that most people were probably relieved that the octogenarian emperor had finally been laid to rest with Theodora in the imperial mausoleum attached to his church of the Holy Apostles, to permit a new ruler to chart his course. Indeed 565 marked the end of a long era, since Belisarius had died in March and Peter the Patrician at about the same time as his master.

It has been observed, quite appropriately, that Justinian was 'conscious of living in the age of Justinian', a view that can be traced back to hostile comments in Procopius' *Secret History* that Justinian 'was not interested in preserving established institutions, but always wanted to innovate in everything', and 'If there was anything that he could not change forthwith, he at least put his name on it.'[106] Innovation was not regarded favourably in antiquity, and Justinian had taken pains to present many of his legal changes as justified by return to ancient precedent.[107] In both the project to codify the law and to construct S. Sophia Justinian was prepared to take considerable risks, attempting to achieve what many regarded as impossible. The same is true for the Vandal expedition, which was opposed by many of his senior advisers, including his chief financial officer, John the Cappadocian.

The image that Justinian proclaimed, and wished to have propagated, was that with divine assistance he could accomplish what others found impossible. As Procopius stated in the *Buildings*, in the context of the construction of the Nea Church in Jerusalem when it appeared impossible to transport columns of appropriate size to the site, 'when we assess everything by human ability, we consider that many things are to be judged impossible, but for God nothing whatsoever can be hopeless

---

104. Corippus *In Laudem Iustini* 1.275–90.
105. Proc., *Buildings* 1.10.16–17.
106. Honoré, *Tribonian* 16; Procopius, *SH* 6.21, 11.2.
107. Lee, *From Rome* 254–5; Maas, 'Roman History'.

or unachievable'.[108] Comparable problems involving the main piers and arches of S. Sophia and the management of Dara's water supply, which baffled the professionals, were also resolved by Justinian with God's help.[109] Justinian could even declare, shortly after the recovery of Sicily in 536, that with divine favour he might regain all lost Roman territories as far as the Ocean,[110] possessions that had been lost by the negligence of his predecessors. Military successes were inevitably more ephemeral than the complete overhaul of Roman Law or construction of a grand cathedral, but the campaigns of Justinian's reign are important in their own right in contributing to the political and religious shape of Europe.

---

108. Proc., *Buildings* 5.6.21.
109. Proc., *Buildings* 1.1.67–78, 2.3.1–15.
110. Justinian, *Novel* 30.11.2.

Chapter 2

State of the Nation

T he realm inherited by Justinian in 527 comprised the eastern half of the Roman empire, stretching from the Adriatic in the west to the Euphrates and head waters of the Tigris in the east, from the Danube and Transcaucasia in the north to the first Nile cataract in the south. Its provinces, which collectively constituted the most prosperous and secure parts of the Mediterranean world, had been ruled separately from the west since the division of the empire at the death of Theodosius I in 395, and indeed for much of the preceding century. The two halves had remained closely integrated, for example sharing the same laws, so that an edict issued in one half had effect in the other and with a ruling elite that moved easily between the two. In the mid-fifth century, however, as the west had come under increasing pressure from tribal invasions, eastern emperors had not been able to intervene effectively to sustain the rule of their western colleagues. The emperor in Italy had progressively lost control of resources, especially when the Vandals seized the prosperous North African provinces, and so could not maintain and move armies or preserve his authority. When the Scirian military commander Odoacer deposed Romulus Augustulus in 476 and returned the imperial regalia to Constantinople with a message to the effect that no new appointment was required, the news had little impact in the East, certainly nothing to compare with that of Alaric's capture of Rome in 410.[1]

International position

Geopolitically Justinian's empire was by far the most powerful state in Europe. This strength was based on a number of factors: the comparative weakness of most of its near neighbours; the overall efficacy of its administrative structures, especially considering the problems caused by the

---

1. For a clear account of these events, see Heather, 'Western Empire'.

size of the empire in a world where communications were slow and central authority was inevitably eroded as distance from the capital increased. There was also the resilience of its urban and agricultural bases, as well as of the economic networks that tied its regions together; the empire-wide structure of the Church, whose shared faith helped to uphold imperial integrity, and the social and cultural cohesion of its ruling class. The solidity of the eastern empire is demonstrated by its ability to weather catastrophes such as destructive foreign invasions, massive earthquake damage, and, worst of all, the onset of bubonic plague.

In the West, most former imperial territories were now controlled by four major tribal groupings, the Vandals in Africa, Ostrogoths in Italy, Visigoths in Spain, and Franks in Gaul.[2] Although these kingdoms have a specific tribal name, each of them was in fact an agglomeration of different tribal units, which the ruling family tried to forge into a more unified and stable whole with varying degrees of success. Military victory and its accompanying booty brought greater prestige, which might be underlined by the standard manifestation of royal power, the issuing of codified laws, but the absence of a strong leader or of successful campaigning could lead to challenges from within the family or the fractious nobility that soon fragmented the superficial unity of the kingdom.[3] This is demonstrated by the rapid implosion of the successful Ostrogothic state at the death of Theoderic.

In each kingdom the majority of the population comprised the rural inhabitants of the former Roman provinces, who now simply worked the land for a new class of rentier owners. In each there were also survivors of the former Roman elite, who dominated the church and might contribute to administering the state; these could lend an aura of Roman respectability, as Cassiodorus did most successfully for the Ostrogoths. One other significant fact about these kingdoms was that, with the exception of the Franks who had adopted orthodox Nicene belief, the rulers had been converted during the reigns of Constantius II and Valens with the result that they subscribed to Homoian Christianity and are often for convenience referred to as 'Arian'. As a result, there was tension internally with the Catholic church hierarchy and, potentially, externally with the orthodox empire in the east.

---

2. For an overview, see Heather, *Fall*, or more briefly Collins, 'Western Kingdoms'.
3. Cf. Shaw, 'War' for this fragility.

Justinian's empire shared its eastern frontier with Iran, the other 'great power' of the western Eurasian world, which had been ruled since the early third century by the Sasanid dynasty.[4] After 150 years of regular warfare, Persia appeared to have reached a *modus vivendi* with its western rival in 387 by agreeing a partition of Armenia. In the fifth century, there were only two brief interruptions to the peace, not least because Persia was threatened on its north-eastern frontier by the Hephthalites or White Huns. The Sasanids made a massive investment in defences in the Gorgan plain to the south-east of the Caspian, where they constructed a wall of fired bricks extending for 195km,[5] but when Peroz went on the offensive the Hephthalites defeated and captured the Shah, forcing the Sasanids to pay tribute.[6] It was believed, at least by the Sasanids, that Rome and Persia had collaborated in defending the passes across the Caucasus, with Rome contributing towards Persian expenses on the basis that prevention of raids by Hunnic and other groups north of the mountains was a mutual benefit. In the decades before Justinian's accession the Persian realm had experienced considerable internal disruption as a result of Kavadh's conflicts with his nobility. These had led to him being overthrown by his nobles and briefly imprisoned, before he fled to the Hephthalites and was reinstated with their support. This disruption included the Mazdakite movement, which advocated common ownership of property and the overthrow of traditional family links; it was for a time supported, or tolerated, by Kavadh as a means to undermine the power of the nobility.[7] Once Khusro was safely installed on the throne in the 530s, he crushed the Mazdakites and initiated a series of financial and military reforms that were intended to increase royal power, central resources and national security.

The empire's third main area of international interaction was the Danube, where the Roman frontier had been swept away in the 440s by Attila's Huns.[8] When Attila's federation rapidly collapsed after his death in 453, the empire continued to be troubled by its constituent elements. The main ones were Gothic groups, until they were either incorporated

---

4. For an overview, see Wiesehofer, *Persia*; more detail in Rubin, 'Sasanid Monarchy', and 'Reforms'; Howard-Johnston, 'Great Powers'.
5. Lawrence & Wilkinson, 'Borderlands' 117–18; Sauer et al, *Imperial Frontier* ch.2 and 23.
6. Proc., *Wars* 1.3–4.
7. Payne, 'Cosmology' 4–5, 28–30, asserts that only in 590 did the Iranian nobles waver in their support for their king, but the chronological parameters of his study exclude consideration of the extensive Mazdakite problems of the late-fifth and early-sixth centuries.
8. See Thompson, *Huns*; also Heather, 'Huns'.

into Roman structures or led west to Italy by Theoderic, Gepids and Lombards who established themselves on the middle Danube, and various Bulgar Hunnic groups that lived to the north of the Black Sea. The empire could control some units, such as the Heruls, through the grant of vacant land near the Danube, but new people arrived to fill any space vacated to the north of the river. By Justinian's reign Slavs and the more obscure but broadly similar Antes had entered Roman horizons and were starting to cross the river. The process of restoring Roman control after the fifth-century ravages had begun under Anastasius, pushing north from the Thracian plain and west from the Black Sea, but much more remained to be done under Justin and Justinian, for whom the region was important as their homeland.

Apart from these three major areas of interest, the empire also had to attend to specific issues on its northeastern and southeastern borders. In the northeast, relations had to be managed with Armenians, Laz, Tzani, Iberians, and other Transcaucasian people, many of whom were potential allies as Christians although socially and culturally most were closer to Persia.[9] In the southeast the desert frontiers of Palestine and Arabia were variously troubled and protected by Arab tribes, of whom the most important for the sixth-century empire were the Jafnids or Ghassanids, who received imperial support as a bulwark against the Lakhmid federation, which was a client of Persia.[10] In the Arabian peninsula, competition between Rome and Persia might be pursued by proxies, with religion as a key issue: Christians received assistance from the Axumites in Ethiopia, where the empire maintained diplomatic ties, while a Jewish leader in Arabia could hope for support from the Lakhmids and Persia.[11] In southern Egypt the frontier was intermittently troubled by raids from the nomadic Blemmyes and Nobades.

The question of whether the Roman empire had an overarching grand strategy for managing its international relations and frontiers has been much debated.[12] We rarely have information about the processes for

---

9. Thomson, 'Armenia'; Braund, *Georgia*.
10. Whittow, 'Jafnids'; Fisher, 'Political Development'.
11. Conrad, 'Arabs'; Bowersock, *Throne*.
12. Luttwak, *Roman Strategy*, deals with the empire down to the early fourth century; numerous responses, largely hostile, are conveniently summarized in Kagan, 'Redefining'; Luttwak, *Byzantine Strategy*, covers the reign of Justinian and has been much more favourably received. For an overview, see also Whitby, 'Ancient Rome'.

imperial decision-making,[13] and so have to make inferences about policy from the dispositions of fortresses and troops and from the literary evidence. It is reasonable to assume that the emperor did attempt to maintain a front line of defence along the frontiers where these were clearly demarcated, as by the Danube. Major fortified cities, for example Dara and Amida in Upper Mesopotamia, were supported by networks of smaller forts in between and also by defences at places along the main routes to the interior, for example Edessa in the East or Serdica in Thrace. This approach did not, however, prevent emperors from trying to project Roman authority beyond such formal limits, with the result that frontiers were zones rather than fixed lines. This was particularly relevant for those areas, for example between Palestine and the Euphrates or in reconquered North Africa, where there were no clear divisions and local inhabitants were accustomed to moving to and fro across notional borders. Roman economic power reached outwards, attracting individuals or groups to serve in Roman armies, and Christianity also extended Roman influence beyond formal borders, but a *modus vivendi* had to be established with local leaders to ensure peace and stability.

Internal structure

The empire's territory was made up of three main land blocks: the Levant, Asia Minor and the Balkans. The provinces of the northern and central Balkans had been impoverished by repeated warfare in the fifth century, but most of the remainder of the empire was prosperous. In Asia Minor many of the cities of the Aegean littoral were flourishing reservoirs of resources and human talent for Constantinople, while on the Anatolian plateau extensive estates provided livestock for the empire's needs and income for major private landowners. In the Levant, the Nile valley grew the grain that fed Constantinople's population while Palestine and Syria exported oil and wine; in much of this area population densities reached their ancient peak in the early years of Justinian's reign. Certain areas were less fully under imperial control than the majority: Justinian was spared problems in Isauria, the region centred on the Taurus mountains in southern Anatolia, thanks to the energetic reassertion of official authority

---

13. Justinian's decision to attack the Vandals is a very rare exception (see Ch.6), and even then we have to rely on the account in Procopius, who, though not present at high-level discussions, could have learned the details from Belisarius.

by Anastasius in the 490s, but the Samaritans in Palestine twice revolted, in 529 in an uprising focused on Neapolis triggered by Justinian's religious repression, and again in 555 at Caesarea where they combined with local Jews. In 558 the Tzani, warlike inhabitants of northeastern Anatolia whose incorporation into the empire and conversion to Christianity had been celebrated early in Justinian's reign, revolted and had to be pacified over again.

The empire's armature or skeleton was provided by a combination of sea-lanes and the Roman road network. The busiest sea routes linked Alexandria and Gaza via Cyprus or southern Anatolia to Constantinople, while lesser routes crisscrossed the Aegean or tied in the Black Sea littoral. The risk of bad weather reduced traffic at sea from late autumn to early spring, while the Vandal occupation of Carthage had brought control of Roman ships and maritime expertise, enabling them to pursue piratical raids which sometimes affected the eastern empire. On land Constantinople was connected to the east by two strategic highways, a more northern one through Ankara and Caesarea (Kayseri) towards the Armenian frontier and a more southerly one that crossed the Taurus via the Cilician Gates, before heading east towards Edessa (Urfa) or south to Antioch (Antakya). In the Balkans the comparable routes were the old Via Egnatia that led west via Thessalonica and then over the Pindus mountains to the Adriatic at Dyrrachium, while a more northerly route ran through Philippopolis (Plovdiv) and Serdica (Sofia) towards the Danube at Singidunum (Belgrade). In earlier times this route had continued via Sirmium towards northern Italy across the Julian Alps, but this western part of the journey was now controlled by the Gepids or Ostrogoths.

It was possible for information or military reinforcements to travel quickly, especially by sea at the right time of year and with a favourable wind, but equally it was possible for communications to be disrupted. Along the main highways the empire supported an extensive infrastructure of way-stations, the larger *mansiones* providing accommodation while the smaller *mutationes* held replacement animals. This massive system underpinned the movement of official business through the *cursus publicus*, warrants for whose use were eagerly sought and often obtained improperly by people of influence. The faster side of the *cursus publicus* provided posting horses, pack animals, light carriages, and mule carts; the slow side, the *cursus clabularius*, offered ox-drawn carts for moving official goods, for example supplies and equipment for troops or materials for imperial constructions. The cost of this system was high and already in the fifth century Emperor

Leo had acted to reduce its coverage, while Justinian took further steps to restrict its operation in Asia Minor to the strategic highway to the Persian frontier.[14]

In terms of the speed of travel, a message from the eastern frontier could probably reach Constantinople within a week, although critical information could have travelled more quickly if relays of riders continued through the night. An important individual naturally travelled more slowly than professional dispatch riders, and a tight limit for the journey of an ambassador from the Tigris to Constantinople and back – a round trip of about 2,500 kilometres – was the seventy days that Khusro allocated to Rufinus in 531. The oxen of the *cursus clabularius* will not have covered more than 20km in a day, if that, while the horses of the *cursus publicus* would have permitted Rufinus to go as much as twice as far. This pace of life meant that emperors had to grant considerable autonomy to their local representatives, provincial governors and military commanders.

Constantinople

Constantinople was the hub for this world, the imperial and religious centre for the East and by far the largest city in Europe with a peak population of up to 500,000. The city was situated on the tongue of land between the Sea of Marmara and the Golden Horn, where it was protected by three separate sets of defences. The innermost was the wall of Constantine that had marked out the limit of his new imperial city in the 330s; although this was now superseded, the wall did distinguish the densely inhabited areas inside from the more suburban regions outside.[15] In 413 a triple line of fortifications was completed about a mile further west on the peninsula: these are known as the Theodosian Walls, although the young Theodosius II would have had little input into their creation, for which credit belongs to the praetorian prefect Anthemius. An external moat was overlooked by a lower outer wall or *proteichisma*, while the main wall, a traditional late Roman construction of concrete braced by six separate bands of five-brick courses and faced with limestone blocks, rose about 30 metres above the moat. This wall was overtopped by 96 towers that rose a further 3-4.5 metres above the wall and projected between 6

14. Proc., *SH* 30.1–11; John Lydus, *de Mag.* 3.61.
15. See Mango, *Développement*.

and 11 metres.[16] At their northern end near the Golden Horn the walls eventually incorporated the defences of Blachernae, an area of importance as a suburban residence for the emperor as well as the site of a major church to the Virgin.

In Justinian's reign the land between the Constantinian and Theodosian walls was the location for the elite's villas, as well as monasteries, cemeteries, market gardens, and open-air cisterns. In the mid-fifth century a further set of defences was constructed about 60km west of the capital that ran from the Black Sea to the Sea of Marmara near Selymbria (Silivri). These protected the whole European side of the Bosporus, whose prosperity had risen as the growth of the capital led to the construction of luxury residences along the waterway and extramural monasteries, as well as some important elements of the city's extensive water supply system.[17]

The focus of the city was the Great Palace, located in the southwest on the slopes overlooking the Sea of Marmara where it benefitted from cooling sea breezes in summer.[18] Adjacent to it lay the Hippodrome, where the emperor met his people on race days and other formal occasions, with the back of the imperial box, the Kathisma, directly connected to the Palace by a passage.[19] Nearby was the Great Church of S. Sophia where the emperor worshipped most regularly in the presence of his people; again this could be reached from the Palace by a protected walkway. The backbone of the city was the Mese, a colonnaded avenue that ran from the open space of the Augustaeum outside the main entrance to the Palace, the Chalke, through the Forum of Constantine – whose site is marked by the porphyry pillar now known as the 'Burnt Column' – past the Tetrapylon, a junction with a major road running north-south through the city, and the Forum of Theodosius, adorned with triumphal arches with palm-tree decorations on columns, to the Capitolium near the Church of S. Polyeuctus and the aqueduct of Valens. Here there was a major fork, with the Mese continuing closer to the Sea of Marmara through the Forum of Arcadius, with a decorated

---

16. The most detailed discussion is Tsangadas, *Fortifications* ch.1. Nothing survives from the Constantinian wall, but much of the Theodosian land walls still encircle central Istanbul.

17. Whitby, 'Long Walls'; these walls are also known as the Anastasian Walls, and he is often given sole credit for their construction, but the name reflects the fact that they had to be substantially restored during his reign.

18. For the operation of the court, see McCormick, 'Emperor'.

19. For the emperor Theodosius I in the Kathisma, see plates 5, 10, 15, and plate 17 for the key monuments that lined the spina (the central divider in the Hippodrome) with S. Sophia.

column comparable to the extant Trajan's Column in Rome, through the Constantinian Wall and on to the Golden Gate in the Theodosian Walls.[20] From the Capitolium the northern branch passed S. Polyeuctus and continued through the forum dominated by the Column of Marcian, then near the Holy Apostles, and finally through the two sets of walls.

Constantinople's large population could only be supported by the regular import of massive quantities of grain, oil, wine and other foodstuffs, for which extensive harbour and storage facilities were needed.[21] The first harbours were located on the Golden Horn, but the larger harbours of Julian and Theodosius were soon developed on the Sea of Marmara. Each required long wharves and substantial granaries to permit the rapid unloading of the hundreds of ships that transported grain from Egypt or oil and wine from the Levant. Registered inhabitants of the capital were entitled to regular rations, as had been the case in Rome, and this was an envied privilege so that movement to reside in the city had to be controlled and the numbers of recipients restricted.

An equally pressing need, granted that the city had no permanent streams or other water supplies, was an abundance of water, both for personal consumption and for the baths and fountains that were essential aspects of civilized Roman life. In addition to numerous covered cisterns, of which most were fairly small although the surviving Basilica Cistern (Yerebatanserai) near the Hippodrome is substantial, massive open-air cisterns were constructed between the Constantinian and Theodosian walls in the mid-fifth century. A very extensive network of channels, tunnels and, where necessary, aqueducts, crisscrossed the hinterland, stretching out to the Long Walls and beyond, reaching close to the modern Turkish frontier with Bulgaria.[22] Security of supply was a constant concern for emperors, since shortages of grain, water, wine or oil provoked disturbances, including embarrassing chants in the Hippodrome over bread and even murders when inhabitants fought for water at the fountains.[23] As a result, a regular ceremony in the imperial calendar was a procession to inspect the granaries.[24]

---

20. On this processional route, see Mango, 'Triumphal Way'; also Matthews, *Constantinople* ch.6.
21. For discussion of all aspects of the functioning of Constantinople, see the papers in Dagron and Mango, *Constantinople*.
22. For comprehensive discussion, see Crow et al. *Water*; for cisterns, see also Ward et al. 'Cisterns'.
23. Malalas 18.95 (wine), 121 (bread), 139 (water); Marc.Com. *s.a.* 524 (oil).
24. Const.Porph., *de Caerimoniis* 2.51.

Organization and security were the responsibility of the City Prefect, who oversaw the running of the fourteen regions into which the city was divided.[25] Although the Prefect was a very senior official with a large staff under him, the most serious events often exceeded his ability to cope. When rioting progressed beyond the regular disturbances of the Hippodrome or minor unrest, imperial guards had to be brought in to restore order. Dedicated wardens could cope with the frequent minor fires that inevitably broke out in such a densely-populated space with its wooden buildings, but major conflagrations or the massive destruction from the 557 earthquake could only be made good through imperial intervention.

Controlling the number of residents was a perennial problem: to survive the city required a regular inflow of people from the healthier countryside, but the attractions of urban life with the chance for subsidized food supplies were a powerful magnet, while legal and religious matters, as well as insecurity in the Balkans, also drew people in, often for extended periods. In 535 Justinian legislated to raise the prestige and effectiveness of the Prefect of the Watch by establishing the new role of Praetor of the People, while in 539 he created the office of *quaesitor* with the responsibility to scrutinize everyone coming to the capital, verify their business and means of support, and ensure that they left promptly after the conduct of their affairs; there were special regulations for visiting bishops.[26]

Chief Officers

One reason for the congestion in Constantinople was that the administration of the empire, both secular and ecclesiastical, was concentrated in the city. Within the Palace there were three main offices, the most important being that of the *magister officiorum*. He was in charge of the majority of the palace guards, the *scholae* and *domestici*, was responsible for all aspects of the administration of the palace, controlled admissions to imperial audiences as well as the *cursus publicus* (public post) and couriers who brought official business to the capital, supervised the billeting of soldiers and production of weapons in the state arms factories, directed the *agentes in rebus*, officers who were dispatched into the provinces to conduct all manner of business, and oversaw the major palatine bureaux. The other

---

25. For discussion of the regions, see Matthews, *Constantinople* ch.5.
26. Justinian, *Novels* 13; 80 (*quaesitor*); 6.3; 123.9 (bishops).

two officials, the *comes sacrarum largitionum* and *comes rei privatae*, handled imperial finances. The former received customs dues, commutation of military levies, and the output of mines and textile factories, which he then distributed as coin, whose minting he controlled, or as plate or uniforms. In addition to a large palatine staff, he also controlled the operations in the provinces required to collect his revenues and minerals. The other office, as the title indicates, managed the emperor's private estates that had been built up through bequest, confiscation, or annexation of heirless property, to the extent that the emperor perhaps owned about 15 per cent of land in the provinces.[27] Revenues in rents were used to meet the emperor's more private expenses, including the support of the imperial household. Alongside these three, legal business was conducted by the *quaestor sacri palatii*, to give the role its full title, using officials in the bureaux controlled by the *magister*, while, in an example of the creation of parallel structures to ensure that mutual competition reduced the risk that any officer became over-mighty, the *comes excubitorum* commanded the most prestigious unit of guards and so could counter-balance the *magister officiorum*. The imperial bedchamber was run by the eunuch *praepositus sacri cubiculi*, who gradually acquired some of the revenues of the *res privata*.

Technically outside the palace, though naturally closely linked to it, the key official was the praetorian prefect of the Orient,[28] the empire's chief financial official with responsibility for collecting tax revenues and levies, providing for the needs of the armies, and ensuring the food supply of Constantinople and other major cities. The prefect calculated the empire's financial needs, of which by far the largest single part related to military expenditure, determined what manpower was required to fill the ranks, and oversaw the distribution of supplies and pay to military units. This task was exceptionally complex and required a substantial staff in the capital, allocated to numerous departments or *scrinia* within the two major subdivisions of finance and justice. To control local matters outside the capital the prefecture was divided into dioceses, each under a vicar or deputy, with these in turn being split into provinces under a governor; these officials had offices that mirrored that of the prefect in the capital. Within the provinces much of the business of tax-collection

---

27. The guesstimate of Lee, *From Rome* 227.
28. There was also a praetorian prefect of Illyricum, based at different times in Thessalonica and Justiniana Prima; his operation will have mirrored, though on a much smaller scale, that of the prefect of the Orient. In due course prefects were appointed to Africa and Italy.

was carried out at city level by the local *curiales*, city councillors, a duty that offered opportunities for enrichment but was more often unwelcome, since the *curiales* would be held liable for any shortfall in revenue. The prefect handled a substantial amount of legal business that was referred upwards from provincial governors and diocesan vicars.

Although there was a variety of taxes, by far the most important was the land tax that was assessed through formulae which varied between provinces; this factored in the quality or productivity of land, its area and type of crop and the associated manpower, with the detailed census being conducted at local, usually city, level. In theory provinces were reassessed on a cycle of fifteen years or indictions, which came to be used as an important dating mechanism, but in practice there is no evidence that such a massive task was ever undertaken across the empire. In theory, again, the combination of all this local information on tax capacity permitted the praetorian prefect to construct a balanced budget, with the predictable expenses of the armies and capital being aligned with the tax productivity of the provinces, so that in any given year an appropriate rate of assessment could be imposed. In practice the system was far less perfect, with supernumerary levies being exacted in order to make up for shortfalls, whether that was in the original calculation or as a result of losses in the extraction process. By the sixth century much of the tax was levied in coin, although it was always possible to demand produce. Regardless of how the revenue arrived, much of the income was used to purchase supplies, probably at advantageous rates, that were needed to support the armies.

Although this description might suggest a fairly clear demarcation of duties between an emperor's senior officials, the reality was different, markedly so. The interests of the praetorian prefect overlapped with those of the *magister* in the matter of military supply and those of the *comes sacrarum largitionum* with regard to coinage, while the *comes rei privatae* and the *praepositus* both had interests in imperial estates. Such duplication of responsibility was deliberate, since it was very much in the emperor's interests to maintain an administrative polyocracy, where no single office had clear superiority but officials at different levels competed with each other for power and influence, ultimately ensuring that the emperor remained supreme.[29] We can observe the effects of this approach through

---

29. John Lydus, *de Mag.* 3.66–7. For discussion, see Kelly, 'Emperors' 150–6, 169–75; Barnish, Lee and Whitby, 'Government' 170–81.

the eyes of John Lydus, a career civil servant who grumbled as he observed his position in the judicial wing of the prefecture being restructured in 539.[30] The changes had resulted in judicial officials being overshadowed by their financial colleagues, allegedly in line with the priorities of John the Cappadocian.[31]

A system of this size and complexity was inevitably open to abuse and imperial legislation was repeatedly issued to crack down on malpractice. This repetition of legislation does not, however, demonstrate a disregard for the law and imperial authority, since laws were repeated because petitioners believed that imperial intervention would bring about change.[32] Detailed records were kept both centrally and locally, but it must usually have been difficult to track down a particular document when needed, for example by searching through the files kept in the substructures of the Hippodrome at Constantinople. Justinian was publicly concerned with administrative efficiency and legislated to raise the prestige of some provincial officials by increasing their salaries substantially.[33] His reforms were, of course, bitterly criticized by Procopius in his *Secret History*, but that might reflect the fact that the emperor was attempting to rebalance in limited ways a system that had always privileged those with wealth and status, both in terms of securing access to justice and obtaining the desired results.

Cities

In the provinces the efficacy of imperial administration depended to a considerable extent upon the vitality of the network of cities. In Late Antiquity the classical city of the High Empire came under pressure through the effects of inflation, religious change, tribal invasion, and the magnetic location of imperial power.[34] In the western empire many cities had contracted significantly well before the end of imperial rule, but in the East this process was much slower. Imperial legislation might suggest that the local ruling class of *curiales* was under remorseless pressure as individuals attempted to avoid their obligations or escape from them by entering

---

30. Justinian, *Novel* 82.
31. See Maas, *Lydus* ch.2, esp. 33–5.
32. Harries, *Law* 77–88; Whitby, 'Role'; for the older, negative assessments of administrative changes in late antiquity, see Jones, *LRE* 1045–58, and especially MacMullen, *Corruption*.
33. E.g. Justinian, *Novels* 24–5 on Pisidia and Lycaonia.
34. Overview of changes in Lee, *From Rome* 202–7.

imperial service, but the weight of evidence is somewhat misleading: the *curiales* were the people best placed to complain about apparent breaches of, or loopholes in, the laws regulating their activities, and so would petition the emperor for legislative redress. The creation of the massive imperial administration and a new Senate at Constantinople in the fourth century required the regular inflow of members of the provincial educated elite, but local *curiales* wanted some control on this movement as well as the substantial benefits that it brought to individuals. John Lydus and Evagrius both looked back to the demise of effective city councils during Anastasius' reign, when the praetorian prefect Marinus was said to be a particular enemy of the *curiales*.[35] Procopius blamed Justinian for removing the revenues that underpinned the salaries of local teachers and doctors.[36]

Despite the pessimism of these authors, city councils continued to exercise responsibilities. Justinian's legislation in 535 to compel the most significant locals to take in rotation the post of *defensor civitatis*, to oversee the effective running of their city, reflects his commitment to cities as the key units of local administration as well as his awareness of the problems they were facing.[37] The public life of cities in the early empire had been intricately bound up with the conduct of religion, with temples dominating most urban centres and revenues from estates being used by *curiales* to support festivals and building projects. Thus the triumph of Christianity undermined a substantial element of the traditional economic and social fabric of the cities, but the new centres of religious power did replace this. The Church became increasingly important as a local landowner and as the resources of the secular elite declined the clergy joined the ranks of the local notables, the *ktetores* or owners; in many cities the local bishop was the most powerful individual, the person to represent the city in moments of crisis.

The most serious threat to cities was invasion, in part because of the possible sack of the urban centre, but equally importantly through the ravaging of the rural hinterland on which most cities depended for sustenance. In the northern Balkans cities had been weakened by repeated Hun attacks, either being captured or having their territories regularly ravaged. When Justinian came to construct his prestige urban project at his birthplace, now renamed Justiniana Prima, the strong circuit of walls

---

35. John Lydus, *de Mag.* 1.28; Evagrius 3.42; *de Mag.* 3.49 (Marinus).
36. Proc., *SH* 26.6–10.
37. Justinian, *Novel* 15. For a sensible and positive assessment of the continuing vitality of cities in the sixth century, see Whittow, 'Ruling'.

initially enclosed an area of under seven hectares, tiny for a classical city and providing room for only a small population, especially since much of the interior was occupied by administrative buildings, a basilica and seven other churches. Here security and survival were paramount.

Where cities have been extensively excavated in the eastern provinces the picture is very different. The best examples are Ephesus and Sardis in Asia Minor, Aphrodisias in Caria, Apamea in Syria, and Caesarea in Palestine.[38] In each city it is clear that traditional urban life with broad streets, flourishing commercial areas, and places for public entertainment existed alongside the new provision of churches through the sixth century, or in the case of Apamea until the Persian sack of 573. The anecdotes in the *Life* of Symeon the Holy Fool suggest that much the same was true of Syrian Emesa.[39] What links these six cities is that they were all provincial capitals and it is reasonable to postulate that the presence of a governor and his support staff consolidated the vitality of such sites.

What happened outside these privileged cities is less clear, not least because archaeologists are naturally attracted to the most important sites, but the smaller city of Corycus on the southern coast of Anatolia also flourished along with numerous inland villages, and surveys of the extensive remains of villages in the limestone massif inland from Antioch reveal that the area was densely settled, with new building work continuing into the later sixth century and levels of occupation being sustained into the seventh. Similarly surveys in modern Greece show that it was more densely settled in the late Roman period than in the earlier empire, with smaller farmsteads than in previous centuries but a more intensive exploitation of the countryside that generated surpluses for export.[40] The settlement of marginal land in upland Syria and in the wadis of Palestine indicates that population levels there were also high. Cities were at the apex of focused economic and social pyramids. The interdependence of city and hinterland is revealed by events at Myra in 542, where the local bishop, Nicholas of Zion, advised famers not to bring their produce to the city market for fear of contracting plague, with the result that the city came

---

38. See discussions in Foss, *Ephesus* and *Sardis*; Rouché, *Aphrodisias*; Balty, 'Apamée'; Raban and Holum, *Caesarea*; overview in Lee, *From Rome* 205–7.
39. For discussion of the *Life* and translation, see Krueger, *Symeon*.
40. The best overview is Ward-Perkins, 'Land' esp. 320–7; Foss, 'Countryside; Foss, 'Lycian Coast' 47–8; Dauphin, 'Pavements'; Sodini, 'Dèhès'; Curta, *Edinburgh History* 38–40; Alcock, 'Roman Imperialism'.

close to starvation until saved by the saint.[41] If the broad underpinning of local agriculture was disrupted, as was happening in the Balkans, cities would gradually be strangled unless they could depend on regular support from the imperial centre. Another impoverished part of the East was Cyrenaica, eastern Libya, which had been plagued by tribal incursions.[42]

If a city was destroyed, whether by enemy attack as at Amida in 503 and Antioch in 540, or by earthquakes as at Antioch in 527 and 528, significant recovery was possible through a combination of imperial assistance and the migration of population from a flourishing hinterland. In those areas where cities were widely scattered, for example central Anatolia, provincial governors might struggle to control the large landowners who dominated their estates with bands of armed retainers, and they received little help from the managers of the extensive imperial properties in the area, a situation that Justinian attempted to remedy through his provincial reorganizations. Even here, though, the miracles in the *Life* of Theodore of Sykeon convey an impression of flourishing villages in Galatia at the end of the century.[43]

To sustain effective and fair administration in the provinces, emperors had to know what was happening and to ensure that their image was known and respected in all places. Governors contributed to the dissemination of the image through their role in propagating laws and they were supposed to submit regular reports, but reliance solely on official channels of communication might not lead to the truth reaching the emperor's ears, as a notorious example of collusion between governors and investigators in fourth-century Africa demonstrates.[44] However, alternative sources of information were available. Under Justinian acclamations chanted in provincial capitals were transmitted to Constantinople,[45] and the Blue circus faction, which looked to Justinian as its patron, would report on matters if it could see advantage to itself; furthermore, bishops or monks might also report on abuses. Regular inclusion of the emperor's name in church services will have strengthened his local reputation, a replacement for the

41. See Magoulias, 'Lives' 69–70.

42. Mattingly, *Tripolitania* 171–217.

43. Translation of most of *Life* in Dawes and Baynes, *Byzantine Saints*, and discussion in Mitchell, *Anatolia* II ch.19, esp 122–34.

44. Ammianus Marcellinus 28.6; discussion in Matthews, *Roman Empire* 383–7.

45. This dates back to an edict of Constantine in 331 (*Cod. Theod.* 1.16.6), with the praetorian prefect being tasked with conveying the chants.

allegiance established in former times through celebration of the imperial cult, and it has also been suggested that the circus factions contributed as well through chanting that inevitably mentioned the victorious ruler.[46] All this could not have resulted in a perfect system, but since Justinian's legislation proclaimed his concern for justice and efficiency there was an incentive for reports of infringements to be submitted.

Economy

In addition to the health of cities, another indication of the vitality of Justinian's empire is the evidence for economic activity.[47] The majority of economic exchanges will have been local, as peasants and other producers supplied food and other necessities to neighbouring cities, receiving in exchange the coinage that they needed to pay their taxes. The evidence of rows of shops in Sardis and Apamea can be backed up by stories in the *Life* of Symeon the Holy Fool. This seventh-century text has several stories of Symeon's deliberately bizarre behaviour in the market of Emesa, where he made a nuisance of himself by disrupting commerce, eating produce he had not purchased, and giving away goods that he did not own.[48] Much long-distance activity related to the state, namely the provisioning of Constantinople and logistical support for the armies; this was always subject to the vagaries of harvests and the intervention of bad weather, but there is no evidence for the sort of structural stasis that prevented the fifth-century western empire from pursuing its wishes.

Literary evidence for economic activity is rare and patterns of trade have to be reconstructed primarily from the evidence of pottery, the remains of the amphorae that were used to transport bulk goods such as oil, wine, fish sauce, and high-quality table wares. Pottery survives in very substantial quantities since jars broke quite easily, but thereafter their fragments were almost indestructible and incapable of reuse (unlike metal or glass). Evidence from shipwrecks, of which increasing numbers have been explored in the Mediterranean, indicates that bulk cargoes of amphorae

---

46. Liebeschuetz in his review of Alan Cameron, *Circus Factions*, in *JRS* 68, 1978, 199.
47. The best overview of economic activity in the late empire is Ward-Perkins, 'Specialized Production'; also Sarris, *Economy*.
48. See Krueger, *Symeon* esp. ch.7.

were regularly accompanied by other goods, so that it is reasonable to infer broader patterns of trade from the discovery of pieces of amphorae.[49]

Distribution of coinage is another indicator of activity: although the state produced coins for its own purposes, primarily to pay the troops and to collect taxes, its existence then facilitated a range of economic exchanges as, for example, soldiers spent their stipends or farmers sold their produce to obtain coin to meet tax demands. Marble is another durable object whose place of origin can be identified; in the late antique world the grey-striped marble of Proconnesus in the Sea of Marmara came to dominate the market for church decoration, for example columns and chancel screens.[50] Finally papyri from Egypt reveal highly complex economic activity in the towns and villages of the Nile valley. Although Egypt is sometimes set aside as a special case, this view is becoming increasingly difficult to sustain.[51]

The combination of this evidence has led to the rejection of the older view that the whole Roman empire had lapsed into irreversible decline during the fifth century. Trade across the Mediterranean and beyond was inevitably affected by developments such as the emergence of the Vandals as a piratical naval power, but it continued to flourish. Overall, whereas in much of the West economic activity largely shrank into local horizons, societies in most of the East were richer and more complex into the late sixth century. This complexity of combined interlocking local, regional and long-distance networks, of which the first two can best be studied in Egypt while the last is charted by the pottery evidence, points to a flourishing state of affairs. It is more than coincidence that amphorae identified as coming from northern Syria and Palestine, mostly for oil and wine respectively, are widely distributed at the same time as the evidence of field surveys demonstrates very high levels of settlement in these areas. Syrian oil was shipped to Vandal Africa, the wine of Gaza was widely esteemed for its quality, while the fine red-slip pottery produced at Phocaea on the Aegean coastline is another example of specialist production for wide distribution. When Procopius was sent to Syracuse by Belisarius to find out information about Vandal preparations, the cover story for his espionage was that he was buying provisions in the market there. At Syracuse he happened to meet a fellow citizen of Caesarea who had

49. Overview in Lee, *From Rome* 235–9.
50. Dodge and Ward-Perkins, *Marble*.
51. Overview in Keenan, 'Egypt'.

settled in the west as a merchant, quite possibly in the export of wine from Palestine, and this man had a staff who travelled widely on his business.[52]

The trade discussed above was maritime. According to an influential model of the ancient economy the costs of transport by land made the movement of goods over significant distances prohibitively expensive for anyone other than the state.[53] There are, however, stories that offset this negative picture. John of Ephesus records the activities of two honest but successful traders, the brothers Elijah and Theodore, who accompanied caravans to Persia, and of Addai who created a vineyard in Mesopotamia that attracted merchants from Cappadocia; in the latter case the traders were certainly moving heavy bulky produce.[54] Goods for which we have very little evidence – for example perishable items such as wool and leather – will probably have had a similar impact on particular areas, but they rarely survive, so that we can only guess at the supply chains that underpinned the state factories for producing clothing, shields, and other military equipment. The state was concerned about the acquisition of strategic materials, as is indicated by a story in Procopius about Justinian's interest in improving access to the luxury item of silk, used for the ceremonial robes worn at court. Early in his reign, in the context of diplomacy to persuade the Christian Ethiopians to support the Romans in their war against Persia, Justinian suggested to the king that he could make money and help the Romans by moving into the Indian silk trade, so that the Romans no longer had to enrich their enemies through this commerce. The initiative failed, since Persian traders regularly pre-empted the Ethiopians at Indian harbours, but the emperor's interest was sufficiently well-known for some monks to approach him in 551 with an offer to smuggle silk worm eggs.[55]

Although our knowledge of the Justinianic economy is fragmentary, what we know indicates the persistence of a powerful and prosperous system that tied cities to their countryside, connected frontier armies to provincial centres of production as well as to the imperial core, and linked areas of specialist output with wider Mediterranean markets. It was

52. Proc., *Wars* 3.14.3–9.
53. Finley, *Ancient Economy*; Jones, *LRE* 841–2, based on the charges in Diocletian's Edict on Maximum Prices.
54. John of Ephesus, *Lives* pp. 576–85; 129–30. Muhammad, before the start of his prophetic activity, travelled with caravans transporting grain between Syria and Arabia.
55. Proc., *Wars* 1.20.9–12; 8.17.1–8.

underpinned by a currency that was fairly stable, with the gold *solidus*, minted at 72 to the pound, being used for official salaries;[56] this provided the standard while the bronze currency, which had been overhauled by Anastasius, preserved a stable relationship with gold and serviced the normal transactions of life. This currency united the empire and served as a vehicle for publicizing imperial messages. Gold and bronze were minted at Constantinople and Thessalonica, and in due course at Carthage and Ravenna, while Nicomedia, Cyzicus, Antioch, and Alexandria produced only bronze. From the mid-540s and intermittently over the next 150 years, some issues of *solidi* were struck at a slightly lighter weight, of 20–23 *siliquae* as opposed to the standard 24. Because many of the lightweight *solidi* have been found to the north of the Danube it used to be thought that they were produced to reduce the expense of payments to tribal groups or to facilitate trade, but this is implausible since most such transactions will have been done by weight and the reverse marking on these *solidi* clearly indicates their different weight. A more plausible explanation is that they were used to pay certain internal salaries and pensions in an effort to trim costs when the plague or other financial pressures had reduced imperial revenues.[57]

Christianity

The Church constituted another network that supported the coherence of the empire. Some scholars, working in the tradition of Gibbon, have believed that Christianity contributed to the decline of the empire by creating a large new class of unproductive mouths, withdrawing much-needed manpower from the system of military recruitment, and undermining the warlike spirit of the Romans by opposing military service or advocating acceptance of defeat as justified divine punishment for human misdeeds. The evidence, however, is not compelling. The Old Testament provided plenty of prototypes of successful fighting in God's name, so that the Bible could be harnessed to imperial military need with the Romans becoming the new Israel. In crises emperors were prepared to conscript monks, especially those who had seen this as an escape route from service, and the considerable size of ecclesiastical establishments has to be

56. For a Justinianic *solidus*, see Plate 9.
57. See Hendy, *Monetary Economy* 492–4; Sarris, 'Plague' 175–7.

set alongside the unquantifiable staff that underpinned the innumerable temples to local and imperial divinities in the early empire.[58]

What Christianity did offer was an organization that paralleled the structures of the state, with patriarchs in the largest cities (Constantinople, Alexandria, Antioch, and Jerusalem), who presided over groups of provinces in each of which a metropolitan bishop was located in the provincial capital, with the metropolitan being responsible for the bishops in each of his province's cities. Bishops varied considerably in wealth and hence power, with the richest having stipends of over 30 pounds of gold per annum, while at the other end of the scale, where the majority of bishoprics were probably located, there were official categories for those with incomes of under 2, between 2 and 3, and between 3 and 5 pounds.[59] The bishops of a province and the metropolitans of a diocese were supposed to meet annually, thereby tying together these larger units, while the traffic of clergy and monks from the provinces to the capital was such that Justinian had to legislate to ensure that bishops had written support for a visit from their metropolitan and could only secure an imperial audience through the Patriarch of Constantinople.[60] Since the Church became a very substantial landowner, bishops were important figures in their cities, being involved in appointing and monitoring public officials, against whom they might need to protect their communities, financing public works, and implementing regulations.[61] In crises they emerge as the *de facto* community leaders, for example taking responsibility for negotiations at Sura in 540 after the city's garrison commander was killed.[62]

The Church offered ideological as well as structural support for the empire. God would grant success to rulers who upheld orthodoxy, as Justinian proclaimed in his legislation and as Christian leaders and writers regularly insisted when arguing for their particular point of view. Shared religion could reinforce links with external states, for example Lazica and Axum.[63] It helped that the majority of the empire's enemies were either non-Christian or heretics, so that divine favour would naturally support the orthodox. At a local level a bishop might sustain morale and

---

58. Whitby, 'Emperors' 175–9; 'Army and Society' 528.
59. Justinian, *Novel* 123.3 of 546.
60. Justinian, *Novels* 6.3 of 535; 123.9 of 544.
61. Liebeschuetz, *Decline* ch.8.
62. Proc., *Wars* 2.5.8–21.
63. Lee, *From Rome* 277–9.

restrain the panic of the civilian population, as Thomas did at Apamea in 540 by parading the city's relic of the True Cross while Khusro's army approached from the ruins of Antioch.[64] Stories of miraculous escapes could give inhabitants the confidence to contribute energetically to their city's defence:[65] at Sergiopolis in 542 a heavenly army was said to have appeared on the battlements, while at Edessa the *acheiropoietos* image of Christ – one not made by human hands – came to be credited with destroying the Persian mound when it threatened to overtop the walls in the 544 siege.[66]

Not all aspects of Christianity were positive, however. The converse of the strength of orthodoxy was the division of heresy and schism. Justinian's measures against heretics caused his own 'Arian' soldiers to mutiny,[67] and subsequently his attempts to force through his decisions on the so-called Three Chapters provoked strong opposition in reconquered Africa. The most substantial issue was that of the opponents of Chalcedon in the East: the 'Nestorians', followers of the condemned Patriarch Nestorius, were almost entirely located outside the empire, mostly within the Persian realm, but the Miaphysites, at the other end of the religious argument, constituted much of the population of Egypt and the frontier provinces in Syria, Mesopotamia and Armenia. After attempts to negotiate an agreement had failed and bursts of coercion had proved futile, in the 540s the Miaphysites had begun to create their own ecclesiastical structure so as to ensure that there were bishops to ordain priests who could perform baptisms and other rites. This did not immediately create secular problems under Justinian, but at Edessa in 609/10 Khusro II believed that these doctrinal divisions offered an opportunity to win over some local populations,[68] and these could be seen as contributing to the success of Arab invasions, the divine punishment for successive emperors' 'heretical' commitment to Chalcedon.

---

64. Proc., *Wars* 2.11.14–27; Evagrius 4.26.
65. Whitby, '*Deus nobiscum*'.
66. Evagrius 4.27–8, writing over 40 years later. In each case it is noticeable that Procopius did not record the rescue miracle (*Wars* 2.20.11–15; 2.27.1–17), though in the context of Khusro's approach in 540 he noted that Edessa enjoyed divine protection through Christ's letter to King Abgar (2.12.26), so that he would probably have recorded the miracle stories if they had been in circulation.
67. Proc., *Wars* 4.14.12–14.
68. Agapius 460 (for the context, see Hoyland, *Theophilus* 66–7): Khusro offered to spare Nestorians and Jacobites (i.e. Miaphysites) but threatened with death those who refused to abandon the Chalcedonian faith.

Education

Although the Church strongly disapproved of the traditional system
of secular education, since it was based on a canon of classical texts, for
example Homer, that presented stories of the Olympian deities, this
continued in reasonable health into the reign of Justinian. This mattered
because, though there could be no such thing as a national curriculum, a
fairly uniform empire-wide approach to education created a shared Greek
cultural background for the cadre that provided the majority of the empire's
administrators and senior officers. It also entrenched a snobbishness that
despised those outside the charmed circle, even those whose considerable
learning did not extend to perfect pronunciation.[69]

The first stage in the process was to learn basic reading and writing
with a local elementary teacher, of whom most were based in cities.[70]
Those who could afford to continue to the next stage studied with a
grammarian who would concentrate on imparting correct expression, both
orally and in writing, through study of a select group of classical texts;
these were copied out and then explained by the teacher. The third stage
was the study of rhetoric, through which pupils learned to compose their
own elegant speeches by close study of a selection of model texts and a
rhetorical handbook. Only a tiny fraction of the population could afford
this full experience, but these men – and it was overwhelmingly men who
benefitted – were equipped with a common body of literary knowledge that
allowed them to understand recondite allusions or literary jokes,[71] marking
them off from the majority of the population.

After this tripartite training some students progressed to further study.
Law was a favoured route for those interested in an official career which
involved attendance at one of the schools at Beirut, Constantinople or
Alexandria. Philosophy was more specialist, with the Academy at Athens
focusing on Neoplatonic teaching while at Alexandria a broader approach
was adopted, with Aristotelian commentary being an important element.

---

69. Thus Procopius (*SH* 20.17) sneered at Junillus, who as *quaestor* (542–8) and author of
doctrinal tracts (*PLRE* III.742) must have had an excellent education, but he was a Latin-speaker
whose attempts to speak Greek provoked laughter among his subordinates.
70. Summary in Browning, 'Education' 856–63.
71. For example, the term used to denigrate bowmen in Procopius' introduction, *toxotai*, in
contrast to the reputable *angemachoi* and *aspidiotes*, Homeric words for close-fighters and shield-
men (*Wars* 1.1.8), achieves its full force if the audience recalls that the word was used only once
in Homer, to refer to the cowardly Paris: see Van Nuffelen, 'Wor(l)ds' 42.

For a few in the Greek East, Latin was also studied, with John the Lydian being the prime example of someone whose reasonable but not perfect knowledge of the language made him an exception; one of his many reasons for detesting John the Cappadocian was that the prefect did not use Latin in his dealings.[72]

In an empire where different languages such as Coptic, Syriac, Armenian or Thracian were widely spoken by local populations, this education tied together the elite through a shared Greek culture. The origins of historians illustrate this phenomenon with authors coming from Panium in Thrace, Myrina in Asia Minor, Philadelphia and Epiphaneia in Syria, Caesarea in Palestine, and Egypt; only Menander came from the capital. Each year aspiring sons of the curial class in the cities moved to Constantinople in the hope of imperial preferment, to seek other forms of patronage, or to pursue a lucrative legal career. For some the move will have been brief, whereas others stayed to make their careers while still retaining an attachment to their native city and region, as Zoticus did in assisting his fellow provincial, John from the Lydian city of Philadelphia, with employment and marriage.

Justinian has been held responsible for initiating a decline in secular higher education.[73] An important element in this negative view is the closure of the philosophical school at Athens, seven of whose leading teachers briefly migrated to Persia in the hope of receiving more enlightened patronage from Khusro I, an incident recounted by Agathias.[74] The context was Justinian's action against pagans in 529, when particular attention was devoted to those involved in teaching and perhaps even a specific edict aimed at Athens; it does, however, seem that many of the philosophers returned to Athens after their brief sojourn in Persia.[75] Action against pagans, which continued to the end of Justinian's reign,[76] is not the same as an attack on, or disregard for, education. It is true that Justinian appointed as praetorian prefect John the Cappadocian, whom Procopius despised for his lack of education, but John, like Peter Barsymes, was a skilled financier and Procopius' snobbery reflects his own disregard for practical expertise.[77] Justinian is known to have patronized

---

72. John Lydus, *de Mag.* 2.68.
73. Lemerle, *Byzantine Humanism* 77.
74. Agathias, *Hist.* 2.30–1.
75. Malalas 18.47; *Cod. Iust.* 1.11.10.2; 1.5.18.4 (general); Malalas 18.42 (Athens). Summaries of the considerable debate in Sheppard, 'Philosophy' 841–3; Browning, 'Education' 863–5.
76. Malalas 18.136.
77. Proc., *Wars* 1.24.12.

the chronicler Marcellinus Comes and he commissioned John the Lydian to write an account of the Roman victory at Dara. He probably also, directly or indirectly, commissioned the *Buildings* of Procopius in the 550s and Paul the Silentiary's poem for the rededication of S. Sophia in 562. His *Novels* demonstrate that he valued effective communication adorned with appropriate cultural references, while his doctrinal endeavours presupposed the existence of a body of educated clergy, whose training would have begun in the standard secular system.

Challenges

Justinian's empire was united by different powerful bonds, but its prosperity faced substantial challenges: quite apart from warfare, environmental change and natural disasters have been blamed for undermining its economic and hence military stability. There is insufficient evidence for climate change to sustain an argument that this could have caused the variety of regional rises and falls in prosperity that can be seen across the Mediterranean. The abnormally cold year of 535/6, possibly caused by a massive volcanic eruption in Indonesia that led to failed harvests across Europe, is a particular case.[78] Whether it contributed to triggering the outbreak of bubonic plague in 542 is based on complex speculation and the plague is better treated as a disaster in its own right. It has also been contended that the clearance of land for intense agricultural exploitation that extended into marginal lands resulted in the dumping of alluvial deposits in river valleys, thereby damaging the productivity of the latter. There is evidence for alluvial deposition in the late Roman or post-Roman period, but this is impossible to date more precisely: in Asia Minor this had been carrying on for centuries as the city of Miletus, a major port in the fifth century BC, gradually became landlocked.

Different parts of Justinian's empire were shaken by earthquakes, with the most substantial, or best reported, being at Antioch in 527 and 528, and Constantinople in 557 and 558, but in each case with a much wider impact. At Antioch in 527 Procopius records that 250,000 perished,[79] but the city still recovered substantially, thanks to imperial support. The same

---

78. For an argument that maximizes the impact of climate change, in particular an alleged 'Late Antique Little Ice Age' of the mid-sixth century, see Harper, *Fate* ch.7, but the response of Haldon et al. 'Plagues (1)' details substantial problems of method and interpretation that seriously undermine Harper's thesis.
79. Proc., *Wars* 2.14.6.

was true at Constantinople, with Justinian taking a personal interest in the reconstruction of S. Sophia's dome and leaving the capital – perhaps for the first time in his reign – to supervise work at the Long Walls. Whether the shell-shocked inhabitants of Cos, whom Agathias observed in 551 wandering amidst the ruins,[80] rebuilt their city is unknown, and there must have been places where the relief of taxation for a few years was insufficient to restore the area's prosperity.

Terrible as these events were, they pale into insignificance in comparison to the 'Justinianic' Plague that reached Egypt in mid 541 and Constantinople in spring 542, where it raged for four months. It had left the capital by March 543, when Justinian issued a law declaring that God's 'education' was over and that wages should return to pre-plague levels,[81] but it continued to sweep through western provinces over the next two years.[82] During Justinian's reign it returned to the capital for six months in 558 and to the Levant in 560–61, and then periodically thereafter until the mid-eighth century. We have two detailed, independent accounts by Procopius and John of Ephesus, both of whom witnessed the plague's impact on Constantinople and Asia Minor. From these it appears that the plague was bubonic, with swellings in a victim's groin or armpits, though with some manifestations of pneumonic and septicemic variants.[83] To contemporaries the mortality seemed almost beyond calculation, with deaths said to be running at 5,000 a day in Constantinople to peak at over 10,000,[84] villages along the highways of the east being depopulated, and crops left to rot in the fields. Normal burial arrangements were overwhelmed, large pits were dug, and bodies were thrown into towers in the wall of Sycae (Galata) across the Golden Horn. Work came to a standstill as people abandoned their jobs and Constantinople ran the risk of starvation as the supply and distribution of food was affected. Even Justinian caught the plague, as did the historian Evagrius as a schoolboy. Much of the bronze coinage struck in Justinian's 15th and 16th regnal years

80. Agathias, *Hist.* 2.16.1–6.
81. Justinian, *Novel* 122.
82. The bibliography is substantial. A convenient overview is Sarris, 'Plague'; also Stathakopoulos, *Famine* ch.6, and, at greater length, the contributions to Little, *Plague*.
83. Proc., *Wars* 2.22–3; John of Ephesus, as preserved in the eighth-century *Chronicle* of Pseudo-Dionysius of Tel-Mahre (trans. Witakowski, 77–87). These descriptions clearly point to bubonic plague, *Yersinia pestis*, but aspects of the accounts of its spread occasion some doubts that are rehearsed inconclusively by Hordern, 'Plague'.
84. These rates are probably considerable exaggerations, or could not have persisted for very long, unless mortality was very much higher than in more recent plagues.

(August 541–3) may depict the emperor with puffed out cheeks, arguably in an attempt to represent the swollen glands of a bubonic sufferer, and suggests the severity of the affliction, even for the lucky survivors.[85]

Even allowing for some understandable exaggerations in eye-witness descriptions, the plague was horrific and sparked rumours of supernatural intervention, but the overall impact on the empire was much less extreme.[86] Mortality in the densely-populated capital is bound to have been very high, but overall comparison with other pandemics, including the medieval Black Death, suggests that somewhere between 20 and 30 per cent of the population perished. That means that the death toll in the empire was several million people, but, as with the Black Death, there were some benefits: wages rose since labour was in shorter supply, while in Egypt landowners had to grant better terms in order to secure tenants to farm their lands. It might be expected that the elimination of about one quarter of the population would have had a serious impact on military recruitment, but there is in fact no clear evidence for this, and in the aftermath of the plague Justinian's armies campaigned with reasonable success in Italy, North Africa, and the East.[87] In part this was because the plague stuck at a high point in population in many areas, and mortality will have been heaviest in cities, while military recruitment tended to focus on rural and upland areas where the more scattered distribution of population probably reduced the plague's impact.

It has been suggested that Justinian's own brush with death brought about an intensified focus in the latter part of his reign on religious matters and the establishment of orthodoxy, since the plague was clearly divine punishment for human error;[88] this is possible, although orthodox doctrine and ecclesiastical unity had been major concerns for Justinian from the start of Justin's reign. It is also likely that the empire's reduced population could not immediately generate the same tax revenues for the state as previously. The evidence for this is the resort to issuing lightweight *solidi*, although there are no other signs such as requests for tax remissions over the next decade. Safe conclusions are, first, that the plague, even if it

---

85. Pottier, 'L'empereur', who suggests that these different coins were produced between May and October 542, after which the imperial iconography returned to normal.

86. For an extreme interpretation of the plague, see Harper, *Fate* ch.6, but note the response of Haldon et al. 'Plagues (3)' who observe that Harper 'crafts a convincing narrative based on rhetorical flourishes but little evidence'.

87. Discussion in Whitby, 'Recruitment'.

88. Meier, *Zeitalter* 340–1.

benefitted individual farmers and workers in the short term, did nothing to strengthen the overall structures of the state; and second, that even though the onset of bubonic plague in 542 did not trigger an instant social and economic collapse, repeated visitations for almost two centuries after Justinian's death eroded the ability of some regions to recover, especially when they were weakened by warfare or other troubles.

Justinian had inherited an empire in a strong financial condition: Procopius claims that at his death Anastasius left 320,000 pounds of gold in the treasury,[89] and this is unlikely to have been reduced much under Justin I since there was little military action before 527 and few extravagant building projects. This massive sum might have been inflated by Procopius to sharpen the critique of Justinian's profligacy, but it also reflects the ability of the empire's tax base to generate a revenue surplus. At Justinian's death, however, he bequeathed debts to his successor and there are possible signs of financial unease in his latter years. In 562 a group that included bankers plotted to kill Justinian, for the conspiracy only to be discovered at the last moment.[90] What had upset these financiers is unknown, but Justinian had been spending heavily on making good the damage from the 557 and 558 earthquakes, the peace agreement with Persia in 562 required the dispatch of almost 3,000 pounds of gold as the first instalment, while the Bulgar Kutrigurs continued to ravage the Balkans. In the circumstances too many bills were perhaps being left unpaid, which is the implication of the celebration organized in the Hippodrome by Justin II to mark the repayment of his predecessor's forced loans.[91] This would suggest that any difficulty was short-term, relating to the flow of revenue, rather than structural.

These problems do not contradict the overall impression of a prosperous empire for most of Justinian's reign. At his death the empire had enjoyed comparative peace on all its major frontiers for over two years, something that had not happened at any earlier point in his reign, and indeed a decade during which, despite the Kutrigur raids into the Balkans, the level of military activity had been lower than during any comparable period earlier in the reign. Justin II certainly inherited many challenges, but he also assumed control of an empire in which expenditure on warfare should have been at its lowest level for half a century.

---

89. Proc., *SH* 19.7.
90. Malalas 18.141; Theophanes 2357.15–238.18.
91. Corippus, *In laudem Iustini* 2.360–404.

Chapter 3

Sources

In terms of the weight of evidence, the reign of Justinian is one of the best-attested periods of antiquity and certainly the most thoroughly reported reign of the Byzantine era. This is, however, in large part because of the volume both of legal writing associated with Justinian's project to codify Roman Law and of doctrinal works relating to the major ecclesiastical controversies of his reign, which culminated in the ecumenical council of 553. Even so, we are relatively well informed about the military events of his reign, thanks to the works of Procopius, which provide the richest account of Roman campaigns since the termination of the *Res Gestae* of Ammianus Marcellinus in 378. Abundance of evidence does not necessarily remove problems and, as on other occasions, as for example with Thucydides' account of the Peloponnesian War in the fifth century BC, the influence on our perceptions of a single source of apparent authority demands a critical approach. Consideration of our evidence for the wars of Justinian is dominated by the problems of Procopius, who is one of the great historians of the ancient world and arguably the greatest of Byzantine historians.[1]

Procopius was born, probably in about 500, into a family in the Palestinian city of Caesarea that was sufficiently wealthy to support a traditional education. The neighbouring city of Gaza could have provided this, while Beirut could have given him the legal education that led to him qualifying as a *rhetor*. In 527 he was appointed as *sumboulos* or *assessor* to the new *Dux Mesopotamiae*, Belisarius, whose personal secretary he may have become; as *assessor* he will have overseen an office that probably expanded as Belisarius undertook increasingly important roles.[2] Procopius

---

1. For succinct discussion of the problems with ancient sources for Roman warfare, see Lee, *Warfare* 20–9; this excellent recent book provides a lucid social history of Roman warfare from the Republic to the late Empire.

2. For discussion of the evidence, see *PLRE* III Procopius 2. Lillington-Martin, 'Procopius' 158–62, has suggested that he was elevated to a more important role in 533 at the start of the Vandal expedition, since he starts to use *paredros* to describe his position, a term that is applied to senior imperial advisers such as the *quaestor*. This is possible, but the evidence is not decisive.

accompanied Belisarius on his campaigns for about the next fifteen years, being accepted as an associate who could be entrusted with sensitive and important tasks during the Vandal and Gothic campaigns. Thus in 533 Belisarius instructed him to go ahead to Syracuse to discover information on the Vandals' movements, while in 537 he was sent out of besieged Rome to collect much-needed reinforcements and supplies in Campania.[3] Unsurprisingly, perhaps, Procopius' contributions are reported to have had an uplifting effect on his commander. At some point in the 530s, quite possibly soon after Belisarius defeated the Persians outside Dara in 530, he decided to compose a history, for which his official position gave him access to excellent information, though also an incentive to be biased towards his employer, as is evident in his account of Belisarius' defeat at Callinicum in 531.

The seventh-century Coptic chronicle of John of Nikiu refers to him as patrician and city prefect, and it is independently attested that a man called Procopius held the office of prefect of Constantinople in 562/3. These honours are not impossible for the historian, perhaps being granted in return for delivery of the successful panegyric in the *Buildings*, but it is also telling that Greek authors, including Agathias who knew him reasonably well, refer to him as *rhetor* and do not mention a higher rank.[4] Certainty on this issue is not possible.

Overall he produced eight books of the *Wars*, of which the first seven, divided between Rome's three enemies of Persia (Books 1–2), Vandals (3–4), and Goths (5–7), were made public in 551, while Book 8, which combined actions on all campaign fronts, extended his narrative to the start of 553. Major events away from the frontiers, such as the Nika Riot and the Plague, are interwoven into the Persian narrative,[5] while events in the Balkans, which are not accorded separate treatment, perhaps because Belisarius never campaigned there, are introduced into the Persian and Gothic narratives at appropriate points but then form part of the general account in Book 8. In the late 540s, as he was finalizing the first seven books of *Wars*, Procopius also began work on his notorious *Secret History*.

---

3. Proc., *Wars* 3.12.3; 6.4. For intelligent discussion of Procopius' references to himself in *Wars*, see Ross, 'Narrator', who identifies that the first-person singular is used, in Herodotean fashion, to corroborate surprising information (e.g. the temple of Orestes: 1.17.13–20) or special personal reflections, whereas the third person is employed for most activities.
4. John of Nikiu 92.20; Full discussion in *PLRE* III, Procopius 2 at p.1066.
5. Proc., *Wars* 1.24; 2.22–3.

By this time his views of Justinian and even Belisarius had changed to become much more negative and in this work he claimed to be recording a true account of actions and motives, information that was too explosive to be included in a work for public consumption. This text does not provide a historical narrative but first presents a diatribe against the misdeeds and wickedness of Justinian and the depravity of Theodora. The second half of the work covers economic, social, and religious issues that the imperial couple exploited to damage the empire through their collaborative rivalry.[6] In the first five chapters Belisarius is presented as a pawn of his wife, Antonina, and hence at the mercy of Theodora's whims. It offers some alternative explanations for military events, for example Belisarius' behaviour during his eastern campaign of 541, when he allegedly declined to advance deep into Persia because he was awaiting the arrival of his wife.[7]

Somewhat later than the *Wars* and *Secret History* Procopius produced a final work, the *Buildings*, possibly in response to an imperial commission, that is devoted to an account of Justinian's construction works.[8] In six books this project first covers Justinian's buildings in Constantinople, mainly churches starting with S. Sophia but also with an evocation of the maritime beauty of the city's location (Book 1); then works in the eastern provinces, mainly defensive improvements, starting at the key fortress of Dara but also some measures to control flooding (2–3); next the Balkans (4), where two long lists simply name places built or repaired by the emperor without any specific detail;[9] then Asia Minor and Palestine (5), with attention especially to roads and bridges and the churches of the Holy Land; and finally North Africa (6).

It has been asserted that the work is unfinished because there is no treatment of Italy and the material in the Balkan lists would have been worked up into a narrative presentation, but the argument is not compelling. Justinian in fact supported very little construction work in Italy, with the famous church of San Vitale in Ravenna being financed by Julius Argentarius

---

6. Proc., *SH* 14–30.

7. Proc., *SH* 2.18–25.

8. The specific date of *Buildings* is disputed. Procopius refers to the great bridge over the Sangarius as being under construction and nearing completion (5.3.9), a project that began in 559/60 (Theophanes 234.15–18) and was completed before the end of 562 (Paul the Silentiary, *Ekphrasis* 928–33). On the other hand, he does not mention the collapse of the dome of S. Sophia in 558 or the reconstruction that was also completed in 562. For different views, see Whitby, 'Bridge', and Greatrex, 'Dates'.

9. Proc., *Buildings* 4.4, 11.

(banker), while the sheer volume of the site names in the Balkans precluded the provision of specific information on each. Of greatest relevance to the military events of the reign is the information, on occasion quite specific, about Justinian's attention to the upkeep of defences along the empire's frontiers, and especially his concern for the Balkans, granted the lack of detailed treatment in *Wars*. The work does also provide incidental evidence for Justinian's restructuring of military commands in the east.[10]

The contradiction between the venom in the *Secret History*, where Justinian is the destructive prince of devils, and *Buildings* where he is the benevolent protector of his people and regular recipient of divine support and guidance, used to cause some perplexity but is now better understood in terms of genres and audiences. The *Buildings* was a panegyric, in which fulsome praise was expected, while it is notable that Justinian's substantial expenditure on construction works is not mentioned in the *Secret History*, though it might have been criticized as wasteful extravagance. It is possible that in the second half of the 550s, when Procopius clearly decided not to continue the narrative of the *Wars* to cover the defeat of the Franks in Italy and actions in Transcaucasia that Agathias would later narrate, or extend the *Secret History*, the topic of building works proved attractive to him, with the result that he devoted himself to gathering the information and presenting it in an effective panegyric. This long-standing 'Procopian problem' is no longer a major issue for scholars.[11]

The *Wars* is a traditional history, often referred to as a 'classicizing' history since Procopius positioned himself in the sequence of Greek historians that now stretched back almost a millennium to Herodotus and Thucydides in fifth-century BC Athens. The topic of such works was primarily public military and diplomatic actions. These had to be presented in the appropriate literary style, with the accompaniment of rhetorical speeches that might be used to introduce some of the author's personal views – especially if he wanted to distance himself from comments that might cause offence to the powerful – and the adornment of digressions on historical or geographical matters or natural disasters.

As is common in such works, Procopius opened the *Wars* with a statement about the importance of the events he was narrating to save them from oblivion, which he illustrated by contrasting the denigration

---

10. Proc., *Buildings* 2.6.9; 3.1.28–9.
11. Cameron, *Procopius* ch.1.

of archery in Homer with its contemporary importance, and a profession of his commitment to truth and accuracy.[12] The language and style had to be suitably classical. For Procopius the key stylistic models were Xenophon and especially Arrian, who both composed in elegant flowing Greek, but intellectually a key influence was Thucydides, whose presentation of specific events he might copy in his own account of the bubonic plague; he made no attempt, however, to imitate Thucydides' deliberately convoluted style. Authors were expected to explain as well as record events. For Procopius this involved presenting the context for Justinian's military actions through brief surveys of antecedent events from the mid-fifth century onwards. For this information he relied on the fifth-century historian Priscus of Panium, whose work only survives in extracts, and probably also on the lost work of Eustathius of Epiphaneia, while the second-century writer Arrian provided the geographical information on the Black Sea with which Book 8 opens.

One result of this classical frame was that novelties had to be presented through suitable periphrases or with apologies for their unfamiliarity.[13] Thus contemporary tribal enemies are subsumed under suitable classical names, so that the Goths become Getae or the Huns Scythians. Technical terms, for example for military equipment or specific ranks and offices, are explained as if the readers were completely ignorant of their signification. This affectation of ignorance extends to matters of religion, since Christianity was obviously not something that could have been understood by the contemporaries of Thucydides. Thus the monks responsible for the Persian capture of Amida in 503 are referred to as 'those who are the most ascetic of the Christians, whom they call monks', or the bishop whose dream helped to trigger the African campaign as 'one of the priests whom they call bishops'.[14] This oblique approach does not contradict the view that Procopius was a typical sixth-century believer, a conclusion firmly established by Averil Cameron,[15] which has withstood a more recent attempt to argue that he was a closet pagan who encoded an esoteric philosophical message in his narrative.[16]

Both the *Secret History* and *Buildings* are set within an explicitly Christian world view, and the same is true for *Wars*, even if this is not always so clear. A good example in the *Wars* is Procopius' decision to record

---

12. Proc., *Wars* 1.1.
13. On Procopius' language, see Cameron, *Procopius* ch.3.
14. Proc., *Wars* 1.7.23; 3.10.18.
15. Cameron, 'Scepticism'; *Procopius* ch.7.
16. Kaldellis, *Procopius*; refutation in, among others, Whitby, 'Religious Views'.

the miraculous parade of the True Cross at Apamea in 540, of which the result was that 'God saved Apamea', although he describes the relic with a characteristic circumlocution as 'a portion of the cross on which it is agreed that Christ once willingly endured his punishment'.[17] For Procopius all human affairs were under the control of God, even if it was not always possible for mortals to comprehend divine reasoning, as Procopius remarks in an agonized comment on Khusro's destruction of Antioch in 540.[18]

Procopius does, on occasion, mention Christian matters when they impinge on historical events. Thus the fact that the battle of Callinicum was fought on the day before Easter, so that the Roman soldiers were weakened from their fasting, is explained: 'Christians honour this feast in particular, being accustomed not only to abstain from food and drink on the day before but also to extend the fasting for much of the night.'[19] He also records the prominent part played by eastern bishops in negotiating with Khusro in 540,[20] but there are limits to what he includes. He does note the geopolitical impact of religion in terms of allegiances in Transcaucasia, where Christianity distanced the Iberians and Laz from the Persians, or in securing help from the Ethiopian and Himyarite rulers who should 'collaborate with the Romans in fighting the Persians because of their concord of belief'.[21] But there are also omissions: he comments that Justinian's restrictions on Arian worship were exploited to undermine the allegiance of some Roman troops,[22] but makes no mention of how the complexities of post-Chalcedonian doctrinal disputes affected loyalties in North Africa in the 540s and 550s or how Jewish-Christian rivalry entangled the Ethiopians and Himyarites in South Arabia. At no point does he refer to the Miaphysite stance of the Jafnid leader, Harith ibn-Gabala, although this influenced the nature of the confederation's attachment to the empire and intersected with the Christian dynamics of the eastern provinces. It is perhaps relevant that Thucydides had eschewed religious aspects of the Peloponnesian War, so that specifically doctrinal matters could have no place in Procopius' secular narrative.

---

17. Proc., *Wars* 2.11; quotations from sections 14 and 28.
18. Proc., *Wars* 2.10.4–5.
19. Proc., *Wars* 1.18.15.
20. E.g. Proc., *Wars* 2.5.13–18; 6.17–25; 7.14–8.1.
21. Laz: Proc., *Wars* 1.12.2–5; 2.28.26–30. Ethiopia: 1.20.9.
22. Proc., *Wars* 4.14.10–15.

In the context of a religious dispute in Ulpiana that prevented an army from crossing the Balkans to support the Lombards, Procopius states that he intended to write about the matters 'on account of which the Christians fight between themselves';[23] this suggests that he planned to compose an ecclesiastical history, but, if so, there is no other evidence for the project. If he had produced this work, it is likely that he would have adopted a fairly tolerant view of religious difference, in line with several ecclesiastical historians, for example Evagrius.[24] At least in the *Secret History* he criticizes Justinian's religious persecutions as a device to destroy mankind under the pretence of securing unified belief,[25] and he eschews the sort of debate in which Justinian revelled:

> For although I am well versed in what was in dispute, I will not mention them at all. For I consider it an insane folly to examine what the nature of God is. For I think that even human affairs cannot be accurately grasped by humanity, and certainly not what relates to the nature of God. Accordingly, for my part I will play safe by keeping silent on these matters, with the sole intent that what has been honoured should not be discredited. For I would not say anything else at all about God than that he is comprehensively good and holds all things in his power. But let each person say whatever he thinks he knows about these things, both priest and layman.[26]

Acceptance of the incomprehensibility of God was a basic tenet of Christian belief.

This is relevant to one of the most problematic passages in Procopius, his musing on the catastrophe of the Persian capture and destruction of the great city of Antioch. This begins with a comment on the random operation in the world of *tyche*, fortune, fate or luck, which elevates or destroys people without any apparent logic.[27] This is then expanded:

> But I become dizzy as I write about such a great calamity and transmit it to future times to remember, and I cannot understand

23. Proc., *Wars* 8.25.13.
24. Evagrius 1.1; Whitby, 'Religious Views'.
25. Proc., *SH* 13.7–8.
26. Proc., *Wars* 5.3.5–9.
27. Proc., *Wars* 2.9.13.

why it should be the will of God to exalt the fortunes of a man or place and then to cast them down and destroy them for no cause that is apparent to ourselves. For it is not right to say that with Him all things are not always done with a reason...[28]

A contradiction has been identified in this passage between the apparently independent operation of *tyche* and the omniscience of the Christian God,[29] but his perplexity is in fact a thoroughly Christian response to the problem of evil in the world that had troubled theologians such as Augustine.[30] Men as well as places had their ups and downs: when the brave Gothic leader, Totila, was eventually defeated and killed, Procopius inserted further reflections on the incomprehensibility of human fortune.[31]

The *Wars* is a substantial work, 540 large pages in Kaldellis' recent revision of the standard Loeb translation, and its composition will have occupied several years, probably two decades overall; it would be surprising if Procopius' views did not evolve during this period. In the same way that the reign of Justinian swapped the optimism of the 530s for the gloom of the 540s, so too Procopius' views changed after Belisarius' triumph over the Ostrogoths. The cataclysm of the plague, which must have affected many of Procopius' relatives and acquaintances, or his realization that Belisarius lacked the backbone to stand up to the wiles of Antonina and Theodora, may have played their part, but the decisive issue probably was Khusro's destructive rampage through Syria in 540. Critical comments on Justinian's ambitions and control begin to intrude, though most of these are safely located in the mouths of foreigners and so can be excused as the sort of things that enemies would say. Ambassadors from the Ostrogoths and Armenians criticized Justinian's insatiable ambitions when urging Khusro to attack the Romans, while the Utigur Sandil castigated his treatment of the trans-Danubian tribes.[32] There are, even, some direct criticisms of the emperor, for his lack of attention to the Gothic war, willingness to tolerate his generals' misdeeds, and failure to ensure that his armies were paid on time.[33] It is noticeable that these

28. Proc., *Wars* 2.10.4–5.
29. Kaldellis, 'Historical'.
30. Whitby, 'Religious Views'.
31. Proc., *Wars* 8.32.28–30.
32. Proc., *Wars* 2.2–3; 8.19.
33. Proc., *Wars* 7.36.4–6; 8.13.14; 8.26.6–7.

explicit comments are restricted to the latest parts of *Wars*, which would have been written in the context of parallel work on the *Secret History*. The events of the 540s forced Procopius into serious reflection on the challenge for a Christian author of reconciling belief in an all-powerful God, in whom benevolence and mercy were key attributes, with the random nature of human affairs that included major disasters.

The early 540s see a change in the focus and tone of Procopius' narrative. The successes of the 530s are presented as a good story, in which Belisarius is the obvious protagonist. There are differences of emphasis: the reconquest of Africa is reported with particular stress on the Romans' good fortune and the fulfilment of Christian predictions, whereas in the year-long siege of Rome an epic tone is adopted with attention to single combats, heroic displays of bravery, and graphic accounts of horrific wounds. In each case Belisarius is centre stage, with the siege of Rome in particular highlighting his personal courage, intelligent leadership, and command of the besieged inhabitants. After 540, however, Belisarius is much less prominent, in part because he was entrusted with fewer missions by Justinian, but more importantly because his campaigns were generally unsuccessful after 542. By contrast Book 7 and the western portions of Book 8 are dominated by the Gothic king, Totila: he is the central figure, a good and effective leader of his people who behaves properly. Even Belisarius cannot devise a strategy to counter the Gothic successes for reasons that Procopius could not grasp, whether it was just *tyche* or whether God thwarted him in order to permit Gothic affairs to flourish.[34] Even though Book 8 concludes with the defeat of Totila's successor, Theia, at Mons Lactarius, the real conclusion of the *Wars* is the defeat and death of Totila at Busta Gallorum, an event that the victorious Roman general, Narses, correctly attributed to God.[35]

The key problem in our inevitable dependence upon Procopius is the compositional one: what has he chosen to narrate, or not to narrate, how has he slanted his presentation to create certain impressions on his readers? It does, for example, appear that he might chose to ignore events in which Belisarius did not participate, for example in 529 or the latter part of the 542 eastern campaign. Study of Procopian narratives remains in its infancy, although important steps are now being taken.[36] Something

---

34. Proc., *Wars* 7.13.15–18.
35. Proc., *Wars* 8.35 (Mons Lactarius); 8.33.1 (Narses).
36. Whately, *Battles*; contributions to Lillington-Martin & Turquois, *Procopius*.

as simple as Procopius' deployment of numbers is a case in point. Although this aspect of Procopius has been singled out for praise, as an improvement on the general run of ancient historians who rarely provide specific numbers, the reality is less straightforward. Procopius is sometimes imprecise, on occasions his numbers are fantastic, and his use of the term 'myriads', 'ten thousands', may be intended to signal the need for caution, but he deployed this information to underline messages that he wanted his narrative to convey, for example the destruction caused by Justinian's actions.[37] The same can be said about specific information on names and titles. In his accounts of battles, in the Vandal campaign he places weight on morale in deciding conflicts, whereas in most other battles the tactical deployment of troops is at least as important.[38]

As a writer working within a very long tradition, the influence upon him of his great predecessors is an important factor. In this respect, Thucydides is the key figure: Procopius' account of the bubonic plague was influenced by Thucydides' report of the plague at Athens, and ambassadors' complaints to Khusro about Justinian's insatiable energy recall those of the Corinthians to the Spartans about Athenian ambitions. The hopes and frustrations of Belisarius' attempt to force his way up the Tiber recall the similar emotional swings of the doomed Athenian attempt to escape the Great Harbour of Syracuse, while the narrative of the Gothic Wars is structured in Thucydidean fashion according to the year of the war, as opposed to the regnal years of Justinian that are used for the Persian and Vandal campaigns. Such historiographical overtones should not be interpreted as evidence that the literary tradition has distorted contemporary reality, rather they illustrate how the cultural context enriches the presentation of the narrative. Similarly, Procopius' geographical excursuses can be traced back to Herodotus and rely on Arrian, but the information he presents is relevant to the understanding of his campaign narratives.

Procopius' *Wars* were continued by Agathias, writing after Justinian's death under Justin II and Tiberius, whose *Histories* in five books extends the narrative down to 559. Agathias came from the Asia Minor coastal city of Myrina, where his family – like that of Procopius – had the resources

---

37. Treadgold, *Historians* 218–20 for praise of Procopius' information; Whately, *Battles* 125–7, 171–7 for a properly nuanced analysis.
38. For an important conclusion of the detailed investigations, see Whately, *Battles* 231–5.

to equip him with a good classical education, of which part was pursued at Alexandria.[39] Like his predecessor he trained as a lawyer, but, unlike him, he practised as a barrister in the Royal Stoa at Constantinople. As a writer he first became known as a poet, his earliest work being the *Daphniaca*, nine books in hexameters with erotic myths as the subject. This is lost, but a collection of contemporary epigrams, known for convenience as the *Cycle* of Agathias, can be reconstructed in large part because it was incorporated into the *Greek Anthology*. Agathias himself wrote several of the epigrams, some of which are on the traditional topic of love, although there are also family subjects, one that accompanied the dedication of a gift to the Archangel Michael, a group on the construction of a public lavatory, possibly at Smyrna, which Agathias had financed in his role as Father of the City, and one commemorating Justinian's bridge over the Sangarius. Many of the other authors in the *Cycle* were clearly friends, including Paul the Silentiary as well as several fellow lawyers. The *Cycle* was opened by a long epigram in praise of an anonymous emperor, who, from the dates of the latest epigrams, has to be Justin II.[40]

Poetry was Agathias' first and greatest love, as he explains in the preface to the *Histories*, and this has been held against the quality of his historical work. He was, though, then influenced by the greatness and vicissitudes of contemporary events to contemplate applying himself to something more useful than mere poetry. This move received strong encouragement from his friends and especially the imperial notary, Eutychianus, who urged that poetry and history were not really that different and that this project would be good for his reputation and status.[41] Unlike Procopius, Agathias had no direct experience of war or diplomacy that might have helped him to present and explain events. Rather, he continued to work as a lawyer, which, he complained, relegated historiography to a part-time activity and prevented him from improving his style by reading the great authors of antiquity.[42]

Agathias covered three main areas of military activity: the conclusion of major campaigning in Italy as Narses defeated the Franks, which is introduced with an excursus on the Franks, continuing clashes between Romans and Persians in Transcaucasia, and the 559 invasions of the

39. Cameron, *Agathias* ch.1.
40 *Anthologia Palatina* 4.3; discussion in Cameron, *Agathias* ch.2.
41. Agathias, *Hist.* pref 7–13.
42. Agathias, *Hist.* 3.1.2–6.

Balkans.[43] These military accounts are separated by various digressions, to which Agathias clearly devoted considerable attention since they were occasions to display his erudition. They included the earthquake of 551, including his personal observations on the island of Cos and account of a visit to Tralles,[44] an account of Persian customs that ends with the story of the visit by the Athenian philosophers to Khusro's court, a history of the Sasanid dynasty, supposedly drawn from Persian archives,[45] and the earthquakes of 557/8.[46] The narrative of events is also broken up by the expected speeches, which Agathias exploited to express views on the war in Italy, rehearse the arguments for allegiance to Rome or Persia, and present a formal Roman legal investigation into the unsanctioned assassination of Gobazes, king of the Laz.[47] As to the actual narrative of events, Agathias does overall present a reasonably clear account and was prepared to include specific descriptions of military equipment, the understanding of which Procopius, with his greater familiarity, perhaps took for granted.

Agathias presented his account as an explicit continuation of Procopius, going so far as to summarize the contents of *Wars* in his preface. His approach to religious matters is similar to that of Procopius, with literary circumlocutions being accompanied by clear references to Christian material and views. He too was tolerant of religious diversity as well as of divergent human customs, with regard to which each nation views its own practices as the best.[48] Human understanding has its limits, 'It is enough, if indeed we could know only this, that everything is arranged by a divine mind and a higher will.'[49]

One important divergence from Procopius is in his attitude to Emperor Justinian: whereas Procopius had been constrained in his public writing from expressing negative views that he had developed during the later 540s, Agathias was writing under emperors for whom the shadow of Justinian was a challenge. As a result, opportunities to highlight his

---

43. Agathias, *Hist.* 1.1–2.14 (Franks); 2.18–4.23 (Transcaucasia); 5.11–23 (Balkans).
44. Agathias, *Hist.* 2.15–17.
45. Agathias, *Hist.* 2.23–31 (customs); 4.24–30 (history); Hoyland, *History* 8–9, suggested that Agathias' boast about archives was designed to raise his credibility in comparison with that of Procopius; full discussion of the digression in Cameron, 'Sassanians'.
46. Agathias, *Hist.* 5.3–10.
47. Agathias, *Hist.* 1.5; 16 (Italy); 3.8–14 (allegiance); 4.2–11 (Gobazes).
48. Agathias, *Hist.* 1.7.3; 2.23.8–9.
49. Agathias, *Hist.* 2.15.13; for the correct interpretation of this clause see Brodka 'Faktoren' 163; Whitby, 'Religious Views'.

failings could be useful. In the context of the Kutrigur invasion that breached Constantinople's outermost defensive line of Long Walls in 559, Agathias commented on the decline in Roman military manpower, both in terms of numbers and of status and reward. He blamed Justinian for this collapse, saying that in his old age he preferred to hold his enemies at bay through diplomacy rather than confront them boldly, as he would have in his early years.[50] Whatever truth there is to the criticisms, the subtext for readers is that this approach was the origin of the empire's contemporary problems in the Balkans.

Agathias ceased working on his *Histories* in about 580/1, most probably because he died, and certainly before the accession of Maurice in 582, whom he mentions without signalling that he would become emperor. His work was continued by two authors. John of Epiphaneia, though presenting himself as the continuator of Agathias, in reality focused on the Persian war that began in 572 and offers no information relevant to the final years of Justinian; only the first few chapters of his account survive, though the shape of the remainder can be inferred from the narrative of Theophylact Simocatta, which followed it closely. The other continuator was Menander Protector.[51] His account does not survive either, but in this case we are fortunate to possess very substantial passages in the collection of historical excerpts commissioned by Constantine Porphyrogenitus in the tenth century. Most of these concern diplomatic activity, since two of the extant titles of Constantine's collection relate to embassies to and from the Romans. As a result, we have an exceptionally long account of the negotiations that led up the agreement of the Fifty-Year Peace in 562 and there is also some information on the empire's earliest dealings with the Avars as they approached the Black Sea to enter Roman diplomatic horizons.[52]

An extract from Menander that is quoted in the tenth-century Byzantine lexicon, the *Suda*, describes the genesis of his history. Like Procopius and Agathias he had trained as a lawyer, but then preferred to indulge in the distractions of popular entertainment; from this wasted life of indolence Menander was rescued by Emperor Maurice, whose commitment to literature led him to offer financial rewards to its practitioners. Menander,

---

50. Agathias, *Hist.* 5.13.5–14.5.
51. See the introduction to Blockley, *Menander*, for discussion of most aspects. As a Protector, Menander would have belonged to the imperial guards, although it is possible that the title was honorary, a reward for composition of his history.
52. Menander fr.6 (peace treaty); fr. 5 (Avars).

who was beginning to tire of a life of penury, seized his chance. This portrait of dissolute youth may well be an exaggeration designed to extol the role of Maurice as patron and Menander certainly devoted himself to the collection and recording of detailed information. His account of the 562 peace talks runs to 600 lines of text, which include the actual terms of the treaty and codicils, and is far more detailed and informative than any account of diplomacy in Procopius or Agathias. It is possible that Menander was assisted in his enterprise by the fact that his brother, Herodotus, another law student who fell out of love with his studies, probably served on embassies during Justin II's reign and so knew how to access the best information.

Granted the incomplete state of Menander's text, it is not possible to say much about his views or biases. He does, however, have an interesting assessment of Justinian's policies for dealing with the empire's tribal neighbours:[53] this starts along the lines of Agathias' critique of the aged emperor's lack of vigour, which led him to seek means other than bold confrontation to defeat his enemies, but then proceeds to state that he would still have crushed them by wisdom rather than by war if death had not carried him off first. Just as Agathias' comments on Justinian reflect contemporary imperial policies of robust rebuttal of diplomatic demands and, if necessary, confrontation, so too Menander's more nuanced approach is in line with Emperor Maurice's attempts to defend the Danubian provinces while avoiding open conflict, for which he lacked the resources in the 580s. The quality of information and clarity of description in the extant passages of Menander make the loss of his full account all the more regrettable.

Apart from this sequence of three traditional historians, the next source in terms of importance is the Greek *Chronicle* of John Malalas, a text that has its own complications and challenges.[54] The *Chronicle* is an account of world history that in its current form stretches from the Creation and Adam through to the reign of Justinian, narrating events in very different levels of detail in eighteen books; for current purposes only the last two books that cover the reigns of Justin and Justinian are of relevance. Nothing is known about the author, or first author, beyond what can be inferred from the extant text. He was probably born in about 490, since

---

53. Menander fr.5.1.17–26.
54. For full discussion, see the contributions to Jeffreys, *Studies*.

he could access oral sources stretching back to the reign of Zeno (467–91). The word 'malalas' is Syriac for the Greek *scholasticus* or *rhetor*,[55] which indicates that the person had trained as a lawyer, a background that, as we have seen, is common among historians in the late empire. Chronicles used to be held in contempt as naïve, non-literary, or 'monkish' creations, but Malalas was a person of good education, who wrote in what was probably standard bureaucratic Greek. The *Chronicle* was also underpinned by an intellectual interest in the age of the world, since Malalas was concerned to demonstrate that there was no basis for contemporary fears that the world would end when it reached its 6,000th year, which for many people was due to occur in the early sixth century.

The Antiochene focus of the post-Biblical parts of the first seventeen books strongly suggests that the author was an inhabitant of Antioch-on-the-Orontes, the third city of the eastern empire and seat of the *magister militum per Orientem* and *comes Orientis* as well as of a Patriarch; hence the city provided employment to a considerable number of bureaucrats. It is likely that the author served in the office of the *comes Orientis*, or some comparable functionary, which gave him access to official information. At some point the author moved from Antioch to Constantinople; this might have been as late as 535 when the office of *comes Orientis* was abolished,[56] although the exceptional detail of the account of the Nika Riot in January 532 suggests that the move had occurred before then. Although many chronicles only present brief statements of events, for the years when he was a contemporary witness Malalas does include some extensive reports of warfare, rioting, and natural disasters.

The *Chronicle* originally existed in several versions. It is very possible that its earliest one terminated in 528, shortly after the accession of Justinian, but this was promptly continued, most probably by the same author, down to 533. At that point the regular updating of information ceases, or at least there is a dramatic change in the level of detail recorded for each year, and the account only gradually becomes less sparse in the 550s, in due course providing fuller narratives for a number of events at the end of the decade and the early 560s. This continuation of the text, for which a different author may have been responsible, probably terminated at Justinian's death in 565, although this cannot be absolutely

---

55. Indeed, both Evagrius and John of Ephesus refer to him as John the *rhetor*.
56. Just., *Novel* 8.5.

certain since the last pages of the single manuscript are lost and the text breaks off in 563.

A further issue is that this manuscript preserves only an abbreviated version of the original, whose full text we can reconstruct to an extent as a number of later authors had access to it in its complete state. Of these secondary witnesses the most important for Justinian's reign are:

- The *Chronicon Paschale*, a Constantinopolitan chronicle compiled in the late 620s which had access to a version of Malalas that terminated in 533 shortly after the Nika Riot, of which it presents a detailed and important account.
- Theophanes, whose early ninth-century *Chronographia* drew on a text of Malalas that extended down to 565.[57]
- Excerpts in the historical collection commissioned by Constantine Porphyrogenitus, one of whose few extant titles is *de Insidiis*, 'On Plots', which provides information on urban rioting, including events in Justinian's final years that are lost from the Malalas manuscript.
- There is also a medieval Slavonic translation of the unabridged Malalas, although that is of little use for current purposes, since it was based on the very first version of the *Chronicle* and so does not extend beyond Justinian's first year as emperor.

It is fortunate that the convoluted nature of this significant text has been set out clearly in the translation overseen by Elizabeth and Michael Jeffreys and Roger Scott as well as in the edition of the text by Johannes Turn.

With regard to the wars of Justinian, Malalas and his tradition are important on two counts. First, the information provided on urban rioting, especially at Constantinople, and official responses is invaluable since, with the exception of the Nika Riot, such events did not impinge on traditional histories, and even the Nika Riot is viewed by them from an elite perspective. Second, his bureaucratic service at Antioch did give Malalas access to reports of contemporary military and diplomatic action. Thus, we possess some information that is independent of Procopius, for example the establishment of a *dux* at Palmyra as part of the reorganization

---

57. Thus Theophanes provides important evidence for the material lost from the end of the manuscript of Malalas.

of commands on the eastern frontier. His most significant information is the account of the battle of Callinicum in 531: Malalas presents a version that gives a much less favourable picture of Belisarius' actions than does Procopius and may have been based on the enquiry into the defeat, but it would be unwise to assume that this must be the whole truth since even an official report on events might well have been slanted to favour one of the various competing interests.[58]

Other historical accounts include a Latin chronicle by Marcellinus *comes*, a native of Illyricum who served in the retinue of Justinian in the latter part of the reign of Justin.[59] His work, which is presented as a continuation of the fourth-century chronicle of Jerome, initially terminated in 518, but he then continued it to 534, after which it was extended by a different author until 548. Information in Marcellinus takes the form, typical for chronicles, of brief notices of events entered under their consular year; unsurprisingly, it shows particular interest in events in the Balkans and favour towards Justinian.

Victor of Tunnuna, a North African bishop who was exiled for his opposition to the Three Chapters initiative, produced a chronicle that reached the end of Justinian's reign, whose brief notices occasionally provide information not preserved elsewhere. Book 4 of the Greek *Ecclesiastical History* of Evagrius Scholasticus, another inhabitant of Antioch, covers the reign of Justinian and contains a certain amount of information on secular matters as well as doctrinal dealings. Much of the military material is derived from Procopius, though this was selected in order to highlight miracles and other specifically Christian aspects.[60] Evagrius does, however, provide independent information on the Persian invasions of the early 540s.[61] He describes the display of the relic of the True Cross at Apamea, which his parents had taken him to witness, introduces the miraculous intervention of the *acheiropoietos* icon of Christ into the narrative of the salvation of Edessa from the Persian siege of 544, and offers a different version of the Persian failure to capture Sergiopolis in 542. These accounts are significant as evidence for how some people chose to interpret recent historical events.

---

58. Malalas 18.60.
59. For full discussion, see Croke, *Marcellinus*.
60. See the discussion by Whitby in the translation of Evagrius, especially at xxviii–xxxi.
61. Evagrius 4.26–8.

The Syriac text now referred to as *The Chronicle of Pseudo-Zachariah of Mitylene* is something of a hybrid that combines aspects of a chronicle and a church history.[62] The person who compiled the work was an anti-Chalcedonian monk from the region of Amida. In the 560s he brought together a number of earlier accounts, including the early Justinianic *Ecclesiastical History* by Zachariah, bishop of Mitylene, various documents on ecclesiastical matters, and an unidentifiable text or texts on the reign of Justinian. It is this last category that is most relevant to the current discussion, since it provided Pseudo-Zachariah with a fair amount of information for his account of the Persian war of 527–32 in Book 9 that offers some supplement to Procopius; for example, the brief account of Callinicum is independent of both Procopius and Malalas. There is also an isolated notice of a barbarian raid that sacked the village of Diobulion in 554,[63] after which Justinian sanctioned a public tour of an icon of Christ in order to raise funds for reconstruction.

The Syriac *Ecclesiastical History* of John of Ephesus, another monk from the region of Amida who was used by Justinian to convert pagans in Asia Minor and became the anti-Chalcedonian bishop of Ephesus, originally covered events of Justinian's reign in its second part. This is now lost, although much of its content can be reconstructed from the subsequent tradition of Syriac historians, in particular from the eighth-century *Chronicle* of Pseudo-Dionysius of Tel-Mahre.[64] John provided an extensive account of the Justinianic plague, which is a useful alternative eye-witness account to that in Procopius, as well as some information on other secular matters.[65] John also composed a hagiographical collection, *The Lives of the Eastern Fathers*, which preserves accounts of heroes of the Miaphysite resistance to Chalcedon in the sixth century. This records information, inevitably biased, on attempts by Justin and Justinian to re-establish unity among the eastern churches through a combination of coercion and discussion.[66]

---

62. See the extensive discussion by Greatrex in the introduction to the translation of Pseudo-Zachariah.

63. Ps.-Zach, *HE* 12.4b.

64. See Van Ginkel, *John*, and Witakowski's introduction to the translation of Pseudo-Dionysius.

65. Part Three of John's *History*, which does survive relatively intact and covers the post-Justinianic period down to 588, presents a combination of lengthy, albeit sometimes confused, reports of both religious and secular matters.

66. For discussion, see Ashbrook Harvey, *Asceticism*.

One final literary text to be mentioned is the *Iohannid* of Corippus, a hexameter poem in eight books that celebrates the achievements of John Troglita. John was one of Belisarius' officers in the 533 Vandal expedition and then remained in Africa as a *dux*, serving under Solomon and Germanus until at least 537. After a period of service in Mesopotamia, for which Corippus provides some details to supplement Procopius, he returned to North Africa as *magister militum* and it is his subsequent campaigns against the Berbers in the late 540s, events only recorded briefly by Procopius in the later chapters of Book 4, that comprise the bulk of the poem. Corippus' text breaks off after John's victory at the Plains of Cato and the death of the Berber leader Carcasan, though this highpoint probably marked the conclusion of the poem. Both as an epic poem and a panegyric there are bound to be limitations to the accuracy and clarity of Corippus' account of events, but he does describe much more fully than Procopius the stages and setbacks that led up to John's eventual triumph.

Some insight into the organization and tactics of sixth-century Roman armies and their enemies is provided by military manuals, of which the most useful are the *De Re Strategica* by Syrianus *magister* and the *Strategicon* attributed to the emperor Maurice. The two works of the Anastasian military author Urbicius are of little relevance, since his *Tacticon* is a brief summary of the second-century AD *Ars Tactica* of Arrian, while the *Epitedeuma*, *Invention*, presents a personal suggestion for a portable anti-cavalry device and falls into the category of bright ideas of dubious application. Syrianus' *De Re Strategica* is part of a tripartite text, whose other components are a treatise on military oratory and a technical analysis of naval warfare. It used to be dated to the reign of Justinian on the basis that its latest specific reference is to a tactic deployed by Belisarius, but that only provides a *terminus post* and the most convincing context is now seen as the ninth century, not least because in the text the empire's main opponents are Arabs rather than Persians.[67]

This late date notwithstanding, Syrianus can provide insight into sixth-century approaches to warfare since the tradition of military handbooks was extremely conservative: thus the description of the operation of light and heavy cavalry reflects standard Roman practice stretching back

---

67. Rance, 'Date'.

at least to the second century AD.[68] The tactic attributed to Belisarius relates to his treatment of superior enemy forces, when he would identify his opponents' probable line of advance, destroy provisions along that route to force them to divide into several columns spread across a wide area, and then attack these divisions separately.[69] This is certainly sound tactical sense, but cannot actually be connected directly with any campaign described by Procopius. The closest is the account of Khusro's invasion of Syria in 542, when Belisarius encamped at Europus to cut his direct line of retreat, inconveniencing the Persians since they could not return along their invasion route through Commagene (Euphratesia) where they had already consumed all provisions;[70] although this contains elements of the tactic in Syrianus, there are also clear differences.

The *Strategicon*, or *Book of the General*, of Maurice is to be dated to *circa* 600, but contains observations on the operational thinking of Roman commanders that are relevant to the reign of Justinian, even if they derive from a period when resources were even more constrained than they had been in mid-century. Whether it was actually produced by Emperor Maurice is unknowable, but it does reflect official ideas about how generals should operate, providing an 'introduction for those embarking on command'.[71] The first ten books focus on cavalry tactics, most probably drawing lessons from Roman experience in campaigns against the Persians in the 570s and 580s, after which Book 11 contains four chapters that analyse how the Romans should aim to defeat their four main groups of enemies: Persians; Scythian races including Avars and Turks; blond-haired races including Franks and Lombards; Slavs and Antes. Although Goths have disappeared from the empire's main adversaries, the chapter on Franks and Lombards is relevant to their treatment. This recommends the use of archery to weaken the impact of the cavalry charge, their most potent weapon, tactics that are broadly in line with those of Narses at Busta Gallorum. With regard to the Persians, Maurice's advice is the opposite, to come to grips as quickly as possible to deliver the weight of the Roman charge and reduce the effect of superior Persian archery that, for example, helped to decide the outcome at Callinicum. The final book, Book 12, which draws on experience in the Balkans in the 590s, represents

---

68. Syrianus 35.18–23.
69. Syrianus 33.33–9.
70. Proc., *Wars* 2.20.24–21.20.
71. Maurice, *Strat. Pref.* 24; see Rance, 'Battle' 347–8; also Syvänne, *Age* 16–19.

a certain shift in focus. It first covers infantry tactics and then turns to camps and hunting.[72] Although the work postdates Justinian's campaigns, the treatment of formations and tactics is still of some relevance.[73]

Most of the *Strategicon* is devoted to cavalry matters, organization, training, and tactics; the training of horse archers receives attention, which links with Procopius' introductory praise for the power of Roman mounted bowmen.[74] The limited space devoted to infantry, which is only discussed in Book 12, cannot be used as evidence for its reduced role in the sixth century, since the whole treatise advocates the importance of a balanced or mixed force, in which the solidity of an infantry phalanx underpins the fluidity of attacking cavalry. Treatments of set-piece battles in the traditional histories rarely describe specific tactical moves, but there are occasions when it is possible to identify actions that align with the *Strategicon's* advice in Book 4 on ambushes and about fighting in groups, *drungisti*:[75] the decisive impact of relatively small units of concealed cavalrymen is described by Procopius at Dara, Satala, and Busta Gallorum.[76]

Justinian's extensive legal activity casts light on military affairs in two distinct ways. The first is the insight provided by the legislation into Justinian's mindset and ambitions, since the preambles to laws preserved in their entirety (as opposed to being excerpted in the *Codex*) explain the rationale for a particular piece of legislation. Here the necessity of divine favour for Justinian's endeavours is a recurrent theme if he was to accomplish the obligations he undertook when God granted him the empire. It is revealed that at the summit of his success in the 530s Justinian even hoped that God would permit him to recover all territories that his predecessors had lost.[77]

There are also several laws that deal with provincial reorganizations that in some cases impacted upon military commands. The establishment of the Praetor of Thrace in 535 was meant to improve the oversight of Constantinople's Long Walls by abolishing competing vicariates, while the creation of the *quaestura exercitus* in 536 was probably intended to improve logistical support for impoverished frontier provinces by linking

---

72. Maurice, *Strat.* 12.A-B (infantry); 12.C-D (camps and hunting).
73. See Rance, 'Maurice's *Strategicon*'.
74. Proc., *Wars* 1.1.12–15.
75. See Rance, 'Drungus', esp at 116–18.
76. Proc., *Wars* 1.14, 33, 39–40; 1.15.9–17; 8.31.7.
77. E.g. prefaces to Justinian, *Novels* 85–6; *Nov.* 30 for extreme optimism.

them with safer and richer Aegean coastal provinces.[78] In 535–6 there were also several provincial changes in Asia Minor, one of whose motives was to improve internal security; several adjustments were needed later to close loopholes.[79] The re-establishment of imperial control over conquered territories in the West is recorded in some detail.[80] Through its selection of laws that are still relevant, the *Codex* provides important information on the basis for military recruitment, although the overall significance of this is disputed, as well as on the continued importance of *limitanei*, which suggests that Procopius' criticism of Justinian for undermining them is excessive.[81]

The sources discussed so far all record events from a Roman perspective. A complete understanding of Justinian's wars would require insight into the military, political, social, and ideological structures of their main enemies, information that is sadly lacking. For the Sasanids there is no contemporary narrative of events from their perspective, and indeed it is doubtful if there was any tradition of historiography, despite attempts to credit Khusro I with establishing one during his reforms of the Iranian state. What Khusro, however, does appear to have patronized is the creation of epic narratives about the Sasanids' mythical predecessors, the Kayanids, which cast light on contemporary political cosmology and the Iranian view of the world, including relations with Rome.[82] Writers on the Sasanid past in the early Islamic centuries had access to this material, as well as formal information about regnal lengths and, possibly transmitted orally, other stories. Armenian historians, who do provide some information on Persian affairs, though not necessarily from a positive perspective, are lacking for the sixth century until the seventh-century text of Pseudo-Sebeos begins its account with events of Maurice's reign.

We are better informed about the structures of Sasanid society and especially its overhaul by Khusro I, thanks largely to *The Letter of Tansar*, a work attributed to a third-century priest but actually dating from three

---

78. Justinian, *Novels* 26; 41.
79. Justinian, *Novels* 24–5, 28–31 (AD 535–6); *Edict* 8 (548); *Nov.* 145 (553). Succinct discussion in Jones, *LRE* 280–1, 294.
80. Africa: *Cod.Iust.* 1.27 (AD 534), with *Novels* 36–7 on Church affairs (535); *Nov* 75 (537) on Sicily; Pragmatic Sanction for Italy (554) *Appendix* to *Novels* 7.
81. Recruitment: *Cod.Iust.* 12.23, 43; *limitanei*: 31.4, 46.4; Proc., *SH* 24.12–14. See Chapter 4 for discussion.
82. See the discussion in Payne, 'Cosmology' 13–22; also Wiesehöfer, *Persia* 158; *contra* Hoyland, *History* 3–23, esp. 21, on the dating.

centuries later.[83] Kings presided over a pyramid of nobility, who formally owed allegiance to the crown but in reality might compete, especially if a ruler was weak or unsuccessful.[84] These nobles provided the king with the cavalrymen who constituted the backbone of Sasanid armies and so could determine royal success. Khusro appears to have revised the structure of Sasanid defences by creating four great regional commands to cover threats from the south-west (Arabs), west (Rome), north (Caucasus), and north-east (Hephthalites, Turks), and to have reduced his feudal dependence on the highest nobility to fill his armies by organizing cavalry units under his direct authority that were drawn from the ranks of the *dekhans*, or lesser nobility. Recruits who could not provide their own horse and equipment were given the necessary land to do so.[85] From the sixth century we do not have a triumphal royal inscription along the lines of the third-century *Res Gestae Divi Saporis*, nor is there a monumental royal rock relief between those of Narses (303–9) at Naqsh-i Rustam and Shapur II (309–79) at Bishapur and the early seventh-century reliefs of Khusro II at Taq-i Bustan. Why Khusro I did not commemorate his victories in this traditional way is unknowable, but the earlier reliefs do portray the standard equipment of Persian cavalrymen.[86]

Evidence from within the Vandal kingdom was produced by Romans who had stayed during the conquest in the 430s or who returned to reclaim what property they could. Some were prepared to serve in the royal palace to run the administration of Vandal territory. Much was written by Catholic clergy who suffered pressure or persecution for most of the Vandal period, the fullest account being by Victor of Vita in his *History of the Persecution in the Province of Africa*, published in the late 480s, which recounts the persecutions under the first two Vandal rulers, Geiseric and Huneric. It is quite possible that these writers have exaggerated the levels of religious tensions in order to defend their own claim to orthodoxy, and that life for the majority of the former Roman population was less confrontational.[87]

---

83. Payne, 'Cosmology' 22–4.
84. On this constantly shifting balance, see Whitby, 'Persian King'; Payne, 'Cosmology' 22–30, argues for much greater alignment between nobility and kings, but does not consider the issues raised by the Mazdakite movement.
85. Howard-Johnston, 'Great Powers'.
86. Full discussion in Farrokh, *Armies*.
87. For this approach, see Whelan, *Being Christian*, esp. ch. 2 and 5; for the traditional acceptance of Victor's representation, see Moorhead's introduction to his translation of Victor.

A more relaxed image of life under the Vandals is provided by some of the poets in the *Latin Anthology*, for example Luxorius who was still writing under Gelimer.[88] Most Vandals were settled in the immediate hinterland of Carthage, which provided a focus for the life of the privileged elite. Not all poets were so fortunate: Dracontius was gaoled for composing a panegyric of a foreign ruler but not doing so for the Vandal king, though an elegiac poem requesting pardon probably obtained his release, after which he settled in northern Italy. This evidence points to the fragility of the *modus vivendi* established between the Vandal conquerors and their Roman subjects, who constituted the majority of the population, hence the receptivity of the latter to a return to Roman rule. At the same time, the determination of the church leadership in matters of faith to preserve their views, regardless of the discomfort this might create, is relevant to the troubles that Justinian would experience with African opponents of his doctrinal initiatives.

With regard to the Ostrogothic kingdom in Italy, although we do not, unsurprisingly, have a narrative of their defeat, we are substantially better informed about the internal affairs of the kingdom, its relations with the majority Roman population, and especially the public image that it wished to project, internally and internationally. In no small part this is due to the writings of Cassiodorus, who served the Ostrogothic regime in various roles, including as *quaestor* and *magister officiorum* under Theoderic, and praetorian prefect during the early stages of Belisarius' invasion. By 538 he had left Ravenna for Constantinople, where he remained for about two decades before returning to his family estate in southern Italy to reside in his monastery near Squillace. He composed a long history of the Goths at Theoderic's behest, which, though lost, underpins the *Getica* of Jordanes; this work invented the notion of a long-standing tribe of Ostrogoths under the leadership of the Amals, Theoderic's family, who morphed from parvenu warlords into an ancestral dynasty.[89] Cassiodorus' *Variae* collect the Latin letters, edicts, and other documents that he drafted for Gothic rulers from Theoderic to Witigis. In dealings with the emperor in Constantinople, Theoderic was suitably deferential while also underlining his divine right to rule,[90] but in letters to other rulers in the

---

88. Clover, 'Felix Karthago' 151–4.
89. The substantial confusion caused by Cassiodorus' myth-making was resolved by Heather, 'Cassiodorus'; see also Heather, *Goths and Romans* and *Goths*; Van Nuffelen & Van Hoof, *Jordanes* 60–4.
90. Cass., *Variae* 1.1.

West he adopted a superior position[91] which he attempted to consolidate with suitable gifts, for example a water clock and sundial for Gundobad the Burgundian king.[92] Overall Cassiodorus was at pains to present a picture of a cultured and effective regime, one that had very strong Roman overtones in spite of its anti-Nicene stance in religion. Theoderic acted to safeguard the buildings of Rome, which were not necessarily a priority for its current inhabitants, and espoused the virtues of music, while Theodahad defended the benefits of religious pluralism.[93]

The chronicle known as part two of the *Anonymous Valesianus* presents a largely positive view of Theoderic's rule and his virtues, although the final chapters record the troubles of his last years. The *Liber Pontificalis* contains lives of all popes,[94] with information on their dealings with both successive emperors and Ostrogothic kings, a balancing act that was on occasions difficult. In particular the *Lives* of Silverius and Vigilius record some information on the reconquest from a non-Procopian perspective and naturally cover their troubled relationship with Justinian. The *Collectio Avellana*, which was compiled in the 550s, preserves papal correspondence, both incoming and outgoing, including letters between Hormisdas and the court of Justin down to 521. Another illuminating author is the Gallo-Roman aristocrat Ennodius, who became Bishop of Pavia in 515 and was twice sent to Constantinople as an ambassador. He composed a panegyric of Theoderic, a *Life* of his episcopal predecessor, Epiphanius, that records his public political activity including several embassies as well as his spiritual excellence,[95] hymns, epigrammatic inscriptions, and a collection of poems on subjects such as a boat trip on the Po, a defence of the study of non-Christian literature, and a marriage hymn.

The most famous work to be composed in Ostrogothic Italy is Boethius' *Consolation of Philosophy*. This was written in prison after he had fallen foul of Theoderic in 523 in the context of competition to succeed the ageing king and of worries about the improvement of relations between Catholic Romans and Constantinople after Justin's support for Chalcedon had ended the Acacian Schism. The *Consolation* argues, through the female personification of Philosophy, that in spite of the

---

91. Cass., *Variae* 3.1–3.
92. Cass., *Variae* 1.45–6; for discussion of the diplomatic letters, see Gillett, *Envoys* 177–85.
93. Cass., *Variae* 1.25; 2.40; 10.26.
94. For discussion of the collection, see Davis' introduction to his translation.
95. For discussion of the diplomatic activity, see Gillett, *Envoys* 152–69.

apparent injustices and inequalities of this world, divine providence is in control of everything. Before his fall Boethius had been a loyal servant of Theoderic, being entrusted with the investigation of tampering with the coinage, producing the water clock sent to the Burgundians, and finding a lyre-player for the Frankish ruler, Clovis.[96] He was honoured with the western consulship for 510 and in 522 his two infant sons occupied both consulships, one as the eastern nominee, a signal honour. Boethius wrote numerous works on Aristotelian philosophy, including several translations, arithmetic, music, and theological topics and was one of the great intellectuals of the Roman empire. His execution in 524 casts an unpleasant shadow over Theoderic's reign and is a reminder that, despite the best efforts of Cassiodorus and others to present an image of stable civility for the regime, Ostrogothic control in Italy was never totally secure.

Ostrogothic Ravenna provided an impressive location for the royal court, not nearly as grand as Constantinople but surpassing whatever was available to Franks, Visigoths, or Vandals, and it was further embellished under Theoderic with the construction of S. Apollinare Nuovo and the Arian Baptistery, both adorned with lavish mosaic decorations. The spectacular gospel text known as the *Codex argenteus*, written in the imperial colours of gold and silver ink on purple parchment, was a product of Gothic patronage. The court was supported by the settlement of many of the Ostrogothic warriors in the Po valley and neighbouring Picenum, although, unlike the Vandal settlement in Africa, estates were granted in many other parts of Italy, with Ostrogothic troops clearly serving as garrisons in key locations.

Some of the sources discussed above deal with Justinian's interventions in ecclesiastical matters, in particular Evagrius and John of Ephesus, but there is a wealth of other evidence both from Justinian's own perspective, including correspondence with the papacy, some laws, and doctrinal statements issued by the emperor, and from those of his various adversaries. Central to these disputes is the substantial documentation associated with the Ecumenical Council convened by Justinian in Constantinople in 553.[97] On the anti-Chalcedonian front, there is the correspondence of Severus, Patriarch of Antioch, which records doctrinal discussions with imperial representatives and texts relating to various

---

96. Cass., *Variae* 1.10, 45; 2.40.
97. Translated in Price, *Acts*.

internal disputes such as the Tritheist issue, which split the Miaphysites in Justinian's reign. At the opposite end of the spectrum clergy, especially in the Latin-speaking West, who were uncomfortable with the compromises that Justinian was prepared to tolerate in his attempts to broker a deal with Miaphysites in the East, produced a substantial corpus to refute Justinian's drive to condemn the Three Chapters. The issues and their history are presented succinctly in the *Breviarium* of Liberatus, an archdeacon at Carthage who accompanied his bishop, Reparatus, to attend the 553 Council and then probably followed him into exile at Euchaïta, where he wrote his account in the 560s. Hagiography provides a different perspective. In addition to John of Ephesus' anti-Chalcedonian collection, Cyril of Scythopolis composed lives of various Palestinian holy men who supported Chalcedon. Patriarch Eutychius of Constantinople's interactions with Justinian, which began when he was plucked from provincial obscurity to lead the church in the capital and chair the Council of 553 and ended with dismissal in Justinian's final year for his opposition to the emperor's Aphthartodocete initiative, are presented in a positive light in the *Life* composed by Eustratius in the 580s.[98]

Archaeology provides some assistance for understanding Justinian's wars, in large part through the survival of fortifications at some important sites, especially on the eastern frontier. The impressive walls of Amida (Diyarbakir) are largely medieval but represent the size of the Roman city. At Edessa (Urfa) parts of the line of the curtain walls that twice defied Khusro survive, as does the extra-mural dam constructed by Justinian to reduce the risk of flooding by the river Scirtus. The late Roman walls of Antioch (Antakya) are recorded in eighteenth and nineteenth century engravings, their course can still be traced on the steeper parts of Mount Silpius, and the Iron Gate that regulated the flow into the city of the Parmenius torrent survives almost to full height, including the work that Justinian contributed in order to rectify its deficiencies. At Martyropolis (Silvan) much of the sixth-century circuit is preserved, and at one point it proved possible to observe how the earlier defences were strengthened, broadly in line with Procopius' description of Justinian's work at the site.[99]

The most extensive late-Roman remains in the east are at Dara, where in addition to parts of the lower level of the circuit wall there survive the

---

98. Whitby, 'Church Historians'; Stallman-Pacitti, *Cyril*; Averil Cameron, 'Models'.
99. Proc., *Buildings* 3.2.11–14; Whitby, 'Antioch'; id., 'Martyropolis'.

measures to regulate the water supply, grain stores, water cisterns, and unidentifiable internal buildings that provide the basis for the modern village.[100] They convey an impression of this heavily-defended site, which was able to withstand Khusro's energetic siege in 540.

Away from the east, the late Roman walls of Rome provide the most illuminating commentary on Procopius' narrative of events. Although many of the gates do not survive, much of the curtain preserves the appearance that would have been familiar to Belisarius during the two sieges that he withstood; there is even limited evidence for the merlons that he added in 536/7, and for the emergency repairs undertaken after Totila had slighted the defences in 547.[101]

In North Africa there is a certain amount of inscriptional evidence for the efforts of Justinian's governors to restore the defences of settlements that the Vandals had deliberately neglected or slighted,[102] but these did not play a major role in subsequent Justinianic campaigns. Apart from the relevance of walls to sieges, there is no help from battlefield archaeology, mainly because none of the major engagements of Justinian's reign can be located so precisely: even the location of the battle of Dara in 530, which might appear to have been immediately south of the gates in the south walls, has been challenged.[103]

---

100. Whitby, 'Dara'; see Plates 11-13.
101. For a thorough account of the defences, see Richmond, *City Wall*, on Belisarius' work in particular, see 38–42, 264–7, and for merlons 72, 89.
102. Collected in Durliat, *Les Dédicases* 7–59.
103. For discussion, see Ch.5. XXX.

Chapter 4

The Sixth-century Army

Thanks to the survival of extensive contemporary narrative histories as well as imperial legislation, we are reasonably well informed about the nature and operation of Justinian's military forces, a contrast with the situation in the preceding century when the evolution from the fourth-century Roman armies that are known through Ammianus Marcellinus, the *Notitia Dignitatum*, and the Theodosian Code is unclear. That is not to say that there are no uncertainties or disagreements about some key matters, for example the balance between types of forces, whether central versus local, infantry or cavalry, Roman as opposed to non-Roman, and about recruitment.[1] There is a popular perception that Roman armies underwent an inexorable change from the infantry legions of the Republic and early Empire towards the heavy cavalry of the medieval world, with the balance having already shifted by the sixth century. It is also believed that local troops declined to the status of part-time soldier-farmers and that non-Romans provided most of the effective troops. All these views will be questioned.

There is an issue with terminology, since Procopius and his successors as historians deliberately avoided technical language so that troops and units are often referred to by non-specific terms, such as *stratiotai*, 'soldiers', rather than by the actual type of their unit, whether that was *arithmos* or *meros*. Furthermore, Procopius did not always record everything that he knew: thus in describing Narses' dispositions at Busta Gallorum he notes that 8,000 archers were placed on the wings with 1,500 cavalry placed at an angle on the left wing.[2] But he does not provide figures for the troops commanded by Narses and Valerian on the wings or for the dismounted Lombards, Heruls, and other non-Romans in the centre. Just as he recorded that fifty infantry had occupied the tactically important hill in advance

---

1. Full discussion in Jones, *LRE* ch.17; Whitby, 'Army'.
2. Proc., *Wars* 8.31.2–7.

of the battle,[3] so for the battle he provided numbers for the elements that would be important in the subsequent fighting, but not for the rest of the army.[4] It is frustrating that Procopius could easily have provided us more specific information, but we have to work with what we are given.

At Justinian's accession the empire's armies were divided between five major commands: the two *magistri militum praesentales*, whose troops were based in the vicinity of Constantinople on either side of the Bosporus, so that their commanders were in the 'presence' of the emperor, and three regional *magistri* for Illyricum, Thrace and the East (*Oriens*). In 528 the last of these commands, the massive *Oriens*, was subdivided when a new *magister* was created for Armenia and Lazica, the northeastern sector of the frontier from the Tigris headwaters to the Black Sea. The Long Walls of Constantinople were under the authority of a deputy, vicar, of the European *MM praesentalis*, but Justinian found that this officer devoted most energy to competing with the vicar of the praetorian prefect, who was responsible for civilian matters in the area, so that in 535 he allocated the combined duties to a Praetor.

In due course re-conquered lands in the West were placed under *magistri* for Africa, Italy, and Spain. The supernumerary title of *magister militum vacans* was used to give individuals increased authority for particular operations. The provinces under the authority of the regional *magistri* were commanded by *duces*, though Egypt and some central Anatolian provinces were under a *comes rei militaris*. Justinian's reorganization of the Armenian frontier resulted in the number of dukes in the East being increased from seven to eleven, while new ones were created for Africa.

The dispositions of units under these commanders can be inferred, to an extent, from the *Notitia Dignitatum*, a late fourth-century official list that includes the locations of different types of military units throughout the empire. Its evidence is not straightforward, since the lists underwent various up-datings in the early fifth century. Also, even in their latest version they antedate Justinian by a century, during which time some new units were established although most existing ones continued to operate. In particular Justinian himself was responsible for creating several new units, often as a result of successful campaigns in which prisoners were taken, for example the *Numidae Iustiniani*, a unit of Berbers from Africa which is recorded in Egypt, the *Equites Perso-Justiniani*, created from the former

3. Proc., *Wars* 8.29.13.
4. For discussion of Procopius' use of numbers, see Whately, *Battles* 125–7, 171–7.

garrison of Sisauranon who served in Italy, the *primi Felices Iustiniani* who are found in Africa, or the *Iustiniani Vandali* who fought the Persians in the 540s, all the units being deployed at some remove from their point of origin.[5] The *Notitia* does, however, highlight the importance of the distinction between central palatine units and local provincial ones, and also gives a broad indication of how the troops under the command of, say, the *MM per Orientem* were distributed in the provinces and cities under the command of his subordinate dukes.

Categories of Troops

The army of the fourth century had been divided into two broad categories, the *comitatenses*, which were mobile forces that accompanied emperors on campaign and so might be switched from the Rhine frontier to the Euphrates, and garrison troops commanded by a duke and assigned to particular provinces or cities; the latter are most often referred to, at least by modern scholars, as *limitanei*, though in the sources they are also called *burgarii*, *castrensiani*, or *ripenses*. The *comitatenses* enjoyed superior conditions, possibly because, while visibility to the emperor could bring rewards for distinguished service, the mobility this entailed was not necessarily popular and the more static *limitanei* had greater opportunities for securing local economic benefits. On occasions units were moved from one category to the other, with *limitanei* becoming *pseudocomitatenses* or *comitatenses* losing their superior pay and materials (e.g. extra horses), although the switch was not always recorded with a formal change of title. This basic division of soldiers, *stratiotai*, persisted into the sixth century, although the *comitatenses*, sometimes referred to as *katalogoi* from the registers that underpinned recruitment, can now be split into two categories – those who served in the praesental armies and were based near the capital (*palatini*) and those commanded by the regional *magistri*. The latter were no longer fully mobile, with their field of operation normally restricted to the region commanded by their *magister*; they might be stationed with *limitanei* as when Justinian strengthened Palmyra,[6] and they regularly fought alongside the frontier troops.

One important aspect of the *limitanei* is that part of their pay had been replaced by a grant of land, whose produce and revenues provided for the

---

5. References in Jones, *LRE* ch. 17, nn. 111, 119.
6. Malalas 18.2.

needs of the soldiers and their families. This, along with the fact that they did not enjoy all the legal privileges of the *comitatenses*, has led to them being dismissed as no more than part-time second-class soldier-farmers. In his *Secret History* Procopius claimed that Justinian devalued them by allowing the pay of those on the eastern frontier to fall into arrears by four or five years, and then forcing them to forego their pay altogether when peace was made with the Persians, so that he removed from them the very name of soldiers.[7] The assertions of the *Secret History* have to be treated with caution and this evidence is open to other interpretations. Ownership of property did not make a soldier an amateur: under the Republic, ownership of property had been the key qualification for the privilege of serving in the armies that conquered the Mediterranean, and did not entail that the owner actually did all, or even very much, of the work on his land. Even genuine farm-workers could have some military value, as the mobilization of peasant militias in Lucania in 547 and Totila's actions to counter Roman successes demonstrate.[8] Procopius' critique of Justinian undoubtedly contains exaggerations, and it is possible that the produce from the land allocations of *limitanei* was intended to cover living expenses in peace-time, with payment only made for service away from their base.[9]

At any rate, it is clear that Justinian valued *limitanei* sufficiently to re-establish their deployment in Africa after the Vandal conquest with the allocation of lands to cultivate.[10] Justinian's Code also incorporated the provisions of the Theodosian Code relating to the training and monitoring of the *limitanei*, which suggests that he expected them to be capable of fighting. The numerous sieges during Persian wars will have involved some *limitanei* in the defence of their cities, including their own families and property, often successfully. Later in the century the Fourth Parthian legion, a unit of *limitanei* stationed in Syria according to the *Notitia*, fought at the battle of Solachon (586), where one of its members distinguished himself for valour, and the unit stationed at Asemus on the Danube frontier was so impressive that an unsuccessful attempt was made to incorporate it into the mobile army.[11] Finally, Egyptian evidence from the end of the sixth century reveals that service in units of *limitanei* was a hereditary

---

7. Proc., *SH* 24.13–14.
8. Proc., *Wars* 7.22.1–6, 20.
9. See Whitby, 'Recruitment' 112–13; Lee, *Warfare* 59.
10. *Cod.Iust.* 1.27.2.8.
11. Theophylact, *Histories* 2.6.9; 7.3.1–7.

privilege for which recruits were prepared to pay, so that Justinian had not destroyed their credibility.

Since the fighting ability of the *limitanei* is assumed to be inferior, the co-location with them of *comitatenses* has been taken as a sign that the quality of the latter had also declined. However, the arrangements for re-conquered Africa reveal that *limitanei* were envisaged as the front line of provincial defence, with the *comitatenses* being held in reserve to offer support where needed.[12] This was how Roman frontiers had been defended for over 200 years and for the strategy to work as well as it did under most circumstances the frontline troops had to be good enough to hold up enemy invasions, while the back-up troops being assembled from regional bases also had to be effective.

Another argument used to assert a decline in the quality of Roman soldiers is the prominence of non-Roman troops in narratives of warfare: this has contributed to a belief that these 'barbarians' were the most effective units in sixth-century armies and indeed came to constitute the bulk of Roman forces, with negative consequences for discipline, reliability, and ethos.[13] In part this is a question of context, since the expeditionary forces used to recover Africa and Italy were bound to contain significant elements that had been enrolled specifically for the mission, alongside contingents from eastern armies that had been reassigned to the venture. The new units will undoubtedly have been recruited on the basis of quality as well as their specialist skills; since horse archery was prized as a tactical advantage over Gothic lancers, there will have been numerous Hunnic troops and these were likely to be used prominently in battle. It is also possible that, just as in the Republic and early Empire non-citizen units, *auxilia*, played important roles in battle and suffered heavier casualties than citizen legionaries, generals in the sixth century placed non-Roman units in positions of particular danger.

The traditional way to enlist non-Roman troops in late antiquity was as federates. These functioned as ethnic units under the leadership of their own chief and might range in size from a few hundred to a major warband of 10,000, for example the Goths who followed the two Theoderics in the Balkans in the 470s,[14] who in theory became Roman soldiers when

---

12. Co-location at Palmyra (Malalas 18.2) may well have been because there were no suitable bases for *comitatenses* to the rear within suitable marching distance, say 100 kilometres or 4 to 5 days' march.

13. E.g. Teall, 'Barbarians' esp. the conclusions at 321–2.

14. Proc., *Wars* 8.5.13–14.

their leader was granted the title of *magister militum*. Such foreign units continued to exist in the Justinianic armies, for example the Huns and Lombards who served in Africa and Italy, although they are now termed *summachoi*, allies. Procopius comments that the nature of federate service had changed so that anyone could be enrolled in these units; although he provides no further details, he records Romans as commanders of a federate unit, which does represent a change from earlier practice.[15] At some point in the sixth century the federates were reorganized into their own *moira*, brigade, under a *comes foederatorum*, who is first securely attested in 546.[16]

It is possible that the blurring of distinctions between federates and regulars occurred as a result of the settlement of tribal groups within the empire in return for military service, as for example the Heruls who had been located near Singidunum on the Danube, or the Lombards further upstream.[17] The Heruls often served as allies under their own leader, for example Fulcaris and Philemuth who led Herul contingents in Italy, but Procopius comments that some of the Heruls had even become Roman soldiers enlisted among the federates,[18] and some of their commanders have Roman names. The conquered Vandals were moved from Africa to be enrolled for service in Justinian's eastern wars in five cavalry units of *Iustiniani Vandali*. There were also, undoubtedly, some individual non-Roman volunteers, though these might most often have been enlisted in the private retinues of individual commanders, or been men of high status who became officers, like the Persian Aratius.

Alongside non-Roman units another feature of Justinianic armies is the prominence in the narratives of the personal attendants of senior commanders, their *bucellarii* or 'biscuit-men', named for the hard, twice baked bread (*bucellatum*) that formed the basis for military rations. These retainers can be traced back to the fifth-century entourages of commanders, often of non-Roman origin, from which their use spread to senators and other leading men.[19] Emperors legislated to prevent such retinues from

---

15. Proc., *Wars* 3.11.3–5.
16. Proc., *Wars* 7.31.10. Artabanes (see *PLRE* III Artabanes 2) held the post concurrently with that of MM *praesentalis*; whether he continued in the role when he was sent to Sicily in 550 as *MM per Thracias* is unknown, but in both roles it would certainly have been helpful for him to have held authority over federate contingents.
17. One consequence of the weakened distinction between federates and regulars is that in the later sixth century a new elite unit, the Optimates, was created.
18. Proc., *Wars* 7.33.13–14.
19. Liebeschuetz, *Barbarians* 43–7; Whitby, 'Recruitment' 116–19.

being maintained in cities and on estates,[20] but Justinian recognized that there were limits to the ability of provincial governors to crack down on these bodyguards. The extent to which all these retainers were purely private is debatable, since some landowners in Egypt were given official sanction to recruit *bucellarii*; these then received an official salary in return for performing some imperial administrative business, while those enrolled in the retinues of generals took an oath of loyalty both to their individual commander and to the emperor and were also paid by the state. They were not entirely under the control of their commander, since in 542 the *bucellarii* of Belisarius remained in the east when he was recalled to Constantinople and had still not rejoined him when he was transferred to Italy in 544. Belisarius had to beg Justinian for them to be sent to him.[21]

Numbers might be substantial, since Valerian, *MM per Armeniam*, was sent by Justinian to Italy in 547 with over 1,000 of his bodyguards. That said, the suggestion of Procopius that Belisarius maintained 7,000 retainers at his personal expense is regarded as impossibly high;[22] this assertion comes in the passage where Procopius praised Belisarius at the height of his powers as the outstanding Roman general. Although Procopius has probably exaggerated the numbers, his assessment of their excellent quality is plausible, since enrolment in a commander's retinue was one possible reward for distinguished service in battle.[23]

The imperial guards are a special case. The largest unit was the *scholarii*, 3,500 in total enrolled in seven *scholae*, although from the late fifth century the 300 strong excubitors were the elite guards unit with responsibility for protecting the entrances to the Palace;[24] the emperor's personal guards were forty *candidati*. Proximity to the emperor was a privilege and individuals were prepared to pay to be enrolled in the *scholae*, to the extent that Justinian exploited this during Justin's reign by creating a supernumerary body of 2,000 reservists. After his accession, however, he soon dismissed these without compensation, according to the critical Procopius to whom we owe this information.[25] Agathias decried the military effectiveness of the *scholarii*

---

20. *Cod.Iust.* 9.12.10.
21. Proc., *Wars* 7.10.1.
22. Proc., *Wars* 7.1.18–20.
23. E.g. Proc., *Wars* 8.29.28.
24. Imperial guards with their spears and oval shields are depicted on the Obelisk of Theodosius and the San Vitale mosaic of Justinian: see Plates 10 and 3.
25. Proc., *SH.* 24.15–20.

when they were called upon to defend the capital against the Kutrigurs in 559, charting their decline from a force of experienced former soldiers into a parade-ground unit suitable only for imperial ceremonies.[26] This negative assessment chimes with his critique of Justinian's failure to attend to military matters and is in line with Procopius' accusation that Justinian extorted money from individual *scholarii* by listing them for campaign service, an unexpected duty from which they had to purchase exemption.[27] There will have been some truth in these criticisms,[28] but guards were regularly deployed to repress rioting in Constantinople and so had some fighting capacity, and individual *scholarii* are attested on campaign in the narrative histories.[29]

The final element of the Justinianic military establishment to note is the navy, although it must be admitted that little is known about it in the sixth century. At Constantinople the dockyards on the Golden Horn housed the most powerful naval force in the Mediterranean, one that maintained the barrier between Europe and Asia and protected the capital's coastline, which was not yet defended by a full set of sea walls. It had access to some form of 'Greek fire', a highly inflammable substance that was used in 515 to thwart the attempt by Vitalian to capture the city from the sea.[30] The standard vessel was the dromon, a ship propelled by a single bank of oars, probably twenty-five on each side, with sails being used for longer journeys.[31] The navy escorted the expeditionary forces to the West – where Belisarius was grateful not to have to confront the strong Vandal fleet based in Carthage – maintained communications between the Roman coastal strongholds in Italy at the height of the Gothic revival in the 540s, and crushed the small Gothic fleet near Ancona in 551. It also played an important role in sustaining the Danube frontier, preserving links with Roman outposts along the river and thwarting attempts to cross to the south bank, at least when the river was not frozen. It is, however, true that warfare in the sixth century was essentially land-based.[32]

---

26. Agathias, *Hist.* 5.15.2–6.
27. Proc., *SH.* 24.21–3.
28. For example Jones, *LRE* 658, accepts that they were ornamental, but for the argument to the contrary see Mary Whitby, 'Occasion' 465–6.
29. E.g. two *comites scholae*, John and Diogenes, are recorded fighting at the battle of Cotyaeum in 492, presumably accompanied by their units: Theophanes 138.10.
30. Malalas 16.15.
31. For very full discussion, see Pryor and Jeffreys, *Dromon*; also Cosentino, 'Naval Warfare' 331–3, 338.
32. Cf. Shaw, 'War' 144.

Recruitment

The processes through which Justinian's armies were recruited have occasioned considerable debate. In the fourth and early fifth century it is clear from the Theodosian Code that conscription through a regular levy, *dilectus*, conducted in the provinces was the basic method.[33] This was, unsurprisingly, unpopular both with landowners, who were grouped into units called *temones* or *capitula*, whose members were responsible for providing a recruit that might deprive them of an agricultural worker, and with individuals, especially at times of severe pressure as in the late-fourth century after the losses at Adrianople. As a result the Code contains a long chapter devoted to closing loopholes in the system.[34] These provisions were not, however, incorporated into the Justinianic Code, as a result of which scholars have postulated a fundamental change at some point between the mid-fifth century and Justinian's accession: it is supposed that military service became sufficiently attractive that the need for conscription faded, since there were usually sufficient volunteers to fill the ranks. The improvements have been ascribed to a 50 per cent increase in pay under Anastasius, or to a more general economic rebalancing in which military service came to be perceived as more desirable, as a result of higher levels of rural under-employment combined with the expectation of local service for the majority of recruits into both the *limitanei* and regional *comitatenses*.[35]

There are, however, other ways to explain the differences between the two legal codes.[36] The bulk of the legislation in the Theodosian Code relates to particular military crises in the late-fourth and early-fifth centuries, whereas Justinian was codifying regulations for a simpler system operating in steady state. Justinian in fact preserved the recruiting units of landowners, *temones*, whose rotating president had the unwelcome responsibility of supplying the recruit; if conscription did not exist, the relevance of these units would be unclear. It was necessary also to preserve legislation to prevent the enlistment of unsuitable recruits such as slaves, *coloni* (tied tenants), and *curiales*,[37] while the *Digest* contains a reference to the *dilectus* in the context

---

33. For an overview of Roman imperial practice, see Lee, *Warfare* 72–4.
34. *Cod.Theod.* 7.13.
35. Treadgold, *Army* 153–5; Jones, *LRE* 669–70, although he does admit that 'the revolution... is a surprising one'.
36. Discussion in Whitby, 'Recruitment' 75–87.
37. *Cod.Iust.* 10.42.8.

of a son being mutilated to prevent his conscription, an indication that this issue continued to require legal attention even though Justinian's Code had not incorporated the relevant Theodosian texts.[38] Finally Justinian restricted the possibility of commuting the supply of a recruit for a payment in gold, a privilege that was now guaranteed only for imperial estates, which indicates that he wanted his system to supply physical bodies.[39] All this indicates that there is no need to postulate a major but totally unrecorded change in this fundamental aspect of imperial administration.

While conscription provided some of the necessary recruits, it is also the case that volunteers were welcome, and indeed it is arguable that these two apparently distinct approaches to recruitment in fact usually operated in tandem. Effective conscription required the co-operation of the local elites – landowners who supplied bodies to the army or who, in certain circumstances, might even lead a local group into military service if the rewards were appropriate.[40] Although military recruitment should, in theory, have been distributed across the empire's provinces roughly in proportion to their populations, which were recorded for tax purposes, it is probable that practice varied. Units of *limitanei* will usually have been recruited locally, and we can observe the unit stationed at Syene in Upper Egypt at the end of the sixth century maintaining a waiting list of those keen to enjoy the benefits of imperial service.

The regional *comitatenses* may also, in part, have been recruited locally, but it is clear that certain regions of the empire were favoured for recruiting purposes, with it being possible to focus demand on these areas by permitting other provinces to commute recruits for gold. The central Balkans had been a prime recruiting ground since the third century, in the fifth century Isauria, the mountainous region of central Anatolia, emerged as important, while in the sixth century Armenians, Tzani, Laz, and Iberians from northeastern Anatolia and Transcaucasia also become prominent. What unites these areas is that they are all upland regions, where there were abundant supplies of healthy young men for whom the imperial army was the best available employment. From the empire's perspective enrolment in the army helped to defuse potential problems in areas where the emperor's authority was not always paramount, by removing young

---

38. *Digest* 59.16.4.12.
39. *Cod. Iust.* 11.75.3.
40. For this approach, see Whitby, 'Recruitment' 66–8, 83–6.

men who would otherwise have been underemployed and attaching them to imperial structures.[41]

That said, all these recruits did need to be trained in Roman ways. One of the alleged factors in the Roman defeat at Callinicum in 531 was the inexperience of the unit of Isaurians from central Anatolia: these had only recently been recruited from the land and Procopius observes they were mostly from the neighbouring province of Lycaonia, with the implication that they were poorer quality than true Isaurians. In 544 Belisarius complained to Justinian about the inexperience of soldiers he had recently recruited in the Balkans.[42]

In addition to conscription and volunteering there was probably an element of hereditary service, even though references to this have also not been taken over fully from the Theodosian into the Justinianic Code. At least this still operated under Anastasius and its confirmation by Maurice in the late-sixth century was regarded as a benefit within an otherwise unpopular package of military changes.[43] If nowhere else, hereditary service will have continued in the *limitanei*, since only this would allow the continued lawful occupation of the estates allocated to the active soldier.[44] There is in fact, however, some reference to hereditary service in the Code in the chapter 'Concerning the sons of military officials who die in warfare'.[45] Its first subsection imposes the duty of hereditary service on the sons of any official bound by an oath, whether the father is still in post or not; the second subsection states that sons of centurions ought to follow their fathers' position, while the third records the privilege that sons of those killed on active service should inherit their fathers' position up to the rank of *biarchus*, thereby providing support to the dead man's family.

Those who argue against continuing hereditary service have to interpret the first subsection as applying only to civilian officials rather than soldiers, but this then means that the chapter has no coherence; it is easier to postulate that the men bound by an oath in the first subsection do include soldiers, since these were men who had sworn

---

41. Cf. Shaw, 'War' 155.
42. Proc., *Wars* 1.18.39–40; 7.12.4–5.
43. Jones, *LRE* 668, suggests believes that it lapsed, but this seems implausible, granted that it is attested later in the century and was a standard aspect of many professions in the late Roman world.
44. Haldon, *Recruitment* 21.
45. *Cod.Iust.* 12.47.2.

an oath of allegiance.[46] To permit the son to inherit the benefits of his father's rank, which appears to have been repeated by Maurice as a concession to sweeten unpopular reforms,[47] was clearly an advantage for some individual soldiers. On the other hand it could have disrupted promotion mechanisms, if current soldiers in lower grades were prevented from moving up through the hierarchy, and it would appear to upset the operational balance of a unit since promoted soldiers were expected to have the experience to undertake harder tasks such as standing in the front ranks. These problems could have been avoided if the son did not inherit the full obligations of his father's rank and his new position was supernumerary, but we do not have that sort of detailed information.

Based on assumptions about the size of the military establishment, discussed below, it is likely that the army in steady state needed each year about 7,500 recruits into the *comitatenses* and 6,000 into the *limitanei*, with more required to replace casualties. Hereditary enrolment supplied some, perhaps most, of the *limitanei*, as well as some of the *comitatenses*, but the empire would still have to find several thousand recruits each year.[48] How sustainable this was depends on assumptions about the size of the empire's overall population, about which we can only guess. One plausible assessment is that before the plague the eastern provinces had a population of about thirty million, dropping towards twenty million by later in the century once the full effects of the plague had been felt.[49] A population resource of this size should have been capable of generating the annual quota of recruits. At the same time, a system that functioned reasonably well in steady state would be put under pressure if it had to find, say, the equivalent of two or three years' normal supply at short notice, either to replace battle casualties or to create an army for new duties, for example in the West. Other factors such as the popularity of the anticipated campaign, the reputation of the individual commander, and specific local circumstances such as external threats, would all influence the ease with which recruits could be secured.[50]

---

46. For this argument, see Whitby, 'Recruitment' 80–1.

47. Theophylact, *Histories* 7.1.7.

48. Discussion in Whitby, 'Recruitment' 83–5; for the broader situation from early to late empire, see Lee, *Warfare* 77–9.

49. Mango, *Byzantium* 23, noting that the drop to 20 million probably occurred after Justinian's reign.

50. See Proc., *Wars* 7.39.12–25 for the powerful impact on recruitment of the re-appointment of Germanus to command an expedition to Italy in 550; also 8.26.14–17 for the positive reputation of Narses.

Army Units

The units that these recruits joined varied. The formations known from the *Notitia*, infantry legions whose size is estimated at about 1,200 men and 600-strong cavalry *alae*, continued to exist in many cases, although the former might now be termed *tagmata*, 'formations' or regiments. Other terms in use were *numerus* and *arithmos*, 'number', and *katalogoi*, 'registers'. The strength of the new cavalry formation of *Numidae Iustiniani* is recorded as 508, which might represent an under-strength *ala*.[51] It is possible that units formed on a specific regional basis, for example the Isaurians, were recruited into larger units. At Callinicum in 531 the Isaurian contingent numbered at least 2,000, Belisarius was accompanied to Italy by 3,000 Isaurians in 535 and a further 3,000 Isaurian reinforcements arrived at Naples in 537.[52] In 538 the Isaurians were sufficiently numerous to be operating in different locations, with some defending Ancona and Rimini while others were available to be dispatched to Milan.[53] It is possible that these Isaurians comprised a number of units of the standard legionary size of around 1,000 men, which were brigaded into a *moira*, but the Procopian narrative suggests they were a single unit that could be subdivided as necessary. The size of non-Roman contingents varied, but it might be the case that 600 was seen as the appropriate size for an effective unit of Hunnic cavalry.[54] In the late sixth century, but most probably under Justinian as well and earlier, units were grouped into larger formations, the brigade or *moira* of 2–3,000 men and the division or *meros* that was 6–7,000 strong.[55]

In contrast to this speculation, we have a detailed insight into one sixth-century unit, thanks to the reconstruction of a Greek inscription from Perge on the south coast of modern Turkey. This preserves the greater part of the local translation of a Latin edict from Anastasius relating to military service, in particular corrupt queue-jumping in the promotion hierarchy, as it was implemented for the local unit.[56] It is unclear whether the edict was restricted to the province of Pamphylia or had universal effect, but the latter seems likely. In addition to the imperial law, which is reinforced

---

51. *Pap.Lond.* 1663.
52. Proc., *Wars* 1.18.5; 5.5.2; 6.5.1.
53. Proc., *Wars* 6.11–12.
54. Proc., *Wars* 1.13.20; 3.11.11.
55. Maurice, *Strat.* 1.4.10–12, 23–6.
56. For this text see the important article by Fatih Onur, 'Military Decree', which presents the results of his painstaking reconstruction of the text.

by an address from the *magister militum*, the inscription contains the unit's muster roll, with a full list of the quota of officers and promoted soldiers together with the amount of *annona* to which they were entitled. The unit contained:

- 1 tribune and one junior tribune, who probably received 24 and 10 *solidi* each.
- 20 *ordinarii* at 8 *annonae*.
- 20 Augustales at 6, with a further 30 at 5, and 70 at 4 *annonae*.
- 60 Flaviales at 4, and 140 at 3 *annonae*.
- 10 *signiferi* and 10 *optiones* at 3 *annonae*.
- 50 *veredarii* at 3, and a further 225 at 2 *annonae*.
- 10 *vexilarii*, 10 *imaginiferi*, 2 *librarii*, 3 *mensores*, 4 *tubicines*, 8 *cornicines*, 2 *bucinatores*, 1 *praeco*, 2 *armaturae duplares*, and 4 *beneficiarii*, all at 2 *annonae*.
- 136 *torquati semissales*, 256 *bracchiati semissales*, and 20 *armaturae semissales*, all at 1.5 *annonae*.
- a less certain number, but probably well into the hundreds,[57] of *munifices*, *clerici*, and *deputati*, all at 1 *annona*.

With the exception of the two most senior officers, the rest of the unit received the bulk of their remuneration in kind (*annonae*) with limits on what they were permitted to convert to gold *solidi* (*adaeratio*). This indicates that the edict must have been issued before 498 when Anastasius commuted the distribution of *annonae*, uniforms, and equipment for gold. The unit must have been substantially larger than the accepted size of 1,200 for a legion: if the promoted men had at least as many non-promoted rank-and-file soldiers under them, then the unit was at least double this.

The list of grades is more extensive and detailed than any other evidence that we possess, but is also not entirely consistent with the rates established by Justinian for *limitanei* in reconquered Africa, where a shorter hierarchy (setting aside the most senior position of *adsessor*, a civilian rather than a military position) runs from *primicerius*, *numerarius*, *ducenarius*, *centenarius*, *biarchus*, and *circitor* to *semissalis*.[58] Although certain

---

57. The figure for *munifices* ended in '59', but the preceding figure or figures are lost; for the *clerici* and *deputati* it is possible that the figure ended in the digits '73', but again with one or more preceding digits. See Onur, 'Military Decree' 187.
58. *Cod.Iust.* 1.27.2.

aspects of the inscription, specifically the limitation on *adaeratio*, no longer applied in Justinian's reign, the text reveals several things: the close scrutiny of the military establishment through regular muster rolls; the complex structure of a unit; and the limitations to our knowledge about the diversity of the army, in that this unit, for which we have unique detailed information, does not entirely correspond to the assumptions that have been made about size and structure from other scattered evidence.

Officers and Commanders

Most of the promoted positions in these units, including many of the junior officer positions, although not always the commanding tribune or *primicerius*, were filled through gradual internal promotion. The chaotic, noisy conditions of ancient battle made it imperative that there was a strong bond between the rank-and-file and their local leaders, so there were operational benefits to extended common service. Senior officers, however, were appointed by the emperor and Justinian clearly took into account a range of considerations: personal loyalty was vital, probably even more so than ability, although that was also relevant; outsiders might be attractive as men who would have to depend on the emperor for their careers. In the case of the units with a particular geographical focus or a non-Roman contingent, a fellow countryman or tribesman was often needed. One consequence of the emperor's concern over loyalty was that different commanders might be instructed to keep an eye on each other, with the resulting suspicions leading to problems in the field.[59] It was rare for an individual to receive supreme authority, as Belisarius did as *strategos autokrator* in Africa (but not apparently in Italy) and subsequently Narses when concluding the Gothic campaigns.

Belisarius and Sittas, Justinian's first two appointments as *magistri militum*, had both been members of his personal bodyguard before his elevation, his *bucellarii*, and then been tried out as provincial *duces*; in spite of Belisarius' defeat at Callinicum, his loyalty in the Nika Riot confirmed his credentials. Germanus, appointed to command the expedition to Italy in 550, was Justinian's cousin, and his son Justinian and son-in-law John (nephew of Vitalian) were among his supporting commanders; the latter already had a long record of service. The Persarmenian brothers, Aratius and Narses, who deserted to the Romans in 530, held commands in the

59. E.g. Proc., *Wars* 6.22.1–5, 30.1–2.

West through into the 530s, while another Persarmenian, the eunuch Narses, had an even more glittering civil and military career into the reign of Justin II, after he too had decisively helped Justinian overcome the Nika rioters. The Heruls were regularly led by Pharas and Philemuth, along with other tribesmen, Aluith, Visandus, and Verus, the last name being a useful reminder that nomenclature is not always a reliable guide to ethnic identity. The leaders of smaller tribal groups, such as the Gepid Mundo, might be entrusted with command of Roman troops.

Not all Justinian's choices are so explicable, as Procopius commented with regard to the selection of the aged Liberius to lead a relief expedition to Italy in the winter of 549/50.[60] A puzzling case is the Armenian Artabanes, who had deserted the Persians in the early 540s after fighting successfully for them in the 530s. After commanding a small Armenian contingent in Africa, he quickly rose to become *MM per Africam* and then, on his return to the capital, *MM praesentalis*. In 549 he was discovered to be plotting against Justinian, but, escaping serious punishment, he was appointed *MM per Thracias* in 550, as which he commanded forces in Sicily and Italy. Quite why his disloyalty was overlooked is unknown, but he had at one point been seen as a possible husband for Justinian's niece, Praeiecta, a match that was thwarted by his existing marriage in Armenia.

One important facet of Justinian's generals that has received attention recently is the question of the networks that supported these leaders.[61] In the same way as Justinian often appointed commanders with whom he had some relationship, so generals such as Belisarius and Narses had certain associates whom they trusted – though with the difference that they could not always determine who their colleagues would be. From the troubles that plagued Belisarius in Italy in 538–40, it emerges that the eunuch Narses had close links with John (nephew of Vitalian), the Armenian brothers Aratius and Narses, and Justin, whereas Belisarius could rely on the support of Valerian (colleague in Africa), Martin (commander in the East in 531 and in Africa), Uliaris (officer in Belisarius' bodyguards), and Ildiger (son-in-law of Antonina).

Affiliation was not permanent: thus John the Glutton, one of Belisarius' officers in Italy who accompanied him to the East in 541, then accused him of treacherous talk in 542, probably after Belisarius found fault

---

60. Proc., *Wars* 7.37.26–7.
61. See Parnell, 'Networks', and at greater length, *Justinian's Men*.

with his conduct of a raid across the Tigris. After 542 this John is found alongside Narses in 545 and 552. These networks clearly stretched much further, with second-tier commanders having their own groups, but we lack the information to identify these. They mattered because commanders decided on strategy and tactics in council with senior officers,[62] who were to be treated with courtesy,[63] and then had to rely on these subordinates to carry through the plans as ordered.

Terms and Conditions

It is clear that conditions of service for soldiers were relatively favourable, even if not quite as generous as supposed by those who believe in a volunteer army. The key element in financial reward was the donative, the accession donative paid at the start of a new reign of five *solidi* plus one pound of silver (equivalent overall to nine *solidi*) and the quinquennial donative of five *solidi*. Procopius asserts that Justinian declined to pay the latter, so that the troops went without for thirty-two years,[64] but such radical destabilization in the early years of his reign seems unlikely. It has, therefore, been suggested that Justinian converted the quinquennial donative into an annual payment of one *solidus*.[65] It seems improbable that soldiers still received an annual *stipendium*, but in addition to their ration (*annona*), whether paid in cash by *adaeratio* or in produce, soldiers received cash allocations for equipment, uniforms and, where appropriate, horses. Kit and mounts came from state factories (*fabricae*) that specialized in different items and from stud farms on the Anatolian plateau or in Thrace, while clothing was provided through a special tax, the *vestis militaris*, and produced in part by *fabricae* and in part by individual taxpayers. It is possible that the allocations deliberately exceeded the value of the various items, but soldiers could preserve cash by economizing on these matters, albeit at the risk of leaving themselves poorly prepared for action, and it was a benefit if a commander offered to replace at his own expense material lost in battle.[66]

Promotion within a unit based on length of service led to an increase in rations, up to five *annonae* for the senior officer, *primicerius*, in a unit

---

62. E.g. Proc., *Wars* 6.16.
63. Maurice, *Strat* 8.2.97.
64. Proc., *SH* 24.27–9.
65. Jones, *LRE* 670.
66. Proc., *Wars* 7.1.8.

in Africa, although the rates in the unit at Perge were more generous. *Comitatenses* qualified for the full benefits of veteran status after twenty years of service, *limitanei* after twenty-four, although there are examples of individuals choosing to serve longer. Those discharged as a result of wounds enjoyed the same legal privileges, most importantly tax exemption for themselves and their families if they had served long enough. A major benefit for all soldiers was the enhanced status that service brought, which might be translated into tangible benefits through, for example, the exploitation of billeting arrangements.

Numbers

For all its detailed information, the *Notitia Dignitatum* does not shed light on the overall numbers in the late Roman army, since there is nothing to indicate the complement of an infantry legion or a cavalry vexillation. Estimates are made based on assumptions as to the size of these units,[67] for example that a legion was about 1,000 to 1,200 men and cavalry units about half that number, but we do not even know whether they had a standard size. The unit at Perge must have been at least 2,500 strong and quite possibly over 3,000, which suggests there was variation. We do have one specific figure for the overall manpower in the Justinianic armies: Agathias, in the context of an attack on Justinian's disregard for the empire, asserted that, whereas the empire had once been defended by 645,000 men, this had now been reduced to no more than 150,000.[68] The rhetorical setting for this information is crucial and the contrast of 'then and now' has been sharpened both by distorting the two figures and by taking the establishment of the entire empire, West as well as East, as the point of departure. It is also likely that Agathias has excluded the *limitanei* from the figure he offers for Justinian, on the basis that Justinian's critics did not regard them as proper soldiers.[69] If these adjustments are applied, Agathias' figure of 150,000 would permit the existence of six armies under the eastern *magistri* in the range of 10–25,000 *comitatenses* each, with a comparable army

---

67. A detailed reconstruction is valiantly attempted by Jones, *LRE* 679–84.
68. Agathias, *Hist.* 5.13.7–8; see above for discussion. We also have a specific figure for the size of the Diocletianic establishment, i.e. *circa* 300: John Lydus states that that there were 389,704 in the armies and a further 45,562 in the navies, a total of 435,266 (*de Mensibus* 1.27), though he goes on to accuse Constantine of doubling the size of the military, which is not credible.
69. Whitby, 'Recruitment' 73–5.

in Italy, a smaller force in Africa, and a very small detachment in Spain. On that basis Jones concluded that there had been a slight reduction in the military establishment, from about 170,000 to 150,000 under Justinian.[70]

This is plausible, though not certain. It must also be borne in mind that there will have been a difference between the muster rolls and actual fighting strength: Procopius alleged that Justinian's *logothetes*, officials who were charged with reviewing the composition of units, deliberately left the names of the deceased on the rolls which prevented others from moving up to higher grades and allowed emperor and officials to share the savings in pay.[71] On the other hand, it is likely that sixth-century units were no more under-strength than their fourth-century predecessors. Agathias' figure would not include all the various allied contingents and *bucellarii*, which in combination would add several thousand troops to the total. On that basis, the Justinianic military establishment was, perhaps, not much smaller than its predecessors in the fourth and fifth centuries.

This overall figure needs to be calibrated against the specific information that we have for armies on campaign in the sixth century. The army assembled under Anastasius for the campaign of 503 is said to have numbered 52,000 men and, according to Procopius, was the largest force ever assembled to fight the Persians.[72] It was commanded by three *magistri militum* plus the *magister officiorum*, operated in separate detachments, and was so large that it required special logistical arrangements at Edessa. This monstrous army was only formed by combining the forces allocated to several commanders, and a more normal size for a large operational army in the East would have been the 25,000 who fought at Dara in 530, when the *MM per Armeniam* was separately commanding about 15,000 men further north, or the 20,000 in the 531 campaign that culminated at Callinicum.[73] Even armies of this size will have entailed summoning contingents from a number of provinces under the command of the particular *MM*.

In the Balkans, where the logistical infrastructure was less robust, a large field army operating away from the hinterland of Constantinople was probably in the range of 10–15,000, although larger forces had been used under Anastasius. Belisarius was sent to Africa with 10,000 infantry, 5,000 cavalry drawn from the *comitatenses* and federates, plus a

---

70. Jones, *LRE* 684.
71. Proc., *SH*. 25.5–6.
72. Ps.-Joshua, *Chronicle* 54; Proc., *Wars* 1.8.1–5.
73. Proc., *Wars* 1.13.23; 15.11; 18.5.

further 1,000 Herul and Hun horse-archers, but with only 7,500 regular troops and allies in the first instance to Italy,[74] although in each case with his own *bucellarii* and those of his officers in addition. The discussion of army sizes in Maurice's *Strategicon* regards the range of 5–6,000 to 10–12,000, or 15,000 as proportionate, with a force above 15,000 or 20,000 as less usual.[75] By the 590s the empire's resources had been diminished, primarily through repeated visitations of plague but also from loss of control in the Balkans, so that it is reasonable to infer that army sizes half a century earlier would have been a bit larger than these.

Equipment and Tactics

We have little specific evidence for the equipment of the sixth-century Roman army, but equally there is no evidence for significant changes between the third and seventh centuries, so that it is legitimate to draw on information from across these centuries to produce a composite picture. Most of our information comes from images of soldiers, for example illustrations in manuscripts of the Bible or other texts, sculptures on monuments, or depictions in. mosaics or on silverware. The consistency of the picture across the different media provides some reassurance of its accuracy.[76] Infantry were equipped with spear, sword, helmet, oval shield, and in some cases with bows. Body armour was normally a mail corselet that protected the wearer to below the waist, though for some the corselet was made from scales of metal or horn (*lamellae*) and others wore metal breastplates. That infantry still wore body armour contradicts the assertion of Vegetius, writing *circa* 400, that Emperor Gratian (375–83) had acceded to a petition from the troops that they be permitted to stop wearing armour and helmets since, as a result of the failure of training, they found these too heavy.[77] Vegetius was keen to highlight the decline in standards and competence of the contemporary army and has probably extrapolated a general rule from a particular instance, since it was known for commanders to use troops with lighter or little protection on difficult terrain where agility was key.[78]

---

74. Proc., *Wars* 3.11.2, 11; 5.5.2–4.
75. Maurice, *Strat.* 3.8; 10.
76. See Elton, 'Forces' 286–95; Syvänne, *Age* 43–51.
77. Vegetius, *Epit. rei Milit.* 1.20. For succinct discussion of Vegetius, see Rance, 'Battle' 344–5; for fuller treatment, see Milner's introduction to his translation of the *De Re Militari*.
78. E.g. Maurice, *Strat.* 12.B.20.

Although there were some specialist units of archers and slingers, for example the light-infantry Berbers and Isaurian slingers and javelin-men in Lazica in 555,[79] it is likely that most Roman infantry units were formed from troops of different types.[80] The experienced promoted soldiers who stood in the front ranks and as rear markers for each file were more heavily equipped, for example with larger shields, stronger helmets, and greaves to provide extra protection for the lower leg. Those in the middle ranks were more lightly equipped and might fire arrows, javelins, lead-weighted darts, or sling-shot.[81] This permitted the unit to form a shield wall or *fulcum*, a version of the classical Roman *testudo* or tortoise:[82] the front rank locked its shields together, shield boss to shield boss, while those in the second rank raised their shields over the heads of the front rank and rested them on their shield bosses, thereby protecting their faces and upper bodies.[83] Such a solid unit, bristling with the spears of the front three ranks projecting through the shield wall,[84] could withstand a cavalry charge while also laying down a barrage of missiles that would disrupt the onrush. The ability of fifty infantry to withstand a series of Gothic charges by standing shoulder to shoulder to defend the route that led up to the important hill at Busta Gallorum demonstrates the effectiveness of such a formation.[85]

As to cavalry, late Roman armies had a few units of heavily armoured cataphracts, whose horses also had some frontal protection, but it is unclear whether these still existed in the sixth century when operational flexibility was prized. The cataphracts have seized the imagination as antecedents of medieval knights, but such units were always exceptional and their operational effectiveness, as opposed to their considerable psychological impact, was questionable. The distinction between units that relied on a shock charge and those that disrupted opponents with

---

79. Agathias, *Hist.* 3.20.9.
80. Units of archers might be created for special purposes by withdrawing the best archers from the regular units, as happened at Busta Gallorum: Proc., *Wars* 8.31.5; cf. also Maurice, *Strat.* 12.B.9.3–8.
81. Agathias, *Hist.* 2.8.4–5; Maurice, *Strat.* 12.B.4.5–8. If this sort of mixed-arms unit sounds implausible, it does resemble the mixed phalanx that Alexander the Great was believed to have been developing towards the end of his life (Arrian, *Anabasis* 7.23–3–4).
82. See the important discussion of Rance, 'Battle' 366–7, on which the above is based.
83. Maurice, *Strat.* 12.B.16.33–8.
84. Maurice, *Strat.* 12.A.7.49–57.
85. Proc., *Wars* 8.29.11–28.

missiles had eroded, and, as in infantry units, the heaviest protection may have been reserved for those in the front ranks. So too had the distinction between *cursores* – offensive units that aimed to disrupt the enemy with charges, often in a wedge-shaped formation, and missiles – and *defensores*, cavalry formed up in closer order to provide stability to the flexible *cursores*.[86] Some non-Roman units were more specialist, with Arab allies relying on hit-and-run tactics rather than close engagement or Huns being expert at archery and lassoing. If put under severe pressure, or when facing challenging opposition, Roman cavalry would dismount in order to achieve the stability of an infantry formation.[87] At Busta Gallorum Narses ordered his Lombard, Herul, and other non-Roman troops to dismount to make it harder for them to flee in the face of the Gothic charge.[88] Cavalry carried spears or two-handed lances, bows, swords, and in some cases a small shield hung around the neck.

Procopius singled out Roman horse-archers, *hippotoxotai*, for special praise, using them in his introduction to the *Wars* to demonstrate the superiority of contemporary warfare over the classical period when archery was despised.[89] His eulogy is undoubtedly exaggerated and it is likely that few Romans had the expertise in both horsemanship and archery to shoot accurately to either side while riding at full speed, but the image was an ideal towards which soldiers could be rigorously trained. The most effective mounted archers were Huns, and it was the example of their heavier composite bows, high-arched saddles,[90] and techniques that the Romans were following. Maurice wanted all his Roman cavalry to achieve a reasonable level of competence in archery in order to counter the Avars, successors to the Huns as horse-archers from central Asia.[91] Superiority in archery enabled the Romans to win their major victories

---

86. Maurice, *Strat.* 3.5.63–76.

87. Proc., *Wars* 8.8.30–4.

88. Proc., *Wars* 8.31.5.

89. Proc., *Wars* 1.1.8–16. For discussion of the literary context for Procopius' preface, see Basso and Greatrex, 'Preface', who highlight Procopius' claim that these contemporary archers were superior in courage as well as in equipment. Kaldellis, *Procopius* 17–24, argues that Procopius' discussion of horse-archers is an ironic digression, whose concealed intention was to point to the un-Roman nature of these troops, who were therefore not to be esteemed, but he ignores the context that Procopius provides (*Wars* 1.1.6, 16); he also misunderstands his supposed Platonic antecedent, as Petitjean, 'Classicisme', points out.

90. These saddles made the adoption of the stirrup, probably later in the century from experience of the Avars, an advance of limited significance: see Rance, 'Battle' 358.

91. Maurice, *Strat.* 1.2.28–36.

in the West, where opponents preferred to fight at close quarters, and even against the Persians whose skill in archery was renowned. Procopius commented on the greater penetrative force of Roman archers, whose slower rate of fire was offset by its efficacy.[92]

The narrative of Procopius can convey the impression that cavalry was all that mattered in late Roman warfare, since it is cavalry units that delivered victory at Dara in 530 and in engagements with the Vandals, to the extent that Procopius credited victory over the latter to the 5,000 cavalry that Belisarius took with him.[93] At Dara, Belisarius appears to have had so little confidence in his infantry that he stationed them behind a protective ditch. At Ad Decimum the victory was decided long before the infantry arrived on the scene, and outside the walls of Rome during the siege of 537 it was the cavalry's hit-and-run tactics that unsettled the besieging Ostrogoths. In each case there were particular reasons why the infantry did not play a significant role, although they were responsible for capturing the Vandal camp after Tricamerum.[94] It is also possible that Belisarius himself was less adept at handling infantry formations than Narses, who used them effectively later in the Italian war against both Totila and the Franks. It has been noted that the *limitanei* included many more cavalry units than did the *comitatenses*,[95] which reflects the fact that the former needed to be able to patrol the frontier regions whereas the latter had to be capable of moving rapidly to confront problems: infantry could preserve their fighting ability after a long forced march much better than horsemen.

Late-Roman infantry were different from the heavily-armed legionaries of the Republic and Early Empire, when they provided the prime offensive force through volleys of short, heavy spears (*pila*) and a ferocious charge, while the cavalry operated on the wings and rarely made a decisive contribution. The distinction between tradition and contemporary reality is picked up in an anonymous work of Justinian's reign, a dialogue in which one of the speakers, Thomas, asks 'Why, Menas, must we therefore accept as incontrovertible that the infantry is more important in war than the cavalry?' Menas argues that infantry, as the historic backbone of Rome's greatness, must take precedence, whereas Thomas insists that he wants to

---

92. Proc., *Wars* 1.18.31–4.
93. Proc., *Wars* 4.7.20–1. For rhetorical effect, Procopius ignores both the non-Roman cavalry and the *bucellarii* who accompanied the expedition.
94. Proc., *Wars* 4.3.19–24.
95. Treadgold, *Army* 50–3.

discuss 'what is now the dominant practice in war'.[96] The infantry of the later empire was primarily used for defensive purposes. This does not mean that it was of little importance, since it provided a stable platform from which the offensive cavalry could launch attacks and then regroup if necessary.[97] Deterring or frustrating cavalry attacks was a vital role in pitched battle and infantry had to be well-trained to succeed. In the defeat at Callinicum, Procopius describes how a relatively small unit of infantry formed themselves into what is clearly a *fulcum* – although he does not use the technical term – and resisted repeated Persian attacks while the rest of the Roman army crossed the Euphrates. At Busta Gallorum a shield wall of fifty infantry secured a crucial success for Narses.[98]

A number of late Roman soldiers were proficient in operating machines for firing projectiles. Procopius provides a description of one, which he calls a *ballistra*, that was used at the siege of Rome in 537.[99] This consisted of a bow whose arms were wound back by its handlers so that on release it projected a bolt, half the length but four times the thickness of a normal arrow, at least twice the length of a standard bowshot with impressive penetrative force. It is possible that this describes the torsion-powered *ballista* known from fourth-century texts, although it more probably refers to a tension-powered *arcuballista*.[100] Such machines were sufficiently mobile to be mounted on wagons and deployed on the battlefield, although there is no specific evidence for this happening in the sixth century.

For offensive sieges the troops had the capacity to construct stone-throwing 'onagers', wild asses, as well as battering rams with their protective mantlets. In describing the construction by some Sabir Huns of a special lightweight covered, ram for use on difficult terrain at Petra in 551, Procopius commented that both the Romans and Persians still had great numbers of engineers of their own.[101] In frontier cities and many interior ones as well, civilian inhabitants were organized into militias that could

---

96. *Dialogue on Political Science* 4.30–9. This fragmentary text adopts what can be termed a senatorial standpoint in critically commenting on aspects of Justinian's reign: see Bell, *Social Conflicts* 274–6.
97. This is similar to Alexander the Great's tactics of using the Macedonian phalanx as the solid anvil that pinned enemy forces and permitted the cavalry to deliver aggressive hammer blows.
98. Proc., *Wars* 1.18.45–8; 8.29.11–28.
99. Proc., *Wars* 5.21.14–18.
100. Discussion in Marsden, *Artillery* ch. 7, esp. 246–8: torsion machines were powered by twisted sinews, tension ones by arms that were bent back.
101. Proc., *Wars* 8.11.27–32.

support the professional *limitanei* and *comitatenses* to protect their homes, though when deprived of this expert leadership, as at Topirus in 550, their best efforts might prove futile.[102]

Some, perhaps many, Roman soldiers came from areas or people with a strong native military tradition, but even for them training was vital in order to inculcate them into Roman ways and accustom them to Roman discipline.[103] Vegetius inevitably bemoaned failures in training as a key factor in the decline of Roman armies, but it is clear from Maurice's *Strategicon* that training regimes in theory continued into the late sixth century. Most of the *Strategicon* is concerned with cavalry, but the book on infantry refers to the importance of practice to improve skills with different missiles and to become expert in the various Roman routines.[104] With regard to cavalry the information in Maurice is, to an extent, influenced by experience of confronting the Avars and so represents developments subsequent to Justinian's reign, but the provision of large-scale exercises that were designed to provide a taste of real battle and demonstrate the importance of good co-ordination was a constant from earlier times. Archery drill was particularly important given the greater significance of mounted archers in the battle line, while organized hunts provided a realistic setting for honing a variety of skills.[105] Training had to be continuous and a new commander might well want to ensure that his troops were capable of fighting as he wanted.

Most armies of any size were combined forces, with a preponderance of infantry. Belisarius invaded Africa with an army of which about 40 per cent were cavalry, 6,000 recorded horsemen out of 16,000, but also with several hundred *bucellarii* in the commanders' retinues, who will probably have been mounted. In Maurice's *Strategicon* the possibility of an army having more cavalry than infantry is envisaged, but it is clear that the opposite was the norm with a proportion of two-thirds infantry being proposed, while a force is said 'not to be unbalanced' even if the cavalry only constituted a quarter.[106]

102. Proc., *Wars* 7.38.9–17.
103. See Rance, 'Battle' 371–5.
104. Maurice, *Strat.* 12.2–3, 14–17 with a summary at 12.24.
105. Maurice, *Strat.* 1.1; 3.5; 12D.
106. Maurice, *Strat.* 12.A.7.5–12.

Logistics

That armies fight on their stomachs is a truism and Roman forces were underpinned by a complex logistical system that ensured that, for most of the time, supplies reached their intended destinations as and when needed.[107] The situation was obviously much easier for the army in peacetime when units would be located near their established bases, with manoeuvres and other training activities during the campaign season probably occurring within their province, or at least nearby. In these circumstances the *limitanei* were probably expected to support themselves from their allocated estates, while supplies could be channelled to the units of *comitatenses* from the tax revenues of their own or adjacent provinces. A special case was the Danube frontier, where the provinces of Scythia and Moesia were incorporated by Justinian into the new administrative unit of the *quaestura exercitus*. One of this unit's key functions was probably to allow the devastated frontier regions to be supported by the resources of Cyprus, the Aegean islands, and Caria, which could easily be transported to border fortresses thanks to the Roman control of the sea and Danube river.[108]

The assembly of a major army was a different matter. The text known as the *Chronicle* of Pseudo-Joshua the Stylite – an early-sixth century account written by an inhabitant of Edessa, probably a monk – records the exceptional arrangements that were needed to support the enormous army assembled by Anastasius for the eastern campaigns of 503 and 504. The city's bakers, who were expected in the first instance to meet the troops' needs, could not cope, so that Appion and then Calliopius, both praetorian prefects, supplied wheat to the city's households with orders to produce *bucellatum*, the standard double-baked biscuit, at their own expense. In 503, 630,000 *modii* (bushels) of wheat were used at Edessa; in 504, 850,00 with further bread supplies being arranged from Alexandria in Egypt; and in 505 630,000 *modii* were used locally with much more being supplied by bakers throughout the region.[109]

Pseudo-Joshua also remarks on the care with which the Roman army besieging Amida was supplied, so that its camps were well-provided with

<hr>

107. Lee, 'Food Supply' 290.
108. Lee, 'Warfare' 408–9. Sarantis, 'Military Provisioning', argues that agriculture in the Balkans was not as seriously disrupted as often assumed; this is probably correct for areas south of the Stara Planina, but closer to the Danube the situation is likely to have been more precarious.
109. Ps.-Joshua, *Chronicle* 54, 70, 77.

food, drink, shoes, and clothing, in marked contrast to the starvation and cannibalism within the city.[110] It was easiest for armies to operate near an effective supply base, as Anastasius' generals responded when the emperor complained in 505 about their failure to attack Nisibis effectively: the nearest fortresses were far away and too small to receive the army, and they lacked the water and vegetables to support them. Their proposed solution was to construct an advanced operations base at Dara[111] which Anastasius duly undertook. Its remains include several large cisterns and a massive granary, and it is a reasonable inference that one of the main functions of the city's population was to provide supplies and other support for the soldiers. The combination of Dara and other strengthened bases at Theodosiopolis, Martyropolis, and Citharizon in Armenia enabled Justinian's armies to operate effectively along the frontier in upper Mesopotamia and Armenia.

Armies on the move away from reliable supply bases created greater challenges.[112] The expeditionary force to Africa in 533 had to carry its own supplies for the journey, which resulted in problems because the *bucellatum* had not been properly cooked,[113] and then relied on markets on Sicily that the Ostrogoths had permitted. On campaign in enemy territory an army might hope, at the right season, to live by ravaging the land, but this was rarely an option for the Romans. In Africa Belisarius was very careful to treat the inhabitants with respect, punishing those who seized produce by force, since he wanted the locals to see his army as liberators rather than conquerors; the result was what he desired, with the inhabitants arranging markets and providing for the soldiers' needs.[114] In Italy the attitude of the inhabitants to their Ostrogothic overlords was less hostile than that of the Africans to the Vandals, so that it was harder for Belisarius to break existing connections between producers and the regime until he was clearly winning. During the 537 siege of Rome Belisarius had to send Procopius to Campania to arrange for supplies to be shipped to Ostia; in the event grain and wine were conveyed by sea, while a large wagon train carried grain up the Via Appia.[115] On the other side, Witigis found it impossible to

110. Ps.-Joshua, *Chronicle* 77.
111. Ps.-Zachariah, *HE* 7.6.
112. Lee, 'Warfare' 410–12.
113. Proc., *Wars* 3.1311–20.
114. Proc., *Wars* 3.16.1–8; 17.6–7.
115. Proc., *Wars* 6.4.1, 19–20; 5.2–3.

supply his large army outside Rome in 537/8, while the Franks near Milan in 539 suffered severely since the empty land offered limited supplies.[116]

Roman command of the sea was a crucial advantage, which Totila countered when besieging Rome in 546 by basing ships on the islands that could monitor traffic from Sicily and bridging the Tiber below the city.[117] Eventually at the height of Totila's success, Belisarius was reduced to moving from one isolated coastal stronghold to another, since these were the only places where his troops could be supported.[118] Totila also began to exploit the naval resources that had fallen under his control, organizing attacks on Sicily and Corsica, and a ravaging expedition across the Adriatic that disrupted supplies to Narses.[119] Campaigning in the Balkans presented many of the challenges of an overseas expedition, at least when an army ventured away from the security of Constantinople's Long Walls or the Danube supply line. Under Anastasius we hear of an army of 10,000 being accompanied by 520 wagons,[120] which slowed its advance to the speed of its ox transport and so made it vulnerable.

Roman Participation

The prominence of non-Romans and quasi-private soldiers in Roman armies has raised questions about the commitment of Romans to military activity and the resulting identity and discipline of these troops, the extent to which Justinian's armies remained genuinely Roman, and whether the dilution of the Roman element had brought about problems with order and obedience. A gap between civilian and solider is seen as a major factor in the demise of the empire in the West and its decline in the East: the main defence against barbarian invaders was entrusted to mercenary barbarians, while continuing Roman involvement in military activity was primarily for local or regional benefit, since commitment to the unified empire had evaporated as the distant central government had annexed local administrative responsibilities.[121] Although the discussion above has touched on a number

---

116. Proc., *Wars* 6.6.1, 25.16–18.
117. Proc., *Wars* 7.13.5–7; .18.7–10.
118. Proc., *Wars* 7.35.1.
119. Proc., *Wars* 7.37–4–5; 8.22.17–32.
120. Marc.Com. *s.a.* 499.
121. See Liebeschuetz, *Barbarians* 17–21, for the essential argument; also Southern and Dixon, *Army*; Ferrill, *Fall*. For the counter argument, see Whitby, 'War and State'.

of these issues, it is worthwhile in conclusion to this chapter to confront the accusation that the Romans had become progressively 'demilitarized'.

As ever, there is some basis to these accusations. Military service was unpopular in parts of the empire, especially the West, in the late fourth and early fifth centuries. That does not mean that this still applied in the sixth century, even if one rejects the belief that the eastern empire had been able to abandon conscription. Justinian did draw on substantial non-Roman resources for his campaigns, but the overwhelming majority of his *limitanei* and probably the majority of the regional *comitatenses* will have been recruited internally. The plague of 542 has been seen as a decisive factor in pushing Justinian to rely on non-Roman troops to an inappropriate and destabilizing extent,[122] but after initial disruption to military activity, among Persians as well as Romans, the evidence for Roman recruitment over the next half century does not substantiate the argument.[123]

When troops mutinied or declined to fight, the standard reason was economic, either the absence of pay or arguments about land ownership.[124] Particular reasons can be given for these failures: the absence of pay for *limitanei* during a period of peace, problems in maintaining armies in areas that could not support troops locally, especially recently re-conquered areas, or the disruption to administrative normality caused by the plague. Ringleaders of mutinies were treated harshly, but the majority of ordinary soldiers were pardoned, the same mixture of responses that had been employed from the early days of the empire: trained soldiers had always been too valuable a resource to be squandered if they could be cowed into obedience.[125] Roman troops did not always perform well in battle, for example at Callinicum where the Isaurian contingent, which had been prominent among those grumbling about Belisarius' reluctance to fight, crumbled under pressure,[126] but the military successes of the Republic and early empire masked numerous reverses and examples of poor performance. In this respect the armies of the sixth century were not much different from those of preceding centuries.

There are instances of problems with non-Roman troops: en route to Africa Belisarius impaled two Huns who had murdered one of their comrades,

---

122. The key argument of Teall, 'Barbarians'.
123. See Whitby, 'Recruitment' 103–10.
124. Proc., *Wars* 2.7.37; 4.26.10–12; 4.18.2–9; Lee, 'Food Supply' 284–7; *Warfare* 101–4.
125. Whitby, 'Army' 311–12; *contra* the argument of Kaegi, *Unrest* 72.
126. Proc., *Wars* 1.18.38–40.

provoking a response that they had not enrolled to be subject to Roman laws, a view that resonated even with some Roman soldiers.[127] At Busta Gallorum Narses dismounted his allied cavalry to prevent them from fleeing so easily, and shortly afterwards sent home the Lombards whose lawless behaviour was unacceptable.[128] At Casilinum Narses had a leading Herul killed for murdering a servant, which angered the Heruls 'as barbarians' so that they initially decided not to fight.[129] These incidents demonstrate both the problems that could arise when integrating external units into the Roman army, but also the determination of Roman commanders to uphold discipline throughout their forces. There is no sign that the fighting capacity of Roman armies was impaired by these events, indeed at Casilinum the Heruls joined the Roman line just in time for the battle.[130]

In conclusion, it should be stressed that Justinian's armies remained effective Roman fighting forces. Expansion in the west inevitably stretched resources more thinly and problems arose, as they had often done throughout the empire, when it was necessary to sustain major campaigns on more than one frontier. Justinian did not campaign in person, but as emperor he took key decisions over appointments and resources, made strategic choices and even directed tactical responses.[131]

---

127. Proc., *Wars* 3.12.8–10.
128. Proc., *Wars* 8.31.5; 33.2–3.
129. Agathias, *Hist.* 2.7.2–4.
130. Rance, 'Battle' 374.
131. Proc., *Wars* 8.21.6, 26.12–17 (appointment of Narses and support for his expedition to Italy); 3.10 (invasion of Africa); 8.26.1–2 (Justinian orders the garrison at Thermopylae to sail to Croton in Sicily).

Chapter 5

Persian Wars

The Persian war under Anastasius, which had broken out after he had rejected demands from King Kavadh for financial contributions towards the defence of the Caucasus, had effectively ended in 506 when a fixed-term truce was agreed for seven years.[1] Things had started badly for the Romans, with the loss of Amida in January 503, and even the deployment of very substantial forces had not allowed them to recover the city or achieve anything more than raids into Persian territory.[2] The truce permitted the Romans to press ahead with the construction of their new forward base opposite Nisibis at Dara, which the unsuccessful generals had requested, and the strengthening of Theodosiopolis (Erzerum) in Armenia. Kavadh was distracted by fighting against the Huns, perhaps in the Caucasus, and, by the time he protested at what he saw as a breach of a fifth-century agreement against new fortifications in border areas, Dara was already equipped with walls that were sufficiently high to deter an assault. The end of the truce in late 513 did not lead to a resumption of hostilities.

Anastasius' final years witnessed a number of developments in Transcaucasia that would ultimately be significant in the resumption of fighting in the 520s and remain an important source of discord throughout Justinian's reign and beyond. Although under the early empire the Romans had controlled Colchis (Lazica) in the west and Iberia in the east and these links had been strengthened in the first half of the fourth century by

---

1. Proc., *Wars* 1.9.24. The full range of sources for events is translated, or at least listed, in Greatrex and Lieu, *Eastern Frontier* 78–134.

2. Greatrex, *Rome* 74–6, states that Procopius downplayed Roman successes under Anastasius in order to magnify Belisarius' victory at Dara, but the truth is that there was nothing to compare with this victory in pitched battle and the Romans could only recover Amida in 506 through the terms of the truce.

conversion to Christianity, Roman authority actually decreased.[3] In part this was the result of Sasanid ambitions to recover all the ancestral lands of their Achaemenid predecessors in the fifth and fourth centuries BC, in part because the impact of Julian's disastrous invasion of Persia in 363 and problems in the Balkans in the 370s led the Romans first to accept Persian control over most of Armenia in 378 and then to withdraw their troops from Iberia. The attachment of the Iberian court to the Sasanids turned Lazica into a frontier region, one that was connected historically and religiously to Rome but culturally to Armenia, Iberia, and hence to Persia. In the 470s the Sasanids achieved their ambition of asserting authority over the Laz court, which gave them access to the Black Sea as well as control of the western passes over the Caucasus through which Huns and other groups could threaten Roman territory.[4] The most famous route across the Caucasus was the central Darial pass that led into Iberia; popular belief credited Alexander the Great with the construction of a Great Iron Gate in the mountains to keep out invaders, who were equated with the Biblical hordes of Gog and Magog, but it was the Persians who developed an extensive system of fortifications in the fifth century to control access, especially through the Darial pass and near Derbend near the Caspian.[5]

Christianity, however, sustained a link with Rome for Armenians and Laz in particular, which became stronger when Persian kings attempted to enforce participation in Zoroastrian rites. Ties with Persia had also been undermined during internal conflicts in Persia after the death of Peroz and into the early years of Kavadh, when Persian society was rocked by the Mazdakite movement that challenged accepted social relations and property ownership. These distractions had allowed the Transcaucasian peoples considerable independence, which it was difficult for Kavadh to reverse.

At his accession, Justin will have sent the customary notification to Kavadh via a major embassy, and it is plausible to speculate that Kavadh responded in the customary return embassy by repeating the requests for money that Anastasius had been ignoring.[6] It has been suggested

---

3. For Transcaucasia in the third and fourth centuries, see Braund, *Georgia* ch.8, and for the fifth century pp. 269–75.
4. Cf. Proc., *Wars* 2.15.27–9 for the articulation of these benefits to Khusro when Laz envoys sought his support in 541, and see Braund, *Georgia* 273–4.
5. Lawrence & Wilkinson, 'Borderlands' 109–16. The Derbend Wall extended 45 km inland from the Caspian, far into the mountains, while to the south the Ghilghilchay Wall stretched at least 27 km. Both walls and the Darial fort are dated to the fifth century. For the difficulties of the Darial pass, see Bruce Mitford, *East* 617–20.
6. Greatrex, *Rome* 130–1.

that the symbolism of payments was more important than their financial contribution.[7] The ability to present the Romans as tributaries was undoubtedly very attractive, but Kavadh's finances were sufficiently tight, since he was having to make payments to the Hephthalites, that extra income from the west would have been welcome.[8] It is probably not a coincidence that al-Mundhir, leader of the Lakhmid Arabs who were attached to the Persians, chose to invade Roman territory and ravage Osrhoene, probably in 519, as a way of applying pressure on Justin. This will not be the last time that a proxy was used to harm opponents without risking a direct confrontation, and Kavadh employed the Lakhmids again to press his demands for annual payments from Justin.[9] This raid was probably the occasion on which two Roman commanders, the *dux* Timostratus and John, were taken captive.[10] Negotiations for their release were entrusted to the experienced diplomat, Abraham, who met al-Mundhir at Ramla, south-east of the Arab capital of Hira. Also at the meeting were envoys from Dhu Nuwas, the Jewish king of the Himyarites in the south of the Arabian peninsula. Dhu Nuwas had recently repulsed an attempt to remove him by an expedition sent across the Red Sea by Ella Asbeha, king of the Christian Ethiopians, and had then slaughtered significant numbers of Christians in the city of Najran. Dhu Nuwas tried to draw al-Mundhir and the Persians into his conflict, probably hoping that, because the origins of his conflict with Ethiopia lay in the killing of Roman traders, he might receive support on the principle of my enemy's enemy. At any rate, he did not succeed in this and the Martyrs of Najran, as they became known thanks to the efforts of Symeon of Beth Arsham to publicize their fate, galvanized Christian opposition to his rule in Himyar.

Increasing Tensions

In the early 520s there were various tensions between Rome and Persia, but also a reluctance to allow these to spill over into full-scale war. What

---

7. Colvin, 'Comparing' 207–9; more fully in Payne, 'Cosmology'; Payne argues that receipt of Roman payments confirmed the mythical-historical role of Eranshar (Iran) as ruler of the world, which is very plausible, but does not mean that the money was not also useful.
8. Even for Khusro, who strengthened the fiscal structures of his realm, access to additional amounts of gold facilitated the recruitment of Sabir mercenaries. Persia was very rich, but its budget maintained a fine, Micawberesque, balance.
9. Ps.-Zach., *HE* 8.5a.
10. Proc., *Wars* 1.17.43–5.

happened to change this is presented differently in our two main sources, Malalas and Procopius, whose accounts deal with distinct issues but are amenable to being conflated into a coherent composite account. Malalas focused on developments in Transcaucasia, whereas Procopius largely ignored these to narrate Justin's humiliating rejection of Kavadh's request that he should adopt his third son, Khusro, in order to smooth his succession to the Persian throne. It has been suggested that Procopius omitted events in Transcaucasia because he knew that they had been reported in Malalas and so would be available to his readers,[11] but it is most implausible that he would present such an incomplete account that relied on another, unnamed, source for full comprehension. Colvin has proposed that Procopius did not want to acknowledge that the Persians had a reasonable claim to Lazica and other Transcaucasian territories, since accepting that they had valid grievances would undermine his drive to portray them as repeated aggressors.[12] With regard to Malalas' silence on the adoption discussions, it is possible that these were carried on at a high level that bypassed the office of the *comes Orientis* in Antioch, so that Malalas did not have access to information.

A composite account runs as follows. In 521 or 522 the new king of the Laz, Ztath, refused to be crowned in the traditional way by Kavadh, since this would entail participation in Zoroastrian rites whereas Ztath had recently embraced Christianity. It would appear that for half a century the Laz ruling house had renounced Christianity as part of their rapprochement with Persia, although many of their subjects remained Christian. Ztath now travelled to Constantinople, where he was baptized, given a distinguished Roman wife, Valeriana,[13] crowned by Justin, and dispatched home with lavish gifts. There may also have been friction with Persia over control of the Laz local empire in the Caucasus, where the Laz exerted authority over the Suani, Scymni, and Abasgi who inhabited the Caucasus foothills, whereas the Sasanids preferred these peoples to be independent and hence amenable to Persian influence.[14]

Kavadh sent a diplomatic protest that Justin had interfered in Persian internal affairs, which Justin rejected on the basis that he had merely

11. Greatrex, *Rome* 142 n.8.
12. Colvin, 'Comparing' 205–9.
13. Cf. Proc., *Wars* 8.9.8 for another marriage between Laz royalty and a Roman aristocratic lady, and Braund, *Georgia* 286, for the importance of this tactic in cementing allegiances in the region.
14. Braund, *Georgia* 276–80.

welcomed Ztath into the true faith.[15] Kavadh then secured the support of Zilgibi, a Hunnic leader, for an expedition against the Romans, but Justin managed to thwart this by informing Kavadh about previous Roman dealings with Zilgibi, who had received gifts from Justin to collaborate against the Persians, and warning him that the Huns would betray the Persians; when Zilgibi acknowledged receiving Justin's gifts, Kavadh killed him and many of his army.[16] Justin's apparent honesty over their mutual Hunnic ally prompted Kavadh to resume peace discussions.

At this point it is legitimate to turn to Procopius,[17] since the adoption proposal needs to be located at some point between the defection of the Laz and that of the Iberian Gourgenes in 524/5. Kavadh, who was now in his 70s, wanted to secure the succession for his third son, Khusro, passing over the claims of the eldest, whose close connections with the Mazdakites posed a threat to the social order. His second son, who was blind in one eye, was disqualified from ruling even though he had a reputation as a good warrior. He therefore offered to set aside his legitimate grievances if Justin would adopt Khusro and thereby strengthen his claim. Apparently, the request was being favourably received until the *quaestor*, Proculus, objected on legalistic grounds that a formal adoption would give Khusro a claim to the Roman throne; adoption 'by arms', which had been used when Zeno adopted Theoderic and Justin Eutharic (Theoderic's son-in-law), was possible.

The patricians Hypatius and Rufinus, who had both previously negotiated with Kavadh, were sent to the frontier to discuss peace and oversee the ceremony, while Khusro had travelled north up the Tigris to be available when required.[18] Discussions, however, faltered over the attachment of Lazica and broke up when the Romans made clear that Khusro would only be adopted in the manner appropriate for barbarians, a slight that the Persian king could not tolerate. It is difficult to see how Proculus' objection, even if it had some legal validity, could have had any practical force; it is therefore hard not to see this as a device to thwart negotiations, unless adoption 'by arms' could have been presented to the

---

15. Malalas 17.9.
16. Malalas 17.10.
17. Proc., *Wars* 1.11.1–30.
18. Croke, Justinian' 53, alleges that Hypatius' actions were directed by malice for Justinian, but there is in fact no suggestion of this in Procopius and Croke's discussion is badly confused.

Persians as a standard and honourable route, something that was impossible after the Roman delegates reacted to the question of Lazica being raised.

Even now Kavadh was not in a position to renew war with Rome, since Gourgenes, the king of Iberia, had sought help from Justin in reaction to Kavadh's attempts to perform Zoroastrian rites in his country. Kavadh was probably responding to the defection of Lazica by trying to break the link with Rome that Christianity created for the Iberians. Justin promised to help and sent Probus, nephew of Anastasius, to recruit Hunnic mercenaries, but to no avail. Subsequent Hunnic forces sent from Constantinople were too weak to oppose the Persian invasion, so that the Romans focused on protecting the frontiers of Lazica, to which Gourgenes and some of his nobles had fled before they travelled to appeal directly to Justin. The chronology of these events is uncertain, but the initial approach was probably in about 525, with the failed efforts to assist Gourgenes extending through 526 and even into 527. Justin's reliance on Hunnic troops to support the Iberians reflects his reluctance to commit to an open confrontation with Kavadh that the use of Roman forces would have entailed, but the result was that he failed to keep his undertakings to Gourgenes.

Even in Lazica, where Justin attempted to strengthen the frontier with Iberia by placing Roman troops in the fortresses of Sarapanis and Skanda, he was unsuccessful. According to Procopius the remote location made the forts difficult to support and the Roman soldiers were not prepared to subsist on the millet that grew locally; as a result, when the Laz ceased their efforts to keep the troops supplied, the Romans departed and the Persians took over possession.[19] This may not be the whole story, since it is quite possible that the removal of native garrisons from two key frontier fortresses was not welcomed by the Laz and may reflect Roman suspicions about Laz loyalties. Granted that Sarapanis could be reached by a navigable river, the explanation that both forts were difficult to supply is unconvincing. In this region the top Roman priority was to deny the Persians access to the Black Sea, which could be achieved as long as Lazica remained within the Roman orbit; beyond Lazica, the attachment of other peoples, such as the Iberians, was useful in denying their resources to the Persians, but control of their territory was less important. Hence the Romans were prepared to relinquish the inland forts that offered access to Iberia but

---

19. Proc., *Wars* 1.12.15–19; 8.13.15–19.

consolidated their authority on the coast by upgrading the fort of Petra (near modern Tsikhisdziri) into the city of Petra Pia Iustiniana.

Early Hostilities

In 526 the Romans were active elsewhere on their north-eastern frontier as open war became more likely. Two of Justinian's young guardsmen, Belisarius and Sittas, conducted a successful raid into Persarmenia, but a second raid was defeated by the Persarmenian brothers Narses and Aratius.[20] Even this may not have prevented further discussions about peace in the winter of 526/7, since Pseudo-Zachariah records that negotiations broke down again over Kavadh's demand for 500 pounds of gold a year to pay for the defence of the Caucasus.[21] The massive earthquake which destroyed Antioch in May 526 and claimed 250,000 lives, was probably distracting the Romans and encouraging them to defer open conflict.

In 527 Libelarius led an army on Nisibis, the city surrendered by the Romans in 363 as part of the agreement that allowed Julian's army to escape from Persian territory;[22] its recovery remained an objective for Roman emperors throughout the sixth century. Libelarius withdrew without achieving anything, presumably because the Persians did not venture outside their city walls while his army was not equipped for a major siege, but part of this initiative was probably an attack on the Persian fort of Thebetha, located about 50km to the south-south-east of Nisibis, by the *dux Mesopotamiae*, Timostratus.[23] The capture of Thebetha would have allowed the Romans to increase pressure on Nisibis, but in spite of breaching the walls Timostratus was unable to capture it and his troops then suffered badly from thirst while withdrawing across the desert towards Dara; Timostratus himself died, perhaps after the return of the expedition.

---

20. Proc., *Wars* 1.12.20–3.
21. Ps.-Zach., *HE* 8.5.a,
22. There is some confusion over the posts held by these commanders. Libelarius is usually referred to as *MM per Orientem*, but Procopius states that Belisarius succeeded him in charge of the troops stationed at Dara, i.e. as *dux Mesopotamiae* (*Wars* 1.12.24). On the other hand, Pseudo-Zachariah (9.1b-2a) refers to Timostratus as both *stratelates*, which usually represents *MM*, and *dux* on the frontier, i.e. *dux Mesopotamiae*, as which he was succeeded by Belisarius after his death. In 525 Libelarius had been a *dux* at Edessa, presumably therefore of Osrhoene, and it is possible that he continued in this position, briefly inheriting Timostratus' command of Mesopotamia in addition to his other ducate.
23. For this section of the Persian frontier, see Lawrence and Wilkinson, 'Borderlands' 106–9.

Justin's next move was to order the silentiary Thomas, who came from Apadna and so had local knowledge and presumably connections, to oversee the construction of a fort at Thannuris, located on the east bank of the Euphrates and believed to be suitable for deterring Arab raids. Thannuris was placed to observe, and even thwart, any attacks that might come up the Euphrates, the main route for invasions from the south, and then continue along the Khabur towards Upper Mesopotamia rather than striking west towards Syria. Substantial materials were gathered at the site, but the initiative was thwarted by Arabs and Kadisini from Singara and Thebetha.[24]

After the failure at Thannuris, another attempt was made to construct a new fortress further north at Melabasa,[25] the name for the mountainous region south of the Tigris in the northwest part of the Tur Abdin. Its purpose would have been to increase Roman pressure on Arzanene, the area of Persian territory north of the river and west of the Batman. This too was thwarted when Kavadh sent an army under Gadar the Kadisine, who defeated the Romans. Pseudo-Zachariah gives the date as the fifth indiction, i.e. August 527 at the latest. Although Belisarius was already in post as *dux*, it is unclear whether he was involved in this reverse, although the Melabasa hills were located within his area of authority. Also in 527, it is probable that Sittas coerced the Tzani,[26] highlanders in north-eastern Anatolia whose territory bordered Lazica, into submission to the Romans. Their fierce independence and remoteness had enabled them to defeat various attempts, which may have been going on for several years, but Sittas overcame them and then won them over by diplomacy, with their allegiance being confirmed by conversion to Christianity. This success would have facilitated Roman operations in Lazica, although that area currently remained quiet, and secured a useful source of good troops.

On ascending the throne in August 527, Justinian continued the policy of strengthening Roman frontier arrangements. In the south the new *comes Orientis*, the Armenian Patricius, was given funds to rebuild Palmyra,

---

24. The Kadisini inhabited the Jebel Sinjar to the north of Singara.

25. Ps.-Zach., *HE* 9.5.a

26. The date is uncertain since Procopius states that they were suppressed before the current war (*Wars* 1.15.24), but also while Justinian was emperor (*Buildings* 3.6.6). These indications can be reconciled by supposing that Sittas completed his task in late 527. Greatrex, *Rome* 130 n.28, without explanation, ignores the statement in *Buildings* that Justinian was emperor when Sittas defeated them. Although important operations were currently underway in Upper Mesopotamia, it remained possible for the Romans to field a substantial army in the Armenian sector of the frontier.

including its churches and baths; a *numerus* of troops, i.e. *comitatenses*, was to be stationed there, while the *dux* of Phoenicia based at Emesa was to advance his command there,[27] bringing with him his *limitanei*. All this was intended to increase Rome's ability to respond to the raids of al-Mundhir and his Arabs in an area where the transhumant tribal life militated against hard frontiers.[28] There was further trouble in this sector in early 528. Harith, leader of the Kindite Arabs who were allied to Rome, quarrelled with the *dux* of Palaestina Prima, Diomedes, and withdrew eastwards into what is termed the 'inner *limes*'; there he was attacked and killed by al-Mundhir. Justinian ordered the frontier *duces* and Arab allies under the Jafnid phylarch Harith to retaliate, which they did successfully, taking numerous captives, burning four Persian fortresses, and forcing al-Mundhir to flee east, temporarily.[29]

To the north of the Tigris, Justinian strengthened the defences of Martyropolis (Silvan), now renamed Justinianopolis, which had been too weak to resist the Persians in 502, and transferred there a *numerus* of *comitatenses* from the eastern army.[30] This was part of the northern sector of the frontier, the key element of whose reorganization was the creation of a new *magister militum per Armeniam et Pontum Polemoniacum et gentes* based at Theodosiopolis. Sittas was appointed to this role and allocated troops from the two praesental armies as well as the army of Oriens, the latter presumably being the units of the eastern army already stationed in Armenia. Eventually the new *MM* had authority over six *duces* based at Tzanzakon, Horonon, Artaleson, Citharizon, Melitene, and Martyropolis. The first two supervised the territory of the Tzani, whereas the next pair controlled routes through the highlands of Armenia, Melitene was near a major crossing-point on the Euphrates while Martyropolis faced the fertile Persian territory of Arzanene, where the king owned property and could watch the route south over the Taurus through the Bitlis pass. Citharizon and Horonon were new bases whose creation was a further major improvement to frontier arrangements.[31] At the same time the civil provinces of Armenia were reorganized, with the frontier areas, which had previously been

---

27. Malalas 18.2.
28. Liebeschuetz, 'Arab Tribesmen'.
29. Malalas 18.16.
30. Malalas 18.16; for some evidence for Justinian's work, which is described at Proc., *Buildings* 3.2, see Whitby, 'Martyropolis'.
31. See Howard-Johnston, 'Citharizon'.

under local satraps, being grouped into the new province of Armenia IV.[32] These changes were undoubtedly facilitated by the recent pacification of the Tzani but also reflected Justinian's interest in Transcaucasia, the location of the *gentes* in the *MM*'s full title.

Justinian secured two further successes in the north where he won over Boa, a widow who led a band of Sabir Huns after her husband's death; she prevented two other Sabir leaders from taking their warriors to help the Persians, handing over one of them to Justinian to be executed at Constantinople.[33] North of the Black Sea near Bosporus a Hun king by the name of Grod converted to Christianity, travelling to Constantinople for baptism with Justinian as sponsor. Although his followers rejected the change and killed Grod, the overall result was an increase in security at the Roman outpost of Bosporus.[34]

Procopius says nothing about these activities in the *Wars*, not least because Belisarius played no part in them,[35] but his next item of information fits the context of strenuous efforts to build new forts near the frontier. Justinian instructed Belisarius to construct a fortress at Minduos, 'on the left as one goes towards Nisibis', namely somewhere on the southern flank of the Tur Abdin that rises on the left of the route from Nisibis to Dara. In Upper Mesopoatmia the Tur Abdin plateau had considerable strategic importance since it separated the Tigris basin, where Amida and Martyropolis confronted the Persians beyond the Batman, from the plains of Beth Arabaye across which a major route ran east from Edessa and Constantina, passing a bit to the south of Dara, towards Nisibis and the Tigris. The Romans controlled the easiest routes across the plateau, whereas Persian links with Arzanene ran from the northeast and they had no direct access from Arzanene to Beth Arabaye.

The Persians ordered work to stop, probably invoking the fifth-century agreement that banned frontier constructions, and when Belisarius' forces were unable to drive them away, Justinian ordered two *duces* from Lebanon, the young and reckless Thracians Buzes and Cutzes, to move north to support him. A battle ensued near the building works, in which the

32. Jones, *LRE* 280–2.
33. Malalas 18.13.
34. Malalas 18.14.
35. Less surprisingly, he does not mention the order at the start of Justinian's reign, perhaps received by Belisarius as local *dux*, that the exiled Miaphysite monks should be allowed to return (John of Ephesus, *PO* 18 p.619).

Persians triumphed, taking Cutzes and numerous others captive, with the result that they were able to raze what had been constructed.[36] The same events involving Belisarius, Cutzes and Buzes, as well as other commanders including Basil and the Arab Atafar, although without mention of fortress building, are located by Pseudo-Zachariah in the desert of Thannuris, namely to the south of Nisibis.[37] Malalas too records this Roman defeat when Cutzes, the former *dux* of Damascus, Sebastian with a contingent of Isaurians, Proclianus the *dux* of Phoenicia, the *comes* Basil, Belisarius, and the Arab Atafar confronted a substantial Persian army, said to number 30,000, under the command of Kavadh's son, Xerxes;[38] Malalas noted both the death of Atafar, as does Pseudo-Zachariah, and the capture of Cutzes.

It is clear that all three sources are describing aspects of the same sequence of events. Procopius has certainly failed to provide any details on the defeat, which Pseudo-Zachariah ascribed to the failure of the Roman commanders to observe that the Persians had dug several concealed trenches in and around their encampment. The result was that the Romans impetuously rushed into the trap. While Belisarius managed to escape to Dara with his cavalry, the infantry suffered heavily and were killed or captured. A reconciliation is possible along the following lines: obeying imperial instructions, Belisarius was engaged in protecting construction activity on the southern flank of the Tur Abdin, but in response to the news of the approach of a large Persian army he was instructed to march south to join a number of frontier *duces* from Syria and Lebanon. The combined army, which did not have a clear overall commander since the senior individuals were the frontier *duces*, came upon the Persian army, but suffered a serious reverse. It was not, however, a complete disaster, since Malalas records that some Persian generals were killed and the Persians returned home after the battle rather than stay to follow up their victory. Belisarius' move south would have allowed the Persians in Nisibis to dismantle the construction works at Minduos. This does not solve all problems, since Procopius specifies that the battle occurred at the construction site of Minduos, but it does make sense of the involvement of commanders from further south on the frontier.[39]

---

36. Proc., *Wars* 1.13.2–8.
37. Ps.-Zach., *HE* 9.2.b.
38. Malalas 18.26; the Persian prince was presumably Zames, since his elder brother, wrongly called Peroz, is said to have been fighting in Lazica.
39. For a somewhat different solution, see Greatrex, *Rome* 156–9, who rightly concludes that the 'site of Minduos eludes final resolution'.

It is unclear when relations with Persia moved from a phoney confrontation pursued via intermediaries and through construction works, to open hostilities, but 529 is plausible: the Roman effort to fortify Minduos was viewed by Kavadh as a serious threat, on a par with Dara, and in this year he must have embarked on mobilizing the large forces that operated in 530 from Nisibis as well as in Armenia. Justinian responded to the reverse at Minduos by ordering several senators to leave Constantinople with their forces, presumably their private retinues of *bucellarii*, to defend a number of eastern cities, including Amida, Edessa, and Beroea, while the patrician Pompeius was sent out with a large force of Illyrians, Scythians, Isaurians, and Thracians.[40] The latter army appears to have contingents drawn from the two regional armies in the Balkans, supplemented by Hunnic mercenaries and Isaurian recruits from Anatolia.

Notwithstanding these preparations, Justinian also restarted peace talks, in part because the winter was exceptionally severe but also perhaps because a new earthquake caused further damage at Antioch and Laodicea (Latakia) as well as across southwestern Anatolia. In March 529 al-Mundhir raided Syria as far as the territory of Antioch, before retiring with his booty at the approach of Roman commanders; in response Justinian transferred a substantial force of infantry, the Lycocranitae, from Phrygia and replaced Hypatius with Belisarius as *MM per Orientem*.[41] He also elevated Harith, leader of the Jafnid Arabs allied to Rome, to what Procopius terms 'king' in order to have authority over most of the other Arab phylarchs and organize effective opposition to al-Mundhir.[42] Arab groups settled in Roman frontier provinces followed their own phylarch, but there was no scope for overall coordination until this appointment for Harith.[43] A major Samaritan revolt broke out, with the rebel leader Julian even presiding at chariot races in Neapolis, but the *dux Palestinae* with an unnamed Arab phylarch suppressed the uprising with considerable bloodshed; the

---

40. Malalas 18.26.
41. Malalas 18.32, 34.
42. Proc., *Wars* 1.17.46–8.
43. See Liebeschuetz, 'Arab Tribesmen' esp. 79–80. Shahîd's massive *Byzantium and the Arabs in the Sixth Century*, of which volume 1 alone runs to over 1000 pages (in two parts), is much less helpful than its title would suggest, since in the main it reprises the author's discussions over the previous 40 years, defending his interpretations against academic challenges or adapting them in the light of new evidence. A constant concern for Shahîd is to demonstrate the importance and integrity of Rome's Arab allies in the face of what he regards as malicious misinterpretation by the likes of Procopius. For his discussion of Harith's elevation, see pp. 95–109.

phylarch is said to have sold 20,000 young captives into slavery in the east.[44] In July Justinian's envoy to Persia, the *magister officiorum* Hermogenes, was sent back with a letter addressed in a calculated insult from 'Kavadh, king of kings, of the rising sun' to 'Flavius Justinian Caesar of the waning moon' that demanded the resumption of payments as stipulated by ancient records of the agreement to provide mutual assistance.[45] Kavadh urged Justinian as a pious Christian to avoid bloodshed and gave him one year to produce the money.[46] This was not a request that Justinian was going to accept right now, but he did send Hermogenes and the patrician Rufinus to continue negotiations; Rufinus waited at Hierapolis, while Hermogenes continued to join Belisarius at Dara and arrange the army there.

530 Campaign

Procopius says nothing about the events of 529 and instead moves directly from the capture of Cutzes to the battle at Dara in 530. Both sides knew that it was unlikely that negotiations would succeed and so had assembled troops, 25,000 at Dara on the Roman side and 40,000 on the Persian side at Nisibis under the command of Peroz of the house of Mihran (Procopius uses the family name).[47] Procopius describes the Persian advance from Nisibis as 'sudden',[48] which might seem surprising since everyone was expecting a confrontation, but this might refer to the fact that Kavadh's letter of 529, written in July, had promised the Romans one year to provide the necessary money, whereas the battle at Dara was fought in June.[49] As they approached from the south, they would have seen the walls and buildings of Dara straddling the low foothills of the Tur Abdin scarp.[50] Belisarius and Hermogenes prepared to receive the Persian attack by protecting their position to the south of the city walls with a line of ditches,[51] set back in the

---

44. Malalas 18.35.

45. Whitby, 'Diplomacy' 126; Maksymiuk, 'Two Eyes' 601.

46. Malalas 18.44.

47. The 70,000 claimed by Malalas (18.50) might include the army that Kavadh sent to Armenia.

48. Proc., *Wars* 1.13.12.

49. Theophanes 181.1.

50. See Plate 11 for the view from the church at Ambar, about 3km south of Dara.

51. Discussions in Greatrex, *Rome* 169–85; Haldon, *Wars* 28–35; Syvänne, *Age* 463–4. Most reconstructions infer that the central section of the ditches was withdrawn, thereby inviting the Persians to advance into a killing ground, but the sketches at Greatrex, *Rome* 172, 179 and 182–4, show them projecting.

centre and with passages so that Roman forces could advance and retreat but through which it would be difficult for the Persians to follow. Although the ditches meant that much of the Roman army would be static – and hence at risk from Persian archery – it appears that Belisarius had insufficient confidence in the quality of the majority of his troops to risk them in an open clash with the larger Persian army. Their position might also have been protected to an extent by the artillery mounted on the large southern towers in Dara's defensive circuit, whose range would have been three or four times that of the Persian bowmen.[52] Granted the inferiority of the Roman army in numbers and probably overall quality, it might seem surprising that Belisarius and Hermogenes chose to fight outside the city walls. In part this might be because their army of 25,000 was too large to be accommodated within the city, although in that case some of the troops might have been stationed in the river valley to the north of the city. It is therefore possible that Justinian's major improvements to the defences were still in progress, so that the city was not yet ready to withstand a major siege.[53]

The Persians were arrayed in a traditional tripartite formation, their right wing commanded by Pityax, the centre under Peroz, and the left under Vareshman;[54] behind this front formation of cavalry was drawn up the Persian infantry, which was not expected to contribute to the victory. On the

---

52. I accept the traditional location of the battle, a short distance south of the city directly on the Persian line of advance from their base at Ammodios, for whose relationship to Dara, see Greatrex, *Rome* 170–1 n.9. I see no merit in the speculation of Lillington-Martin, 'Struggle' 602–11, that the battle should be located further from the city, 2.5 km to the south just to the east of the church at Ambar, on the basis that *pylae*, the standard Greek word for 'gates', can be applied in the plural to a ravine or other narrow passage through mountains where a road could be blocked. There is no such striking geographical feature near Ambar and Lillington-Martin applies the term to a gap over 2km in extent. Also, it was in the Romans' interest to be as close to Dara's walls as possible, Procopius' expression 'the gate (n.b. singular as opposed to the plural used for mountain defiles) opposite Nisibis' refers to the city's south gate that exited onto the road south via Ambar to Ammodios where it joined the main west-east road leading to Nisibis. The Herul cavalry on the Roman left would have been concealed by the hill at the southeast corner of Dara's walls. For the view of the south Watergate, near whch the gate to Nisibis will have been located (probably just east of the extant stretch of the Watergate), see Plate 12; the gate towers will have resembled the towering Porta Appia at Rome (Plate 16), with the first-phase Anastasian horseshoe construction reinforced by Justinian with rectangular cladding and raised with an additional storey.

53. Whitby, 'Dara' 758–9; Lillington-Martin, 'Struggle' 604, doubts that the fortifications would still have been incomplete 25 years after the city's foundation, but overlooks the fact that fortification work had been halted under Anastasius, probably when a truce was agreed in 506, and Justinian had only recently embarked on a major strengthening of the defences. The best-preserved stretch of the walls is that facing north, at the north-east corner of the city (see Plate 13).

54. Pityax is a title, quite possible Vareshman as well: see Greatrex, *Rome* 176 n.22.

Roman side, Procopius records that Buzes commanded the cavalry formation that constituted the left wing, along with 300 Heruls under Pharas, while the cavalry right wing was led by John, Cyril, Marcellus, Germanus, and Dorotheus. At the central end of each wing, but outside the protective ditches, two groups of 600 Huns were placed to support the Roman cavalry if it was forced to retreat, those on the left under Sunicas and Aigan while those to the right were led by Simmas and Ascan.[55] The centre, where the Roman infantry must have been stationed along with further cavalry, was commanded by Belisarius and Hermogenes. Peroz was confident of success and sent a message to Belisarius with instructions to prepare him a bath for the following day.

On the first day the two armies confronted each other without engaging until the late afternoon[56] when some horsemen on the Persian right charged; the Roman cavalry initially withdrew in the face of this attack, but when the Persians halted, perhaps uncertain about how best to approach the Roman positions, Buzes' men turned to charge and drove the Persians back to their lines.[57] The other events of the afternoon were single combats in which Andreas, the bath attendant of Buzes who happened to be a skilled wrestler, killed two Persians, on the second occasion fighting in defiance of an explicit command from Hermogenes. Overnight the opposing commanders exchanged messages, Belisarius urging the Persians to withdraw to allow peace talks to progress while Peroz pointed to Roman bad faith as the obstacle to agreement; both expressed confidence that they had divine support, and Peroz repeated his request that a bath and meal be prepared for him. The Persians were also joined by a further 10,000 troops who had been summoned from Nisibis; it is possible that Peroz had been awaiting their arrival during the first day and so delayed a full assault.

On the second day respective dispositions were broadly the same, although Peroz held half his forces in reserve so that they could be rotated into the battle to ensure their fighters were always fresh, while he also retained the unit of Immortals to engage only on his specific

---

55. Procopius has, typically, given detailed information only about the units that would play a decisive part in the battle.

56. For the Persian practice of delaying an engagement when the enemy were strongly positioned, but also to allow the day's heat to sap opponents' strength, see Maurice, *Strat.* 11.1.32–40.

57. Greatrex, *Rome* 177, sees this as the Romans deploying the standard steppe tactic of faking a retreat only to turn suddenly on pursuers when the latter were disorganized, an approach that Maurice in fact advised should not be used against the disciplined Persians (*Strat.* 11.1.46–8); Procopius' account suggests a more measured response to the Persians, who had halted rather than fallen into confusion.

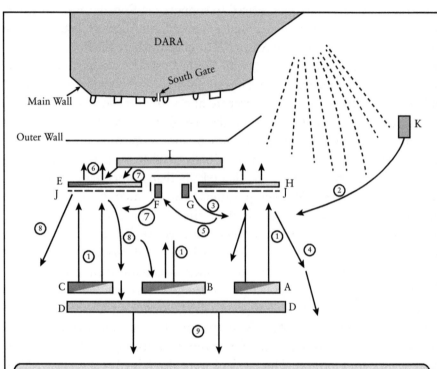

Dara 530, second day

Dispositions

A = Persian right under Pityax
B = Persian centre under Peroz
C = Persian left under Vareshman
D = Persian infantry
E = Roman right under John, Cyril, Marcellus, Germanus, and Dorotheus
F = Hunnic cavalru under Simmas and Ascan
G = Hunnic cavalry under Sunicas and Aigan
H = Roman left under Buzes
I = Roman second line under Belisarius and Hermogenes
J = Staggered Roman ditch with multiple crossings
K = Herul cavalry under Pharas concealed by hill

Phases

1 = General Persian advance after archery exchanges; Roman left buckles
2 = Pharas launches surprise attack on Persian flank and rear
3 = Sunicas and Aigan attack Persian rear
4 = Persian right turns to flight
5 = Sunicas and Aigan ordered to reinforce Simmas and Ascan
6 = Roman right buckles as Immortals reinforce Persian assault
7 = Hunnic cavalry attack Persians from flank and rear, Belisarius moves to stabilize right
8 = Persians left turns to flight
9 = Persian infantry flees under Roman assault

instruction. On the Roman side Pharas proposed that his Heruls should be concealed behind a hill at the extreme left of the Roman line to attack the Persians in the rear.[58] The morning passed without fighting, the Persians wanting to exploit the fact that they ate later than the Romans, who were accustomed to eat before noon and so would be becoming hungry. The battle commenced with an exchange of missiles in which Persian numbers and their ability to rotate their fighters contributed to a heavier fire, although they were shooting into a head wind that reduced the force of their arrows. Once supplies of missiles were exhausted, the armies engaged at close quarters with spears. On the Persian right the Kadisini turned the Romans to flight but were then caught in the rear by Pharas' Heruls and threatened in the flank by the Huns under Sunicas and Aigan, with the result that they fled, suffering 3,000 casualties.

Meanwhile Peroz had been strengthening the Persian left, where he committed the Immortals, and their charge turned the Roman right to flight. In response Belisarius ordered the Huns under Sunicas and Aigan to join those with Simmas and Ascan, whom he reinforced further with some of his own men. Their charge cut the attacking Persians in two and, after fierce fighting when the Roman thrust was in danger of being surrounded by the Persians, Sunicas first killed the standard bearer of Vareshman and then the general himself. The result was a confused flight in which 5,000 Persians are said to have perished. This allowed the Romans to attack the Persian infantry, who also fled with heavy casualties, although Belisarius and Hermogenes restrained their troops from pursuing too far, for fear that the Persians would turn to confront the now disorderly Roman troops and so diminish the victory that had already been won.

This account of the action is based on the detailed narrative in Procopius; Malalas is brief, no more than a dozen lines of text, although he does single out for mention Sunicas, whom he credits with killing a Persian commander called Saros in a duel, and confirms heavy Persian losses.[59] Pseudo-Zachariah has a bit more information: he credits the Hun Sunicas and Simmas, who is termed a Roman chiliarch, supported by forty men, with repulsing the Persians through repeated attacks across the battlefield, while to the east of the city the Heruls with Buzes repulsed

---

58. This will have been the hill on which the north-east angle of the city walls was located, visible at the east edge (right) of Plate 12.
59. Proc., *Wars* 1.13–14; Malalas 18.50.

the Persian infantry. He confirms heavy casualties, which the Persians attempted to conceal by ordering pack animals to come from Nisibis to collect booty but then loading them with corpses.[60] In spite of the victory, it appears that the Persians were able to ravage Beth Arabaye.

Kavadh had also made preparations to invade Armenia, placing under Mihr-Mihroe an army of 30,000 Persarmenians and neighbouring Sunitae that also included a contingent of 3,000 Sabir Huns.[61] On the Roman side Sittas, who had recently been switched from *MM per Armeniam* to one of the praesental roles (as well as being married to Justinian's sister-in-law Comito), had overall authority over Dorotheus, who had succeeded him as commander in Armenia. They managed to disrupt Persian preparations in a surprise attack on the Persian camp, but then could not prevent the much larger Persian force from advancing as far as Satala. Sittas had only 15,000 men with him and so could not confront the Persians in pitched battle. Instead he took 1,000 cavalry to hide in the hills around the city while Dorotheus remained within the walls. When Mihr-Mihroe's troops were already investing the walls, Sittas sprung his trap and charged down in an attack, whose size the Persians could not gauge because of the dust clouds they raised in the dry summer. The Persians formed up in close order and Sittas split his cavalry into two units to maximize their impact, while at the same time the Roman troops within the walls charged out. Fighting was fierce because of the weight of Persian numbers but they eventually retreated to their camp after Florentius, a Roman cavalry commander, led a suicide charge that captured the Persian commander's standard and so disrupted their formation.

The Persians suffered significant losses and withdrew from Roman territory; on his return to court Mihr-Mihroe was humiliated by being deprived of his ornamental headpiece. As a result of this victory an important Persarmenian family defected: first the brothers Narses and Aratius came over with their mother, and the generosity of the welcome they received from Justinian's *cubicularius*, the eunuch Narses who was also Persarmenian, persuaded their younger brother Isaac to join them. Isaac arranged for the Romans to capture the fortress of Bolum opposite Theodosiopolis. Another success was when the Persarmenian Symeon, who supervised a gold mine at Pharangion for Kavadh, decided to stop sending the bullion to the Persians. Although Symeon declined to give the gold to the Romans, the loss to the

---

60. Ps.-Zach., *HE* 9.3.a.
61. On this general, see Maksymiuk, 'New Proposal'.

Persians was still a considerable benefit and they did manage to thwart Persian attempts to recover the resource.

During 530/31 Julian conducted a mission to the Himyarites in south Arabia and the Ethiopians, with the aims of building up Rome's links with Arab tribes to persuade them to act against the Persians, even if only through the latter's Lakhmid allies. He encouraged the Ethiopians to support Roman interests by opening up a trade route to India that would allow the Romans to secure supplies of silk without having to acquire it through Persian middlemen, who gave the profits to the empire's enemies.[62] In Himyar the persecuting Dhu Nuwas had been overthrown in 525 after the Ethiopian king, Ella Asbeha, had ferried an army across the Red Sea in ships, most of which were supplied by Rome, to support a rival, Sumyafa Ashwa (Esimiphaeus). As a result, both peoples were now ruled by Christians and Justinian exploited their shared religion in pursuit of his aims. Neither initiative was successful, since Persian traders always arrived at the relevant Indian harbours before the Ethiopians could and purchased all available silk, while the extent of the desert barrier dissuaded the Himyarites from campaigning north towards Mesopotamia.

531 Campaign

In the latter part of 530 the Romans pursued negotiations through Rufinus and Hermogenes; Kavadh was still aggrieved by the Roman refusal to contribute to the costs of defending the Caucasus and by their fortifications in Upper Mesopotamia, where the continuing affront of Dara was underscored by the failed attempt at Minduos. That said, it did appear that peace might be obtained in return for a payment, so that Rufinus was again dispatched to the east in 531. By then, however, Kavadh's confidence had been restored by reports of the Roman problems with the Samaritans, whose envoys suggested that they could provide 50,000 men in support and hand over their own lands, Palestine and Jerusalem.[63] It is usually assumed that this Samaritan offer was at least a year after the suppression of their revolt, but the exact chronology of its conclusion is unknown and it is possible that the region was still in turmoil. Kavadh was also spurred on by advice

---

62. Proc., *Wars* 1.20.9–12; Malalas 18.57.
63. Malalas 18.54.

The 531 Campaign

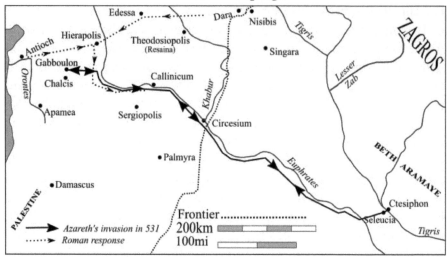

from al-Mundhir that any invasion should be directed up the Euphrates towards the cities of Syria, abandoning the river north of Circesium to strike across the desert towards Sergiopolis (Resafa), a route that al-Mundhir's Arabs had exploited successfully and that bypassed the improved Roman defences in Upper Mesopotamia. As a result, Kavadh gave an army to the Persian Azareth,[64] and sent him up the Euphrates with al-Mundhir.

According to Procopius the Persians invaded Commagene, namely the province of Euphratesia based on Hierapolis. Belisarius heard about the attack when the Persians reached Circesium and after initial doubt – perhaps uncertain as to whether this was a diversionary thrust – came to support the local troops with 8,000 men, of whom 5,000 were Arabs under Harith. Meantime the Persians had encamped at Gabboulon in Syria Secunda, about 15km from Chalcis where Belisarius was barring their advance further west. The *dux* Sunicas with 4,000 men caught the Persians and Lakhmids while dispersed for plundering,[65] and killed or captured some, but this success angered Belisarius who had ordered that there should be no engagement until the whole army had assembled. Hermogenes, who had

---

64. Probably again a title rather than a name.
65. Payne, 'Cosmology 20, asserts, largely on the basis of the *Kings' Book of Kings*, that Sasanid forces were supposed to spare the countryside while targeting Roman towns, but this ignores the substantial evidence that their armies, like most in the ancient world, supported themselves by ravaging their enemies' property.

now reached Hierapolis with 4,000 men under Ascan, Simmas, and Stephanus, managed to reconcile Belisarius and Sunicas. Persian ravaging extended as far north as Batna, but their increasingly perilous position persuaded them to retreat with their booty after capturing and sacking Gabboulon.

Belisarius shadowed their retreat with his army, which now numbered about 20,000, much to the annoyance of many of his men and officers who were keen to engage and were irked by Belisarius' caution. Matters came to a head on 18 April, Good Friday, when the Persians were camped on the south bank of the Euphrates opposite Callinicum; this was the last chance for the Romans to halt them, since further south they would be crossing much emptier country where it would be difficult to support an army. Belisarius, with the agreement of Hermogenes, attempted to persuade his men that it was best to allow the Persians to depart, especially since many Roman troops had been fasting for Easter and reinforcements were awaited.[66] The result was abuse directed at Belisarius, who now reversed his decision and exhorted his troops to prepare for battle the following day.

On his right wing at the southern edge of the battlefield, Belisarius stationed Harith's Arabs on rising ground, next to them a unit of 2,000 Isaurians – or as Procopius observes, more properly Lycaonians – Phrygians, and then the Huns of Ascan.[67] Belisarius occupied the centre with his troops, while to his left the Huns of Simmas balanced those of Ascan; the northern end of the line, adjacent to the Euphrates, was held by the Roman infantry under Peter. On the Persian side Azareth held the right wing while al-Mundhir commanded the left, opposite Harith. The details of the fighting are obscured by the recriminations that followed the Roman defeat, with Procopius certainly presenting Belisarius' actions in the best light whereas Malalas offers an alternative view that may contain its own distortions. Battle opened with the customary missile fire; Procopius implies that the Romans had the better of this since the penetrative power of their weightier bowshots more than compensated for the denser rapid Persian volleys, but Pseudo-Zachariah says that on a cold day the wind was against the Romans, a comment that suggests he believed they came off worse in the exchanges.[68]

---

66. Pseudo-Zach., *HE* 9.4.a, reports that the Persian commander actually asked Belisarius to respect the feast, which the latter was initially inclined to do.
67. For discussion of the battle, see Greatrex, *Rome* 200–7; Syvänne, *Age* 465–7.
68. Proc., *Wars* 1.18.31–4; Ps.-Zach., *HE* 9.4.a.

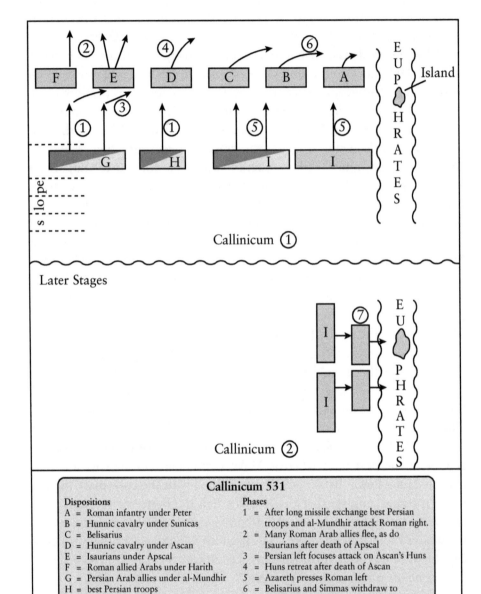

Callinicum ①

Later Stages

Callinicum ②

Callinicum 531

Dispositions

A = Roman infantry under Peter
B = Hunnic cavalry under Sunicas
C = Belisarius
D = Hunnic cavalry under Ascan
E = Isaurians under Apscal
F = Roman allied Arabs under Harith
G = Persian Arab allies under al-Mundhir
H = best Persian troops
I = Persian troops under Azareth

Phases

1 = After long missile exchange best Persian troops and al-Mundhir attack Roman right.
2 = Many Roman Arab allies flee, as do Isaurians after death of Apscal
3 = Persian left focuses attack on Ascan's Huns
4 = Huns retreat after death of Ascan
5 = Azareth presses Roman left
6 = Belisarius and Simmas withdraw to Euphrates
7 = Roman infantry and dismounted cavalry ward off attacks by victorious Persians until nightfall

By mid-afternoon the fight was still balanced, at which point the best Persian troops joined al-Mundhir on the left wing. According to Procopius, Harith's Arabs fled without even waiting for the Persian charge, which allowed the Persians to attack the Romans from the rear.[69] By contrast in Malalas, after fierce fighting, Apscal, commander of the Phrygians, was killed when he charged into the Persians and his horse stumbled after treading on a corpse. As a result the Phrygians fled, followed by many of the Roman Arabs, although Harith and others continued to fight. Malalas acknowledges that there were rumours of treachery by some of the phylarchs:[70] these may have resented the recent elevation of Harith as their overlord or been keen to preserve their own followers from annihilation. This flight exposed the Isaurians and Ascan's Huns; the former lacked experience and fled towards the Euphrates but the latter perished while fighting bravely. According to Malalas, Belisarius withdrew across the river when the Isaurians crumbled, leaving Sunicas and Simmas to cover the retreat with their dismounted horsemen, during which they inflicted some significant losses on the Persians. Procopius on the other hand, reports that Belisarius remained in place with some of his men as long as Ascan's Huns held station, but at their collapse he withdrew to join the infantry on the river bank, dismounting his men and holding off repeated Persian assaults with a shield wall until night fell. He then crossed to an island in mid stream, from where he was brought to Callinicum on the following day. In Procopius the Persians pillaged the corpses before continuing their withdrawal down the Euphrates, whereas in Malalas the pillaging was done on the next day by the Roman soldiers and inhabitants of Callinicum, who recrossed the river.

There is agreement about much of the battle: the collapse of the Roman right wing, with the flight or destruction of the Phrygians and Isaurians, suspicions of Arab treachery, and the effective rearguard action by an infantry shield-wall. On the other hand there is disagreement about the roles of Harith, whether he was among the first treacherous fugitives or fought bravely in spite of being deserted by many of the Arab forces, and of Belisarius, whether he saved his own skin by abandoning his men as soon as the battle turned against him or participated in, indeed organized, the vigorous Roman defensive action on foot. Events were

---

69. Proc., *Wars* 1.18.35–7.
70. Malalas 18.60.

reported by Hermogenes to Justinian, who ordered Sittas to move south from Armenia to offer support and appointed Constantiolus to investigate the defeat. This enquiry resulted in the recall and dismissal of Belisarius,[71] a disgrace that Procopius glides over by saying that he was removed from office in order to campaign against the Vandals.[72] This outcome has often been taken to indicate that Malalas has preserved the more accurate account of the battle, but Greatrex has raised reasonable doubts about this, since the verdict might reflect the unpopularity of Belisarius with his subordinate commanders or strained relations with the likes of Hermogenes.[73] If the Romans were disappointed by the outcome, the Persians were not greatly pleased either since the invasion had achieved little and their losses in the battle had been heavy.

In the wake of Callinicum, Justinian renewed attempts to negotiate peace through Rufinus, to no avail, but an interesting development was an approach to Justinian from the Lakhmid al-Mundhir, who requested that the deacon Sergius should be sent to him so that he could take back peace terms. It is unclear whether al-Mundhir was hedging his bets with regard to the Persians, attempting to squeeze some personal benefits from Justinian, or operating as an intermediary for Kavadh. Justinian also sent the former praetorian prefect, Demosthenes, to the east with money to ensure that cities were equipped with granaries, while the Persians stormed the fort of Abgersaton in Osrhoene after a hard fight in which they had suffered heavy casualties from Roman missiles.[74]

The final actions in the war focused on Martyropolis, the refortified Roman base opposite Persian Arzanene; they are narrated most fully by Pseudo-Zachariah and Malalas,[75] less completely and clearly by Procopius, who may well have had to accompany Belisarius back to Constantinople. The *dux* Bessas defeated and killed Gadar the Kadisine, who had been an effective commander for the Persians, while the *MM* Dorotheus captured a wealthy fortified Persian trading post in Armenia. Kavadh instructed his army to take Martyropolis, but the city was energetically defended to

---

71. Malalas 18.61.
72. Proc., *Wars* 1.21.2; he also obscures it by inserting, immediately after the narrative of Callinicum, his account of Justinian's efforts to secure help from Ethiopians and Himyarites in opening up a route to purchase silk in India.
73. Greatrex, *Rome* 194–5.
74. Malalas 18.61.
75. Ps.-Zach., *HE* 9.5–6; Malalas18.65–6.

the extent that the Persians despaired of capturing it. The arrival of cold winter weather in November, the approach of a large Roman relief army under Sittas, and, most importantly, the death of Kavadh persuaded the besiegers to withdraw. A group of Sabir Huns, who had been recruited by the Persians to support their efforts, arrived too late, but then proceeded to ravage Roman territory as far as Cilicia and the vicinity of Cyrrhus in Syria. During their withdrawal some Huns were confronted by Roman troops and lost their booty.

The accession of Khusro in September 531 gave scope for successful negotiations, since he had to consolidate his hold on the throne in the face of supporters of his two elder brothers. The process is described most fully by Procopius.[76] An embassy led by Hermogenes, Rufinus, Alexander and Thomas met Khusro on the Tigris and agreed terms for an eternal peace, with the Romans agreeing to pay 11,000 pounds (Roman) of gold and to withdraw the *dux Mesopotamiae* from Dara.[77] The money was presented as the price for Persian acquiescence in the existence of Dara and as covering a contribution to defending the Caucasus, as the Persians had long wanted,[78] but being a lump sum could not easily be presented as tribute, the image that the Romans were determined to avoid.

Khusro demanded the return of Pharangion and Bolum but refused to restore the Lazic forts of Sarapanis and Skanda. Rufinus was given seventy days to consult Justinian and return with his decision. At first the emperor was inclined to accept Khusro's conditions, but then decided to insist on the return of the forts in Lazica. Khusro initially balked at this demand and ordered his army to advance, which caused Rufinus considerable embarrassment since he had already started to deliver the gold to the Persians, but Khusro then agreed not to pursue hostilities and the peace was finalized, including the exchange of forts. Another element in the terms apparently, as we learn from Agathias, was that Khusro insisted that Justinian should receive back a group of philosophers from Athens,

---

76. Proc., *Wars* 1.22.
77. In modern terms the amount is just under 8,000 pounds of gold, or 3,640 kg.
78. Braund, *Georgia* 270, argues that the Romans had no interest in defending the Caspian Gates, the Darial pass, since this debouched into Iberia and from there into Persian territory, whereas it was the western passes into Lazica, which the Persians had controlled from the 470s to the early 520s, that mattered to them. This is undoubtedly correct, but that does not prevent the Persians from requesting contributions in cash or in kind towards the garrisons, and the Romans using this as a convenient explanation for financial payments that would otherwise resemble tribute.

who had travelled to Persia in response to Justinian's moves against pagans, and allow them to live without harassment.[79] So ended thirty-one years of war, as Malalas noted, counting from Kavadh's attack on Amida in 502;[80] so too ended the valuable supplements and alternatives to Procopius' narrative that were provided by Malalas and Pseudo-Zachariah.

The cost of this eternal peace might seem high, but in fact it only represented twenty-two years of the rate that Kavadh had repeatedly demanded as the annual Roman contribution to the Caucasus defences, or twenty-six years at the annual rate of 30,000 *solidi* that Justinian agreed at the end of his reign for the Fifty-Year Peace of 561/2.[81] By way of comparison, in 521 Justinian had spent 4,000 pounds of gold on the beast hunts with which he celebrated his consulship;[82] that was clearly a massive amount for such a purpose, but indicates that 11,000 pounds for long-term peace in the East was not astronomical. Justinian was delighted with his deal, which he celebrated in the preface to the second edition of his *Codex Iustinianus*, not least because it permitted him to pursue other opportunities that were opening up in the West. These could only be achieved through the transfer of several units of the eastern armies, which would leave defences there seriously weakened and so was only possible during peacetime. The fortification drive that had characterized Justinian's early years will also have been halted, and with the prospect of a permanent cessation of hostilities the pay of *limitanei* was probably suspended.

As long as the peace held, such economies were not critical, but threats soon emerged. At some point in the 530s, although the chronology of all the embassies is uncertain,[83] Justinian was engaged in diplomacy beyond Rome's southern borders. Two missions were conducted by Abraham and one by his son Nonnosus, to whose account we are indebted for our knowledge of the family's activities, even though all we have is a summary. All related to Qays, the Arab phylarch who led the Kindite and Ma'add tribes. Abraham made a treaty with Qays and took his son Mavia to Constantinople as a hostage, then Nonnosus travelled to both Ella Asbeha and Qays to persuade the latter to come to Constantinople, without success, and finally Abraham did persuade Qays to travel, handing

79. Agathias, *Hist.* 2.31.4.
80. Malalas 18.76.
81. See also the comparative information in Greatrex, *Rome* 216.
82. Marc.Com. *s.a.* 521.
83. See Greatrex, *Rome* 236–8, for a summary of the debate.

his leadership over to his brothers, Amr and Yezid, with Qays being rewarded by appointment as phylarch of Palestine. The strategy behind these missions is not spelled out, but it might appear that, in the wake of al-Mundhir's damaging activities, Justinian was attempting to strengthen Roman control on its southeastern frontier by ensuring the loyalty of the Kindite and Ma'add tribesmen and improving coordination across the frontier. If so, such moves might well have worried al-Mundhir and the Lakhmids.

Justinian's conquest of Africa prompted Khusro to ask for a share of the spoils, on the basis that this could not have been secured without Persian acquiescence, a request that Justinian declined.[84] Marcellinus Comes records an incursion by two Arab chiefs with 15,000 followers in 536; al-Mundhir had refused to allow them to pasture in Persian territory, with the result that they entered Euphratesia, where the local *dux*, Batzas, managed to prevent conflict through a combination of soothing words and firmness.[85] For Marcellinus at Constantinople to have heard about the incident, it must have posed a serious threat. In the same year Justinian reorganized the provinces of Armenia, reassigning some cities to different provinces and in particular incorporating lands in the upper Tigris basin that had previously been controlled by satraps into the province of Armenia Quarta.[86] The preface to his *Novel* placing the two Pontus provinces under a Moderator of Helenopontus proclaims considerable ambitions in Transcaucasia, where Roman control had been consolidated in Lazica with the city of Petra renamed Justinianopolis, the Tzani pacified for the first time, and the Suani, Scymni, Apsili, and Abasgi described as 'friendly and ours, with God's help'.[87] In 537 an infantryman named John seized control of Dara, holding it for four days until other soldiers and some civilians overthrew him; Procopius comments that the incident could have been very grave, if the Persians had not been observing the peace.[88]

The drift towards war accelerated in 539 as a result of a dispute between the two sides' Arab allies. According to Procopius, an argument about grazing rights in the borderlands was manufactured at Khusro's instigation to provide a pretext for war, since he was increasingly

---

84. Proc., *Wars* 1.26.1–4.
85. Cf Liebeschuetz, 'Arab Tribesmen' on the inevitable permeability of the desert frontiers.
86. Justinian, *Novel* 31.
87. Justinian, *Novel* 28.
88. Proc., *Wars* 1.26–5.12.

concerned by Justinian's successes in Italy. Although Justinian sent the *comes sacrarum largitionum* Strategius and Summus, *dux Palestinae*, to resolve the quarrel, they could not agree a solution, with the former keen to avoid giving a pretext for war and the latter insistent that Roman territory should not be surrendered. While Justinian was pondering the issue, Khusro added a further complaint that Summus had attempted to undermine al-Mundhir's attachment to Persia.[89] The opposite to this account in Procopius is presented in Tabari, whose tenth-century Arabic universal history preserves a certain amount of earlier Persian material:[90] unsurprisingly this accuses Harith and the Jafnids of ravaging al-Mundhir's lands, for which Justinian refused repeated requests for compensation from Khusro. Other factors gave further encouragement to Khusro. The Ostrogothic king Witigis paid two priests from Liguria to travel to Persia, where, accompanied by an interpreter of Greek and Syriac they had hired in Thrace, they urged Khusro to attack Justinian before he became too powerful to be challenged.[91] There was also an embassy from disgruntled Armenians whose experience of Roman provincial rule had not been happy, to the extent that they had revolted, killed the proconsul of Armenia Prima, and fled to Pharangium. Sittas was sent by Justinian to restore order but he was killed when reconnoitering incautiously, and his successor Buzes enraged the Armenians further by murdering a leading Armenian whom he had invited for talks. The result was that the Armenians appealed to Khusro, pointing to Justinian's insatiable appetite for expansion, alleging discontent with Roman domination in Lazica as well as Armenia, and noting that his two best generals were unavailable, Sittas being dead and Belisarius unlikely to return from the West.[92] With this encouragement, Khusro's council agreed to prepare for war in 540.

540 Campaign

Realizing that relations were sliding towards a resumption of conflict, Justinian appealed to Khusro to set aside his suspicions and preserve the peace, but to no avail since Khusro detained the envoy Anastasius. At the

---

89. Proc., *Wars* 2.1.
90. Greatrex and Lieu, *Eastern Frontier* 102–3 provide a translation of this Tabari passage (Nöldeke 238–9).
91. Proc., *Wars* 2.2.
92. Proc., *Wars* 2.3.

The 540 Campaign

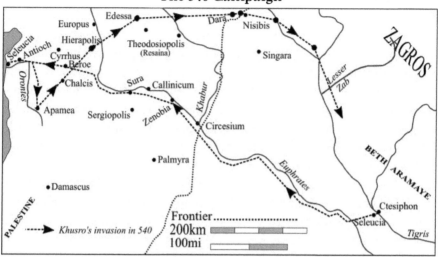

start of spring he led his army up the west bank of the Euphrates, repeating the direction of the invasion in 531.[93] After declining to cross the river to attack Circesium on the grounds that it was too strong and ignoring Zenobia as being insignificant,[94] he reached Sura, which the magi predicted he would capture since his horse had neighed and stamped the ground. On the first day of the attack the Armenian Arsaces, who commanded the garrison, led a determined resistance, but he was killed and the demoralized defenders entrusted negotiations to their bishop. Khusro accepted the bishop's gifts of food and drink and appeared to be amenable to agreeing a ransom for the town, but secretly he was furious that the first Roman place he approached did not open its gates to him but had slain some leading Persians. He ordered the Persians who were escorting the bishop back to the city to obstruct the city gate with a stone; Khusro's army was ready to pounce and the city was pillaged and torched. Khusro now instructed Anastasius to report to Justinian on what he had witnessed and contacted Candidus, bishop of Sergiopolis (Resafa), for him to ransom the 12,000 prisoners from Sura for 200 pounds of gold. Candidus did not have the money to hand but agreed to provide it within a year; apparently few of the ransomed captives survived for long.

---

93. Proc., *Wars* 2.5.
94. For this site, see Blétry, 'Guerre'.

Belisarius was still nominally *MM per Orientem*, but in his absence in Italy Justinian had appointed Buzes as commander over the land east of the Euphrates and given him authority over the whole area until Belisarius returned. Buzes had gathered his army at Hierapolis, from where he decided to set off with his best troops. Although he had talked about guerilla tactics to hamper Khusro's large army and force it to withdraw, Procopius comments that he did nothing and that no-one knew where he went.[95] Justinian meantime had sent his nephew Germanus to the East with 300 men, promising that a large army would follow shortly. Megas, bishop of Beroea, was sent from Antioch to negotiate with Khusro, reaching him at Hierapolis where a ransom of 2,000 pounds of silver had been negotiated. Megas accepted a demand for 1,000 pounds of gold to secure Khusro's return to Persia and hurried back to Antioch to have this ratified, while Khusro's army advanced to Beroea. Here the agreed ransom was 4,000 pounds of silver, but the city could only find half, with the result that the garrison and inhabitants fled to the citadel, allowing the Persians to sack the lower city. The citadel resisted a Persian assault, but those inside were at risk of running out of water since they only had a single spring, which was quickly exhausted by all the animals they had brought with them.[96] At this point Megas returned from Antioch, where Julian, Justinian's *a secretis* who was on an embassy to Khusro, refused him permission to hand over money; he did, however, persuade Khusro to let Beroea off its unpaid ransom and allow everyone to leave the citadel. Procopius observes that the majority of the soldiers went over to the Persians since their pay was long in arrears.[97]

Khusro's attention now turned to Antioch, the greatest city of the East. The fortifications were strong, but a problem had been identified by Germanus: the main city was located on level ground next to the Orontes river, but from there the walls ran up the steep sides of Mount Silpius at whose summit there was a place where the ground outside almost reached the height of the defences.[98] There was no time to cut back the threatening rock or defend it with a tower linked to the main defences, and instead the defenders constructed a wooden platform inside the walls to increase

---

95. Proc., *Wars* 2.6.7.
96. Proc., *Wars* 2.7.1–13.
97. Proc., *Wars* 2.7.37.
98. It might seem strange that the defences of this important city had been left with such a weakness. It is possible that the danger to the walls had been created by the powerful earthquakes of 526 and 527, if they had produced rock slides that altered the configuration of the ground.

the width of their fighting space. Although Germanus departed to avoid becoming the focus of Khusro's attention, the arrival of 6,000 troops from Lebanon under Theoctistus and Molazes bolstered morale and deterred many from fleeing. Khusro offered to spare the city for 1,000 pounds of gold, but the populace taunted the king and came close to killing his envoy.

Khusro directed his attack against the summit of Mount Silpius, where the wall was most vulnerable, and the fierce Roman resistance was undermined when their temporary structure collapsed. Defenders in neighbouring towers abandoned their positions believing that the wall had been breached. Theoctistus and Molazes promptly rode out of the south gate with their troops, followed by some of the citizens, while Khusro paused his advance, probably giving time for Roman soldiers to depart so that resistance would be less strong. Opposition was provided by the circus factions, some of whom had armour, and the Persians were briefly driven back, but then the weight of Persian numbers ensured that the whole city fell with considerable slaughter. The main city was burned, with the exception of the Great Church, whose treasures were regarded as its individual ransom; in addition to the numerous captives and quantities of precious metals, the booty included marbles, precious stones, and pictures, which were transported back to Persia to adorn a new city called Veh Antioch Khusro, 'The Better Antioch of Khusro'.[99]

Roman envoys now agreed terms with Khusro, that he would withdraw for an immediate payment of 5,000 pounds of gold and an annual transfer of 500 pounds thereafter, with hostages providing security for the agreement. Khusro now advanced to the Mediterranean at Seleucia, where he bathed in the sea and offered sacrifices,[100] perhaps to demonstrate that the king of the rising sun now claimed universal dominion as far as the western sea in which the sun set.[101]

Returning to Antioch, he had the sanctuary of the Archangel Michael at Daphne burned, in retaliation for the killing of a Persian noble by a local youth, and then proceeded towards Apamea on the pretext that he

---

99. Proc., *Wars* 2.9; 14.1–4.
100. Proc., *Wars* 2.11.
101. Payne, 'Cosmology' 21, links this behaviour with the chariot races celebrated at Apamea as examples of Khusro acting as ruler of a subordinate Roman kingdom, but purification in the sea, unlike holding chariot races, is not behviour associated with Roman emperors. It is much more likely that this unusual action was directed at an internal, Zoroastrian, audience, who would have understood the cosmic significance of Khusro's solar ceremony.

was curious to see it. Terms were agreed that he would spare the city for 1,000 pounds of silver, although there was little confidence that these would be respected. The local bishop, Thomas, boosted the morale of the inhabitants by displaying the city's relic of the True Cross, which illumined the cathedral with a miraculous light as it was paraded around; the historian Evagrius was taken by his parents as a child of four or five to witness this spectacle.[102] As expected Khusro did not keep his promise and, as soon as he had entered the city with 200 Persian nobles, he ordered that all its wealth should be brought to him; Thomas did, however, persuade the king to allow him to keep the relic of the Cross. Khusro arranged chariot races in the hippodrome, presiding over the contest and supporting the Greens since he was aware that Justinian favoured the Blues. When the Blue charioteer took the lead, Khusro regarded this as an affront and ordered that his chariot should be held back to last place so that the Green faction and himself could be acclaimed as victors.[103]

Khusro now headed east via Chalcis, which ransomed itself for 200 pounds of gold; he also demanded the surrender of the local soldiers, but the citizens hid them. From there he crossed the Euphrates, building a bridge near Barbalissus which he ordered to be destroyed on the third day, a command that was carried out even though the whole army had not been able to cross, so that the remainder had to make their own way back.[104] Khusro's attention now turned to Edessa, which he was keen to capture because of the promise that Christ was believed to have given to the local ruler, Abgar, that his city would not be captured by barbarians. After the Persians camped nearby at Batna, they apparently lost their way and twice returned to Batna to camp. When he finally reached Edessa, Khusro was suffering from a swollen jaw and agreed to ransom the city for 200 pounds of gold.[105]

The Persians continued east, taking with them a multitude of captives from Antioch, which Buzes refused to allow the Edessenes to ransom. Khusro declined to receive a ransom from Carrhae, on the grounds that its inhabitants were not Christians, but accepted an unspecified payment from Constantina, even though he asserted that the city already belonged to the Persians since in 503 the local bishop had offered food and drink to Kavadh. Dara was another city that Khusro wanted to capture and

---

102. Evagrius 4.26.
103. Proc., *Wars* 2.11.
104. Proc., *Wars* 2.12.1–6.
105. Proc., *Wars* 2.12.7–34

so he began a siege, burning the west gates in the outer wall but being unable to penetrate the intermural space where the defenders kept their animals, and then tunnelling under the walls on the south side of the city, the only part of the circuit that was not founded on rock. Progress was good, but after the Persian mine had passed under the outer wall, the Romans were alerted to the danger and dug a countermine at right angles to the Persian approach. This failure prompted Khusro to abandon the attack and accept 1,000 pounds of silver to withdraw. Since Khusro had attempted to capture Dara during what should have been a truce, Justinian renounced his agreement to the peace terms.[106]

Granted the approach by and offer of assistance from Armenians, it might seem strange that Khusro did not attack further north in order to access this resource and exploit discontent with Roman rule. However, in view of the permeability of the frontier, it is most probable that he was well-appraised about conditions in Syria and Upper Mesopotamia and reckoned that he should exploit the element of surprise by attacking there before the Romans could prepare.[107] The invasion demonstrated both the richness of Rome's eastern provinces and the weakness of its defences in the absence of the units of the mobile army dispatched to Italy to support the reconquest. It is impossible to establish what Buzes as the current *MM per Orientem* was attempting to do, although the fact that he resurfaces in Procopius' narrative at Edessa undermines the accusation that he had completely disappeared. Some of the *limitanei* were demoralized by the lack of pay and were willing to desert, but the troops at Chalcis clearly preferred to remain in Roman service. Over winter Justinian acted to shore up defences, sending Belisarius to command against Khusro with the Gothic soldiers he had brought back from the West and appointing Valerian, who had also returned from Italy, as *MM per Armeniam*.

Campaigns of 541-544

In 541 Khusro switched his offensive to Transcaucasia since he had received an embassy from the Laz, whose experience of the extortion of Roman

---

106. Proc., *Wars* 2.13.16–29.
107. For the easy flow of information across the frontier, see Lee, *Information* ch.5, and for a specific contemporary example of free movement, see Greatrex and Lieu, *Eastern Frontier* 98 for translation of the *Life* of John of Tela (bishop of Constantina): John said that he had frequently travelled to pray with the holy men on the Jebel Sinjar and could not tell the difference between the two empires.

governors, especially John Tzibus who had established a monopoly over trade into the new city of Petra that Justinian had built on the coast,[108] and of the billeting of troops, had led them to contemplate switching allegiance. The Laz envoys reassured Khusro, who had heard that the ruggedness of the terrain made access to their country challenging, that he could lead his army through by felling trees to fill in difficult passages, and they promised to provide guides. The Persians duly constructed a road from Iberia, a route of major strategic significance since in due course it permitted the unification of the previously divergent territories of Lazica and Iberia into the medieval kingdom of Georgia. They entered Lazica where Gubazes performed obeisance.

Khusro sent troops ahead to test the defences of Petra, but they were outwitted by John Tzibus, who instructed the defenders to remain quietly within the walls until the attackers were fully committed, at which point the Romans charged out and inflicted heavy losses. Khusro impaled his defeated commander and proceeded to invest the city in person. On the first day of his attack the Romans resisted strongly with their machines and archery, but late in the day John was killed and this demoralized the defenders. Khusro then ordered his troops to undermine two extramural towers that overlooked the only easy approach to the city, the rest of which was protected by the sea or cliffs. He managed to collapse one of the towers, thereby opening the way to an assault on the wall, and so the inhabitants agreed terms for surrender.[109] To prevent Roman forces in Armenia from disrupting his actions in Lazica, Khusro had sent Huns to raid the provinces but these had been defeated by Valerian;[110] it is noticeable that this success, which did not involve Belisarius in any way, is not reported by Procopius in the *Wars*, and is only included in the *Secret History* to contribute to an indirect demonstration of the unfortunate consequences of Theodora's influence in the empire.[111]

Meanwhile in Mesopotamia Belisarius had gathered his forces, which included a substantial contingent of Arabs under Harith, unaware of developments in Transcaucasia. His spies had informed him that Khusro

---

108. Braund, *Georgia* 294–5, plays down the significance of John's interference in trade in comparison to the aggravation caused by the presence of foreign troops, for which the Laz had to pay by providing supplies at subsidized rates.

109. Proc., *Wars* 2.15; 17.

110. Proc., *Secret History* 2.29–30.

111. Proc., *SH* 2.26–37

was campaigning against Huns, which was probably the public explanation for the northern expedition, and so he consulted his council of officers about action. Most commanders favoured an invasion, but the *duces* of Lebanon feared that al-Mundhir would attack Palestine and Syria if their troops were removed. Belisarius overcame these doubts by stating that the Arabs always had a break from raiding of about two months over the summer solstice, when they devoted themselves to religious business, and promised to release the *duces* within sixty days.[112] Belisarius led his army in good order from Dara to Nisibis, camping with most of his men about 6km from the walls. Contrary to his advice Peter and John Troglita, the *dux Mesopotamiae*, camped much closer, within 2km of the city, and then ignored Belisarius' warning to be wary of a Persian attack in the middle of the day. In the midday heat, when the Romans had stood down to refresh themselves with the cucumbers growing there, the Persians charged out of Nisibis, routed the Romans, killing fifty and capturing Peter's standard. They would have inflicted heavier losses if Belisarius had not reacted promptly to the Persian move: his Gothic spearmen charged the Persians and drove them back to the walls, killing 150. The Persians remained within the fortifications, but placed Peter's standard on a tower, insultingly decorated with sausages.[113]

Nisibis was too strong for Belisarius to besiege and so he continued a day's march to the east to invest the Persian fort of Sisauranon, which contained 800 excellent Persian cavalry. An initial attack was beaten back, at which point Belisarius decided to split his forces, sending Harith with his Arabs accompanied by 1,200 Romans, mostly Belisarius' *bucellarii* under Trajan and John the Glutton, to pillage east of the Tigris and report back on conditions there. After learning from prisoners that Sisauranon was short of provisions, since the system of public storehouses operating at Dara and Nisibis was not practised there, Belisarius negotiated a surrender under whose terms the inhabitants, mostly Christian Romans, were allowed to depart while the Persian troops were sent to Constantinople from where they were deployed in Italy.

Harith secured rich booty beyond the Tigris, a region that had not been ravaged for a long time, but then feared that he might be deprived of it if he returned to Belisarius. He therefore tricked John and Trajan into

112. Proc., *Wars* 2.1616–10.
113. Proc., *Wars* 2.18.16–25.

withdrawing their troops through a false story that a large Persian army was approaching, so that they returned separately to Roman territory at Theodosiopolis (Resaina). Meanwhile, with no news from Harith about his progress, Belisarius' men, especially those from Thrace who were not used to the heat of Mesopotamia, were falling sick in the summer heat. The troops from Lebanon were desperate to return to base since the two-month respite from Arab incursions was past, so Belisarius led his army back to Roman territory, transporting the sick on carts. Here he learned about Harith's deceit but was unable to do anything about it. Khusro withdrew from Lazica with his prisoners and booty, leaving a garrison in Petra, while at the end of the year Belisarius was summoned by Justinian to Constantinople where he spent the winter.[114]

In 542 Khusro again led his army up the west bank of the Euphrates, this time targeting not Syria – which he had thoroughly pillaged in 540 – but the untouched wealth of the Holy Land. En route he was approached by Candidus, bishop of Sergiopolis, who apologized for failing to produce the money he had promised for the captives of Sura. Khusro now demanded double, namely 400 pounds of gold, and Candidus, after severe torture, gave orders that his city's sacred treasures be handed over to the Persians. These, however, were insufficient to satisfy Khusro, who sent men ostensibly to search for more but in reality to take over the city. His duplicity was revealed by a Christian Arab in al-Mundhir's forces, probably someone who respected the city's patron saint, Sergius, a particular favourite of Arab tribes whose reputation was strong on both sides of the frontier.[115] When the Persians were refused entry the enraged Khusro sent 6,000 troops to assault the city, whose defenders numbered only 200, but the city was again rescued by the same Arab informant: he told the defenders, when they were about to negotiate surrender, that shortage of water would force the Persians to retire within three days.[116] The escape of Sergiopolis is also recorded by Evagrius, although he attributes it to the miraculous apparition of numerous defenders on the walls and does not mention the Persian lack of water.[117]

---

114. Proc., *Wars* 2.19. In the *Secret History* (2.18–25), Procopius claimed that Belisarius did not penetrate more deeply into Persian territory because he was waiting near the frontier for the arrival of his wife, but the reasons given in the *Wars* for his actions seem plausible enough.
115. On the widespread fame of Sergiopolis, see Key Fowden, *Plain* esp. ch.4–5.
116. Proc., *Wars* 2.20.1–17.
117. Evagrius 4.28.

Khusro's campaigns in 542 and 543

In response Belisarius assembled his forces on the Euphrates at Europus (Carcemish), disregarding an appeal from Buzes and Justus, nephew of Justinian, to take refuge with them at Hierapolis. His position threatened the Persian line of retreat, so that Khusro sent an envoy to complain about Justinian's failure to open peace talks but also to obtain information on the state of Roman forces.[118] Belisarius arranged an elaborate deceit to

118. Bury, *HLRE* 2.106, followed by Kislinger & Stathakopoulos, 'Pest' 94, attributed Khusro's withdrawal to fear of the plague. But, if the disease had already reached coastal Palestine in late summer 541 (Kislinger & Stathakopoulos, 'Pest' 87–8), the Persians would have known about it before planning their invasion. Of course, they might not have appreciated quite how serious the threat was.

impress on the envoy both the quality of his troops and their ability to block the Euphrates crossings, with the result that Khusro decided he had to withdraw. Perhaps fearing a repetition of the defeat at Callinicum, Belisarius chose not to hamper this, thinking it better to secure the Persian departure than risk battle with desperate men, and the Persians rapidly bridged the Euphrates since they had brought the necessary materials with them. Although Khusro had undertaken to depart without causing further damage, he took the opportunity when passing Callinicum, whose defences were being rebuilt, to capture those who had not fled in time.[119] Khusro's withdrawal is probably also the context for Persian attempts to capture Resaina (Theodosiopolis) on the Khabur and Kafr-tut, located between Resaina and Dara. Pseudo-Zachariah reported the capture of other places besides Callinicum, while Agapius provided the two specific names for places attacked unsuccessfully. A rhetorical account of the heroic actions of John Troglita, in first lifting the siege of Resaina by Persians under Mihr-Meroe and then defeating and capturing the Persians when they moved on Dara, is presented by Corippus.[120] By now plague was raging in Constantinople, but there is no indication in the military narrative that it was yet affecting Syria and Mesopotamia, even though it had struck the coastal cities of Palestine the previous year.

At this point there is a chronological issue, since Procopius' account of events, the only one available, falls one year short of the requisite number of notices of a new campaign year between 542 and 545. The traditional solution is to take Procopius' concluding comments on Khusro's 542 invasion and the summons of Belisarius to Constantinople as a virtual year-end notice,[121] with the long account of the bubonic plague located between campaign years.[122] Thus, Procopius' next chapter, dealing with events in the north, relates to 543. An alternative has been proposed that these northern events, including the Roman defeat at Anglon, occurred in

---

119. Proc., *Wars* 2.21.
120. Corippus, *Iohannid* 1.68–98. All the evidence is set out in Greatrex and Lieu, *Eastern Frontier* 111–12. The account of Pseudo-Zachariah does not survive, though the index to Book 10 records that this was reported in chapter 8. Agapius of Membij, a 10th century Syriac writer who drew on earlier sources, many of them lost, ascribed the actions at Resaina to Belisarius and Khusro, but there is no reason to reject the information in Corippus, since it would have been in his interests to give John credit for defeating the Persian king, if the latter had been involved. This is another example of Procopius' failure to mention events in which Belisarius was not involved.
121. Proc., *Wars* 2.21.34.
122. Proc., *Wars* 2.22–3.

late 542 with the 'lost' year being located during the negotiations for the truce of 545.[123] There is, however, nothing wrong with the traditional chronology, which takes account of the considerable disruption caused by the plague, when Justinian's own illness will have compounded the confusion, whereas the revised version postulates an implausibly rapid movement for Khusro's forces in the middle of 542 in contrast to the normal sedate progress of royal expeditions, disregards events in Upper Mesopotamia after the capture of Callinicum, and unduly elongates the exchange of ambassadors in what has become 543/4.[124]

In the *Wars* Procopius reports that Belisarius was summoned back to Constantinople to be sent to Italy to improve the difficult situation there.[125] As with his account of Belisarius' removal from office after Callinicum, Procopius has not told the whole truth here and a different version of events is presented in the *Secret History*.[126] It appears that Belisarius and his fellow *MM* Buzes had been reported by the general Peter and John the Glutton for allegedly holding treasonable conversations about the imperial succession in the event that Justinian succumbed to the plague, a report that outraged the empress Theodora in particular, who took it as a personal insult. It is quite possible that Peter was still fuming about his disgrace at Nisibis in the previous year, when his disregard for Belisarius' orders had led to defeat, while John may well have been reprimanded for allowing Harith to deceive him over the booty secured in their ravaging expedition. Belisarius and Buzes were questioned about these allegations, and, although nothing could be proved, it is alleged that Buzes was effectively kidnapped by Theodora and held in a secret prison within the women's quarters of the palace for twenty-eight months, while Belisarius was removed from office and left in disgrace, fearing for his life until Theodora arranged for his return to favour to be credited to his wife, Antonina.

In 543 (accepting the traditional chronology) Khusro moved from the Tigris valley through the Zagros to the Iranian plateau near Lake Urmiah,

---

123. Proc., *Wars* 2.28.2–3. The argument, advanced by Kislinger & Stathakopoulos, 'Pest', has been accepted by Greatrex & Lieu, *Eastern Frontier* 112–13, and Kaldellis, *Wars* 124ff.
124. The treatment of Kaldellis is confusing, since he notes that the recall of Belisarius, which Procopius records immediately after the capture of Callinicum (*Wars* 2.21.34), occurred at the end of 542, as had the recall in 541. Thus Belisarius' successor, Martin, could not have been in post before 543, but then Kaldellis accepts that Martin was active in Armenia as *MM per Orientem* in 542. For full discussion of this chronological issue, see Whitby, 'Missing Year'.
125. Proc., *Wars* 2.21.34.
126. Proc., *SH* 4.1–39.

where the great Zoroastrian fire temple of Adur-Gushnasp was located at Takht-i Suleiman. There he awaited the Roman envoys, Constantine and Sergius, who had been sent to arrange a treaty, but Constantine had fallen sick and the mission was delayed. At this point the plague reached Persian territory and Khusro now ordered his commander in Armenia, Nahbed, to send the bishop of Dwin to complain to Valerian, *MM per Armeniam*, about the failure of the envoys to arrive. The bishop's brother, however, revealed that Khusro was troubled by the rebellion of one of his sons, while plague was also affecting his army. When this was reported to Justinian, he ordered his commanders in Armenia to invade in the expectation that there would be no resistance. Khusro meanwhile descended to the Tigris valley which had not yet suffered the full force of the plague.

The Roman invasion was somewhat chaotic, since the various commanders based at Theodosiopolis, Citharizon, Martyropolis, and possibly elsewhere failed to co-ordinate their movements so that they advanced on Dwin, the main city of Persarmenia and a busy trading station, in disjointed groups. Nahbed withdrew from Dwin with 4,000 men to the village of Anglon, located just under 20km to the south with a very strong fortress nearby atop a steep peak. Nahbed reinforced the defences of the village with stones, carts, and a trench, while he placed ambushes in some cabins outside its limits. The Romans approached incautiously and were surprised by the news that Persian troops were present, but decided it would be humiliating for such large forces to withdraw, so they formed up on the difficult terrain as best they could. Martin, the new *MM per Orientem*, commanded the centre, Valerian, *MM per Armeniam* the left and Peter the right.

Nahbed had ordered his men to hold station and so battle was joined when Narses, the Persarmenian noble who had defected in 530, drove back the Persians opposite him with his band of Heruls, forcing the enemy to flee uphill towards the fortress. This caused considerable casualties, but Nahbed then sprang his ambushes: Narses was mortally wounded and his Heruls, who fought without helmet or breastplate, were shot down in the confined space. The Roman army disintegrated, abandoning considerable supplies and numerous pack animals in their flight. Casualties were heavy and many more were taken captive, so that Procopius concluded his account with the comment that the disaster was greater than any that had previously befallen the Romans.[127]

---

127. Proc., *Wars* 2.25.15–34.

544 Campaign

In 544 Khusro invaded Mesopotamia with the city of Edessa as his specific target; having failed in his attempt in 540 he was determined this time to prove that Christian confidence in its inviolability was unfounded. Khusro's first action was to send some Huns to drive off the animals that had been herded into the space near the walls above the hippodrome; a confrontation between shepherds and these Huns developed into a larger engagement, until the Persian horsemen were forced to withdraw. Khusro then entered negotiations about a ransom for the city, the main purpose of which seems to have been to demoralize the inhabitants by raising and then dashing their hopes. After a week Khusro ordered the construction of a siege mound with a foundation of timbers from the trees felled in the vicinity, topped with earth and stones. A sally by some Huns in Roman service disrupted the project, but thereafter the Persians kept a closer watch and the mound advanced until it was within range of the walls, when they constructed screens to prevent missiles from affecting the work.

The Romans again attempted to negotiate, choosing as envoy the doctor Stephen who had once cured Khusro, but the response was unwelcome: Khusro demanded the surrender of two Roman commanders, Peter and Peranius, on the grounds that they were his hereditary slaves, or provision of 50,000 pounds of gold, or to admit into the city his men who would search out all valuables. These proposals were unacceptable, so work on the siege mound continued. The defenders tried further negotiations, to no avail since the Persians blamed Justinian for rejecting peace, and their efforts to build up their defences to overtop the mound were equally unsuccessful, with the result that their morale dropped.

The defenders had started to dig a tunnel under the middle of the mound, but the noise of their digging was heard by the Persians, so that efforts were then focused on the lower courses of the mound closest to the wall: timbers, stones, and earth were extracted to construct a chamber that was filled with wood soaked in cedar oil, sulphur, and bitumen. Conversations about peace continued with Martin, as the Persians professed a willingness to settle if only Justinian could be persuaded, but when the mound had reached and overtopped the wall, the Persians declared that they would now concentrate on fighting. The Romans fired their chamber and kept it replenished with fuel. When smoke began to rise from the mound, they hurled pots of burning embers and launched fire arrows, so that the Persians would not identify the real cause of the smoke, which remained undetected until Khusro arrived in the morning and saw the problem. However, attempts to quench the internal fire with earth and water were ineffective, since these just encouraged the sulphur and bitumen to burn more fiercely and by late afternoon the smoke from the mound was visible from Carrhae, about 45km away. In hand-to-hand fighting on the mound the Romans worsted the Persians.

Six days later Khusro almost surprised the defenders with an assault on the walls using ladders, but the Persians were repulsed after a fierce fight. Khusro at once switched his attention to the Great Gate but was decisively driven back by soldiers and locals. Khusro now revealed that Recinarius, who had been kept in the Persian camp for several days, had come from Justinian to negotiate peace and demanded that talks take place on the next day. When the Romans responded that they would need to wait for three days since Martin was unwell, Khusro prepared a further assault. Bricks were piled onto the siege mound, commanders and troops were positioned opposite every gate with ladders and siege engines, while his Arab troops and some Persians were stationed in the rear, not to attack the wall but placed to round up all fugitives as if in a fishing net when the city fell. The initial assaults went well, but the defenders gradually organized themselves, with the local men fighting on the wall and women and children keeping them supplied with stones and cauldrons of boiling oil to be sprinkled with a whisk on the attackers.

The Persians faltered, only to be forced back to the assault by the furious king, but without success since the weight of Roman missiles kept driving them back. Only at the Soinian Gate, the place called Three Towers, did the Persians force their way through the outer wall until they were repelled by a sally of soldiers and locals led by Peranius. Eventually in late afternoon the attack, which had begun in early morning, was called off. The following day was quiet, but the next day Khusro attacked the Gate of Barlaos, only to be quickly driven back. This was the final assault, and Khusro was now, after as much as two months of failed attempts, prepared to agree terms with Martin to withdraw in return for 500 pounds of gold, promising to do no further damage. At some point in the siege, as we learn from a subsequent aside in Procopius – although it is not mentioned in his main account – the Persians had advanced elephants against the walls, but one of the animals was so irritated by the squealing of a pig being dangled from a tower that it ran out of control.[128]

---

128. Proc., *Wars* 8.14.35–7.

This long and vivid account of the siege in Procopius demonstrates the effectiveness of Roman defences when sufficient troops were energetically supported by the local inhabitants.[129] Morale overall was clearly very high, being bolstered in part by the religious conviction that Christ had promised that the city would not be captured. This siege gave rise to a further important miracle story and the invention of a powerful relic, namely the Mandylion of Edessa, perhaps the article that was to become the Shroud of Turin. Evagrius provided an account of the siege with a focus on the construction and destruction of the Persian siege mound; the Romans had difficulties in firing the material in their chamber until the city's precious *acheiropoietos* icon of Christ, one 'not-made-by-human-hands' but imprinted by Christ himself onto a cloth that King Abgar had sent to him, was brought into the tunnel and applied to the kindling, at which point the flames took hold. For Evagrius the burning of the mound terminated the siege and he does not record the subsequent desperate actions narrated by Procopius.[130] It is clear that between the events in 544, or at least when Procopius' account of them written a few years later, and when Evagrius was working on his history *circa* 590, the story of the promise contained in Christ's letter to Abgar had evolved into a miraculous *acheiropoietos* icon, of which this is one of several to come to light in the sixth century.[131]

After Khusro's withdrawal and the deaths of two Roman commanders, Justus and Peranius at about the same time, Justinian followed up the chance to make peace by sending Constantianus and Sergius to Khusro in Ctesiphon.[132] The Romans demanded the return of Lazica, while Khusro asked Justinian to send him the doctor Tribunus, who had previously treated him for an illness; Justinian obliged, dispatching both Tribunus and the money for the truce. There is no indication of any delay in negotiations, as assumed by those who believe that the 'missing year' in Procopius' narrative

---

129. Proc., *Wars* 2.26–7.
130. Evagrius 4.27.
131. For discussion of the evolution of the story, see Whitby, *Evagrius* 323–6.
132. This is the point at which Kislinger & Stathakopoulos, 'Pest', postulate that Procopius has ignored the passage of one whole year. This timing seems most implausible, granted that it was in Justinian's interests to exploit Khusro's failure at Edessa as rapidly as possible. Greatrex, 'Recent Work' 52–4, attempts to explain what he accepts is a 'rather awkward gap' between the siege of Edessa and the dispatch of ambassadors by postulating that Justus and Peranius died several months after the siege, and that the Roman embassy which followed the arrival of their replacements did not reach Khusro until late 544. This involves stretching Procopius' statement that they died 'at about the same time' as the siege ended and ignoring the fact that the Roman embassy could have met Khusro at his summer base, if that was what its timing dictated.

should be located here; indeed, the shape of an agreement had already been determined and it was in the interests of both parties to finalize matters. Khusro rewarded Tribunus well for his services, inviting him to select Roman captives for release and eventually sending him home with 3,000.[133]

Truce, 545-549

The truce, which excluded Transcaucasia, was intended to provide the time needed to agree terms for a full peace, but there were disturbances. Clashes between the respective Arab allies resulted in one of Harith's sons being sacrificed to a deity called Aphrodite, the Arab al-Uzza, by al-Mundhir, in response to which Harith inflicted a crushing defeat on the Lakhmids.[134] Khusro apparently hoped to use negotiations to achieve two important aims, capture Dara and consolidate Persian control in Lazica through a transfer of populations and assassination of King Gubazes. Domination of Lazica would strengthen the Persian grip on Iberia by removing a potential source of support for any revolt; it would also allow the Persians to construct a fleet on the Black Sea, thereby opening up a new line of attack on Constantinople,[135] and give them control of all the passes across the Caucasus so that they could direct any raiders from the north towards Roman territory. The Laz were already disaffected with the Persians by religious disagreements as well as by their exclusion from Roman commerce on the Black Sea, which had previously supplied them with grain, wine, and salt in return for hides.[136]

In 547 or 548 the Persian ambassador, Yazd-Gushnasp, tried to enter Dara with 500 elite followers, who were tasked with setting fire to their lodgings so that in the resulting confusion the Persians at Nisibis could seize the city; but the plan was revealed and the envoy's abnormally large entourage was not permitted into the city but had to remain at Ammodius. Nevertheless, Yazd-Gushnasp was received lavishly by Justinian, even though he did not appear to have any concrete proposals to offer, with the expenses of the mission apparently costing the Romans 1,000 pounds of gold.[137]

---

133. Proc., *Wars* 8.10.13–16.
134. Proc., *Wars* 2.28.12–15.
135. Braund, *Georgia* 297, argues that the danger of such an attack has been overstated since the majority of the Black Sea coastline remained under Roman control.
136. Salt was an issue since, as explained by Braund, *Georgia* 58, the low salinity of the eastern Black Sea made it difficult for the Laz to obtain salt by boiling sea water.
137. Proc., *Wars* 2.28.31–44.

With regard to the Laz, Khusro dispatched Yazd-Gushnasp's brother, Wahriz (Phabrizus), and 300 men with a quantity of timber to build ships, though ostensibly for siege engines at Petra, and orders to assassinate Gubazes. The timber was destroyed by lightning,[138] while the plot to kill Gubazes at a meeting inside Petra was revealed to him by an Iberian intermediary. As a result Gubazes contacted Justinian, offering to revert to his Roman allegiance, and in 548 Justinian sent to his assistance Dagistheus with 7,000 Roman troops and 1,000 Tzani, who invested Petra. Threatened with the loss of Lazica, Khusro dispatched Mihr-Meroe with a large army, said to be over 30,000 strong, to bolster the Persian position. Gubazes advised Dagistheus to continue the siege, but also focus on defending the two narrow routes that led from Iberia into Lazica, one of which he would block himself. Dagistheus, however, only sent 100 troops to the pass he was to defend and, although these fought valiantly, they could not prevent the much larger Persian army from forcing its way through.

At Petra Dagistheus had managed to collapse a section of the wall, but this did not provide access to the interior since the gap was blocked by buildings that abutted the wall. Even when fifty Roman volunteers managed to enter the city and acclaim the victorious Justinian the lack of support forced their retreat. Gubazes, although he had not received from Justinian the money he expected, both for his own salary as a silentiary and to pay the Alan and Sabir allies he had recruited, still defended the pass he was blocking, but Mihr-Meroe could approach Petra via the other route. There Dagistheus and his men abandoned their camp and possessions, which the defenders came out to pillage, but they were surprised by the Tzani, who had not left with their commander; they took the booty and went home via Rize on the Black Sea.

Inside Petra Mihr-Meroe found that the garrison had been reduced to only 150 fit men, with a further 350 wounded and unable to fight. The corpses of the dead had been kept within the city rather than thrown over the walls, to avoid revealing their weakness to the attackers. He at once resupplied the city and strengthened the walls by filling the Persians' linen provision bags with sand to block gaps. Mihr-Meroe left 3,000 men in the city and withdrew, though en route he was ambushed by some

---

138. Braund, *Georgia* 297–8, regards the lightning bolt as the convenient end to an implausible story, since there was no need for Khusro to go to the trouble of transporting timber to Lazica, which was known for its timber resources.

Laz and Dagistheus, who inflicted casualties and captured some of the Persian horses. Mihr-Meroe was keen to keep Petra supplied, which he knew would be difficult since his own army could scarcely be sustained, and so he selected 5,000 men with Wahriz as commander to oversee this logistical operation and then withdrew the majority of his army to Iberia. Justinian at last sent funds to Gubazes and the Sabirs. In 549 Gubazes, with the support of Dagistheus and exploiting his local knowledge, first surprised and annihilated a screening force of 1,000 Persians, after which they fell on the main Persian force, most of whom they captured or killed. The survivors were pursued into Iberia, where a further encounter led to more Persian losses. The victors burned the supplies that had been intended for Petra and stepped up their guard on the passes from Iberia.

This concludes the narrative in *Wars* 2, which Procopius made public in the early 550s, but he takes up the account in *Wars* 8 that he brought to completion in 554. This book opens with events in the north-east, although military actions are preceded by seven chapters in which Procopius demonstrates – with considerable help from the second-century Arrian – his breadth of knowledge on matters of geography, ethnography, and mythology relating to the eastern Black Sea.

In the final year of the current truce, namely late 549, a large Persian army that contained a contingent of Alans under the command of Farrukhan (Chorianes) marched through Iberia into Lazica. Gubazes and Dagistheus led out their troops, with the Laz in particular very keen to fight for their land and families. The Laz cavalry led the march with the Roman cavalry some distance behind and then in the rear Gubazes and Dagistheus with the infantry. When the Laz encountered a well-armed advance party of 1,000 Persians, they at once turned to flight and sought protection with the Roman horsemen. While the two cavalry forces confronted each other, Artabanes, a Persarmenian in Roman service, placed himself in the intervening space with two Roman companions where they triumphed in a duel. When Gubazes and Dagistheus arrived with the infantry, the Roman cavalry commanders ordered their men to dismount and, having little faith in their Laz allies, forced them to do the same. The allied shield wall perplexed the Persians, who could not charge it down, and the battle was continued with exchanges of missiles. Although the Persians and Alans could fire much faster, the shield wall prevented many casualties and the fight was eventually decided when Farrukhan was hit and fell from his horse. As a result the Persians fled to their camp, where, after brief resistance at the narrow entrance to the stockade by a lone Alan, the allies burst in and massacred their opponents. The survivors returned to Persia, though in the meantime a different Persian force, about which we hear nothing else, had managed to resupply the garrison in Petra.[139]

Lazica 550-551

Over winter Laz envoys in Constantinople criticized the performance of Dagistheus, in particular his failure to prosecute the siege of Petra energetically when the Persian defenders had been reduced to a mere handful; the principal issue may have been that Gubazes had lost confidence in the Roman general. Whatever the reason, the result was that Justinian put Dagistheus under house arrest and replaced him as *MM per Armeniam* with Bessas, who had just returned from a less than successful command in Italy. Justinian instructed Bessas to send a strong force against the Abasgi, whose territory lay to the north of Lazica; their experience of Roman rule had led them to select their own rulers and contemplate revolt. Bessas sent John son of Thomas and the Herul Uligag with a large force by boat. The Abasgi had taken refuge on a spur of the Caucasus that ran down towards the sea, where a narrow defile only wide enough for single file movement, appropriately named Tracheia ('Rough') and protected by a strong fortress, provided the sole access to the territory north of the mountains. The Romans first landed south of the defile, but then John ferried some of his men round to the north, with the result that the Abasgi, threatened from both sides, fled in disorder to the fortress. There a fierce struggle developed, but this was ended when the Romans set fire to the buildings.[140]

Gubazes then had to deal with the defection to the Persians of the Apsili, who had previously been subjects of the Laz. Their territory lay in the mountains to the east of the Abasgi, where they had welcomed a Persian garrison into the fort of Tzibile but then regretted the decision. Gubazes sent John with 1,000 Roman troops and he managed to reconcile them with the Laz.[141]

Procopius now records a revolt by Khusro's eldest son Anoshaghzadh, who had already been relegated from court at Ctesiphon and now took

139. Proc., *Wars* 8.8.
140. Proc., *Wars* 8.9.13–30.
141. Proc., *Wars* 8.10.1–7.

advantage of a serious illness that struck the king. Khusro, however, recovered, his troops crushed the revolt, and Anoshaghzadh's eyelids were disfigured so that he could never succeed to the throne.[142] The placing of this account probably reflects when the events became known to the Romans, so that the challenge may have happened a year or two earlier. Over the winter of 550/51 negotiations for a treaty continued, with the *magister officiorum* Peter being sent to Khusro and Yazd-Gushnasp returning to Constantinople, where he accused the Romans of violating the truce because of conflicts between the Arab allies.

In 551 Bessas turned his full attention to Petra, first undermining the section of wall that Dagistheus had managed to collapse, this being one of the few stretches that was not built upon solid rock. The Persians, however, had cleverly repaired the earlier damage, constructing the stone wall on a base of long timbers that were laid on a gravel bed, so that when the Romans dug out the gravel all that happened was that the wall dropped vertically into the hole without collapsing. This demoralized the Romans, who were finding it impossible to bring their rams up the steep slopes to the walls. That problem was resolved by their Sabir allies, who constructed a special mantlet to protect the ram that was sufficiently light to be carried into place by the forty men stationed inside to swing the ram back and forth. Three of these devices were built and made progress against the stonework, with the Romans pulling out loose rocks with hooked poles. The Persians countered by placing on the wall a wooden tower they had previously constructed and hurling down sulphur and naphtha onto the mantlets; the Romans had difficulty in removing these inflammable projectiles quickly enough to prevent their rams from being destroyed.

Bessas then, though a large old man of 70, led an assault on the walls with climbing ladders and, even when he was thrown down and could not rise because of the weight of his armour, he ordered his guards to drag him back by the foot. As soon as he was set on his feet again, he returned to climb a ladder, inspiring his troops with his bravery. At this point the Persians attempted to halt the fighting to allow negotiations, but Bessas suspected this was just a ruse to allow time to repair the defences so that the assault continued. The Persians were now hit by three blows: a further part of their wall collapsed so that the Romans rushed into the breach, a small group of Armenians climbed a precipice that had been regarded as invulnerable and

---

142. Proc., *Wars* 8.10.8–21.

gained the circuit wall, and the wooden tower from which the defenders were hurling their lighted pots itself caught fire in a gust of wind and burned to death those inside it. Persian survivors abandoned the lower city seeking refuge in the citadel, while the Romans took 730 prisoners, only eighteen of whom were uninjured. The following day the 500 Persians in the citadel rejected the offer of terms and, when the Romans set fire to it, they preferred to be burned to death rather than be captured. The fall of the city revealed the great care devoted to its defence: the Romans captured a mass of weapons, so that each of their soldiers received five sets of equipment, and provisions including grain, cured meat, and beans sufficient to feed the garrison for five years. They also discovered why they had failed to cut off the water supply, since the aqueduct had been cleverly constructed with a triple line of pipes, of which the Romans had only cut the top two.[143]

Meanwhile Mihr-Meroe had been marching to relieve Petra, but on hearing of its fall he advanced into Lazica. Bessas failed to follow up his victory at Petra by taking control of the passes into the country, instead preferring to return to Armenia to exploit its riches. The passes were now seized by the Persians, who forded the river Phasis to move against Archaeopolis, the main city of Lazica which controlled its richest agricultural land, while the Laz destroyed the strategically located city of Rhodopolis, whose flat location made it impossible to defend. Mihr-Meroe first forced the Roman soldiers to abandon their camp near the mouth of the Phasis; they withdrew south of the river and destroyed the provisions they could not carry on their boats.

Back at Archaeopolis Mihr-Meroe arranged his attack on the extremely strong position.[144] He had 4,000 Sabirs in his army and he instructed them to construct the portable rams whose impact at Petra had come to his notice. He directed the Daylamite infantry – agile tough soldiers from the Elburz mountains – to attack the steepest parts of the circuit,[145] while he approached the gates with eight elephants that had accompanied his army. The assault made good progress and the city's granary was set on fire by a traitor, but the Roman commanders led a sally that disrupted Mihr-Meroe's attack and one of his elephants ran amok, causing his men to flee, with the Daylamites following when

---

143. Proc., *Wars* 8.11–12. For discussion of Procopius' presentation of Bessas, which contrasts his failures in Italy with his current heroism and determination, see Whately, 'Bessas'.
144. See Braund, *Georgia* 303–4 for a brief description and plan of the site.
145. For their fighting habit, see Agathias, *Hist.* 3.17.7–9.

they saw the panic. Persian casualties amounted to 4,000 and they lost 20,000 horses, mainly exhausted from the rigours of the long march rather than wounds. Despite this reverse, the Persians still controlled most of Lazica, especially the fertile lands, and Mihr-Meroe established himself for the winter in the district of Mocheresis, where he rebuilt the fortress of Cotaeum. This allowed him to disrupt Laz communications with their dependencies of Suania and Scymnia and prevent supplies reaching the garrison in the fortress of Uthimer.[146] The Suanians, who used to receive supplies of grain from Lazica, now joined the Persians and persuaded Deitatus, commander of Roman troops in the region, to withdraw his men; according to Menander, the grain had been halted after a disagreement between Gubazes and Martin, *MM per Armeniam*, but Persian control of access routes might also have contributed.[147]

Over winter a five-year extension to the truce in Mesopotamia was agreed to permit the resolution of disputes about Lazica and the Arabs. The cost was a further 2,000 pounds of gold, with an additional 600 pounds to cover the eighteen months that had elapsed since the end of the previous truce. Justinian's agreement to these terms was not universally popular, since he appeared to have accepted that the Romans could be presented as tributaries to Khusro and the Persians also retained control of most of Lazica.[148] Late in 551 Mihr-Meroe was able to capture Uthimer when a Laz defector persuaded the garrison that resistance was futile. This further consolidated Persian control over eastern Lazica and the Persians also dispersed the Laz and Roman troops that had gathered near the coast, forcing Gubazes to withdraw to the mountains for the winter. There, in spite of a shortage of provisions and an enticing offer from Mihr-Meroe, he continued to resist.[149]

In 552 Mihr-Meroe was reinforced by a large force of Sabirs, whose alliance Khusro had purchased with the money that Yazd-Gushnasp had brought from Justinian to pay for the truce. While Gubazes and the Romans under Martin remained in defensible locations near the coast, Mihr-Meroe attempted to capture an unnamed fortress where Gubazes'

---

146. Proc., *Wars* 8.14.
147. Menander, fr. 6.1.249–67; Braund, *Georgia* 305, notes that there were other routes into Suania, but if the normal one ran through Mocheresis the provision of grain might still have been affected.
148. Proc., *Wars* 8.15.1–20.
149. Proc., *Wars* 8.16.

sister was sheltering, then tried to approach Tzibile, and finally again moved against Archaeopolis, with no success. The Romans, however, ambushed the Persian army as it withdrew from Archaeopolis and managed to kill the leader of the Sabirs.[150] This terminates Procopius' account of events, which is continued by Agathias.[151]

We have no information about activities in 553, but in 554 Mihr-Meroe led his army towards the fort of Telephis, where Martin was blocking progress by fencing off possible routes through swampy terrain. Mihr-Meroe pretended to fall ill, which reduced the Roman efforts, and then a report of his death led them to slacken their watch and retire to more comfortable billets. This permitted the Persians to spring a surprise attack, which forced the defenders of Telephis to retire to the troops with Bessas and Justin, which were camped a kilometre back at Chrytopolia. From there the Persian advance forced them further back to the island stronghold of Nesos, at the junction of the Phasis and Doconus, over 20km from Telephis. Mihr-Meroe declined to pursue and instead reinforced his garrison at Onoguris, a Persian base near Archaeopolis, at which point he fell sick and died.[152]

At some point in 554 an unidentified group of 'barbarians' sacked the village of Diobulion in Pontus.[153] Most probably they were Tzani, who are said to have returned to their lawless ways and had been ravaging Pontus and neighbouring districts,[154] with the result that they had to be subdued again in 557/8. We are only informed about this specific raid since the village church housed an *acheiropoietos* icon, which Pseudo-Zachariah mentioned because he was discussing the better-known Camuliana image and an associated one at Caesarea in Cappadocia. After the destructive raid the villagers petitioned the emperor, who gave them permission to take their icon on a tour of cities in order to raise money for reconstruction, which they were still doing six years later.

Khusro appointed Nachwergan (a Persian title), to command in Lazica, while Gubazes complained to Justinian about the performance of the generals Bessas, Martin, and Rusticus. Justinian dismissed Bessas, but left Martin in charge in Lazica, with Justin and Buzes in support.

---

150. Proc., *Wars* 8.17.9–19.
151. Agathias, *Hist.* 2.18–4.23.
152. Agathias, *Hist.* 2.19.1–22.5.
153. Ps.-Zach., *HE* 12.1.b.
154. Agathias, *Hist.* 5.1.2.

Relations between Gubazes and the Roman commanders remained bad, and the latter sent John, brother of Rusticus, to Constantinople to complain that Gubazes was acting treacherously; Justinian sanctioned his arrest, and, when pressed by John, that he be killed if he resisted. Martin and Rusticus now summoned Gubazes to a meeting to discuss an attack on Onoguris; when Gubazes said that it was for the Romans to make good their past mistakes, John stabbed him and one of the bodyguards killed him. Justin and Buzes were also present, but not knowing about the plot, were distressed by the outcome.[155]

In the latter part of 555 the Roman commanders focused on Onoguris, but on the news that Nachwergan was marching towards Lazica and the Persians in Mocheresis were approaching to reinforce Onoguris, at the suggestion of Rusticus they sent 600 men to hinder this advance while pressing their attack with the main army. The advice of Buzes that a strong force should be deployed against the reinforcements was disregarded. The 600 Romans at first disrupted the Persian army of 3,000, but the latter regrouped on realizing how few their opponents actually were and hotly pursued the Romans back to Onoguris. Their chaotic arrival threw the main Roman army into confusion, with the cavalry at once fleeing whereas the infantry were caught at a narrow bridge over a river. Only the prompt action of Buzes, who led his men back to cover the retreat, saved them. In their flight the Romans abandoned their camp outside Archaeopolis with its considerable supplies for the Persians to loot.[156]

In the light of the murder of Gubazes as well as Roman incompetence, the Laz considered going over to the Persians again, but in the end decided to report matters to Justinian, who immediately established a judicial investigation into Gubazes' fate, led by the senator Athanasius. Rusticus and John were executed in due course, although Martin was spared. As successor to Gubazes, his son Tzath was crowned by Justinian and sent back to Lazica with Soterichus, who was also entrusted with money for the Misimians, neighbours of the Laz and their subjects. There a misunderstanding led to an altercation in which Misimian delegates were whipped; in retaliation they attacked Soterichus' camp by night and killed most of those inside. As a result, the Misimians felt they had to side with the Persians for protection.

155. Agathias, *Hist.* 3.2.1–3.7.
156. Agathias, *Hist.* 5.6–8.1.

In early 556 Nachwergan was advancing on Nesos with an army said to number 60,000. Martin and Justin had stationed 2,000 Sabir infantry on the plain of Archaeopolis to harass his approach, while Nachwergan deputed 3,000 Daylamites to deal with them. Thanks to a last-minute warning from a Laz captive who escaped the Daylamites, the unprepared Sabir were roused from their beds; slipping out of their camp, which they left open, they concealed themselves nearby so that they could surprise the Daylamites when they entered to attack the huts. The result was a massacre, which was compounded when Babas, a Roman commander who happened to be in Archaeopolis, rushed out to join the pursuit.[157] After failing to persuade Martin to withdraw from Nesos, Nachwergan slipped his army across the Phasis on a pontoon bridge constructed on light boats that he had transported with the army, in order to march on the city of Phasis that was located on the coast near the river mouth.

It took Martin some time to appreciate that the Persians had moved on and when he followed them downstream in his ships he found that the Persians had blocked the river with boats and timbers, backed up by their elephants. The Romans had to abandon the river to reach Phasis by land, where they managed to arrive in time to organize the defences. The walls were wooden and in poor condition, so they were bolstered with a moat filled with stakes and an external rampart, while the different commanders were assigned specific sectors. Martin and Justin held the highest points; Angilas commanded a contingent of Berbers, Theodore, the heavy-infantry Tzani; Philomathius led Isaurian slingers and javelin-men; Lombards and Heruls were under Gibrus, and units from the army of Oriens under Valerian. Ships in the harbour had boats filled with archers and slingers hoisted to their mastheads, which overtopped the walls, and other boats were stationed up the river, while Huns in ten skiffs patrolled further upstream to prevent the Persians from surprising them. When Nachwergan arrived, he prosecuted the siege energetically, filling in the moat. An ill-advised Roman sally failed to disrupt proceedings, though the troops managed to force their way back inside the walls.[158]

At this point, Agathias' narrative becomes implausible. He first has Martin assembling his troops for them to witness the arrival of a messenger, who had been instructed to appear as if from a distance to

---

157. Agathias, *Hist.* 3.17.3–18.11.
158. Agathias, *Hist.* 3.19.1–23.5.

announce the approach of a relief army. Martin feigned annoyance at this, asserting that he wanted his own troops to have the glory and booty of defeating the Persians themselves. News of the alleged relief army reached the Persians who sent men to block its advance. Then Justin is said to have been moved by divine inspiration to take the best of his own and Martin's soldiers plus 5,000 cavalry, because he wanted to go to a famous Christian site in the vicinity; he apparently left the city without being seen by the Persians or appreciating that the Persians were about to attack. Only on returning from his prayers did Justin realize what was happening, at which point he attributed his happy absence from the city to divine providence and charged.[159]

The Persians attacked fiercely, but the Roman resistance was equally robust, with effective fire from their catapults and the men at the ships' masts as well as javelinmen and slingers on the ramparts, while large stones were rolled down to crush the mantlets. The cacophony was intense when Justin's men charged, causing the Persians opposite them to retreat in confusion. This led the Daylamites attacking the middle of the wall to turn around to come to their assistance, but the neighbouring Persians thought they were deserting and so fled, pursued by Romans. The right wing of the Persian attack was still in good order. Here their elephants both protected the Persian formations and disrupted the Roman infantry until one of Martin's *bucellarii*, Ognaris by name, drove his spear into an elephant's face, just near the eye. The wounded animal went beserk, trampling Persian soldiers and spreading confusion so that Nachwergan signalled the retreat.

When the Romans returned to Phasis they burned the Persian siege equipment, but the smoke from this deceived the Persian camp-followers who had been cutting down trees nearby. Nachwergan had ordered them to rush to Phasis as soon as they saw smoke to help spread destruction, so that these too perished in large numbers when they obeyed these instructions. The victory was complete and the booty immense. Nachwergan withdrew to Mocheresis under cover of a rearguard of Daylamites; there he left a cavalry force under Wahriz while he retired to Iberia for the winter.[160]

Agathias now recounts the judicial investigation of Gubazes' murder, which resulted in the condemnation of Rusticus and John, who were

---

159. Agathias, *Hist.* 3.23.3–24.9; 25.8–9. For discussion of this implausible account, see Cameron, *Agathias* 46–8, who rightly sees it as an investigation of the effects of misinformation.
160. Agathias, *Hist.* 25.5.1–28.10.

publicly executed. During the winter some leading Misimians approached Nachwergan in Iberia for assistance, since they expected the Romans to avenge the death of Soterichus. In spring 556 a force of 4,000, half of them Tzani, was dispatched to discipline the Misimians, but they were held up in the territory of the Apsili, where a strong Persian force had assembled. Apart from eliminating a detached group of 500 Sabirs, there was little action to report. In Lazica, the Romans recovered Rhodopolis thanks to the Hun Elminzur, who managed to enter the defences while the Persian soldiers were all outside the walls. As winter approached the Persian troops among the Misimians withdrew to Iberia, which allowed the Romans to advance. The Romans tried to come to an agreement with the Misimians, using some Apsili as intermediaries, but these were slaughtered. The Romans forced the passage into Misimian territory, since the latter had failed to protect a key hill that dominated the route, and were then able to deploy on the plains that were suitable for cavalry. The Misimians congregated in Tzakher, their strongest fortress, which the Romans invested, though not sufficiently closely until Martin sent John Dacnas to command. The defenders had to descend from their heights to collect water and this spelled their downfall.

Illus, one of the Isaurians, discovered their route and observed their regular procedure, so that he was then able to lead Roman troops up the mountain to surprise the few sleepy guards on the gate, admittedly after a dropped shield almost revealed their presence; they then set about massacring those inside the walls. At daybreak a sudden attack by 500 Misimians surprised the Romans and forced them back down the mountain, after which John decided to resort to attacking with rams, siege engines, and missiles. Stiff resistance was being overcome when the Misimians approached John to beg for forgiveness, since they had already suffered severe punishment for their misdeeds. John was keen to avoid having to continue campaigning in difficult terrain as winter deepened and so accepted, recovering the money that Soterichus had brought with him and taking hostages. The operation had, apparently cost only thirty Roman lives.[161]

During the lull in hostilities, Justinian deposed Martin as *MM per Armeniam* and replaced him in 557 with his nephew, Justin. His tenure of office was marred by the depredations of one of his entourage who extorted supplies and money, commandeering some merchant ships so that he could dispose of the local agricultural produce for personal

---

161. Agathias, *Hist.* 4.15.6–20.9.

profit. Nachwergan made no move to resume fighting but was recalled by Khusro, who inflicted a traditional punishment for cowardice, since he had fled the battle at Phasis, namely being flayed alive for his skin to be inflated and hung from a pole.[162]

Peace

After seventeen years of fighting the final acts of hostilities had occurred. A truce was agreed in order to permit substantive negotiations for peace, which was to cover the whole of the frontier, at last including Lazica where each side was to retain what it currently held, since Khusro accepted that the difficulties of supplying his forces in the region thwarted effective action.[163] In 558 Theodore took advantage of the truce to campaign south from Lazica against the Tzani, whose return to ravaging their neighbours had been causing problems. Theodore fortified a camp near Theodorias, itself located near Rhizaeum (Rize), from where he issued a call to his fellow countrymen to return to their allegiance. Only a few responded and the rest attacked the camp with initial success, until Theodore managed to slip some troops behind them to take them by surprise. The Tzani suffered 2,000 casualties and as part of the pacification Justinian instructed Theodore to impose an annual tribute.[164] This concludes Agathias' narrative, but fortunately the fragments of Menander cover the subsequent diplomacy at length.

Fragment 6 of Menander preserves an extremely detailed account of the negotiations between the *magister officiorum* Peter the Patrician and Yazd-Gushnasp, the Zikh, which produced the Fifty-Year Peace of 561/2. The Persians preferred a long peace with an annual gold payment, of which thirty or forty years should be paid upfront, whereas the Romans wanted a short peace with no payments. Eventually agreement was reached at fifty years with an annual payment of 30,000 *solidi* (just over 400 pounds), of which the first seven years would be paid at once, with a further three years delivered in year seven. The terms are listed in full:[165]

---

162. Agathias, *Hist.* 4.24.1–25.3.
163. Agathias, *Hist.* 4.30.7–10; Menander fr.2.1–12.
164. Agathias, *Hist.* 5.1.1–2.2.
165. Menander fr.6.1.314–93.

1. The Persians would not permit barbarians to pass through Tzon or the Caspian Gates to attack the Romans and the Romans would not campaign against the Persians there or elsewhere on the frontier.
2. Both sets of Arab allies would respect the terms and not launch attacks.
3. Merchants of both sides would conduct their business through the established trading posts.
4. Ambassadors using the public post to convey messages should receive proper respect; they would not be hindered when trading goods or subjected to taxes.
5. Arab and other foreign traders must pass through Nisibis and Dara and not cross into foreign territory without official permission; any misdemeanours would result in them being hunted down and handed over, together with their goods.
6. Any defectors during the war should be permitted to return home, if they wished; any future defectors during the peace to be returned, forcibly if necessary.
7. Those alleging harm from a member of the other state must settle the matter fairly, meeting at the border in person or through representatives.
8. The Persians will cease to complain about Dara. Henceforth neither state will fortify a place near the frontier.
9. The forces of the states will not attack any people or territory subject to the other.
10. A large force will not be stationed at Dara and the *MM per Orientem* will not have his headquarters there.
11. If a city damages the property of a city in the other state, the offence will be resolved and damages agreed by judges at the frontier; if that failed, the matter will be referred to the *MM*, and if he did not resolve it to the sovereign.

There followed prayers to God to support those keeping the peace and curses on those wanting to alter its terms, together with confirmation that the treaty was to last for fifty years of 365 days. It was agreed that the Christians in Persia would have freedom to worship and bury their dead. Sealed originals of the terms and unsealed translations were exchanged, after which the Zikh returned to Persia. Peter first celebrated Christmas and Epiphany in Roman territory before going to meet Khusro in Beth Aramaye to discuss the status of Suania, which remained disputed after its switch to Persian allegiance in 551, and also to listen to a complaint from Khusro that 'Amr (Ambros), son of al-Mundhir and leader of the Lakhmids, had not received any particular advantage. These issues would remain unresolved to undermine mutual confidence. Following the treaty, in November 563 the Jafnid Harith visited Constantinople to discuss with Justinian which of his sons should succeed him as leader of the federation, as well as raids into Jafnid territory by the Lakhmid 'Amr;[166] we know nothing more about these raids, which would appear to be violations of the second clause of the Fifty-Year Peace.

Thus, almost twenty-two years after Khusro's first invasions shattered the Endless Peace, the two empires had finally reached a new agreement. Justinian clearly did not want the war, which was sprung upon him while significant numbers of eastern troops were still engaged in Italy, and he had to pursue it in spite of the problems caused shortly after its outbreak by the bubonic plague and the resurgence of fighting in both Africa, where the Berbers had to be subjugated, and Italy where Totila revitalized the Gothic war effort. In spite of the massive losses during the campaign of 540, when the payments made by individual cities amounted to 400 pounds of gold and 6,000 of silver, quite apart from the much richer booty that Khusro secured at Antioch and Apamea as well as invaluable material possessions, Justinian had managed to fight the Persians to a standstill in Upper Mesopotamia, where Edessa and Dara both held firm against determined sieges. In the north unrest caused by the consolidation of Roman rule in Armenia and Tzanica had been quelled, while in Transcaucasia Persian efforts to secure a foothold on the Black Sea had been thwarted and Rome re-established authority over most of the Christian peoples there. Khusro had obviously benefited from the payments for the fixed-term truces, but some of this money had just been recycled to allow him to continue fighting. His failure to capture Dara meant that it was not possible for him to seize Roman territory in the Levant. In the end the Persians had been forced to accept the existence of Dara and concede Lazica and adjacent territories to the Romans. There was no clear victor, but problems remained to destabilize the peace when Justin II adopted a more bellicose approach to international dealings.

---

166. Theophanes 240.13–17 = Malalas 18.148.

Chapter 6

The Reconquest of Africa

The eastern empire had been interested in the Vandal occupation of Africa from its very earliest days, as is narrated by Procopius in the opening chapters of his account of the Vandal War. After a geographical introduction, these provide a summary of the decline of the western empire that is largely drawn from the lost account by Priscus of Panium. The Vandals, who comprised a coalition of Vandals and Alans as well as smaller units picked up on their bloody journey from the Rhine, had crossed from Spain into Africa under their leader Geiseric in May 429. Victor of Vita records the story that, when crossing from Spain, Geiseric had gathered his followers, men, women, and children, into seventy groups of 1,000. It was in Victor's interest to magnify the power of the Vandals, so the total number is likely to have been somewhat lower than 70,000. How many fighting men this represented is uncertain, but an educated guess of about 15,000 is plausible, with the remaining numbers made up by their families, servants, and slaves.[1]

In 430 they defeated the general Boniface, whom they proceeded to besiege in Hippo Regius. When the *magister militum* Aspar, the most powerful man in the eastern empire, led an army to rescue Boniface in 431, his arrival raised the siege but he was defeated and numerous captives taken, including the future emperor Marcian, Aspar's *domesticus*. Aspar remained in Africa until 434, probably taking part in the negotiations that in 435 ceded Mauretania and western Numidia to the Vandals. This arrangement did not last and by the end of the decade the Vandals had taken Carthage and controlled North Africa as far as the Libyan Pentapolis. The Vandals were largely settled on confiscated Roman estates in the province of Proconsularis, closest to the capital at Carthage, with their leader Geiseric's family and senior officers receiving the largest grants. Elsewhere, in Byzacena and Numidia there was probably much less change

---

1. For discussion, see Heather, *Empires* 174–7.

to land ownership; even in Proconsularis the majority of the population will have remained in place, with one group of Roman rentier landlords being replaced by Vandal warriors. The role of Proconsularis as the city of Rome's supplier of the basic staples of grain, wine, and oil, ceased, although other African provinces may have continued to export their agricultural surpluses. One significant change was in the religious sphere. The Vandals had been converted to the Homoian Christianity of mid-fourth century emperors, which held that God the Father and God the Son were 'like' or 'similar to' each other, rather than of the same substance as determined at Nicaea.

In 468 Emperor Leo co-ordinated an attack on the Vandals, whose ravaging had extended to Illyricum and the Peloponnese. Heraclius was sent by land to capture the cities of Tripolis, Marcellinus sailed from Dalmatia to recover Sardinia, and a massive naval expedition from Constantinople under the command of Basiliscus, the emperor's brother-in-law, headed for Carthage. The first two elements were successful, but on reaching Africa Basiliscus did not immediately attack Carthage, instead stationing his fleet down the coast, perhaps because he believed that Geiseric was prepared to negotiate. This delay led to a catastrophe, for which Basiliscus was subsequently accused of accepting a bribe. Geiseric waited for a favourable wind and then launched fire ships at the crowded eastern fleet, causing chaos and wreaking immense destruction. Back in the capital Basiliscus took refuge in S. Sophia until his sister, the empress Verina, interceded to secure his pardon. The fiasco is said to have cost the East 130,000 pounds of gold, information that can be traced back to the historian Priscus; although other figures are given, the loss was certainly immense.[2]

Geiseric died in 477, having recently made peace with Emperor Zeno, to be succeeded by his eldest son, Huneric, who continued his father's persecution of Nicene Christians, especially after a doctrinal conference at Carthage in 484.[3] Succession in the Vandal kingdom was to the eldest male in the ruling family rather than necessarily to the eldest son, so that Huneric was succeeded by his nephew Gunthamund, who relaxed the persecution

---

2. Proc., *Wars* 3.6.2. The historian Candidus (fr.2) records 64,000 pounds of gold, 700,000 pounds of silver (equivalent to about 30,000 pounds of gold), plus funds from confiscations and contributions from the new western emperor Anthemius, while John Lydus reports 65,000 pounds of gold and 700,000 of silver. The total was clearly equivalent to well over 100,000 pounds of gold. For discussion, see Mango and Scott, *Theophanes* 181 n.3.
3. Proc., *Wars* 3.7.26; Malchus fr.13.

to some extent. His successor, his brother Thrasamund, who ruled from 496 to 523, adapted this more eirenic approach, trying to win over the pro-Nicene Roman Christians with gifts, judicial decisions, and official posts rather than violence.[4] Thrasamund, however, still closed Nicene churches, exiled bishops to Sardinia, and oversaw the evolution of an African Homoian church.[5] The persecution of orthodox Catholics is chronicled by Victor of Vita in a work that, naturally, presents the impact of the Vandals on the African provinces and the severity of their oppression in the worst possible light, including the application of the emotive term 'Arian' to the Homoian overlords.[6]

Under Zeno and Anastasius the East did not attempt to intervene again in Africa: the Vandals seem to have reduced their raids into the eastern Mediterranean, perhaps because they had to deal with neighbouring Berber tribes. The end of the western empire in 476 meant there was no urgent need to prop up a co-ruler. The East had its own problems, internal and in the Balkans under Zeno, and in Isauria and on the eastern frontier under Anastasius. The Acacian Schism divided Rome and Constantinople, so that successive popes were unlikely to appeal for help from rulers they regarded as heretics. Finally, the massive losses incurred in 468 both had to be rebuilt and acted as warning against a renewed attempt at reconquest.

The accession of Justin in 518 changed matters. Eastern finances had been restored under Anastasius, who bequeathed a useful surplus in the treasury to his successor. Even more importantly the efforts of Justin and Justinian, as committed Chalcedonians, to repair relations with the papacy meant that they were far more interested in western church business than their two predecessors, and that western clergy were more inclined to look to Constantinople for help. Victims of persecution were available in Constantinople to publicize the fate of orthodox African Christians, most famously some whose tongues had been cut out under Huneric but who still retained the power of speech, at least until two of them decided to visit prostitutes and lost that ability; Procopius states that they were still in the city in his time.[7] The accession of Hilderic, son of Huneric and cousin of Thrasamund, in 523 prevented action. He was half-Roman,

4. Proc., *Wars* 3.8.5–8.
5. For discussion of the religious trajectory of Vandal rule, see Merrills & Miles, *Vandals* ch.7; detailed analysis in Whelan, *Being Christian*.
6. Victor of Vita, *Historia Persecutionis*; see Whelan, *Being Christian*, esp. ch. 2 and 5.
7. Proc., *Wars* 3.8.4.

being the son of Eudocia, hence grandson of Emperor Valentinian III, and established good relations with Justinian while distancing himself from the Ostrogoths. He imprisoned Amalafrida, Thrasamund's widow and sister of the Ostrogothic king Theoderic, and killed her Gothic retinue for plotting against the Vandals. After Hilderic was defeated by the Berbers, however, he was overthrown in 530 by Gelimer, an experienced soldier who was also next in line to the throne. Gelimer attempted to establish good relations with Justinian, but to no avail: Justinian criticized his coup, demanded that Hilderic and two of his nephews, the general Hoamer and Euagees, be sent to Constantinople, and advised the Ostrogothic king Athalaric not to recognize him.[8] Gelimer refused to be overawed and instead had Hoamer blinded.

Justinian was enraged and so, by the end of 530, the stage was set for possible action in the west, as soon as affairs in the East permitted. The agreement of the Endless Peace with Persia in spring 532 freed up military resources, while the need for a signal triumph had been reinforced by the crisis of the Nika Riot in January 532. The public demonstration of unpopularity and the support given to a rival from the family of Anastasius might be countered if there was a clear victory over enemies of faith and empire, in a way that the Persian War – for all the celebration of the peace – had failed to deliver.[9] The crucial thing now was to secure the support of his leading officials, the people whose commitment to the project would be needed to ensure that the complex preparations were undertaken effectively.

The unfortunate precedent of Basiliscus' disaster weighed heavily with commanders who might have to lead the expedition, while troops who had recently returned from the East were not enthusiastic about another distant deployment, especially one by sea. However, the strongest opposition came from the praetorian prefect, John the Cappadocian, who would have responsibility for financing the expedition. These views had an effect on Justinian, but his growing caution was then overturned by an unnamed eastern bishop, who informed him that he should not be afraid of protecting the Christians in Africa from their tyrannical rulers, since God had informed him in a dream that he would fight alongside and

8. Proc., *Wars* 3.9.
9. Cf. Brown, *World* 152, who suggests that 'public opinion was mobilized in a crusade against the heretical Arians'.

Head of Justinian from San Vitale. (*Petar Milošević, CC BY-SA 4.0 via Wikimedia Commons*)

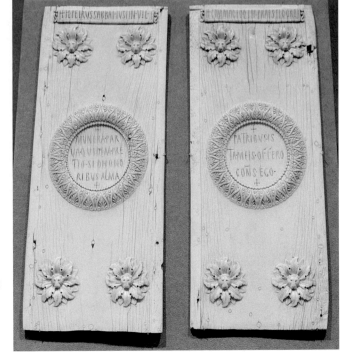

Justinian's full name at the top of exterior leaves of consular diptych; the message in the central roundels reads 'As consul I offer to my fathers (i.e. senators) these presents, small in value but full of honour'. (*By Marie-Lan Nguyen (2011), CC BY 2.5, https://commons. wikimedia.org/w/index. php?curid=127783760*)

Justinian panel from San Vitale. (*Roger Culos – Own work, CC BY-SA 3.0, commons.wikimedia.org/w/index.php?curid=44352375*)

Theodora panel from San Vitale. (*By Roger Culos – Own work, CC BY-SA 3.0, commons.wikimedia.org/w/index.php?curid=44352375*)

Above: Obelisk of Theodosius in Hippodrome, emperor flanked by court, presenting wreath to victor. (*Author*)

Right: Ivory plaque, known as the Barberini Ivory, depicting a victorious emperor, quite possibly Justinian, surrounded by images of triumph. (*Public domain*)

S. Sophia. (*By Arild Vågen - Own work, CC BY-SA 3.0, commons.wikimedia.org/w/index.php?curid=24932378*)

Justinian's Bridge over the Sangarius. (*Author*)

Obverse: Facing bust of Justinian, wearing cuirass with three pellets on breast and plumed helmet with pendilia, r. hand holding *globus cruciger*, shield on l. shoulder. Reverse: Victoria standing facing, holding long cross in r. hand and *globus cruciger* in l. hand. Star in r. of field. (*The Barber Institute of Fine Arts*)

Obelisk of Theodosius in Hippodrome, emperor, senators, and guards. (*Author*)

View of Dara from the south. (*Author*)

View of Dara from site of battle, with south Watergate in centre. (*Author*)

Above: Dara,
towers in north-
east wall from
north Watergate.
(*Author*)

Right: Victory
Medallion from
reconquest of
Africa. (*Public
domain*)

Obelisk of
Theodosius in
Hippodrome,
conquered
enemies present
tribute. (*Author*)

Rome: Porta Appia. (*Author*)

Watercolour (*circa* 1700) attributed to Lambert de Bos showing the main monuments on the Spina of the Hippodrome, with S. Sophia beyond its east end. (*Public domain*)

deliver victory. This restored Justinian's commitment to the venture. It is the first in a series of divine interventions and accurate prophecies that decorate Procopius' narrative of Belisarius' campaign. They all contribute to the impression that this was a victory in which divine favour and good fortune contributed at least as much to Roman success as the general's strong leadership and the quality of his troops.[10]

Preparations and Voyage

In the same way as Basiliscus' expedition had been part of a three-pronged move against the Vandals, so Belisarius' expedition was accompanied by developments in Tripolitania and Sardinia. In the former a local leader, Pudentius, instigated a revolt and transferred allegiance to Justinian, who sent some troops under Tattimuth to support the switch. Gelimer was not in a position to react since he was distracted by events in Sardinia, which he had entrusted to a loyal Goth called Goda. Goda, however, took the opportunity to cease paying tribute to Gelimer and establish his own rule over the island. Apparently, when he became aware of Justinian's preparations for intervention in the west, Goda wrote to the emperor asking for military support for his independence. This explanation for Goda's approach does not quite ring true. Gelimer in Africa was not aware of Justinian's plans in advance of Belisarius' arrival, so it is unclear how a subordinate in Sardinia knew about them, unless he had already been approached by an envoy from the east. That raises the possibility that Justinian had encouraged Goda's rebellion as a means of distracting Gelimer and dividing his forces. Whatever the reality, when Justinian sent Eulogius as envoy with the promise of an alliance and a general to guard the island, Goda rejected the offer on the grounds that he wanted soldiers but not a general;[11] there was clearly a danger that any general would supplant him as local leader.

In the harbours of Constantinople the armada for Africa was assembled, 500 ships with capacities ranging from 3,000 to 50,000 *medimnoi* (roughly 150 to 2,500 tonnes), crewed by 30,000 sailors from Egypt and Ionia, to be escorted by 92 dromons (galleys) whose rowers included 2,000 men who could also fight. The transports carried 10,000

---

10. Scott, 'Classical Tradition' 73–4 proposes that Procopius was indirectly criticizing Justinian through the prudent arguments attributed to John the Cappadocian; cf. also Gillett, *Envoys* 263. However, the demonstration of divine support outweighs the negatives.
11. Proc., *Wars* 3.10.18–34.

infantry and 5,000 cavalry drawn from the *comitatenses* and *foederati* (probably 1,500 and 3,500 respectively), plus a further 1,000 non-Roman troops led by their fellow tribesmen, 400 Heruls under Pharas and 600 Huns under Sinnion and Balas. In addition the expedition included an unknown number of *bucellarii*. Specific figures of 300 are provided for the guards led by John the Armenian and 800 by Uliaris, but we do not know how many Belisarius had overall or what retinues accompanied the other commanders.[12] The *foederati* were commanded by Dorotheus, *MM per Armeniam*, and the eunuch Solomon, Belisarius' *domesticus*. The overall leader of the infantry was John of Dyrrachium, with Theodore Cteanus, Terentius, Zaïdos, Marcian, and Sarapis under him. The cavalry were led by two men from Belisarius' household, Rufinus and Aïgan, alongside Barbatus and Pappus. Other commanders to be named are Cyprian, Valerian, Martin, Althias, John, Marcellus, and Cyril, the last being entrusted with 400 soldiers to support Goda on Sardinia. Belisarius was given supreme authority over the expedition with the exceptional title of *strategos autokrator* and written confirmation from the emperor that his actions had the force of imperial decisions, with the former praetorian prefect of the East, Archelaus, holding a supernumerary prefecture to oversee the expedition's logistics.[13]

Gelimer meanwhile had appointed his brother Tzazon to recover Sardinia, allocating him 5,000 troops and 120 of his best ships. The resources available to Gelimer are unknown, but it is difficult to believe that the numbers of Vandal warriors had not increased quite significantly from the 15,000 who had arrived with Geiseric three generations earlier: the African provinces were prosperous and the Vandals enjoyed life as rentier landlords. A reasonable guess is that Gelimer could command 20,000 mounted Vandal warriors, possibly a few more, plus any Berber support he could obtain. These troops were, however, distributed across the kingdom and so were not immediately available to him.

The expedition's voyage had some eventful moments. Justinian had dispatched an advance party under Valerian and Martin to await Belisarius in the Peloponnese, but shortly after their departure had thought of further orders he wanted to impart; he first summoned them, then thought

---

12. Proc., *Wars* 3.7.1; 19.23. John's and Uliaris' contingents were both drawn from Belisarius' retinue; for the order of battle, see Pringle, *Defence* 51.
13. Proc., *Wars* 3.11.1–21.

better of this interruption to their progress and so countermanded his first instruction by ordering them not to return. This seemed a bad omen, even an accidental curse upon the voyage, which Procopius interprets as being turned aside from Valerian and Martin onto one of the latter's retainers, Stotzas, the future leader of a mutiny who perished in Africa. The main armada under Belisarius, accompanied by his wife Antonina, left Constantinople after being blessed by the Patriarch Epiphanius as it was anchored off the palace, where a recently-baptized Christian was placed on board. Procopius also records a dream that he had, which appeared to predict a successful outcome for the campaign and assuaged his previous worries.[14] After putting in at Heraclea on the Sea of Marmara, the fleet then anchored off Abydus in the Hellespont. There Belisarius had two Huns impaled for killing one of their compatriots after some drunken mockery. This severity offended the Huns, who complained that they had not joined up to be subject to Roman discipline, and they were supported by Roman soldiers who wanted lenience for any future misdeeds, but Belisarius addressed his troops to explain the overriding importance of justice since it is God who decides the outcome of any war. This calmed the unrest.[15]

To keep the fleet together on the voyage Belisarius distinguished the three ships of his command by painting red the upper third of their sails from one corner, presumably in a triangle, and hanging lights from poles in their prow. At the southern tips of the Peloponnese they were fortunate to have calm weather at Cape Malea, since a wind could have caused severe damage to the congested fleet at anchor, and rounded the equally dangerous Cape Taenarum before putting in at Methone on the south-west coast. There over 500 men perished from eating *bucellatum* which had turned mouldy as a result of not being properly fired: this had happened because John the Cappadocian had cooked the dough in the furnaces used to heat the Baths of Achilles. Procopius says that this was a money-saving device, so that John did not have to pay the city's bakers so much or accept the loss of 20 per cent of the weight of the bread, which was the consequence of a thorough double-baking. These accusations may be true, but John might equally have been struggling to produce

---

14. Proc., *Wars* 3.11.22–12.5.
15. Proc., *Wars* 3.12.6–22.

enough *bucellatum* for an expedition of over 50,000 men in a relatively short time and so had to resort to unusual expedients.

From Methone the fleet sailed via Zacynthus, where it took on supplies of water for crossing the Adriatic, and on the sixteenth day touched land in Sicily near Mount Etna. The lightness of the winds had delayed the crossing, with the result that the water supply for most of the fleet had been spoiled. Antonina, however, had managed to preserve her husband's supplies by burying the glass water jars in sand in the hold, away from the sun.[16] Cyril and his 400 men had presumably sailed for Sardinia from Methone.

Once on Sicily Belisarius was uncertain about how best to proceed, allegedly not being sure about the strength and military capacity of the Vandals or what base they would have. It might be thought that such matters would have been investigated before departure, since there were numerous possible sources of information on the Vandals. The main concern might have been the danger that the eastern fleet would be challenged at sea, as the soldiers feared, before they could establish themselves on land: the hundreds of transport ships would be vulnerable and the thousands of horses an encumbrance rather than an advantage. Procopius was therefore sent ahead to Syracuse, on the pretence of purchasing supplies, since the Ostrogothic queen, Amalasuentha, had agreed with Justinian that a market would be provided, but really to see what he could learn about the Vandal plans, whether they were preparing to ambush the fleet as it crossed from Sicily, and where Belisarius might establish the expedition on arrival in Africa.

By chance Procopius met a childhood friend from Caesarea, who was now based in Syracuse for his shipping interests. One of his men had just returned from Carthage and was able to confirm that the Vandals had not yet heard about Belisarius' approach, so that there would be no ambush, that many Vandals had been dispatched to Sardinia to confront Goda, and that Gelimer had so little concern about his coastline that he was staying at a place called Hermione, four days' journey from the sea. Procopius kidnapped the servant to meet Belisarius at Caucana, almost 30km away, promising to return him to his bemused master. There he found the army mourning the death of Dorotheus, but his news about the Vandals restored spirits and the fleet sailed via Malta and Gozo to reach land in September at Caput Vada, five days' rapid travel from Carthage.[17]

---

16. Proc., *Wars* 3.13.
17. Proc., *Wars* 3.14.

Defeat of Gelimer

Once on land Belisarius held a council of war with his commanders. Archelaus spoke in favour of a direct assault by sea on Carthage because of the dangers of their current exposed anchorage and the lack of fortified bases on land since the Vandals had slighted the defences of all cities. Belisarius countered by reminding everyone that the main fear of the soldiers had been meeting the Vandal fleet before they could disembark, so that the best course of action was to unload men and horses and fortify a base where they had landed. This approach was adopted and while digging the trench for the camp a copious spring of water was discovered, which was taken as a good omen for the future. On the next day Belisarius punished some soldiers, who had taken produce from nearby fields, reminding the army that they had come to liberate the Libyans. He then sent his bodyguard Boriades with some of his *bucellarii* to see if they could occupy the nearby city of Syllectum, underlining the importance of demonstrating that they had come to benefit the locals, not to harm them. This initiative was successful and Belisarius was further strengthened by the defection of the man responsible for the public post in Africa, who handed over all the kingdom's horses. A captured official messenger, a *veredarius*, was entrusted with a message from Justinian to the Vandal magistrates at Carthage that proclaimed that war was not being waged against the Vandals but only against the tyrant Gelimer; the messenger found the contents too dangerous to be made public.[18]

Belisarius now advanced on Carthage, taking careful precautions against surprise attacks from Gelimer and others who would be approaching from the south-west or north. He therefore picked out 300 of his *bucellarii* under the command of his *optio*, the Armenian John, with orders to lead the march about 4km ahead of the main body, while the Huns were stationed the same distance inland and instructed to keep pace. Belisarius brought up the rear with his best soldiers, an indication that he expected the main threat to come from Gelimer in the south. The fleet was to travel up the coast, also keeping abreast, using either their main sails or the smaller *dolones* depending on the wind, or rowing when necessary. In this way he advanced about 17km each day, past Syllectum, Leptis Minus (Lamta), and Hadrumetum (Sousse), spending each night at a city or in a secure encampment, until he reached Grasse, about 74km south of Carthage, where Gelimer had a very fruitful estate. Gelimer meanwhile was

---

18. Proc., *Wars* 3.15–16.

making his own preparations, ordering his brother Ammatas at Carthage to kill Hilderic and other prisoners, then gather the Vandals in the capital and prepare to confront the invasion at the suburb of Ad Decimum, where the road narrowed about 15km south of the capital.[19] As for Belisarius, he knew that the Vandals were approaching, since scouting parties from the two forces had clashed, but he now had to part company with the fleet, which rounded the projecting Cap Bon while the army approached Ad Decimum after four days' march.[20]

Gelimer planned a three-pronged ambuscade, allocating his nephew Gibamund 2,000 men to advance ahead of his main force and somewhat to the west, while Ammatas from the north was to block the Roman advance with the Vandals in Carthage and Gelimer closed in from the southwest. Co-ordination was crucial and here the plan failed, since Ammatas arrived at Ad Decimum at midday, earlier than specified, and with relatively few men since he had instructed the Vandals in Carthage to proceed to Ad Decimum as quickly as possible but not in a single body. As a result Ammatas clashed with Belisarius' advance and was slain; his death put his men to flight and they caught up the Vandals, who were advancing from Carthage in disorganized groups of twenty to thirty men, so that John's 300 guards drove them all back to the gates of Carthage with heavy losses. Gibamund meanwhile had reached Pedion Halon, the Plain of Salt (modern Séjoumi), just over 8km from Ad Decimum, where he was confronted by Belisarius' Huns, whose charge easily broke the Vandal formation.

Belisarius was still ignorant of these developments and so fortified a camp for the infantry and baggage 7km from Ad Decimum, so that he could test the Vandals' strength with his cavalry. He therefore sent the *foederati* ahead, following with the remaining cavalry and his own guards. The *foederati* reached Ad Decimum, where locals informed them about events, but they had to confront Gelimer, whose approach from the southwest was announced by a dust cloud. Gelimer, too, knew nothing of what had happened since hills screened both Gibamund's defeat to the north and the Roman camp to the southeast. In a tussle for control of a strategic hill his Vandals routed the *foederati*, who fell back in fear towards

---

19. Pringle, *Defence* 19, proposed that Ad Decimum should be located on the road south from Carthage to Thebeste, roughly on the site of the modern city of Tunis, which is situated between the Lake of Tunis and the salt lake of Séjoumi.
20. Proc., *Wars* 3.17.

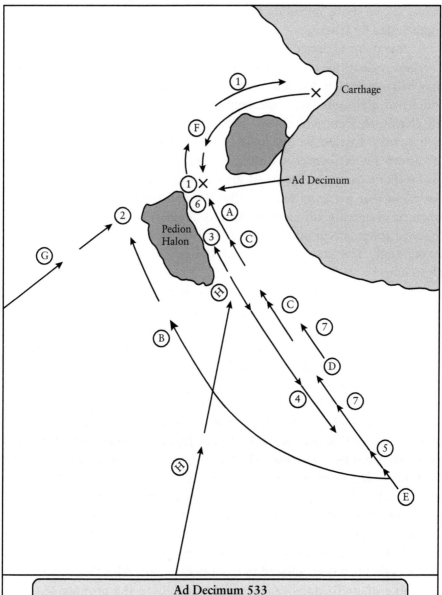

Ad Decimum 533

Dispositions
A = John and advance guard
B = Hunnic flank guard
C = *foederati*
D = Uliaris and 800 guards
E = Belisarius and main Roman army
F = Ammatas and troops from Carthage
G = Gibamund and 2,000 advance guard
H = Gelimer and main Vandal army

Phases
1 = John kills Ammatas and drives Vandals
    back to Carthage
2 = Huns defeat Gibamund
3 = Belisarius sends *foederati* ahead
4 = Gelimer routs *foederati*, whose flight
    disrupts Uliaris' guardsmen
5 = Belisarius fortifies camp
6 = Gelimer stops to mourn Ammatas' death
7 = Belisarius advances to Ad Decimum and
    routs Vandals

Belisarius, en route spreading their confusion to 800 of Belisarius' guards commanded by Uliaris.

At this point Gelimer had the opportunity either to continue north to Carthage, where he could have annihilated John's advance guard, since they had scattered to loot the Vandal corpses, and even destroyed the fleet which had approached too close, contrary to Belisarius' orders, or to pursue the fleeing *foederati* and engage Belisarius before he could restore order in his ranks. Instead he did none of these, but threw away the prospect of victory for reasons that Procopius could not comprehend: on seeing his brother's corpse he mourned his loss and attended to the burial, with the result that his army fell into disorder and could not resist Belisarius when he eventually advanced to Ad Decimum. The Vandals fled west on the road towards Numidia, suffering further losses until the battle ended at nightfall. The scattered units of Belisarius' army regrouped at Ad Decimum.[21]

The Roman inhabitants of Carthage had prepared to welcome the invaders that night, with gates open, lights burning, and the chains that closed the Mandracium harbour removed, while the remaining Vandals sought refuge as suppliants. Belisarius, however, paused since he feared ambushes, while the fleet found shelter from an approaching storm at Stagnum, a harbour about 8km south of Carthage, although one officer sailed into the Mandracium where he pillaged the property of merchants located there. Gelimer had imprisoned a number of eastern merchants, on the grounds that they had encouraged Justinian to intervene, but these were now freed by their jailer. On the morrow Belisarius disembarked the fleet, reminded everyone that there should be no looting since they were liberating the Roman population, and then marched into Carthage, where he ate the lunch that had been prepared for Gelimer the previous day. Belisarius' soldiers were billeted across the city in good order, the remaining Vandals were promised safety, and attention was paid to restoring the city's defences that had been allowed to fall into disrepair. With this easy success a number of predictions came to light, including the promise by Saint Cyprian, the city's third-century bishop and martyr, that he would avenge the appropriation by the Vandals of his church. The Vandal priests had prepared the church for his annual commemoration on 14 September,

---

21. Proc., *Wars* 3.19–20.

so that everything was ready for the festival to be celebrated by orthodox clergy when the day came.[22]

While Belisarius focused on Carthage's defences, Gelimer tried to prevent the Romans from moving out of the city by distributing money among the rural population and offering rewards to anyone who slew a Roman. Some slaves and servants were killed, but when a troop of twenty-two of Belisarius' guards under Diogenes ventured out they managed to fight their way through an encircling force of 300 Vandals. On Sardinia Tzazon, unaware of developments at home, had quickly eliminated the rebel Goda and restored Vandal authority, though in Spain the Visigoth king, Theudis, soon heard of the Roman victory from a merchant, with the result that he rebuffed a request for an alliance that Gelimer had previously sent. Gelimer promptly informed Tzazon that the Romans had recaptured Carthage and recalled him to Africa for an emotional reunion on the plain of Bulla.[23] Gelimer was now strong enough to advance on Carthage, where he demolished the aqueduct and kept watch on the roads. He hoped that Huns or some of the local inhabitants might betray the city, but Belisarius had Laurus, a Carthaginian convicted of treason, impaled and dissuaded the Huns from switching sides by guaranteeing that they would be allowed to return home at the end of the campaign.[24]

By now it was mid-December. Belisarius ordered most of the cavalry and guards to ride out of the city under John the Armenian, while he followed the next day with the infantry and 500 horsemen, eventually camping opposite the Vandals at Tricamarum, about 32km from Carthage. Gelimer and Tzazon exhorted their followers, and then deployed them for battle at midday, taking by surprise the Romans who were preparing their lunch. Belisarius rapidly marshalled his army, the federate units on the left, the other Roman cavalry on the right, while in the centre John commanded Belisarius' personal troops and was joined there by Belisarius himself with the 500 cavalry he had been leading. The infantry were following up at a walk, while the Huns stationed themselves at a distance, in part because they preferred to operate separately from the Romans, in part so they could wait to join the winning side. For the Vandals, Gelimer and

22. Proc., *Wars* 3.21–2.
23. Proc., *Wars* 3.23–5.
24. Proc., *Wars* 4.1.

Tzazon held the centre with their troops and allied Berbers behind them, while the two wings were under unnamed officers.

Apparently the Vandals had been ordered not to use their spears in the battle, but only swords, which presupposed a defensive hand-to-hand combat rather than a frontal charge. For a time the two sides confronted each other across a small stream, until John advanced with some of Belisarius' guards; he was twice driven back, but at the third attempt he led almost all the guards so that a fierce fight ensued in which Tzazon was killed. The whole Roman army now moved forward and routed their opponents, so that the Huns joined in the pursuit back to the Vandal camp; 800 Vandals fell for the loss of 50 Romans. When the Roman infantry finally arrived, Belisarius moved against the camp, at which point Gelimer fled on horseback towards Numidia with a few relatives and retainers. Once his flight was noticed, the rest of the Vandals fled, pursued by the Romans who killed the men and enslaved the women and children. The booty inside the camp was staggering, since the Vandals had benefited from the fertility of their kingdom and pillaging Roman territory.[25]

In the frenzy of pillaging discipline in the Roman army completely disintegrated, with Belisarius incapable of restoring order, and it was only in the morning that he gradually managed to form up his own guardsmen. He sent 200 men with John the Armenian to pursue Gelimer, but after five days John was accidentally killed by Uliaris when he was about to engage Gelimer. This halted the pursuit, with the result that Gelimer could take refuge with the Berbers on the steep mountain of Papua, probably located in the mountainous Kroumire region at the northern end of the border between modern Tunisia and Algeria. Belisarius advanced as far as Hippo Regius, from where he sent the Herul Pharas to blockade Gelimer and prevent supplies reaching him. There he also secured the treasure that Gelimer, in the event of defeat, had entrusted to Boniface to transport to Spain, where he had been hoping to find sanctuary with the Visigoths. It was said that Boniface's ship was repeatedly prevented from leaving harbour or making any progress on the journey, until it seemed that God was forcing him to remain in Africa.

Belisarius now returned to Carthage, where he rounded up the Vandals to be shipped to Constantinople in the spring. Cyril was sent back to Sardinia to recover the island from the Vandals left there by Tzazon,

---

25. Proc., *Wars* 4.2–3.

showing them the latter's head as proof of the Roman victory, and also to seize Corsica. Contingents of guards were sent west along the coast to Caesarea in Mauretania and Septem near the Straits of Gibraltar. Apollinarius, an Italian who had served Hilderic and then fled to Justinian at Gelimer's usurpation, was dispatched to the Balearics, since these were to be administered as part of the diocese of Africa.[26] Troops were allocated to help Pudentius and Tattimuth in Tripolitania against inroads by local Berbers, and finally Belisarius attempted to take over Lilybaeum at the western end of Sicily, on the grounds that this had been transferred to the Vandals as part of the dowry when Amalafrida married Thrasamund. Queen Amalasuentha rebuffed this venture and instead referred the matter to Justinian for arbitration.[27]

Gelimer and his relatives found life on Mount Papua very hard, since they had become accustomed to all the luxuries of Roman civilization whereas the tribesmen who lived on the mountain were inured to the hardships of its cold and wet climate. Pharas failed in an attempt to scale the mountain, losing 110 men in the face of fierce opposition from the Berbers, and so tried to persuade Gelimer to surrender with various promises. Gelimer declined, but asked to be sent a loaf of bread, since he had not seen one for so long, a sponge to bathe one of his eyes that was inflamed, and a harp so that, as a skilled musician, he could sing a lament he had composed over his present misfortune. Pharas granted these requests but maintained a close watch. Eventually hunger, and especially the effect this had on the children, drove Gelimer to seek assurances that Pharas' earlier promises would be honoured, at which he surrendered. Gelimer was laughing uncontrollably when Belisarius received him in the suburbs of Carthage, whether deranged by his hardships or mocking the vicissitudes of fortune, but he was treated with honour until he could be transported to Justinian.[28]

Belisarius was keen to return to Constantinople since he was aware that some of his subordinates had slandered him to the emperor, saying that he was trying to establish a kingdom for himself. In spring 534

---

26. *Cod.Iust.* 1.27.2. Lillington-Martin, 'Strategy' 169–79, speculates that part of the reason for Apollinarius' mission was to secure control of trade routes in the western Mediterranean, especially those that led towards the Atlantic. To me the need to secure all Vandal territory to prevent outlying parts being annexed by neighbours, and the opportunities that this presented to obtain information on events in Spain and Gaul, is sufficient explanation.
27. Proc., *Wars* 4.4–5.
28. Proc., *Wars* 4.6–7.

his imminent departure along with many of his troops and the Vandal prisoners prompted some Berber tribes to raid across the frontiers that were not yet firmly defended. In response Belisarius entrusted some of his guardsmen to the eunuch Solomon, who was now in charge in Africa as praetorian prefect, with orders to suppress these attacks, after which he sailed for Constantinople, where Justinian permitted him the rare honour of celebrating a triumph. Belisarius led his victorious men and captives into the Hippodrome, with Gelimer repeatedly quoting *Ecclesiastes*, 'Vanity of vanities, all is vanity', until everyone prostrated themselves in front of the imperial box; this ensured that Justinian rather than the victorious Belisarius received the ultimate credit for the triumph, an interpretation underlined by the striking of a large gold medallion to celebrate the recovery of the provinces.[29] The royal relatives of Hilderic and the descendants of Emperor Valentinian received rich presents from Justinian and Theodora, while Gelimer was granted considerable estates in Cappadocia.

Settlement and Initial Problems

Meanwhile in the African provinces the process of re-establishing Roman tax registers, which had been destroyed by the Vandals, was started, while Solomon was sent more troops by Justinian.[30] Justinian's thorough reorganization of the recovered territories in 534 is set out in detail.[31] A praetorian prefect for Africa controlled seven provincial governors, more senior *consulares* in Proconsularis, Byzacena, and Tripolitania, with *praesides* in Mauretania Sitifensis and Caesariensis, Numidia, and Sardinia. The *MM per Africam* had five *duces* reporting to him for Byzacena, Tripolitania, Numidia, Mauretania Caesarensis, and Sardinia. The staff in their various offices are listed in detail. Although the legislation sets out two separate hierarchies, Solomon in fact held the positions of both prefect and *MM* and so exercised supreme authority in the provinces. The frontiers were to be protected by the re-establishment of *limitanei*, who would be supported by their allocations of land. In 535 Roman citizens were given five years to reclaim land which had been improperly seized from them or their

---

29. See Plate 14 for a drawing of the medallion, and Plate 15 for the emperor using the Hippodrome to receive submission from conquered enemies.
30. Proc., *Wars* 4.8–9.
31. *Cod.Iust.* 1.27.1, 2.

ancestors by other Roman provincials under the Vandal regime,[32] although properties taken over by the Vandals reverted to the imperial treasury rather than their previous owners, a source of considerable resentment before long.[33] The Catholic Church had all its property returned, while legislation against Arians, Donatists, Jews, and other enemies of orthodoxy was underscored.[34]

Defeating the Vandals was to prove the easiest part of Justinian's engagement in Africa since Berbers and mutineers, sometimes in collaboration, were to plague the provinces for the next fifteen years. The Berbers were already overrunning much of Byzacena and Numidia, where they secured numerous captives and in late 534 even killed two leading men in Belisarius' household, Aigan the Hun and Rufinus, whose attack on some raiders led to them being overwhelmed by a large Berber force. Solomon therefore marched out against the Berbers with all his troops, to confront them at a place called Mammes, where they were encamped on level ground with mountains to their back; these were probably the hills to the west of Kairouan. The Berbers formed a circle of their camels up to twelve deep where they faced the Romans, with their women and children in the middle; some of their horsemen were stationed on the mountain behind them. The Berbers placed themselves between their camels, so that they could dart in and out to hurl their light javelins while relying on the camels to disrupt enemy horses. For a time this worked against the Romans, whose horses threw their riders at the sight and sound of the camels, while the Barber javelins hit their targets, until Solomon ordered his men to dismount and cover themselves with their shields. While the majority of the Romans held their ground, Solomon advanced with 500 men to attack the camels with their swords. They killed about 200 camels which caused the defensive ring to collapse so that the rest of the army poured in, capturing the women, children, and remaining camels.

Berber casualties were said to be 10,000 and Solomon's army returned to Carthage in triumph, but the reverse only stimulated the tribesmen to return to Byzacena in greater numbers. Solomon confronted them at Mount Bourgaon, where they were encamped some way up the western, more accessible, side of twin peaks that were separated by a narrow deep

32. Justinian, *Novel* 36.
33. Proc., *Wars* 4.4.8–10.
34. Justinian, *Novel* 37.

ravine.[35] After the experience at Mammes the Berbers declined to confront the Romans on level ground, whereas Solomon's troops were unenthusiastic about besieging such numerous opponents in desert country. Solomon therefore instructed Theodore, *comes excubitorum*, to take 1,000 men to ascend the precipitous eastern peak by night, so that in the morning he could display Roman flags and start firing on the Berbers from above. The move was successful and the Berbers, finding themselves under attack from Solomon's army moving uphill as well as bombarded from above, turned to flight. In their panic many fell into the ravine separating the two peaks until survivors were able to cross over on the corpses of men and animals. Casualties were said to number 50,000 and captives were so numerous that a Berber boy was sold for the price of a sheep.[36] Solomon again retired to Carthage while the surviving Moors sought refuge either in Numidia with Iaudas, or in Byzacena with Antalas, even though the latter was still loyal to the Romans.[37]

Iaudas had been plundering Numidia from his base on the Aurès mountains to the south and west of Timgad, though Althias who commanded a garrison at Centuriae, a fort near the city of Tigisis, recovered much booty with a force of only seventy Huns, after denying Iaudas access to a crucial well. The Aurès provided the Berbers with a safe refuge, from where, protected by its ruggedness, they could dominate much of the province of Numidia, and so in 535 Solomon marched there, though Iaudas declined to face him. Solomon led his men into the uplands for seven days, until they reached a place called Clipea (Shield) where they waited for three days in the hope of catching Iaudas. However, Solomon became increasingly suspicious that the Berber allies in his army were conspiring with the enemy to ambush him, so that, with his troops running short of supplies, he withdrew to the plains, where he left part of the army to watch the Aurès. He returned to Carthage to prepare an expedition to Sardinia against Berbers, who had been exiled there with their families but were now harassing the Roman authorities.[38]

Solomon's activities in 536 were disrupted when his soldiers mutinied at Easter. One factor was property, since a number of soldiers had married

---

35. There is not enough in Procopius' description to pinpoint the location, but it was probably somewhere in the hills west of Kairouan.
36. As usual when giving an implausibly large figure, Procopius uses the expression 'five myriads'.
37. Proc., *Wars* 4.11–12.
38. Proc., *Wars* 4.14.

Vandal women and expected to secure their inherited estates, whereas Solomon wanted to register these as imperial property captured in war. Another factor was the presence among the Roman troops of at least 1,000 'Arians', including the Heruls, who were angered by Justinian's legislation that excluded all but orthodox Christians from the sacraments and rites such as baptism, which was especially important at Easter. The Vandal clergy fanned the latter resentment and further encouragement was drawn from the return of a unit of 400 Vandals, who had overpowered the sailors when they were being shipped to the eastern front.

A plan to murder Solomon in church on the first day of Easter festivities, 23 March, failed, whether because of the sacrilege involved or Solomon's personal reputation. When the same happened on the next day, the plotters decided that they could no longer stay in Carthage without risking discovery. After the leading rebels had left, Solomon's exhortations for the troops to return to their allegiance appeared to be gaining ground, but on the fifth day, at a mass meeting in the Hippodrome, the troops publicly insulted him and selected Theodore the Cappadocian as their leader. They now started to kill those loyal to Solomon or who had money, with the result that Solomon, accompanied by the general Martin and Procopius the historian, escaped by boat to the shipyard at Misyas, about 65km from the city. From there Solomon sent Martin to advise Valerian in Numidia to secure the loyalty of as many of his men as possible and wrote to Theodore instructing him to govern Carthage; then Solomon and Procopius took ship to Syracuse where Belisarius was preparing to invade Italy.

Outside Carthage the mutineers gathered at the plain of Bulla, where they selected Stotzas, one of Martin's guards, as their leader. He was able to arm 8,000 Roman troops, plus 1,000 Vandals, including those who had just escaped from the east, and march on Carthage. When Theodore attempted to negotiate through Joseph, a member of Belisarius' household, the mutineers killed him and pressed on to invest the city. The defenders were contemplating surrender when Belisarius sailed into the harbour in a single ship with about 100 of his personal guards and Solomon. His arrival transformed morale and the attackers withdrew in disarray, soon to be followed by Belisarius, who had collected 2,000 of the Roman army and reinforced their loyalty with gifts of money. The two armies camped by the river Bagradas near the city of Membresa, about 70km from Carthage. After the expected exhortations from the respective commanders the two sides faced each other, but Stotzas found that a strong wind was blowing into his men's faces. Since this would give a significant advantage to Belisarius in the ensuing exchange of missiles, Stotzas attempted a difficult manoeuvre to reposition his army so that it had the benefit of the wind, but his men fell into disorder while attempting this and Belisarius ordered his men to charge at once. The mutineers fled to Numidia, leaving their stockade with their women and rich booty for Belisarius' men. In the flight there were few casualties, apart from some of the Vandals.

On returning to Carthage, Belisarius was summoned urgently to Sicily to deal with a mutiny in the army there. In Numidia the loyal commanders gathered their forces under the governor Marcellus, but when he confronted the rebels Stotzas was able to persuade his troops to desert. Stotzas then combined the two armies and killed the commanders, even though he had given them guarantees while they sheltered in the sanctuary at Gazophyla, to the west of Tigisis. Justinian now sent his nephew Germanus to Carthage, accompanied by the senators Domnicus, who was to command the infantry, and Symmachus as prefect to control finances. On investigating the military rolls, Germanus realized that only one third of the army remained loyal whereas Stotzas was supported by two thirds. He therefore began a campaign to win back the deserters' allegiance, stating in public that he had been sent by the emperor to right the soldiers' grievances and punish those responsible.

News of this naturally reached the rebels, who gradually began to come over to Germanus, and their friendly reception, which included receipt of their pay even for the period of the mutiny, encouraged others to follow until Germanus at last felt that he had sufficient troops to confront Stotzas in battle. Stotzas had advanced to within 7km of Carthage in the hope that his presence would encourage defections among Germanus' men; but when these did not materialize while the armies faced each other for several days, Stotzas withdrew to Numidia, where Germanus caught up with him at Scalae Veteres. Here Germanus positioned his infantry in the centre of the line, with his baggage wagons behind them to protect his men from attack and bolster their confidence. He commanded the best of the cavalry and the troops who had accompanied him from Constantinople were on the left, while on the right three divisions of cavalry were led by Ildiger, Theodore the Cappadocian, and John Troglita, brother of Papas. Opposite them the mutineers were arrayed in no particular order, with several thousand Berbers behind them under Iaudas, Ortaïas, and other leaders, not all of whom were firmly committed to the rebel cause.

Stotzas first planned to charge Germanus' standard on the Roman left, but was persuaded by the Heruls in his entourage to attack the Roman right on the grounds that the cavalry there would certainly crumble. This indeed happened, allowing Stotzas to assault the infantry formation, but Germanus' group charged Stotzas with swords drawn and were joined by Ildiger and Theodore. Germanus' men began to get the upper hand, although the difficulty of distinguishing between loyal and mutinous Roman troops, with their similar language and equipment, caused considerable confusion until Germanus ordered his men to ask each soldier they encountered to give them his password. Stotzas' troops now fled while Germanus attacked their camp; resistance at the gates was stiff but collapsed when Germanus directed a fresh attack on an undefended sector. At this point Germanus' men disintegrated in a frenzy of looting, while Germanus lamented the danger they had placed themselves in. Stotzas tried to renew the battle with his Berber allies, but they declined and he only just escaped with 100 men. One final attempt to attack Germanus ended in failure as Stotzas' troops preferred to return to their Roman allegiance; Stotzas finally managed to escape to Mauretania with some of his Vandal followers.[39]

Solomon's Campaigns

Although the mutiny was now over, Germanus had to confront a plot against him that was led by Maximinus, one of Theodore's guards. This was revealed to Germanus who outmanoeuvred the plotters, many of whom were killed in the hippodrome at Carthage while Maximinus was impaled outside the walls. In 539 Germanus, Symmachus, and Domninus were recalled by Justinian, with Solomon returning to Africa as praetorian prefect; he concentrated on restoring order across the provinces, repairing defences, and enforcing the laws. In 540 he prepared another campaign to subdue the Berbers on the Aurès. An advance party under one of his guards, Guntharis, was defeated near the deserted city of Bagaïs (modern Baghai) by the river Abigas, which flowed down from the Aurès, and then besieged in its camp. When Solomon approached he sent part of his army to challenge the Berbers, but they blocked up the irrigation channels leading from the Abigas river and diverted its flow onto the Roman camp; as a result the site turned to deep mud and left the Romans at a loss. On

---

39. Proc., *Wars* 4.16–17.

hearing this, Solomon approached, causing the Berbers to retire to the foot of the Aurès where he then defeated them at a place called Babosis.

Many Berbers now withdrew west to Mauretania, but Iaudas with 20,000 followers retreated up the mountain to the stronghold of Zerboule. Before attacking Iaudas, Solomon allowed his army to ravage the farmland around Timgad, an indication that this region had not yet been recovered by the Romans. This respite allowed Iaudas to move most of his Berbers up into the Aurès to take refuge in a sheltered ravine called Tumar, since Zerboule was not strong or large enough to shelter him. Solomon captured Zerboule after three days of bombardment, in which Roman archery killed all the Berber leaders since the parapet was too low to provide protection. Although Solomon had planned to abandon the siege on the next day to concentrate on Iaudas, the Berbers themselves left the fort overnight so that it fell into Roman hands.

There was no good site for a camp near Tumar and the Romans suffered from a shortage of water, with only one cup per day for each soldier, so that the men began to grumble. Solomon attempted to inspire them, but in reality he was at a loss as to how to approach the ravine since the access was steep and narrow. By chance an infantryman, Gezon by name, who was the *optio* or paymaster for his unit, started uphill with some of his men following behind. Gezon killed three Berbers who were guarding the route, which encouraged his men, and soon the whole army was attacking without waiting for the trumpet signal to advance. In spite of their disorder the Romans put the Berbers to flight, killing or capturing most of them, though the wounded Iaudas escaped to Mauretania. To secure the Aurès for the future, Solomon constructed and garrisoned forts, financing this from Iaudas' treasure that he had captured in a tower on the Aurès. Cities, towns, and forts on the north and south flanks of the Aurès massif were repaired and small garrisons will have been installed. Solomon now restored Roman control over the eastern part of Mauretania, the province of Mauretania Sitifensis, and with these successes the provinces enjoyed a few years of peace.[40]

In 543 Justinian sent Solomon's two nephews, Cyrus and Sergius, to join him as the governors of Pentapolis and Tripolitania. A large group

---

40. Proc., *Wars* 4.18–20. The reconstruction of defences is recorded in panegyrical terms in Procopius, *Buildings* 6.4–7. Presentation and discussion of the material evidence in Pringle, *Defence*, 171–339, and Durliat, *Dédicaces*.

of Leuata Berbers came to Sergius at Leptis Magna to receive their customary gifts and insignia and confirm the peace, but an argument at a banquet for eighty leading Leuata resulted in all but one being killed. Their followers were then defeated outside the city, although Pudentius, who had delivered the province to Justinian a decade previously, perished in a rash attack. Berbers were raiding across Byzacena, led by the erstwhile Roman ally, Antalas, who had rebelled after being deprived of his customary payments and the execution of his brother for alleged treachery.

In 544 Solomon marched out from Carthage with his whole army to Teveste (Tébessa), accompanied by his nephews, and then east to a place called Cillium (probably near Babar).[41] Being outnumbered by Antalas, Solomon attempted to secure support from the Leuata, criticizing their defection, but they refused to believe his promises. In the ensuing confrontation, Solomon had the better of the first day's fighting and secured considerable booty, but his failure to distribute this at once upset his troops. On the next day Berber numbers told and Solomon was forced to flee with a few men to a ravine, but, after being injured in a fall from his horse, he was overtaken and killed. Sergius replaced his uncle as commander in Africa but proved a weak and unpopular leader, who antagonized his officers, soldiers, and the Berbers. Antalas even wrote to Justinian, explaining why he was in revolt and offering to make peace if Sergius was replaced by someone better. Meantime Antalas besieged Laribus, a small city on the route from Theveste to Carthage to which Solomon's nephew, also called Solomon, had escaped, until he was bought off for 3,000 *solidi*.[42]

Berber Threats and Roman Mutiny

Antalas had now been joined by Stotzas in raiding Byzacena. They managed to capture the local *dux*, Himerius, who accidentally led his men into the Berber camp when trying to rendezvous with John, son of Sisiniolus; only a few of the Romans resisted under Severianus of Emesa, but most were willing to join Stotzas. Himerius was threatened with death if he did not betray the nearby coastal city of Hadrumetum, which he effected by pretending to be leading Berber captives into it. The city was plundered and garrisoned, but was soon recovered for the Romans when

---

41. Victor Tun. *s.a.* 543 gives the location of the battle, which was not recorded by Procopius.
42. Proc., *Wars* 4.21.

a leading local, Paul, escaped to Carthage and received eighty soldiers from Sergius. By manning numerous ships, whose sailors he dressed as soldiers, and spreading the rumour that Germanus had returned to the province, he tricked his way inside the walls and slew Stotzas' men. For a time the rumour about Germanus gained currency, but when the truth was revealed the Berbers ravaged with increased fury at the deception.

Justinian now sent Areobindus, the husband of his niece Praeiecta, to Africa to split the command with Sergius, the latter taking Numidia while Areobindus campaigned in Byzacena. Areobindus brought with him a contingent of Armenians under the Arsacid royals, Artabanes and John, and was accompanied by Athanasius as the new prefect. Areobindus sent John, son of Sisiniolus, an officer with a good reputation, to confront Antalas and Stotzas near Sicca Veneria (El Kef in western Tunisia), writing to Sergius to order him to bring his troops so that they could fight at full strength. But there was mutual enmity between John and Sergius so that the latter declined to respond, leaving John greatly outnumbered. Early in the fighting John mortally wounded Stotzas with an arrow,[43] but superior numbers then told and the Roman army was put to flight, with John being killed when his horse stumbled. On hearing of this reverse, Justinian recalled Sergius.[44]

Roman authority in Africa was thrown into chaos when Guntharis, the former bodyguard of Solomon and now *dux Numidiae*, planned to rebel against Areobindus, taking advantage of an advance on Carthage by the Berbers in Byzacena under Antalas and Berbers and rebels from Numidia under Cutzinas and Iaudas. Guntharis struck a deal with Antalas to divide control of Africa, with Antalas in charge of Byzacena and Guntharis ruling in Carthage, but, unbeknown to him, Areobindus had won over Cutzinas. Areobindus summoned all his subordinate commanders to Carthage, where Guntharis urged him to go out to fight, intending to murder him in the confusion of battle, but Areobindus deferred this for two days, allegedly being so inexperienced in warfare that he did not even know how to put on his armour.

On the third day Guntharis launched his coup by blocking open the gates on the section of city wall he was defending, in the hope that this

---

43. John is said to have commented that he was pleased that the prophecy with regard to Stotzas, that he would not return from Africa (Proc., *Wars* 3.11.30), had been fulfilled.

44. Proc., *Wars* 4.23–4.

danger would encourage Areobindus to flee, and then persuading other troops to join him with criticisms of Areobindus and promises of money. Areobindus in fact tried to quell the mutiny with the support of Artabanes and his Armenian troops, but soon fled for sanctuary in a monastery so that Artabanes withdrew from the city. Although Guntharis guaranteed his safety, he had Areobindus murdered after dining with him and sent his head to Antalas. The latter, however, was outraged that Guntharis did not keep his promises about sharing power and so opened talks with Marcentius, the *dux Byzacenae* who was holding Hadrumetum. Guntharis was now joined by 1,000 of Stotzas' troops, of whom 500 were Roman soldiers and 80 Huns, and Artabanes then promised obedience so that his Armenians were received back into Carthage. Artabanes was encouraged to act against Guntharis by his nephew Gregorius and the prefect Athanasius, but first he was put in command of troops that Guntharis sent to Hadrumetum to attack Antalas and Marcentius. In an initial encounter Antalas' Berbers were routed, but Artabanes then retired to Carthage, alleging that he feared an attack from Hadrumetum. Artabanes and his fellow conspirators slew Guntharis and his close supporters at a banquet, thereby recovering Carthage for Justinian on the thirty-sixth day of the usurpation.[45]

John Troglita's Campaigns

At his own request Artabanes was recalled to Constantinople, being replaced in 546 by John Troglita, who had been part of Belisarius' expedition and had served under Solomon, so knew the provinces well. Procopius noted his campaigns against the Berbers over the next two years in no more than six sections, concluding with the gloomy observation that afterwards the few surviving inhabitants of the provinces at last found some peace.[46] After his detailed account of Guntharis' coup, which he must have obtained from Artabanes or a close associate, Procopius' information on Africa seems to dry up. John's victories, however, were celebrated by Flavius Cresconius Corippus in a panegyrical epic poem, the *Iohannid*, in eight books of over 4,700 Latin hexameters. Corippus' purpose was to extol John's successes and the details of military events are less clear.

---

45. Proc., *Wars* 4.25.1–28.41.
46. Proc., *Wars* 4.28.46–51.

John's first action was to advance with eight contingents of cavalry and one of infantry to Antonia Castra, a place in Byzacena whose location is unknown, to confront Antalas, whose attempts at negotiation were rebuffed. John was supported by Marcentius, *dux Byzacenae*, as well as the Numidian Berber Cutzinas, who had fallen out with Antalas during Guntharis' coup. Antalas' Berbers retired into the woods and hills, possibly near Kasserine, where they clashed with John's advance guard under Geisirith and Amantius, before withdrawing at John's approach. In the ensuing battle, the Romans were initially successful, but Antalas and one of the other Berber leaders, Bruten, counterattacked, forcing the Romans to retreat until John rallied his men by charging the enemy in person; he was bravely supported by his officers, all of whom apparently wrought heroic deeds. The Berbers were turned to flight, their camp captured with all their possessions, including Solomon's standards that had been lost in 544, and Ierna, one of their main leaders, was killed. John now set about reconstituting the Roman defences in Byzacena, with two *duces* being put in command of the *limitanei*, whose numbers had presumably been augmented.[47]

John returned to Carthage in triumph, but the Leuata Berbers in Tripolitania regrouped under Carcasan and Bruten and threatened to ravage Byzacena, forcing John to march against them again in 547. His forces may have been reduced by the need to dispatch troops west to Septem (Ceuta), which had briefly been seized by the Visigoths according to Isidore of Seville.[48] At his approach the Berbers withdrew south into the desert, where conditions favoured them. The heat and shortage of supplies led to grumbling in John's army, which he had to silence, in part by returning to the coast so that he could be resupplied by sea, though adverse winds prevented ships from putting in. John had probably taken up a position near Tacapes (Gabes), where he could block the relatively narrow passage north into the main part of Byzacena. He was keen to avoid battle but, when news came that the Berbers were heading for a nearby river, he was persuaded to try to deny its water to the enemy and so advanced south-east along the Libyan coast. He had ordered his men to encamp at a place called Marta in the district of Gallica (probably Mareth, 25km south-east of Gabes), to prepare for battle on the next day, but his men apparently disobeyed and while dispersed across the vicinity clashed with

---

47. Corippus, *Iohannid* 4.286–6.52.
48. Isidore, *Hist.Goth.* 42–3; the date of the capture of Septem is unknown, but this suggestion of Pringle, *Defences* 36, is plausible.

the Berbers. A full-scale battle ensued in which John was persuaded to abandon the defensive position he had been preparing on the north bank of a stream and commit his troops on the opposite bank; the Romans, in spite of the bravery of many individuals, were routed with heavy losses, with John himself being wounded.[49]

John found refuge in a coastal city, quite possibly Tacapes, where he gathered the survivors of the rout and then moved to Laribus where he continued to rebuild his army with the help of reinforcements from Carthage. In 548 Carcasan and Antalas ravaged the southern parts of Byzacena, so John advanced to confront them· with the support of considerable numbers of Berber allies under Cutzinas and others. Carcasan and Antalas again withdrew into the desert, but this time John halted his pursuit at a site with good water supplies; from there he sent the tribune Liberatus to observe the Berbers, who were now ravaging the vicinity of Iunca (Chaffar). Captives revealed that the Berber strategy was to wear down the Romans in useless pursuits until their supplies failed, so that John withdrew to encamp on open ground near the harbour of Lariscus (Skhira), to which supplies could be shipped; there he was confronted by further dissent in the ranks, which he again had to suppress.

The Berber force was camped near the Plains of Cato, to which John now advanced his army.[50] He discovered that the Berbers were running low on supplies and so he carefully stopped his men from engaging them prematurely. This inaction convinced the Berber leaders that the Romans were still afraid after their rout the previous year and so they advanced their own camp onto level ground. Knowing that the Romans would be celebrating a Christian festival on the next day, the Berbers decided that this would be a good time to attack. In the Roman camp a priest held a religious service, John leading his men in begging for both forgiveness and help in the coming battle, before the army deployed. A Berber attack on John was repulsed, but another directed at Cutzinas was more successful until John came to the rescue. Roman officers naturally performed heroic deeds and John personally slew Carcasan as the enemy were routed with heavy losses.[51]

---

49. Corippus, *Iohannid* 6.
50. The location is unknown, but may have been in the direction of Capsa (Gafsa).
51. Corippus, *Iohannid* 7–8.

Post-conquest Africa and Spain

The *Iohannid*, whose final lines are lost, concludes with this victory, as does Procopius' account, and the latter has very little to add in the continuation of his narrative in *Wars* 8. Here only three sections are devoted to affairs in Africa, which record the continuing successes of John. These resulted in both Antalas and Iaudas being defeated and subjected, although Procopius concluded the survey with another gloomy comment on local conditions,[52] since by the early 550s he was keen to build up a picture of imperial failure on all fronts. John remained in post in Africa until at least 552, since in 551 and 552 he was involved in attempts to recover Sardinia and Corsica from Totila. Thereafter the information we have on further military campaigns in Africa relates to January 563 when the governor, John Rogathinus, refused to give Cutzinas his customary payment and instead had him killed, with the result that Cutzinas' sons captured some Roman cities and pillaged. In response Justinian sent his nephew Marcian with an army, which managed to restore order.[53] Why Cutzinas had become suspect after years of loyalty is not known, but it is possible that authorities felt that he had grown overconfident and was abusing his privileged position.[54]

This general silence does not mean that the frontiers of the provinces were not always at risk from low-level incursions by the Berbers, but the main source of disruption for the provinces, however, was now religious: the African church strongly opposed Justinian's Three Chapters initiative and many of its bishops were taken to the East and imprisoned for their hostility.[55] This disagreement did not prevent an extensive programme of church construction in Carthage and beyond, as the Nicene faithful, enjoying the restoration of their properties and revenues, reasserted their doctrinal domination.[56]

A coda to the re-conquest of Africa is the acquisition of some territory in south-east Spain in 552. When annexing Vandal territory, Belisarius had taken possession of the Balearic islands and key sites along the coast as far as the Straits of Gibraltar, which brought the Romans into close contact with the Visigothic kingdom in Spain. Relations had existed

---

52. Proc., *Wars* 8.17.20–2.
53. Malalas 18.145.
54. Cf. Heather, *Rome* 273.
55. See Moderan, 'L'Afrique'.
56. Leone, *Townscapes* 209–13.

between Visigoths and Vandals: King Theudis had been approached by Gelimer about an alliance and also for possible refuge, while the Vandal collapse encouraged the Visigoths to occupy Ceuta in North Africa, though they were soon expelled by Roman forces. In 552 dissension within the ruling family, as in Italy, gave Justinian an opportunity to intervene in Spain. After King Agila failed to suppress a revolt in Cordoba, losing his son and royal treasure in the process,[57] the nobleman Athanagild had rebelled. Support was requested from Justinian,[58] who sent the aged Liberius with troops, who helped Athanagild to defeat Agila near Seville.[59] In the process the Romans took control of several cities, some of which Athanagild managed to recapture after succeeding to the throne when Agila was murdered in 555.[60] How far inland Roman control extended is unclear, but there is no evidence that they seized either Seville or Cordoba in the Guadalquivir valley as is sometimes asserted. It is safest to assume that they retained possession of port cities such as Cartagena and Malaga, together with their immediate hinterland. This toehold could have served as the springboard for a full-scale attack on the Visigoths, as Sicily had done with regard to the Ostrogoths, but in Spain the opportunity never presented itself and by the 620s the Romans had been pushed out of their last possessions.[61]

The contrast between the relatively easy conquest of the Vandal kingdom, an organized state of considerable strength, and the protracted struggles against Berber neighbours is explained by the different structures of these opponents. The Vandal occupation of Carthage had transformed them from a heterogeneous itinerant warband into the propertied ruling elite of a centralized state. Their kingdom was run from Carthage, public life revolved around the royal court, and the majority of the Vandals were granted estates in the neighbouring provinces of Byzacena and Numidia. They received the support of some of the Roman provincials, attracted by their patronage or the prospects of service in the administration, but their anti-Nicene religion ensured that there was resentment and opposition that orthodox writers did their best to foment. Therefore, when Belisarius was able to occupy Carthage after a scrappy encounter in its suburbs and then defeat the royal army in

---

57. Isidore, *Hist.Goth.* 45–6.
58. Isidore attributes this to Athanagild, but Jordanes, *Getica* 303 suggests it was Agila.
59. Jordanes, *Getica* 303.
60. Gregory of Tours, *Hist.Franc.* 4.8.
61. For a summary of the situation in sixth-century Spain, see Heather, *Goths* 278–83.

pitched battle, he had deprived Gelimer and his remaining followers of most of their resources, while the restoration of privileges to the Catholic Church and imposition of restrictions on 'Arians' secured local support.

Gelimer did have the mobile elements of the royal treasury loaded onto a ship at Hippo Regius, but this was soon lost; now Belisarius controlled the mechanics of administration, he was in a position to dominate the former estates of the majority of Vandals, and he had possession of many of their families. All that was left for Gelimer was flight, to Spain if he had managed to take ship at Hippo Regius, or with his Berber neighbours. The problem with the latter option was that three generations of life in Carthage had transformed the Vandal warriors accustomed to the hardships of life on the margins of the Roman empire into an elite which, while still prizing military ability, also appreciated the luxuries of civilized Roman life.

The Berbers were the opposite, or are made to appear so in the sources, which present them as fickle outsiders who lived in the harsh conditions beyond the edges of Roman control, in upland areas such as the Aurès massif or in the deserts of Libya. They had leaders who could assemble substantial groups of fighters, but they were also capable of slipping away into regions beyond the reaches of Roman power. The re-establishment of Roman fortified sites around areas such as the Aurès, as Solomon oversaw, permitted authorities to monitor, although not control, the movements of these tribesmen. Relations between the Roman provinces in Africa and their tribal neighbours had always been complicated, depending upon a network of local connections, recognition of the varying needs of tribal groups, regular exchange of gifts, and bestowal of official honours. These links were easy to destroy through clumsy or insensitive interventions, as when Sergius had eighty Leuata representatives killed or Antalas ceased to receive expected rewards. They were hard to construct, since each side was suspicious of the other's different nature, and even harder to sustain in the long term.[62] It was possible for Roman authorities, as both Solomon in the Aurès massif and John Troglita in Byzacena demonstrated, to blunt the military threat from Berber groups, but victory in battle could only be the start for a new process of accommodation.

---

62. Cf. Heather, *Rome* 273.

Accounts of dealings with tribal groups in the fourth century reveal that they were not such complete outsiders as simple narratives present, or that their leaders at least were implicated in the social structures of Roman provincial life.[63] Such accommodation took time and patience, especially on the part of Roman authorities who were more accustomed to obedience. Personal reputation counted for much, as in the cases of Solomon, Germanus, and John Troglita, and these men could establish firm links with leading Berbers, as John appears to have done with Cutzinas, whereas new arrivals parachuted in from a very different environment, for example Sergius or Areobindus, quickly upset matters. Managing the Berbers was a continuous and delicate process as opposed to the short sharp conquest of the Vandals.

Justinian directed the conquest of the Vandals effectively, sending enough troops with an appropriate balance between infantry and cavalry to defeat the enemy and recover Carthage. If he was responsible in any way for Goda's revolt on Sardinia, he had acted successfully to distract Gelimer's attention from a direct attack and remove vital numbers of ships and troops. At the same time Justinian was undoubtedly fortunate on several counts: there was no severe storm that might have crippled the large armada, Tzazon was absent in Sardinia with substantial naval and land forces, and Gelimer failed to grasp the opportunity to transform a setback at Ad Decimum into a clear victory. After Gelimer's surrender, some familiar problems arose that also plagued other campaign theatres: Belisarius' triumph raised suspicions, not least because some of his officers accused him of disloyal ambition. Troops were quickly recalled but only slowly recommitted when matters deteriorated; military pay fell into arrears, perhaps because, as on the eastern frontier, it was believed that *limitanei* did not merit a salary in times of peace, since their estates could support them; some of the choices of commander were wrong, and it was expected that victory in war could be quickly followed by the resumption of normal Roman administration, including the levying of taxation.

Justinian did have to balance his imperial commitments, and, after the invasion of Italy and especially after the resumption of war in the East in 540, the African provinces could not be his top priority. In terms of commanders, loyalty was critical since Africa was sufficiently distant for its controller to have considerable power. Belisarius had proved himself in

---

63. See Matthews, *Roman Empire* 367–76, for discussion of the information in Ammianus.

the Nika Riot, Solomon as a eunuch could not be a threat, Germanus and Areobindus were family. John Troglita is the exception, but he could point to a dozen years of loyal and effective command. Most of Justinian's choices were good leaders, Areobindus being the exception and he paid with his life.

We have little information about the state of the African provinces in the last fifteen years of Justinian's reign, apart from the religious disruption caused by his doctrinal policies. In economic terms it is probable that these provinces recovered some, or even much, of their traditional prosperity, contradicting the gloomy assessments with which Procopius finished his treatment in *Wars* 4 and 8. Carthage appears to have been redeveloped as a port after the reconquest, with the assertions of Procopius' *Buildings* receiving some confirmation from the extensive archaeological study of the site, while at Leptis Minus, another city to have received serious attention, the evidence for continuing commercial activity contradicts the negative views of Procopius. In the early seventh century the African provinces were sufficiently prosperous and stable to form the base from which the family of Heraclius launched its bid to topple the usurper Phocas.

Chapter 7

Italian Campaigns

T he conquest of Vandal Africa, which had long been of interest to the eastern empire, naturally opened up other possibilities in the West: possession of Sicily and Corsica as well as the claim to Lilybaeum in western Sicily brought the empire into much closer contact with the Ostrogoths in Italy. The Ostrogoths had taken power in Ravenna with the support of the eastern empire, being encouraged or sent by Emperor Zeno in 488 to remove Odoacer, who had deposed the last western emperor in 476, and rule Italy for him.[1] Theoderic the Amal, at the head of a large following that perhaps numbered 100,000, including about 20,000 warriors,[2] occupied Ravenna after a long siege under an agreement to share power, killed Odoacer in 493, and then ruled Italy for thirty-three years. His position as king of the Goths was unchallenged, but his Roman constitutional status was less clear, until after two unsuccessful embassies Theoderic secured recognition from Anastasius, this being symbolized by the return of the palace ornaments that Odoacer had sent to Zeno in 476. He did, however, restrict himself to the title of king, *rex*, declining to provoke the East by using that of *basileus*, emperor. That said, his actions in Italy were those of an emperor, for example when deciding between two rival popes in 498, or on his visit to Rome in 500 where he observed all the religious, political, and social niceties of a Roman emperor. His gradual successes in annexing territory outside Italy and establishing a diplomatic supremacy in the West were decidedly imperial.[3]

Relations with the East were generally good, not least because for most of Anastasius' reign the East had more pressing problems: the Isaurians in the 490s, the Bulgars through to 502, the Persians from 502,

---

1. For the context and stages, see Heather, *Goths and Romans* ch.9; id., *Goths* 216–21.
2. Heather, *Goths* 236; Theoderic's band was large, since it had incorporated the followers of the other Gothic leader in the Balkans, Theoderic Strabo, who died in 481.
3. Moorhead, *Roman Empire* 46, Heather, *Goths* 220–35.

and then internal challenges over religion, including the three revolts of Vitalian in the Balkans. A panegyric could float the idea that Anastasius' authority might extend over both Romes,[4] but there was little opportunity for this to be achieved. There were intermittent tensions, for example when the Goth Pitzias captured Sirmium on the middle Danube from the Gepids in 504, and then defeated an eastern army at Horreum Margi in Dacia in 505. In response an eastern fleet of 100 warships with 100 transports carrying 8,000 soldiers ravaged parts of Italy's Adriatic coastline in 508. Overall, however, the mutual recognition of consuls indicates that relations were calm, if not always cordial.

Theoderic focused on constructing a web of alliances, marriages, and influence across the western Mediterranean, and the religious rift between Rome and Constantinople (the Acacian Schism) ensured that the Ostrogoths' attachment to Homoian Christianity did not cause problems especially as, unlike the Vandals, he did not persecute Catholics. Within Italy most of Theoderic's followers were settled in the Po valley, especially in the vicinity of Ravenna, the main focus for the court, and to the north of the river near Pavia (Ticinum) and Verona, where Theoderic built palaces as royal hubs for the Goths living in Liguria and Venetia. There were also significant settlements in Picenum down the Adriatic coast and Samnium in the centre of the peninsula, all of which looked to Ravenna.[5] The process was overseen by Theoderic's praetorian prefect, the Roman senator Liberius, and probably did not cause massive upheaval or resentment since these lands had long been used to support troops in Roman service; at least Liberius' sensitive oversight is praised by both Cassiodorus and Ennodius.[6]

Theoderic cultivated good relations with the Senate, whose talents he needed for his administration and where he built up a significant group of supporters, who had benefitted from his patronage.[7] His rule presented a thoroughly Roman aspect, thanks to men such as Liberius, who served the Goths from 493 until being sent on an embassy to Constantinople in 534, and Cassiodorus, who performed various roles for three decades

---

4. Priscian, *Pan. Anast.* 267. Granted that this poem was written and delivered in Latin, many of the audience capable of understanding the sentiment were probably Latin-speaking fugitives from the West, who would particularly have liked the idea of 'their' Rome being brought under Anastasius' authority. This does not demonstrate that re-conquest was under serious consideration.

5. Wickham, *Italy* 24–5.

6. Cass., *Variae* 2.12; Ennodius, *Ep.* 9.23.

7. Wickham, *Italy* 21–3.

from 507 and whose letters determine our perceptions of the Ostrogothic regime.[8] There may have been senators who preferred not to engage with the Gothic court, and in the Church there were people interested in better relations with the East, though their failure to secure the papacy for their candidate, Lawrence, in 498 demonstrated that they were a minority.[9]

The accession of Justin at Constantinople brought the first sign of change, since as a devout Chalcedonian he was committed to terminating the schism with Rome. Granted that Theoderic's relations with successive popes had been good, this development did not have to occasion an increase in tensions, and his son-in-law, Eutharic, husband of his daughter Amalasuentha, was accorded the signal honour of being Justin's partner in the consulship for 519. The emperor also adopted Eutharic by arms, an indication that he recognized his claim to succeed Theoderic.[10] The problem of succession, however, was to bring the downfall of this prosperous regime, since Eutharic died in the early 520s, leaving an infant son, Athalaric. It is clear that there were different succession options, including a long minority for Athalaric or choice of a different member of the Amal family of suitable age and experience, for example the powerful landowner Theodahad, Theoderic's nephew and son of the late Vandal king Thrasamund and the Ostrogothic princess Amalafrida.

Probably in 522 the patrician and former consul Albinus was accused by the *referendarius* Cyprian of sending Justin letters hostile to the Ostrogothic regime; the affair escalated when the distinguished philosopher Boethius, who was currently Theoderic's *magister officiorum*, intervened on Albinus' behalf, which resulted in the condemnation by the Senate and execution of both Boethius and his father-in-law Symmachus.[11] These events are usually taken at face value, as evidence that Constantinople was developing contacts with significant individuals in Italy, especially amongst a pro-Roman group in the Senate, though Peter Heather has argued that the affair should be seen as part of the succession struggle, since Boethius was connected to Theodahad.[12] Procopius, who in his opening

---

8. For discussion of his reign, see Moorhead, *Theoderic*; also Heather, *Goths* 222–35, for the importance of *romanitas* for Theoderic.
9. The so-called Laurentian schism was resolved by appeal to Theoderic; he unsurprisingly preferred Symmachus, who was opposed to any concessions to the East over the Acacian schism.
10. Cass., *Variae* 8.1.3.
11. *Anon. Valesianus* 14.85–6.
12. Heather, *Goths* 249–54; *Rome* 162–4.

chapter of *Wars* 5 jumps from Theoderic's conquest of Italy to these deaths, regarded them as the one blot on an excellent reign, an error that Theoderic came to regret.[13]

In 526 Athalaric, aged 10 at the most and quite possibly one or two years younger, succeeded his grandfather with his mother Amalasuentha acting as regent. It says something for the reputation of Theoderic and the stability of his regime that his followers, who only a generation previously had been a wandering warband assembled from different ethnic units, for whom military prowess was the critical qualification for leadership, should tolerate even for a brief period the regency of a woman and a long minority. One factor might have been that Theoderic's expansion of Ostrogothic power, which had probably doubled its manpower when he took control of the Visigothic kingdom in 511, meant that there were multiple possible centres of power, some based on the ethnic units that had sunk their identity in Theoderic's band, some based outside Italy. The individual leaders of different groups needed to weigh up their chances of success before making a move.[14] The kingdom did, however, require active leadership, which Athalaric could not yet provide.

Amalasuentha's control of her son's upbringing was challenged, on the grounds that, whereas she wanted him to receive a standard Roman education from a grammarian, leading Goths urged that such cultural pursuits were unnecessary for a leader of the Goths. Amalasuentha appeared to accept the complaints but then picked out three of her leading opponents, whom she dispatched to the frontiers where she had them eliminated. At the same time she had sounded out Justinian about the possibility of refuge in the East and sent a ship with treasure to Epidamnus, an approach that drew the East into Ostrogothic royal dealings even though Amalasuentha eventually decided that she did not need to flee.

This approach to Justinian can be dated to *circa* 533, since in 534 the emperor sent Alexander on a mission to explore why she had not followed her ship across the Adriatic. The embassy had other purposes, the resolution of the dispute over possession of Lilybaeum in western Sicily, which Belisarius had tried to annex as part of the Vandal realm, and protests about both the reception by Uliaris, the Gothic commander at Naples, of ten Hunnic fugitives from Belisarius' army in Africa. In

---

13. Proc., *Wars* 5.1.32–9.
14. Heather, *Goths* 237–42.

addition there was the inroad of Goths into Roman territory in Moesia in the central Balkans, where they attacked the city of Gratiana during a conflict with the Gepids at Sirmium in about 530. Amalasuentha's public response to Justinian's complaints was robust, reminding him that the Goths had given invaluable support to Belisarius' recovery of Africa by providing both free passage and supplies, but writing in private that she was prepared to place all Italy in his hands.

In 533 two bishops, Hypatius of Ephesus and Demetrius of Philippi, were sent by Justinian to discuss a doctrinal issue with Pope John, who responded in a letter of 25 March 534.[15] While in Rome they were secretly approached by Theodahad, who was on poor terms with Amalasuentha because of her desire to thwart his attempts to expand his considerable estates in Tuscany; he offered to hand over Tuscany to the emperor in return for money, senatorial status, and permission to live in Constantinople.[16]

Amalasuentha now summoned Theodahad to confront him about his illegal acquisition of properties in Tuscany, and made him repay those he had wronged, but the worsening health of her son forced her to repair relations with him. After Goths continued to protest about Athalaric's upbringing, he was given other young Goths as companions, but these led him into a life of debauchery and urged him to reject his mother's guidance. His constitution, however, could not tolerate this new behaviour and, after a progressive decline, on 2 October he died while still in his teens. Aware that Athalaric's death would leave Theodahad as the male representative of the Amals, Amalasuentha set about building bridges with him, offering to clear his name of the accusations she had recently upheld as a preliminary to his proclamation as king, though he would be ruler only in name since she stipulated that she would continue to take decisions. Theodahad swore to these terms and on ascending the throne both rulers wrote to Justinian to report developments,[17] but Theodahad disregarded his oaths and imprisoned Amalasuentha on an island in lake Bolsena. He now sent an embassy, led by the senators Liberius and Opilio, to Justinian to defend his actions against Amalasuentha and forced her to support his version of events. Justinian meanwhile, unaware of these recent developments, had sent the lawyer Peter to Italy, ostensibly to

---

15. *Cod.Iust.* 1.1.8.
16. Proc., *Wars* 5.2–3.
17. Cass., *Variae* 10.1–2.

continue discussions about Lilybaeum, but in private to pursue separate conversations both with Theodahad about handing over Tuscany and with Amalasuentha about surrendering the whole of Italy. While en route Peter met the two sets of envoys from the Goths and so paused to await fresh instructions from Justinian, who ordered him to proceed to Italy, where he was to make public his dealings with Amalasuentha, the intention being to create confusion in the Gothic realm. Peter's arrival in Italy coincided with the death of Amalasuentha, in which he played a part if we accept the account in Procopius' *Secret History* that Theodora had instructed him to arrange the queen's death.[18] Some support for this story is offered by letters to Theodora from Theodahad and his wife Gudileva, in which they thanked the empress for sending them Peter and commenting that they had arranged what she had asked about a certain person.[19] Procopius' version in the *Wars* was that she was killed by relatives of the three leading Goths whom she had had murdered for opposing her over Athalaric's upbringing. In public Peter protested about the queen's murder, saying that this would lead to war, but Theodahad added insult to injury by honouring those who had carried out the execution.[20]

Outbreak of War

Justinian launched a two-pronged attack on the Goths in 535. Belisarius was dispatched to Sicily with 4,000 *foederati* and regular troops, 3,000 Isaurians under Ennes, 200 Hunnic allies, and 300 Berbers, plus his own numerous *bucellarii*. In addition, there were the attendants of his subordinate commanders, the Thracians Constantine and Bessas and the Iberian Peranius as well as Valentinus, Magnus, and Innocentius in charge of the cavalry, and Herodian, Paul, Demetrius, and Ursicinus of the infantry. The total number of troops is unknown but might well have approached 10,000. Even that figure, which must be an upper limit for the forces available to Belisarius, would not have been anywhere near enough to overcome the Goths in battle, since the 20,000 warriors whom Theoderic had led into Italy over forty years earlier will have increased during his

18. Proc., *SH* 16.1–5.
19. Cass., *Variae* 10.20–1. Also it is difficult to believe that leading Goths would have reacted favourably to the revelation that their ruler had been secretly planning to hand their kingdom to Justinian.
20. Proc., *Wars* 5.3–4.

prosperous reign. Justinian must have been assuming, or hoping, that the various conversations he had been conducting about a peaceful transfer of power would bear fruit. Ostensibly Belisarius was sailing to Carthage, but en route the fleet would naturally put in to Sicily, where the troops were to disembark and seize the island if this seemed feasible. Belisarius landed at Catana, from where he secured the submission of Syracuse and other cities. Only at Palermo, which trusted in the strength of its defences, did he encounter resistance. This was soon overcome when Belisarius circumvented the strong landward walls by sailing his fleet into the harbour, where boats filled with archers were hoisted to the mastheads; from there they could fire down into the city, which promptly surrendered. By the end of 535 the whole of Sicily had been subjugated and Belisarius was able to enter Syracuse in triumph on 31 December, the last day of his consulship, scattering gold coins to the people.[21] Meanwhile Mundo the Gepid, *MM per Illyricum*, advanced into Dalmatia, where he captured Salona; Mundo had served Theoderic in Italy, but after his death had approached Justinian in 529 and then given loyal service in the Nika Riot.

The capture of Sicily was used by Peter, who was again on an embassy to Theodahad, to pressure him into an accord. Terrified by developments, Theodahad agreed to renounce the Gothic claim to Sicily, send a gold crown weighing 300 litres (about 100kg) each year, provide up to 3,000 Gothic soldiers when required, and accept that he had no authority to execute, or confiscate the property of, any senator or clergy. In addition he had to ask Justinian to bestow promotions to patrician or other senatorial rank, see that the people in the hippodrome and elsewhere would always chant Justinian's name before his own and ensure that no individual statue of him would be erected but only in conjunction with Justinian, who was always to be placed on the right. Theodahad confirmed these undertakings in writing, but soon recalled Peter for further discussions, since he was worrying what would happen if Justinian did not accept these concessions. When Peter said that there would be war, Theodahad wrote to Justinian underlining his passion for learning and offering to hand over Italy in return for estates with an annual income of 1,200 pounds of gold. Peter swore that this offer would only be divulged if Justinian declined the first set of terms, and Theodahad sent a trusted priest, Rusticius, to negotiate on his behalf. Justinian refused the first offer, but gladly accepted

21. Proc., *Wars* 5.5.

the full surrender of Italy, sending Peter and Athanasius to confirm details and then summon Belisarius from Sicily to annex the kingdom.

Progress towards a peaceful handover, however, was disrupted when a large Gothic army entered Dalmatia in late 535 or early 536. They first encountered a scouting party led by Mundo's son Maurice, who was killed after a fierce fight. This prompted Mundo to attack the Goths, which he did successfully, routing them with heavy losses among the nobility but losing his own life in the pursuit. Both sides were left leaderless, the Romans withdrawing from Dalmatia while the Goths occupied various forts apart from Salona, whose defences were weak and inhabitants hostile. The deaths of Maurice and Mundo raised Theodahad's spirits, so that he now rebuffed Justinian's envoys and even put them under guard.[22]

Justinian's response in early 536 was again twofold. Belisarius was instructed to invade Italy and attack the Goths as enemies, while Constantianus, *comes sacri stabuli*, was sent to Illyricum to collect troops and secure Salona if possible. Constantianus gathered his forces at Dyrrachium (Epidamnus) from where he sailed north to Epidaurus. The Goths had meanwhile sent another army to Dalmatia under Gripa, who occupied Salona, but when his spies reported the enormous scale of the Roman expedition he withdrew north to Scardona. This allowed the Romans to recover Salona without opposition and a week later Gripa withdrew to Ravenna, so that Constantianus could take over the whole of Dalmatia. After garrisoning Syracuse and Palermo, Belisarius crossed the Straits of Messina to Rhegium. As he marched through Bruttium and Lucania with the fleet in close attendance on the coast he was welcomed by all the cities, which lacked defences and in any case were hostile towards the Goths. He was also joined by the Goth Ebrimuth, the son-in-law of Theodahad, and his followers. Ebrimuth was sent to Justinian, who welcomed him honourably and gave him patrician rank.[23]

Belisarius now advanced into Campania where he approached Naples, which was held by a strong Gothic garrison so he proceeded with caution. Instructing his fleet to anchor in the harbour, since it was out of range from the walls, he accepted the surrender of a fort in the suburbs and received a delegation of local inhabitants led by Stephanus. He upbraided Belisarius for attacking a Roman city, whose inhabitants were constrained

22. Proc., *Wars* 5.5.1–7.25.
23. Proc., *Wars* 5.7.26–8.4.

by the Gothic garrison, which in its turn could not surrender since Theodahad had control of their families; he urged the invaders to proceed to Rome, since its capture would automatically bring about the surrender of Naples. Belisarius' public response was to urge the inhabitants to grasp the opportunity of liberty rather than fight against it, while allowing the Gothic soldiers the choice of entering imperial service or returning home. In private he offered Stephanus considerable rewards if he could convince his fellow citizens to hand over the city. Stephanus did his best, supported by Antiochus, a merchant from Syria and long-time resident of Naples, but they were opposed by two other leading locals, Pastor and Asclepiades, who insisted that Belisarius must agree to a long list of conditions. When Belisarius agreed to all demands, the inhabitants were minded to hand over their city, until Pastor and Asclepiades again spoke against, urging that the outcome of the war was uncertain, that the Goths would punish traitors, that the city was well provided with supplies, and that Belisarius' willingness to accept all their considerable demands demonstrated that he was not confident of capturing the city. They were backed up by the local Jews, who promised to keep the city supplied, and by the Gothic garrison, which would guard the walls. These arguments prevailed and the siege began.

Belisarius cut the aqueduct, but this did not incommode the inhabitants greatly since there were plenty of wells. Attacks on the walls failed with significant losses, since the defences on the landward side were placed on a steep slope while it was inaccessible from the sea. The defenders sent to Theodahad, asking him to come to their relief, but he remained inactive. Supposedly he had been demoralized by a prediction which a Jew had made: three groups of ten pigs were given Gothic, Roman and imperial names and confined in three huts. In due course it was found that only two of the Gothic pigs survived, whereas most of the imperial ones lived, as did about half the native Romans even though these had lost their hair. On the other hand, granted that the city fell within three weeks, there was little time for Theodahad to organize a response.

Belisarius too was beginning to be upset by his failure to make progress, but he then had some good fortune. In the eastern empire Isaurians had a reputation for being excellent builders, especially in stone, and it happened that one of his Isaurian soldiers was curious to discover the nature of the aqueduct's construction. He therefore entered the aqueduct where Belisarius had cut it and walked towards the city until, close to the circuit wall, he reached a place where the water flowed in a tunnel cut through an outcrop of rock; this tunnel was too narrow for a man to pass, especially if he was wearing armour and carrying a shield, but it was capable of being widened. The Isaurian reported this to his fellow countryman, Paucaris, who was one of Belisarius' *bucellarii*, who immediately told the general. Belisarius rewarded Paucaris and instructed him to collect a team to try to enlarge the passage, which they achieved, not using picks and mattocks that would have been too noisy and probably also too unwieldy within the constrained channel, but by scraping away the rock with iron tools.

Having secured a route into the city, Belisarius made one final attempt at reaching a negotiated surrender and so summoned Stephanus to warn him that he now had the city's capture within his grasp but wanted to avoid the horrors of a sack, especially of such an old and Christian city. When this opportunity was rejected, Belisarius prepared to enter the city by night, selecting about 400 men under the command of Magnus and the Isaurian Ennes, and instructing Bessas to remain with him. He retained near him a large force of soldiers he regarded as most daring, equipped with ladders, and ordered the men in camp to remain at the ready. After nightfall he revealed the plan to Magnus and Ennes and sent them into the aqueduct with two trumpeters who, once inside the city, would cause confusion with their calls and summon their comrades outside. Inside the aqueduct about half of the men took fright and turned back, accompanied by Magnus; Belisarius chose a further 200 men from the troops with him and sent them into the aqueduct with Magnus, at which point the cowards also went back in. To reduce the risk that the approach of the men in armour might be noticed by the Goths on the nearby tower, he ordered Bessas to go forward and engage them in a loud conversation about a possible defection.

The party inside the aqueduct entered the city, but, since the aqueduct was both roofed and carried on high piers, they were uncertain where they had reached and how to descend. At last one soldier laid aside his weapons and managed to climb via an olive tree into the room of a poor single woman, after which he linked the tree and aqueduct with a strong strap that his comrades used to climb down. Three quarters of the night had now passed, but the intruders quickly killed the guards at two towers on the northern defences, the side where Belisarius was waiting, and the ladders were brought up for the assault. These unfortunately were too short to reach the battlements, since the carpenters had not seen the walls, but by lashing pairs of ladders together the ascent was at last made. The seaside walls were manned by the local Jews, who resisted all attempts at scaling since they knew that their earlier opposition to surrender had sealed their fate, but when morning came the attackers moved around the walls and ended this resistance. Initially the city was sacked, with the attackers venting their frustrations after the siege and the Huns in particular not even sparing those who had sought refuge in the churches, until Belisarius restrained them and released the captives. Of the two leading opponents of surrender, Pastor suffered a fit during the attack and died while Asclepiodotus was torn apart by his fellow citizens for bringing on them such hardships. The city came into Belisarius' hands on the twentieth day of the siege.[24]

First Siege of Rome, 537-538

Theodahad's continuing inaction spread unease among the Goths near Rome, which was the obvious next target for Belisarius, and they gathered at Regata, about 50km from Rome, where they elected as king Witigis, who was not from the ruling Amal dynasty but had established a good reputation as a solider. Theodahad fled towards Ravenna, but Witigis sent after him Optaris, who had a personal grudge, to capture him dead or alive; Optaris naturally preferred to take his revenge. Witigis proceeded to Rome, but then persuaded his followers that the most sensible course of action was to go to Ravenna, so that their current conflict with the Franks could be terminated and resources focused on fighting Belisarius. He recognized, the danger that Rome might desert him but hoped that a garrison of 4,000 Goths under Leuderis, who had a reputation for good sense, would keep the city loyal. He also harangued the clergy, Senate, and people to remind them of the benefits of Theoderic's rule, bound Pope Silverius by oaths, and took many senators with him as hostages.

Back at Ravenna he forced Matasuentha, daughter of Amalasuentha, to marry him and then offered to make peace with the Franks by handing over to them the Ostrogothic possessions in Gaul. Although the three Frankish kings, Childebert, Theodebert, and Clothar accepted the transfer, with Theodebert benefitting from the annexation of Provence, they declined to make an alliance since Theodebert had recently agreed to support Justinian in his Italian campaign, but Theodebert later did offer to send non-Frankish troops secretly to aid Witigis.[25]

The alliance between Theodebert and Justinian had been concluded in 535; the initiative came from Theodebert, who had boasted of the

---

24. Proc., *Wars* 5.8.5–10.48.
25. Proc., *Wars* 5.11–13.

extent of his territory that stretched from Pannonia to the Ocean and offered himself to Justinian as a useful and orthodox Catholic ally in the escalating tensions between Ravenna and Constantinople.[26] Good relations with the East had existed from the time of Theodebert's grandfather, Clovis, who had been made honorary consul and probably patrician after he had defeated the Visigoths at Vouille in 507, and Theodebert might have hoped for similar honours to elevate him above his brothers. He ruled the most easterly parts of Frankish territory, with authority that extended into lands in what is now central-southern Germany, where the proximity of the former Roman provinces of Noricum and Pannonia gave him an interest in dealings between Justinian and the Ostrogoths.

Justinian was suitably cautious of the Franks, since his decision to grant Noricum to the Lombards may have been intended to use them as a buffer against the Franks. Their help could have been useful, but when Justinian requested 3,000 troops in autumn 538,[27] probably to strengthen the garrison in Milan, Theodebert deferred his response while envoys travelled back and forth to Constantinople, and eventually sent Burgundians to support the Goths. Even neutrality would have brought some assistance to the Romans, but Theodebert exploited the collapse of Gothic rule to take over the northern fringes of their kingdom, to control the main routes over the Alps, and Venetia in the northeast, from where the Franks were not dislodged until the 560s. Although Agathias praised the Franks for their orthodoxy and for adopting Roman standards of law and administration,[28] this ignored the realities of their behaviour, which was driven by self-interest.[29] In contrast to his positive assessment, Agathias also believed that at the time of his death in 547 Theodebert had been planning to exploit the Roman preoccupation with Italy to lead an army to conquer Thrace and threaten Constantinople itself.[30]

Belisarius left a garrison of 300 under Herodian at Naples and also placed troops in Cumae on the coast. The inhabitants of Rome, eager to avoid the fate of Naples, now sent Fidelius as envoy to invite Belisarius to

---

26. *Epist. Aust.* 18–20.

27. *Epist. Aust.* 19.

28. Agathias, *Hist.* 1.2.

29. Cameron, *Agathias* 50–1, summarizing the long discussion in ead., 'Early Merovingians', esp. App.C at 136–9.

30. Agathias, *Hist.* 1.4.1; his information is, at best, confused, since he says that Theodebert planned to exploit the engagement of Narses and his troops in Italy, i.e. in the 550s several years after his own death.

take over the city, with Silverius being particularly keen on this switch. Belisarius therefore marched up the Via Appia, whose smooth surface of close-fitting stones was still impressive after over eight centuries of use. The Gothic garrison at Rome reckoned that they could not fight Belisarius outside the walls or defend the city in view of the hostility of the inhabitants, and so withdrew north through the Porta Flaminia on 10 December 536 as Belisarius was entering from the south through the Porta Asinaria,[31] sixty years after the end of the western empire. Of the Goths only Leuderis remained behind and he was sent to Justinian to present the keys to the city. Belisarius had to carry out repairs to the defences, since the circuit wall had crumbled in places, providing the merlons on the battlements with side protection, so that defenders would not be hit by missiles, and digging a moat. Although the inhabitants were worried by the prospect of a siege, granted the length of the defences and the challenge of supplying a large inland city, Belisarius continued his preparations, unloading the supplies he had brought from Sicily and forcing the locals to bring in provisions from outside.

Further parts of Italy now came over to Belisarius. No Goths were based in Calabria in the far south or Apulia in the southeast, and these whole regions joined him, although the one specific place that Procopius mentions, Beneventum, does not belong to either region but rather to Samnium. The Goth Pitzias brought over part of Samnium and the Goths located there, although on the opposite side of a river, quite possibly to the north of the Volturno, the Goths refused to join him so that Belisarius spared a few troops to offer support. This put Belisarius in control of most of the peninsula south of Rome and, once preparations for the defence of Rome were complete, he now started to extend his authority north into Tuscany, where he dispatched forces under Constantine and Bessas. The latter took over Narni without opposition from the inhabitants, while the former was welcomed into Spoleto and Perugia. When Witigis sent troops to recover Spoleto, Constantine turned them to flight after a hard-fought engagement against superior numbers, killing most of them.

News of this reverse persuaded Witigis that he had to move from Ravenna, even though he was still awaiting the arrival of the troops that he had recalled from Gaul after his agreement with the Franks. He sent Asinarius and Uligisalus to Dalmatia with orders to recruit an army from

---

31. *Liber Ponificalis*, Silverius 4.

the Swabians in the north and proceed against Salona. While Asinarius recruited more soldiers Uligisalus advanced as far as Scardona where he was defeated, but the Roman commander in the area, Constantinianus, took fright at the combined enemy numbers and so withdrew his garrisons from outlying forts and prepared to defend Salona. The Goths built a palisade around the city and patrolled the seaward side closely with their ships, but in a surprise attack the Romans managed to sink or capture many of the enemy boats, although this just spurred the Goths to invest the city more closely by land. Witigis now discovered how few troops Belisarius had with him to defend Rome and began to regret abandoning the city. Therefore in 537 he moved swiftly to attack, arriving on 21 February,[32] allegedly leading 150,000 cavalry and infantry, mostly armoured, a number that is impossibly high, but which originated in the letter that Belisarius sent Justinian during the siege to ask for reinforcements.[33]

At the news of the Gothic approach, Belisarius instructed Constantine and Bessas to leave suitable garrisons in the places they had taken over but to bring most of their troops to support him at Rome: although his own numbers were critically low, he was planning ahead since he was keen to retain control of the Via Flaminia and did not want to have to besiege such strong locations in the future. At Narni Bessas was surprised by the arrival of a large Gothic advance guard, but he managed to drive it back until superior numbers forced him to retire, after which he withdrew to Rome. Witigis continued his march through Sabine territory, which suggests that he had crossed from the Via Flaminia to the Via Salaria, possibly because Narni was still held by the Romans.

The subsequent siege was to last just over one year and is narrated by Procopius at length,[34] with many specific incidents being described in detail. The key theme that runs throughout his account is the ability of Belisarius, who is superior to everyone, to Witigis in understanding what is best, but also to his fellow officers in identifying key issues and declining to panic at false reports, as well as to the Roman citizens whose morale bounces down and up in accordance with the progress of events.

---

32. *Liber Pontificalis*, Silverius 4.
33. Proc., *Wars* 5.14–16; 24.3. The term used by Procopius at 5.16.11 is '15 myriads', and subsequently Totila reflects on how 7,000 Romans managed to defeat '20 myriads' of Goths (7.21.4). The intention is to highlight the contrast with the limited Roman forces and the Gothic total cannot be trusted: for discussion, see Whately, *Battles* 173–7; id., 'Siege' 266–74.
34. Proc., *Wars* 5.18–6.10.

City of Rome

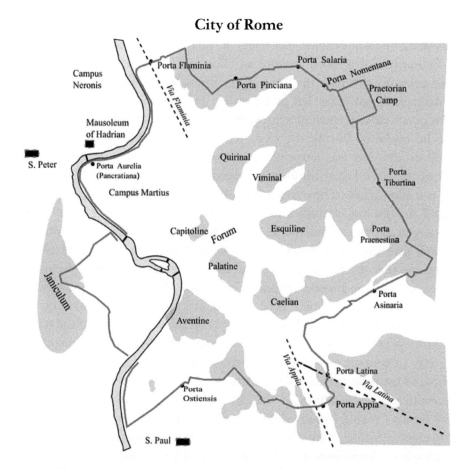

For Belisarius it was critical to bring as many supplies into the city as possible and to ensure that only those actively supporting the defence remained inside. He also had to attend to the risk of treachery, whether from disaffected soldiers or civilians, and plan how to distribute his limited resources around the most vulnerable sectors of the 19km of walls.[35] Witigis, despite his alleged numbers, could not invest the whole circuit, nor could he afford to sacrifice large numbers of his Gothic followers in costly direct assaults. Overall Procopius' extended narrative assumes epic aspects, with acts of individual heroism and information about gory wounds, while

---

35. Richmond, *City Wall*, provides an exceptionally authoritative account of the remains of the walls and gates from their construction under Aurelian in the 270s. The Porta Appia (Plate 16), as strengthened in the early fourth and early fifth centuries, was one of the most imposing gates in the circuit.

Belisarius is presented as a resourceful figure in the manner of Homeric Odysseus, one who is able to outsmart his opponents and inspire his men.[36]

Belisarius failed in an attempt to delay the Goths at a river crossing, most probably that over the Anio on the Via Salaria,[37] when a combination of desertions and panic led to a fortified bridge being abandoned, but a subsequent cavalry encounter provided Belisarius with important insights that he exploited during the siege. He had approached the bridge with 1,000 cavalry, but was surprised to encounter the enemy already on his side of the river. His small force managed to hold its own, provided that it did not allow itself to be overwhelmed by Gothic numbers, and the Goths would provide opportunities to attack when the cohesion of their ranks disintegrated. To defend the walls he appointed an officer to command at each gate and, after Bessas at the Porta Praenestina sent a message to Belisarius that the Goths had broken into the city on the far side of the Tiber, i.e. outside Bessas' sphere of command, he instructed his officers that they should never pay heed to rumours that different parts of the defences had been breached but focus only on their own sector of the wall.

In view of his shortage of troops he recruited the male inhabitants of the city to support his professional soldiers, organizing them into mixed units and providing a salary so that labourers could earn a wage to purchase necessities. Twice a month he changed the keys to the locks on the gates, and he also regularly moved the units of defenders to reduce the risk that close relations might be struck up with the besiegers and give rise to treachery. Musicians played their instruments on the walls at night,[38] while patrols, especially of Berbers, were sent outside the walls after dark, with dogs to raise the alarm if anyone approached. He repeatedly made a public show of his confidence in victory, so that the incredulous civilians thought him mad until events proved him right.

Witigis focused efforts on the north-eastern sector, the five gates from the Porta Flaminia to the Porta Praenestina,[39] against which he built six camps. In order to prevent Belisarius from cutting the Milvian Bridge and

---

36. Whately, *Battles* 190–6.
37. Discussion in Lillington-Martin, 'Struggle' 611–27.
38. The purpose of this is unclear. Perhaps the music was to help the defenders stay awake, perhaps to make it harder for the Goths to start secret discussions.
39. Of these five only the Porta Pinciana and the postern Porta Nomentana survive, the other three having been demolished in the 19th century. For discussion of the surviving remains and evidence for lost structures, see Richmond, *City Wall* 159–69, 185–200, 230. Although similar to the Porta Appia (Plate 16) in basic form, none was as imposing.

depriving the Goths of easy access to the west bank of the Tiber, a seventh camp was built in the Campus Neronis beyond Hadrian's Mausoleum. These camps were surrounded by ditches whose earth was piled up into a high mound topped with sharp stakes. The camp to the west of the Tiber was commanded by Marcias, who had now arrived with the Gothic units from Gaul, while Witigis and five others held those on the east bank. The Goths also cut the city's fourteen aqueducts, while Belisarius took the precaution of filling them in with rubble for a considerable distance to avoid suffering the surprise he had achieved at Naples. He took command at the small Porta Pinciana and the nearby Porta Salaria, a section of the defences open to attack but also suitable for sallies. Bessas held the Porta Praenestina and Constantine the Porta Flaminia, where the gates were blocked by an inner wall of large stones to prevent them being opened, since the proximity of a Gothic camp increased the risk of treachery. The commanders of the infantry were stationed at the other gates.

With the aqueducts cut it was impossible to power the city's water mills and there were insufficient animals to turn the grinding stones. Belisarius, however, devised a solution by constructing floating mills in the Tiber at the bridge that linked the main city with the Janiculum: pairs of boats were lashed together with a distance of two feet in between where a water wheel was suspended. The Goths responded by throwing tree trunks and corpses into the river to break the wheels, to which Belisarius reacted by running iron chains across the river above the bridge so that anything floating downstream was halted there. The city had enough drinking water since the parts further from the river could rely on wells; the drainage system was safe since the sewers discharged into the Tiber, but the public baths could not be used since in the absence of the aqueducts there was insufficient water.[40]

Rome's inhabitants were already disgruntled by the lack of baths, shortages of food, and sleepless nights spent on guard duty, and angered by the sight of the Goths ravaging the surrounding countryside, and Theodahad attempted to exploit this by offering Belisarius the chance to withdraw. When this was rejected he constructed wheeled towers equal to the wall height, which was accurately calculated by counting the courses of stone, equipped with battering rams. Belisarius also prepared the city's siege equipment, arrow-firing *ballistae* on the towers, stone-throwing onagers along the walls, and large spiked wooden constructions called

---

40. Proc., *Wars* 5.19.

wolves that could be dropped on assailants who approached the gates. On the eighteenth day of the siege, i.e. mid-March 537, the Goths attacked, but Belisarius at the Porta Salaria demonstrated how to thwart their advance, killing three leading Goths with three arrows and then directing his men to aim at the oxen pulling the siege towers, so that they were left stranded.

The Goths also attacked the Mausoleum of Hadrian on the right bank of the Tiber. This massive structure, a 14-metre square concrete base topped by a circular drum 10 metres across, had been converted into a fortification to protect the bridge to the Porta Aurelia in the fourth or fifth century by the addition of merlons to the square first storey.[41] There Constantine was in command, although he had crossed to the left bank with some of his men since he feared that the Goths were going to attack the riverside walls, which were weakly manned. The Goths in fact assaulted both the Porta Aurelia and Mausoleum, managing to approach close to the latter since the colonnade that extended from St Peter's concealed their advance until they were too close to be subject to fire from *ballistae* while their large shields protected them from arrows. The defenders were in danger of being overrun, as a heavy barrage of missiles allowed ladders to be brought up, especially as the Goths surrounded the whole bastion so that the garrison always had assailants behind them.[42] At last the defenders broke up the large statues decorating the tomb and dropped chunks on the Goths, forcing them to withdraw. The attack on the Porta Pancratiana, where Paulus led the defence, failed because the walls were sited on a steep rise, while the Goths refrained from attempting the Porta Flaminia, where Ursicinus and the infantry unit of *regii* were stationed, since its sheer slope rendered it inaccessible. Moving clockwise or east around the circuit from the Flaminia towards the Porta Pinciana a section of wall had split without collapsing so that its outer face bulged beyond the main circuit. Belisarius had been dissuaded from demolishing and rebuilding this before the siege on the grounds that St Peter himself had promised the citizens that his personal attention would make it unassailable. An alternative explanation would be the time required for such repairs,[43] but at any event this vulnerable section was never endangered.

The main threat came in the section of wall commanded by Bessas at the Porta Praenestina, where the Vivarium, a space for holding wild

---

41. Discussion in Richmond, *City Wall* 20–6.
42. The first-storey merlons provided scant protection against such cross-fire.
43. As was the case with the extramural rock that threatened the defences of Antioch in 540.

animals with a lower outer wall that lacked battlements or towers, was located immediately outside the main wall, which itself was weak since the mortar in the brick courses was crumbling.[44] The Goths set about mining the outer wall while Bessas and Peranius, the commanders, summoned Belisarius as they feared for the defences. Leaving only a few soldiers on the battlements, he waited for the Goths to break into the Vivarium, then sent Cyprian to lead troops with drawn swords to attack the intruders. The cramped conditions inside the Vivarium impeded the Goths, and, as they fell into confusion, Belisarius opened the gates and put the attackers to flight, burning their siege equipment. At the Porta Salaria a sally also routed the enemy and allowed the Romans to burn their machines. Fighting had begun in early morning and ended late in the afternoon, by which time 30,000 Goths are said to have perished since their large numbers meant that Roman missiles always found a target.[45] That night the defenders on the battlements celebrated their victory in song.[46]

Belisarius now wrote to Justinian to report on developments and request urgent reinforcements if the disgrace of losing Rome was to be avoided. In response Justinian ordered Valerian and Martin, who had been sent out in late December 536 but had only managed to reach Aetolia and Acarnania in western Greece, to proceed rapidly to Italy. In order to preserve food supplies, Belisarius instructed the civilians to send to Naples their women, children, and any servants who could not contribute to manning the walls, also ordering his soldiers to dismiss surplus attendants. Some

---

44. Procopius states that Witigis moved from the Porta Salaria to the Porta Praenestina in order to attack the Vivarium (5.20.10). As a result this enclosure is traditionally located close to the latter gate (Richmond, *City Wall* 184), although there are no obvious remains of such a structure. The most plausible candidate for the Vivarium is the former camp of the Praetorian Guard (disbanded in the early fourth century), which is located between the Salaria and Praenestina as one moves clockwise round the walls. The rectangular camp had been incorporated into Rome's third-century walls, although its outer face lacks the towers that characterize the rest of the circuit, and its defined space would have made an excellent killing ground for Belisarius. The camp was probably within the sector commanded by Bessas at the Praenestina, since Belisarius held the Pinciana and Salaria, in which case Procopius has been slightly inexact in specifying its position, although he perhaps meant no more than that Witigis moved from Belisarius' stretch of defences to that of Bessas. It does seem more likely that the Romans would have exploited a disused structure for their animals rather than build anything new, and it is unwise to assume that Procopius is always precise with regard to topographical details.
45. The casualty figure is implausible, but is in line with the very high total given for Witigis' forces; the word used, *trismurioi* (three myriads), signals the imprecision.
46. Proc., *Wars* 5.20–3.

took ship at Portus while others journeyed by land down the Via Appia without being harassed by the Goths, who were afraid of being ambushed, especially by Belisarius' Berber troops who were adept at rapid attacks. Suspicions of treacherous discussions with the Goths led Belisarius to arrest Pope Silverius and convey him to Greece, while several senators were also dismissed. Apparently during this phase of the siege some Romans secretly attempted to open the bronze doors of the Temple of Janus in the Forum but could only move them slightly. In the Republic and early Empire the doors were opened to signify that Rome was at war, a practice that had lapsed with the triumph of Christianity, and Procopius says that the unknown perpetrators must have had in mind old beliefs.[47]

On the third day after the failed assault, Witigis tightened the blockade by capturing Portus, the city's harbour at the mouth of the Tiber, where he left a garrison of 1,000 men, so that supplies could no longer be unloaded onto barges and hauled upstream by oxen. It was still possible to bring supplies up the left (south) side of the river from Ostia, but this was a much more laborious process since ships had to put in at Antium (Anzio) and transport goods by land. Valerian and Martin arrived twenty days after the loss of Portus, hence in early April 537, bringing with them 1,600 cavalry, mostly Huns, Slavs, and Antes. This reinforcement encouraged Belisarius to go on to the offensive. Three times he gave one of his *bucellarii* 200 or 300 horsemen to display them on a hill near an enemy camp; when attacked, they were to avoid combat at close quarters but fire all their arrows then flee straight for the walls. The Goths lost 4,000 men in these sallies. Witigis thought that he could use these tactics against the Romans and so sent 500 men to occupy a hill just outside the range of missiles from the walls; in response Belisarius gave Bessas 1,000 men who encircled the Goths and shot them down with arrows, until they descended to the plain in disorder where the superior Roman numbers overwhelmed them. Witigis ascribed this defeat to cowardice but a second experiment also ended in heavy losses. Belisarius knew that the Roman superiority in horse-archery gave them a decisive advantage, as long as they avoided encounters at close quarters where Gothic numbers and their reliance on spears would prevail.[48]

These small successes elated the defenders, who now pressed Belisarius to authorize a decisive engagement, abusing him when the disparity in

47. Proc., *Wars* 5.24–5.
48. Proc., *Wars* 5.26–7.

numbers made him cautious. Belisarius eventually agreed, but his plan to catch the Goths by surprise with a sally was repeatedly frustrated, since information was leaked by deserters. As a result, after leaving sufficient men on the walls, he deployed most of his soldiers outside the Porta Pinciana and Porta Salaria, but also gave a cavalry troop to Valerian at the Porta Aurelia supported by an infantry phalanx of Roman civilians at the Porta Pancratiana, to oppose the Gothic camp on the right back of the Tiber and prevent them crossing to join the main battle. At the insistence of their leaders, Principius and the Isaurian Tarmutus, that he should have more confidence in the infantry, he deployed them behind the cavalry to ensure that they did not disrupt it by panicking but be available to cover any retreat. On both sides of the Tiber the fighting at first favoured the Romans, thanks above all to their archery, but Valerian's force disintegrated when given the opportunity to loot the Gothic camp, so that they were driven back to the walls, while numbers eventually told to the east of the river where the Roman cavalry was forced to withdraw and the infantry fled in panic. Most reached the walls in safety, thanks to the heroic self-sacrifice of Principius and Tarmutus, although many had to shelter under the walls since the gates were shut to prevent the Goths from flooding in.[49]

Belisarius now reverted to the small cavalry skirmishes in which the Romans came off better, provided as ever that they did not allow themselves to pursue too far or be locked into fighting at close quarters. Procopius reckoned that there were sixty-seven such engagements during the siege.[50] By late March famine and disease were apparently beginning to affect the civilians, although the soldiers still had grain, since the Goths had at last tightened the blockade on the south side of the city by constructing a fort at the point where the two aqueducts approaching Rome between the Via Latina and Via Appia intersected. As long as there was grain in the fields outside the city, daring individuals slipped out to harvest what they could, but when this was exhausted discontent mounted. The civilians again pressed Belisarius for a decisive battle, but he promised that relief was coming and, probably in early autumn, he also dispatched Procopius to Naples to gather supplies.

He next planned how to apply pressure on the besieging Goths and constrain their supplies by posting Huns near the extramural church of

49. Proc., *Wars* 5.28–9.
50. Proc., *Wars* 6.2.37.

S. Paul and sending out detachments of troops to occupy Tibur (Tivoli), Terracina, and Albano, from where they could harass the Goths. Disease began to affect the Goths, especially at their camp south of the city, but the Huns at S. Paul's were also stricken. Procopius meanwhile had collected supplies at Naples as well as 500 soldiers from Campania, where he was joined by 3,000 Isaurians, who arrived from the East by sea, plus 800 Thracian cavalry and 1,000 regular cavalry under John, who had landed at Dryus (Otranto) and travelled overland. The Isaurians under Paul and Conon sailed for Ostia on grain ships while John accompanied a wagon train up the Via Appia.[51] To cover their arrival Belisarius organized a major diversion at the northern defences, unblocking the Porta Flaminia so that he could launch an unexpected sally to support a force of 1,000 cavalry he had sent through the Porta Pinciana to provoke a Gothic attack. The plan worked well to the extent that the Romans came close to entering the Gothic camp.[52]

News of the approach of Roman relief forces prompted Witigis to attempt to strike a deal with Belisarius, but all offers of concessions were rejected on the grounds that the emperor's wishes had to be respected; as a result it was agreed that the Goths would send envoys to Justinian. The fleet of supplies now reached Ostia and, even though an armistice had not yet been confirmed, the Goths did nothing to hinder the supplies being transshipped and brought into Rome up the Tiber. In late December 537 hostages were exchanged to confirm an armistice of three months for envoys to travel to Constantinople. Shortages of supplies led the Goths to abandon Portus, Albano in the hills south-east of Rome, and Centumcellae (Civitavecchia) on the coast north of Portus, all of which Belisarius took over. This provoked complaints from Witigis that the truce had been breached, but Belisarius just laughed this off and dispatched 2,000 cavalry under John to Alba in Picenum with orders to ravage the land, whose potential defenders had all left for the siege of Rome, if the truce should be broken. Datis, bishop of Milan, and some of that city's leaders came to request a few soldiers with whom they could liberate their city and the province of Liguria.[53]

In a taste of problems to come, an argument now broke out between Belisarius and his subordinate Constantine over some rich booty that one

---

51. It would have entered the city through the towering Porta Appia (Plate 16).
52. Proc., *Wars* 6.1–5.
53. Proc., *Wars* 6.6–7.

of Constantine's guards had appropriated, which resulted in Constantine being arrested after trying to stab Belisarius and then executed. Witigis made three final attempts to capture Rome, first through the aqueduct that entered by the Porta Pinciana, then in a surprise attack at the same gate, and finally by bribing two Romans to intoxicate the guards on the riverside wall so that Goths could land by boat and storm the defences. All these efforts failed, but Belisarius regarded the armistice as clearly broken and so ordered John to ravage Picenum. This he did successfully and, even though he failed to win over Auximum (Osimo) and Urbino, the inhabitants of Rimini invited him in. The Roman occupation of a place so close to Ravenna prompted Witigis to abandon the siege of Rome and Matasuentha in Ravenna to open discussions about betraying the city. The siege of Rome had lasted nine days over one year and ended in mid–March 538.[54]

Defeat of Ostrogoths, 538-540

As he travelled north Witigis left garrisons of 1,000 men at Chiusi and Orvieto and 400 at Todi, with the intention of preventing Belisarius from encroaching further into Tuscany, while east of the Appennines he strengthened the garrison of Auximum with 4,000 men, who could watch Ancona that was now in Roman hands, and of Urbino with 2,000 men, while he placed 500 men in Cesena and Monteferatra. He had moved north slowly since the Roman garrisons at Narni, Spoleto, and Perugia gave them control of the Via Flaminia. Thus Belisarius was able to send 1,000 cavalry under Ildiger and Martin to Picenum, where they were to collect the infantry at Ancona and take them to defend Rimini, from which John and all his cavalry were to withdraw; en route to Ancona they overcame the Goths defending the narrow defile at Petra. In another sign of future problems, however, John declined to obey Belisarius' order, insisting on staying in Rimini with 400 of his cavalry where he was soon put under siege.

Witigis prepared a tower to be wheeled up to a vulnerable section of Rimini's defences, with men pushing it from inside to avoid the problems caused by the vulnerable oxen at Rome. By nightfall it had approached close to the wall, with only a shallow trench in between, but overnight John took a gang of Isaurians who hacked out a deeper obstacle and threw the excavated earth against the city wall as an additional rampart.

---

54. Proc., *Wars* 6.8–10.

In the morning Witigis attempted to counteract this by filling the ditch with logs, but these did not bear the tower's weight and it was only after a hard fight that the Goths managed to withdraw the machine to their camp. Witigis now prepared to starve the defenders into surrender since their provisions were already exhausted. Belisarius sent 1,000 men under Mundila to liberate Milan, Thracians commanded by Paul and Isaurians under Ennes. Travelling by sea to Genoa they proceeded overland to the Po valley, bringing with them a number of small boats to enable them to cross the river. They were confronted by the strong garrison at Ticinum (Pavia), where the local Goths stored their valuable possessions, but overcame them, albeit with the loss of Fidelius, the praetorian prefect. Mundila occupied the strongholds of Bergamo, Como, and Novarra, so that he was left with only 300 troops to defend Milan, which was soon attacked when Witigis sent 10,000 Burgundians, whom he had received from the Franks under their secret agreement to support the Goths.

Belisarius advanced north after Witigis, overawing into surrender the Goths defending Todi and Chiusi, sending the Goths to Sicily and Naples and leaving his own men in the forts. In Picenum Witigis reinforced the Goths at Auximum, ordering them to attack Ancona where Belisarius' garrison under Conon came close to losing the city by rashly confronting the approaching army outside the strong fortifications. When driven back by superior numbers they fled in disorder to the city, where the Goths climbed the walls and were only dislodged by the heroics of two *bucellarii* of Belisarius and Valerian, who chanced to have arrived recently. Further Roman reinforcements under the *praepositus sacri cubiculi* Narses had now reached Picenum, 5,000 soldiers commanded by Justin, *MM per Illyricum*, and the Persarmenian Narses among others, as well as 2,000 Heruls.[55]

Belisarius and Narses took stock of the situation at Fermo on the Adriatic near Auximum.[56] They knew that John desperately needed to be relieved at Rimini, but many officers were unsympathetic to his plight, since he had brought this on himself by disregarding Belisarius' orders to withdraw his cavalry from the city. Narses, however, was well-disposed to John and so Belisarius, after some hesitation caused by the risk that the Gothic garrison at Auximum would attack him from the rear, organized a three-

---

55. Proc., *Wars* 6.11–13.
56. For analysis of the differences between Belisarius and Narses, see Parnell, 'Social Networks' 116–21.

pronged advance with the fleet under Ildiger sailing directly to Rimini and Martin marching up the coast road, while he and Narses took an inland mountain route. The sight and news of the three approaching Roman forces caused Witigis to beat a hasty retreat, leaving behind some of the Goths' possessions and their sick. When Belisarius indirectly reproached John, who was emaciated as were his men, by saying that he should be grateful to Ildiger, John retorted by stating that he recognised his debt to Narses.

This exchange marked the start of a breach between John and Belisarius, while Narses found himself being urged by many to assert his rights viz-a-viz Belisarius: the soldiers would follow him if he were to assume command and he could not have travelled from Constantinople as a close confidant of the emperor only to play second fiddle to a general. When Belisarius attempted to secure agreement to dividing his forces to relieve Milan and besiege Auximum, Narses countered by saying that he would secure Emilia for Justinian while Belisarius could do what he wanted. Even when Belisarius produced a letter from Justinian that stressed that he was in supreme command, Narses still found a loophole to justify him disregarding Belisarius to do what he thought best.[57] This was not a disagreement about strategy, since both Belisarius and Narses recognized the importance of progressively removing territory from Gothic control, but about tactics with Belisarius, who was cautious by nature, giving priority to keeping hold of Liguria by retaining Milan and neutralizing the threat from Auximum, whereas Narses targeted new territories, perhaps in the expectation that the Goths would have to withdraw outlying forces to protect their core territory. It was also a dispute about influence, with officers close to Narses reluctant to facilitate Belisarius' success.[58]

Belisarius sent Peranius to besiege Orvieto while he and Narses moved on Urbino, where they camped on opposite sides of the city. After failing to overawe the defenders into surrender Belisarius prepared protection to allow his men to approach the city gate, but overnight Narses, despite Belisarius' pleas, decided to abandon the siege and withdraw to Rimini on the grounds that John had already failed to capture Urbino when the garrison had been much smaller. Belisarius, however, was lucky since the one spring inside the defences began to dry up, so that after three days the garrison had to capitulate. Narses was not best pleased, but through

---

57. Proc., *Wars* 6.16–18.
58. Parnell, 'Social Networks' 120–2.

John he managed to take over most of Emilia including the city of Forum Cornelii (Imola), although not the fortress of Cesena. Even though it was now December Belisarius marched his army to join Peranius outside Orvieto, which he had heard was low on provisions, while he sent Aratius to remain at Fermo for the winter to prevent the Goths in Auximum from causing trouble. At Orvieto the Goths had been reduced to eating skins and hides softened by soaking, while in both Tuscany and Emilia the failure to harvest grain in two successive summers had reduced the inhabitants to haggard starvation, subsisting on bread made from acorns and even cannibalism. In Picenum 50,000 are said to have perished in the countryside from hunger, with many more deaths in the area 'north of the Adriatic'.[59]

Milan was coming under severe pressure as the Gothic blockade had cut off supplies and a relief army under Martin had halted by the river Po, one day's march from the city. Although Mundila within the city pleaded with him to advance, Martin sent to Belisarius asking him to instruct John and Justin to move from Emilia to support him. They declined to obey unless Narses gave them the order, so Belisarius had to write to Narses to urge the benefits of collaboration in the face of the enemy. Narses did oblige, but John first returned to the Adriatic to secure boats to allow him to cross the Po and then fell ill. All this wasted so much time that early in 539 Mundila tried to agree terms with the besiegers to hand over Milan. The Goths were prepared to guarantee the soldiers' safety but offered nothing for the civilians. Although Mundila urged his men to reject this and go out to fight the Goths, they preferred to accept their own salvation regardless of the fate of the city.

Once in control of the city the Goths put the soldiers under guard, slew all male citizens – allegedly to the number of 300,000 – and presented the women to their Burgundian allies as slaves. When the praetorian prefect Reparatus was discovered, they hacked his body in pieces and fed his flesh to the dogs. Belisarius reported this news to Justinian who recalled Narses; he took with him some of his troops and most of the Heruls declined to remain in Italy after his departure. Witigis expected Belisarius to attack Ravenna in the next campaign season and so started to look for new allies. He failed to interest the Lombards, who stayed loyal to Justinian, and so sent envoys to Khusro to urge the Persians to strike before Justinian became too powerful. Justinian, aware that the Persians

59. Proc., *Wars* 6.19–20.

were contemplating a resumption of war in the East, instructed the envoys that Witigis had earlier sent to Constantinople to return with the offer of a mutually beneficial agreement.[60]

Belisarius' first priority in 539 was to capture Auximum and Faesulae (Fiesole) before approaching Ravenna, to ensure that he could not be caught by surprise attacks. He therefore sent troops to invest Faesulae and others to monitor the Gothic army at Milan while he led 11,000 troops against Auximum, which was very securely sited and held by a strong garrison. Belisarius believed he would have to reduce the city by starvation, and this led to daily skirmishes over fodder that the Goths needed for their horses. The Goths worked out how to ambush the Romans when they tried to prevent them gathering supplies, frustrating Belisarius who could not recall his men even when he could see them coming into danger. Then Procopius recommended that he exploit the different notes of cavalry and infantry trumpets, using the former to sound an advance and the latter for retreat. The defenders managed to smuggle a message to Witigis begging for assistance, which he promised, but he then failed to act, since he both feared Belisarius' army and reckoned the lack of provisions in Picenum made it impossible for him to lead his army there. Meanwhile the defenders of Faesulae, after initially holding their own, were being closely blockaded and also sent to Witigis for help. He instructed Uraias to lead the Goths at Milan to relieve them, but their advance was thwarted by the Roman force sent to watch his actions.[61]

Theodebert, king of the Franks, had been following events in Italy and decided that now was the time to take advantage of the attritional conflict between Goths and Romans. He therefore led a large army, said to number 100,000, most of whom were infantry though the royal escort were mounted, over the Alps into Liguria. The Goths at first thought they had arrived to support them and so welcomed them, allowing them to cross the bridge over the Po at Ticinum, but once inside the Gothic camp Theodebert's men attacked the Goths and drove them to flight. The Romans, who had been monitoring Gothic movements, thought that Belisarius must have routed them, but they were soon disabused and retired to Tuscany. The Franks, however, could not capitalize on these successes since they ran short of supplies and dysentery carried off one third of their army, so that Theodebert withdrew across the

60. Proc., *Wars* 6.21–2.
61. Proc., *Wars* 6.22–4.

Alps. Meanwhile Auximum continued to hold out, frustrating Belisarius whose troops had to operate in an empty land, while the defenders had their hopes buoyed by a promise of imminent assistance from Witigis that a traitor in the Roman army had smuggled through the lines. Even the discovery of this treachery and the public burning of the culprit did not lead to surrender, so Belisarius acted to cut off their water supply.

The defenders relied for part of their needs on a small extramural spring whose flow was collected in a cistern; in order to damage it, five Isaurians were smuggled inside to hack a drainage hole, but the move was discovered and provoked a fierce response from the Goths. Although the Romans managed, after an intense struggle, to drive back the defenders, it proved impossible to damage the cistern and so Belisarius resorted to polluting it with corpses, poisonous plants, and burning asbestos; the Goths still had a well within the walls, but its supply did not meet their needs. Famine had eventually forced the defenders of Faesulae to surrender and Belisarius now paraded them in view of Auximum to increase pressure. The Goths tried to insist on being allowed to withdraw to Ravenna with their possessions, much to the annoyance of the Roman soldiers who believed that their protracted efforts should be rewarded with the booty, but at last terms were agreed under which the Romans received half of the possessions while the Goths submitted to the emperor.[62]

These successes allowed Belisarius to focus efforts on Ravenna towards the end of 539, so he stationed troops on both banks of the Po to prevent supplies being brought downstream. This resulted in the capture of a large number of boats that had been loaded with grain in Liguria but were stranded by a sudden drop in the river level. The Franks again tried to exploit the situation in Italy by offering massive support to Witigis if he agreed to share control with them, but Belisarius persuaded him that negotiations with Justinian offered better prospects. Even so Belisarius aimed to maintain pressure by winning over Gothic towns in Venetia and their forts in the Cottian Alps. When Uraias, who was still leading a Gothic force outside the blockade of Ravenna, moved to intervene in the Alps, the fact that John and Martin had gained control of the forts inhabited by the families of the Gothic soldiers led his troops to desert and take service under John. Conditions in Ravenna worsened when the city's granaries caught fire, whether by lightning or treachery is unclear.

---

62. Proc., *Wars* 6.25–7.

Two envoys from Justinian now arrived, Domnicus and Maximinus, with an offer to allow Witigis to retain half the royal treasure and rule Italy north of the Po, while Justinian received the rest of the peninsula. These terms were acceptable to Witigis and his court, but when the envoys returned to the Roman camp Belisarius declined to add his signature to the agreement, which led the Goths to suspect treachery. Although Belisarius' officers were keen to have the terms ratified, the delay led to fresh proposals from the Goths, first from the nobility and then also from Witigis, to the effect that they would surrender completely if Belisarius agreed to become emperor of the West. Belisarius let it appear that he was receptive to this arrangement and swore not to harm the Goths, though he reserved the oaths about ruling Italy and the Goths until he was in the presence of Witigis and his leaders. Belisarius took the precaution of sending off the three commanders whom he knew to be most hostile to himself, John, and the Persarmenian brothers Narses and Aratius, to secure provisions, taking with them the praetorian prefect Athanasius who had just arrived from Constantinople, while he marched his army into Ravenna and arranged for a grain fleet to dock at Classis, Ravenna's port.

Once inside Ravenna, Belisarius dismissed to their homes all the Goths who lived south of the Po, since he was confident that the Roman garrisons distributed throughout the peninsula would prevent them from combining into an army. He also wanted to reduce Gothic numbers at Ravenna since they outnumbered their new Roman masters. The Gothic garrison at Tarbesium (Treviso) in Venetia now surrendered, as did other forts in the region, although at Verona Ildebad delayed. Some of Belisarius' officers began to slander him to Justinian, who recalled him in order to face the Persians, and the news of his imminent departure disconcerted the Goths, who had been expecting him to stay and rule. As a result some nobles approached Uraias, a nephew of Witigis, offering him the kingship but he urged them to appoint Ildebad. Once this was done Ildebad offered to submit to Belisarius if he confirmed that he would rule Italy, as he had promised, but Belisarius surprised the Goths by preferring to remain a subject of Justinian.[63]

---

63. Proc., *Wars* 6.28–30.

Gothic Revival, 541-544

Belisarius returned to Constantinople with Witigis, the Gothic nobles and royal treasure to considerable public acclaim, but in Italy, as in the re-conquered African provinces, the realities of victory and Roman rule soon created resentment. Procopius held the logothete Alexander 'Scissors' especially responsible, since he annoyed both civilians by demanding the return of money they had made during the Gothic regime and the soldiers by reducing their compensation for wounds. Individual commanders also took the opportunity to enrich themselves, in contrast to Belisarius' scrupulous respect for property in Italy. Ildebad was still based at Tarbesium in Venetia, where he routed Vitalius when the latter attempted to check the growth of his support. His rule, however, soon ended, after he had angered the Goths by executing Uraias for alleged treachery after a quarrel between their wives; Ildebad was murdered at a banquet by one of his guards over a personal quarrel. He was briefly succeeded by the Rugian Eraric, but he could not command the allegiance of the Goths, who turned to Ildebad's nephew Totila for their next leader. Eraric was killed after reopening negotiations with Justinian about splitting control of Italy.[64]

Justinian reproached his commanders in Italy for failing to exploit the situation, and so they assembled their troops at Ravenna and early in 542 marched on Verona with 11,000 men. A local had persuaded a guard at one of Verona's gates to surrender the city, with the result that Artabazus and a group of Persian captives that Belisarius had sent from Sisauranon entered the walls and drove out the garrison. The main Roman army, however, delayed its advance while the commanders argued about the booty, with the result that the Goths were able to recapture the city. Totila now assembled 5,000 Goths and, despite exhortations from Artabazus that his small numbers should not be despised, the Roman commanders remained inactive. Totila prepared for battle by secretly posting 300 men behind the Roman position, who were to spring their ambush once the armies were fully engaged; the result was chaos in the Roman ranks and a rout with heavy losses. After this victory Totila sent an army to besiege Justin in Florence, but he managed to summon reinforcements from Ravenna. Their arrival led the Goths to raise the siege, but again dissension among the Roman commanders undermined efforts: John was left to confront the Goths with his personal troops and, when they were driven back, their flight spread

---

64. Proc., *Wars* 7.1–2.

to the rest of the army, which scattered for refuge. Totila's power grew as his good treatment of prisoners persuaded many to join his cause.[65]

Throughout 542 Totila extended his authority over much of Campania, Samnium and southern Italy, settling down to besiege Naples and capturing Cumae; he was enriched by booty and also began to collect taxation directly from the territories under his control. The Roman commanders each now focused on holding their individual city, without concentrating their forces to confront Totila, so Justinian, dismayed by the crisis, sent a large fleet under Maximinus with reinforcements of Thracians and Armenians, but this delayed in Epirus rather than sail to Italy. Further support was dispatched under Demetrius, who sailed for Sicily where he loaded supplies to relieve Naples, but since he only had a few troops he decided to sail first to Portus for more soldiers. The demoralized troops there, however, refused to follow him, and when he eventually sailed to Naples Totila was ready to attack his fleet of transports with dromons and captured their cargoes. When Maximinus finally reached Sicily, he too responded to the desperate appeals from Naples, but his fleet was driven ashore in a storm and fell into Gothic hands. In 543 conditions inside Naples forced the defenders to accept Totila's offer of terms and he again displayed his humanity in the captured city: he rationed food for the civilians, gradually increasing the quantity to ensure that they did not gorge themselves to death, and provided horses and transport animals for the garrison to travel to Rome under escort after it had been prevented from sailing by adverse winds.[66]

Roman commanders continued to maltreat civilians while their soldiers became increasingly insubordinate. The deteriorating situation in 543 prompted Constantianus, who held Ravenna, to write to Justinian with the backing of the other generals to say that they could not continue the war. Totila meanwhile wrote to the Senate at Rome, reproaching them for preferring 'Greek' to Gothic rule and pointing out the divine support that was favouring his cause. Although John who commanded the city refused to publicize the letter, other messages were posted by night around the city promising that the Goths would not harm Roman civilians. Justinian now sent Belisarius back to Italy and, since he had to leave his *bucellarii* in the East, he recruited 4,000 troops in the Balkans, led them

---

65. Proc., *Wars* 7.3–5.
66. Proc., *Wars* 7.6–8.

to Salona, and prepared to sail for Ravenna. He did manage to prevent Dryus from surrendering to Totila; the city had been under siege and agreed to submit if relief did not arrive by a specified date, but Belisarius sent in a fleet with supplies for a year and a new garrison, although 170 men were lost in an engagement outside the walls while ravaging. Belisarius sailed for Pola at the head of the Adriatic, where Totila discovered just how few troops he had with him by sending spies who pretended to be messengers from Bonus, the commander at Genoa.

Belisarius in Italy, 544-549

In 544 the Goths captured Tibur after a dispute between the inhabitants and their Isaurian garrison led the former to open the gates, though this did not save their lives; possession of Tibur prevented supplies from being brought into Rome from Tuscany. Belisarius, after unsuccessfully appealing to Totila's followers to return to imperial service, recovered Bononia (Bologna) and other forts in Emilia, but was weakened when the troops which Vitalius, *MM per Illyricum*, had brought to Italy decided to return home since they had not received pay, provisions were in short supply, and their families in the Balkans had been captured by raiders. Totila failed to recover Bononia but Belisarius could not reinforce his garrison at Auximum, since the city lacked the supplies to support the 1,000 troops he sent, and his soldiers were ambushed by Totila as they were withdrawing by night, with the loss of 200 men. At Pesaro Belisarius had better fortune, since he was able to restore the defences that Witigis had slighted early in the war by shipping in new iron gates and improving the walls sufficiently to resist an attack. Overall, however, the Romans had to remain on the defensive throughout 544, so that Totila could select which places he would attack next, choosing Fermo and Ascoli in Picenum.[67]

In 545 Belisarius sent John with a letter to Justinian begging for money and soldiers as well as the return of his *bucellarii*, who were still retained in the East, but John achieved nothing apart from marrying the daughter of Justinian's nephew, Germanus. Meanwhile Totila accepted the surrender of Fermo and Ascoli and also took over Spoleto and Assisi in Tuscany, the former by agreement with the local commander, Herodian, the latter after killing the commander Sisifrid and most of the garrison

---

67. Proc., *Wars* 7.9–11.

during an unsuccessful sally. Only at Perugia did he fail, since, though he had the local commander, Cyprian, murdered by one of his guards, the garrison chose to hold out. Towards the end of 545 Totila was in position to invest Rome, where he killed some of the garrison by luring them into an ambush. Famine began to take hold in the city, since after the capture of Naples Totila had posted ships both there and on the coastal islands to catch supply vessels that might attempt the voyage from Sicily. Only in Emilia did he experience failure, since the region's main city, Placentia (Piacenza), rebuffed his invitation to surrender.

Over winter Belisarius withdrew from Ravenna, where he left Justin in charge, through Dalmatia to Dyrrachium in the hope of receiving an army from Justinian, to whom he had reported the latest developments. He did send a few troops with Valentinus and Phocas to reinforce the garrison under Innocentius at Portus with a view to harassing the Goths besieging Rome. They attempted to coordinate their activities with the garrison at Rome under Bessas, but he declined to authorize a sally to support them. One attack on the Gothic camp secured minor success but a second was revealed in advance to Totila, with the result that Valentinus and Phocas perished with most of their soldiers.

Early in 546 Pope Vigilius, who was currently in Sicily after being summoned by Justinian to discuss his response to the Three Chapters initiative, organized a fleet of supplies for Rome, but this relief was captured by the Goths who had now seized the harbour at Portus. In spring Totila finally received the surrender of Placentia, where starvation had resulted in cannibalism, while at Rome the lack of supplies led to the dispatch of the deacon Pelagius to negotiate a truce. Totila's terms were tough, no lenience for the Sicilians who had betrayed the Goths when under no pressure, the destruction of Rome's defences, and that all slaves who had fled to the Goths would remain at liberty. Pelagius could not accept such demands, so the siege continued. Inside Rome the civilians begged Bessas to release some of the supplies he was holding for his soldiers, but the latter were making too much money from selling their rations to the richer inhabitants so that others were increasingly reduced to eating nettles and faeces. Some killed themselves while a few paid to leave the city, though many of these were too weak to take advantage of the opportunity or were killed by the Goths.[68]

---

68. Proc., *Wars* 7.11–17.

At Dyrrachium Belisarius was eventually joined by John and Isaac with an army of Roman and foreign soldiers. John's preference was to cross the Adriatic and proceed by land, whereas Belisarius believed the situation at Rome was so desperate that they should sail there directly. In the end it was agreed that Belisarius would sail to Rome while John recovered Calabria and marched to join him. A storm forced Belisarius to put in at Dryus and the sight of his fleet led the Gothic besiegers to retire to Brindisi, though they also alerted Totila about Belisarius' approach. A change in the weather allowed Belisarius to embark for Rome, but there Totila had taken steps to isolate the city by constructing a timber bridge across the Tiber over a narrow point downstream from the city, with a wooden tower and strong garrison on either bank. Meanwhile John crossed the Adriatic where he recovered the city of Canosa in Apulia. One of the leading locals, Venantius, complained about the treatment the inhabitants had previously received from the imperial army but promised to bring over the whole of Lucania and Bruttium in return for guarantees of better behaviour. Totila posted 300 soldiers at Capua with orders to shadow John if he marched on Rome, and this risk of encirclement dissuaded John from advancing as agreed with Belisarius; instead he turned aside into Bruttium and Calabria where he overcame the Gothic forces.

Although Belisarius repeatedly urged him not to be prevented from coming to Rome by a mere 300 soldiers, John settled down at Cervaro in Apulia. Belisarius, though he lacked the troops to confront the Goths in the open, prepared to force a passage up the Tiber: 200 dromons were given extra protection on their sides, soldiers were to march up both banks of the Tiber, and a pair of broad boats were lashed together to support a tower to overtop the Gothic structures. Belisarius instructed Isaac, the commander at Portus where Antonina and their supplies were, not to leave the defences under any circumstances whatsoever, while he summoned Bessas to make a sally to distract the Goths. Although Bessas declined to co-operate, Belisarius' advance went well as his men drove back the Goths who were protecting an iron chain that Totila had stretched across the Tiber to prevent ships even approaching his bridge. At the bridge a fierce fight developed around the towers, but Belisarius brought up his own floating tower which dropped a lighted fire-boat onto the tower on the right bank, setting it alight and burning to death as many as 200 Goths inside, so that a start could be made on dismantling the bridge.

At this point misfortune struck, since Isaac had left the defences of Portus on hearing that Belisarius was advancing so successfully and attacked the nearby Gothic camp; although he was initially successful, the Goths rallied, slew most of his men and captured him. When Belisarius heard that Isaac had fallen into enemy hands, he inferred that Portus itself had been captured and so rushed to recover it, as well as his wife, while the Goths there were still disorganized. The opportunity to break through to Rome was lost and Belisarius was laid low with a fever.[69]

Inside Rome the numbers defending the walls had shrunk, as fewer and fewer civilians were strong enough to contribute, and the oversight of the guards had grown lax, allegedly because Bessas only cared for making money from selling supplies. At the Porta Asinaria four Isaurians established contact with Totila and agreed to betray the city. Rome fell on 17 December 546. As the Goths entered most of the Roman soldiers fled with Bessas, accompanied by some senators. Within the city other senators took refuge in S. Peter's while 500 ordinary citizens, apparently all that remained from the earlier population, sought sanctuary in other churches. The Goths killed a few Romans, but Totila stopped this after an appeal from Pelagius and harangued his men to behave properly since this would ensure divine favour. Totila sent Pelagius and Theodore to Justinian to arrange peace, but Justinian responded that Belisarius had full power to make these decisions.

In Lucania Tullianus, with the support of 300 Antes whom John had left with him, defeated a force of peasants that Totila sent against them. Therefore, early in 547 Totila decided to march there once he had demolished the walls of Rome, but he halted this project after being upbraided by Belisarius for this thoughtless destruction of such a great city. He now set out for southern Italy to confront John and the Lucanians, taking with him the senators he had captured but sending their wives and children to Campania. John withdrew from Apulia, soon followed by Tullianus after his peasant supporters returned to their fields when they received promises from their former masters that they would own the land they cultivated; Roman raids, however, still prevented Totila from enjoying complete control of Apulia.

Such see-saw exchanges were replicated elsewhere in the peninsula, not least because there was a regular flow of individuals and information between the two sides: Totila's followers included large numbers of former Roman soldiers as well as Goths who had at some point sworn allegiance

---

69. Proc., *Wars* 7.18–19.

to the emperor, while Belisarius' men might be seduced by Totila's good reputation and overall success. Belisarius recovered Spoleto after a pretended deserter won over some of the guards who were defending the amphitheatre, which had been turned into a fort after the city's main walls had been demolished. From Portus Belisarius took 1,000 men to reconnoitre Rome and, although he was ambushed after a deserter revealed his plan, he managed to fight his way out. In the south John consolidated his hold on the region by walling off the isthmus between the harbours at Tarentum to place the inhabitants in safety. On the other hand, Totila occupied the strong fortress of Acherontida (Aceranza) in Lucania with 400 soldiers and then marched on Ravenna.[70]

Belisarius followed up his reconnaissance of Rome by moving his army from Portus to occupy the city. Within twenty-five days he had managed to construct makeshift rubble barriers at the sections of wall that Totila had demolished and stocked the city with provisions brought up the Tiber from Portus. The availability of food attracted those living nearby to move in, since they had been suffering shortages. Totila promptly advanced on Rome to eject Belisarius, thinking that this would be easy since he had destroyed all the gates and Belisarius had not had time to have replacements made. The gates, however, were protected by caltrops scattered outside, while defenders stood in the entrances and manned the adjacent walls. The Goths launched three attempts but were beaten back on each occasion with considerable losses, so that the leading Goths began to reproach Totila for his stupidity in not razing the city completely and permitting Belisarius to recover it. As a result Totila withdrew, destroying the Tibur bridges apart from the Milvian bridge, which was too close to Rome, and refortifying Tibur as a safe place for his valuables.

Totila first moved to reinforce the siege of Perugia, which he hoped to capture since supplies were running short, but he was then diverted south by the news that John had liberated many of the senatorial families who were being held in Campania, sending them to Sicily for safety. By avoiding the main roads, the Goths evaded John's scouts and reached his camp in Lucania unannounced. Totila attacked by night, routing the Romans but only inflicting 100 casualties since most were able to escape to nearby mountains and withdraw to Dryus. Procopius comments

---

70. Proc., *Wars* 7.20–3.

that if he had waited for dawn the Goths could have destroyed the Roman army, but he was driven to precipitate action by anger at John.[71]

By late 547 Justinian was in a position to commit more troops to the West, now that the truce with the Persians had reduced the scale of fighting in the East. These reinforcements arrived piecemeal and Totila destroyed most of a band of 300 Heruls, who had advanced incautiously from Dryus towards Brindisi. Belisarius received orders to move south to combine Roman forces, which he did, sailing with 700 cavalry and 200 infantry via Sicily to the Gulf of Taranto, where he was forced to put in at Crotone by a storm. Totila surprised the Roman cavalry, which had been sent out to secure supplies, killing many and persuading Belisarius to sail back to Sicily. In early 548 a further 2,000 infantry joined Belisarius in Sicily, while Justinian ordered Valerian, the *MM per Armeniam*, who had been sent west with more than 1,000 of his own men, but had spent the winter in the Balkans, to cross the Adriatic. Even so Belisarius still wanted more troops and sent Antonina back to Constantinople to beg for help, using her influence with Theodora; however, she arrived after the death of the empress on 28 June 548 and therefore urged Justinian to recall her husband.

Belisarius now based himself at Dryus, from where, in collaboration with Valerian and John, he tried to relieve the garrison at Rusicane near Thurii. However, his fleet was first scattered by a storm and, after it had regrouped at Crotone, Totila was ready to prevent the ships from coming in to land. Problems at Rome, where the soldiers had killed their commander, Conon, because he had been making money from selling supplies, forced Belisarius to return to the city, while John and Valerian proceeded to Picenum in the hope that a threat there would force Totila to raise the siege of Rusicane. Totila was sufficiently confident to dispatch 2,000 soldiers to reinforce the Goths in Picenum while he remained in the south to receive the surrender of Rusicane, most of whose garrison were glad to join him.[72]

Totila's Successes, Justinian's Reactions, 549–551

After surveying the problems of the empire in Europe, where Totila controlled most of Italy, the Franks had crossed into Venetia and seized

71. Proc., *Wars* 7.24–6.
72. Proc., *Wars* 7.27–30.

much of it from the Romans, the Gepids occupied Sirmium and Pannonia, while the Lombards had been given territory in Noricum from where they ravaged Illyria and Dalmatia, Procopius records Belisarius' departure from Italy after a frustrating and unsuccessful five years in charge. In 549 a raid by Gepids and Slavs into Venetia defeated the Roman troops there, while Totila sent a fleet against Dalmatia. This was led by Indulf, a guardsman of Belisarius who had switched sides, and after plundering two sites south of Salona he defeated the Roman fleet sent to oppose him. In Italy Totila set about gaining complete control. He approached Rome where Belisarius had left a garrison of 3,000 soldiers under the capable command of Diogenes. After capturing Portus he settled down to a siege, which eventually ended on 16 January 550 when some Isaurians at the Porta Ostiensis, disgruntled by the lack of pay and aware that other Isaurians who had helped Totila had been richly rewarded, arranged to betray the city. Many of the garrison perished, since Totila had anticipated that they would flee towards Centumcellae on the coast, the only fortress left in Roman hands in the region, although 400 cavalry took refuge in the Mausoleum of Hadrian and 300 others sought sanctuary in the city's churches; almost all these soldiers joined Totila when given the chance. In contrast to his actions after his previous capture of the city, Totila decided to try to resettle Rome with a mixture of Romans and Goths, demonstrating his new interest by holding a race meeting.[73]

Totila's next target in 550 was Centumcellae, but the garrison under Diogenes declined to surrender. He had also prepared a substantial fleet, 400 warships as well as other vessels he had captured with cargoes and crews, and planned a campaign against Sicily. At Reggio he failed to subdue the garrison, but the Goths did capture Taranto and Rimini, the latter by treachery. Justinian had been dithering about how to respond to Totila's successes: he had refused to admit a Goth envoy who suggested that hostilities should end on the basis that the Goths would agree to fight against the empire's enemies, contemplated appointing the elderly Liberius to command in Italy, then considered his nephew Germanus. He finally reverted to Liberius but did not sanction the departure of the new expedition even after various preparations had been made. Totila crossed into Sicily where he attacked Messina without success but then ravaged most of the rest of the island; he also secured Reggio after the garrison was starved into submission.

---

73. Proc., *Wars* 7.33–6.

The dire news from Sicily at last brought a response from Justinian: Liberius was instructed to sail there immediately and rescue the island, but soon Justinian decided to replace him with Artabanes, whom he appointed *MM per Thracias* and sent out with some soldiers to take over the fleet, while Germanus was given overall authority in Italy. Germanus married Matasuentha, granddaughter of Theoderic, in the hope that she would win over the Goths and launched an energetic recruitment drive in the Balkans. This attracted the *bucellarii* of other commanders and numerous tribesmen from along the Danube, he was permitted by Justinian to enroll some of the cavalry units in Thrace, and the Lombards promised 1,000 soldiers. News of this encouraged Roman soldiers serving Totila to send word to Germanus that they would return to their allegiance as soon as he reached Italy, while at Centumcellae Diogenes was inspired to continue resistance. Just before he set out on the march west, Germanus suddenly died and Justinian ordered Germanus' son, Justinian, and his son-in-law, John, to lead the army to Italy. Liberius meanwhile had reached Sicily, where he put into the harbour at Syracuse, which was under siege, but not being able to leave the defences, he sailed on to Palermo to avoid using up the city's supplies. Totila, after plundering most of the island, withdrew to the mainland in order to confront John and Justinian when they arrived. They had decided to pass the winter of 550/51 at Salona, after being delayed in their march across the Balkans by Slav raiders, who were suspected of operating in league with Totila.[74]

In spring 551 Justinian instructed John to remain at Salona, since he had decided to appoint the eunuch Narses as commander in Italy as he feared that John would not secure the obedience of senior officers. Narses left Constantinople well-supplied with men and money but his journey across the Balkans was delayed at Philippopolis by an incursion of Kutrigurs. Meanwhile Totila had sent 300 warships across the Adriatic on a ravaging expedition; they plundered Corcyra (Corfu) and the nearby Sybotae islands before ravaging the mainland around Nicopolis and capturing several ships, including some destined for Italy with supplies for Narses. He also sent an army into Picenum to capture Ancona, providing forty-seven warships to cut it off by sea.

In this desperate situation Valerian at Ravenna sent to Salona to appeal for rapid help and John, disobeying Justinian's instruction to remain there,

---

74. Proc., *Wars* 7.37–40.

manned thirty-eight warships and crossed to Scardona, where he was met by Valerian with a further twelve ships. They advanced to Senigallia, about 20km up the coast from Ancona, where they encountered the Gothic fleet. Much of the ensuing battle resembled an engagement on land, with exchanges of missiles and hand-to-hand fighting when the ships came to close quarters, but the Romans managed their ships better whereas the Goths either crowded together and so impeded their own efforts or allowed a vessel to be isolated and rammed by the Romans.[75] Most of the Gothic ships were captured or sunk, but eleven escaped to land where their crews burned them before joining the troops besieging Ancona and then withdrawing with them to Auximum. On Sicily, Artabanes, who had at last arrived to replace Liberius, forced all the Gothic garrisons on the island to surrender as their supplies ran out. Totila, however, sent his fleet to take over Corsica and Sardinia, which they subjected to tribute and then defended against an attempt by John Troglita in Carthage to recapture them. On the mainland the Frankish king Theodebert had seized control of the Cottian Alps, parts of Liguria, and much of Venetia. After his death his son Theodebald rejected an embassy from Justinian that offered an alliance in return for his withdrawal from Italy.[76]

Narses' Campaign, 552-553

Justinian continued to pay attention to matters in Italy, ordering the garrison at Thermopylae to take ship and sail to Crotone to relieve its hard-pressed defenders. Their arrival not only saved the city but persuaded the Goths in Taranto and Acherontia to surrender. At the start of the 552 campaign season Narses was finally ready to leave Salona at the head of a substantial army that, apart from his own recruits, included the troops gathered by Germanus, 3,000 Herul cavalry, 2,500 Lombard fighters with 3,000 attendants, 400 Gepids, and several Persian deserters. On reaching Venetia they were opposed by the Franks, who controlled the region, and also discovered that their march towards Ravenna would be blocked by a strong Gothic army stationed at Verona. The Gothic commander, Theia, had made preparations to cut the inland road in the belief that Narses could never lead an army of

---

75. Sarantis, 'Tactics' 202–3, defends the view that the Romans attacked the Gothic fleet with traditional rams that could sink ships.
76. Proc., *Wars* 8.21–4.

his size along the coast. John, however, who knew the region, believed that the coastal route was possible, in spite of the numerous rivers that had to be crossed, and the army reached Ravenna by building a bridge of boats across every river on their journey. After nine days at Ravenna Narses advanced south, passing by Rimini where the Gothic commander, Usdrilas, had tried to delay him by damaging the bridge. Although Usdrilas was killed by Heruls during a sally, Narses chose not to be delayed by a siege, since it was vital to confront the main Gothic forces as soon as possible, before his own large army was distracted by side issues or disrupted by logistical problems in an impoverished landscape. He therefore continued south, leaving the Via Flaminia for minor routes to avoid the Gothic garrison at Petra Pertusa that dominated the main highway.[77]

Totila had been waiting near Rome for Theia and his army; after all but 2,000 had arrived and on hearing that Narses had bypassed Rimini, in early summer Totila advanced his army to Taginae at the foot of the Appennines while Narses camped about 20km away on a plain in the foothills called Busta Gallorum. Narses offered Totila a chance to make peace, but when this failed the envoys agreed that they would fight in eight days, a suggested delay that did not fool Narses. The next day found the two armies encamped in close proximity, where they both wanted to control a small hillock that prevented the Roman position from being encircled.[78] Narses acted first, sending fifty infantrymen by night to take it, and throughout the next day these men beat off repeated Gothic attacks by forming a shield wall to block the narrow approach from the Gothic camp.

When the armies formed up, Narses and John held the left wing near the important hillock while the other Roman troops were stationed on the right wing under Valerian, John the Glutton, and Dagistheus; the two wings were strengthened by 8,000 archers on foot, drawn from the regular units. In the centre Narses placed the Lombards, Heruls, and other non-Roman troops, making them all dismount to ensure that they could not rush off in flight, but also to provide a solid defensive formation to receive Gothic charges. At the very left of the Roman line Narses stationed 1,500 cavalry at an angle with orders for 500 of them to go to help anywhere that the Romans were pushed back while the remaining 1,000 were to ride behind the Gothic infantry when it attacked. Totila deployed opposite

---

77. Proc., *Wars* 8.25.24–28.13.
78. Discussions in Haldon, *Wars* 37–40; Syvänne, *Age* 471–2.

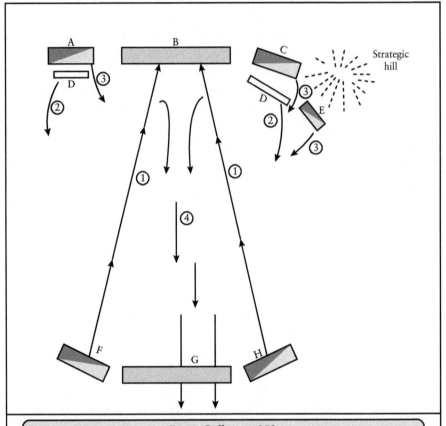

Busta Gallorum 552

Dispositions
A = Roman right under Valerian, John the
      Glutton, and Dagistheus
B = Roman centre formed of dismounted
      Roman allies including Lombards and Heruls
C = Roman left under Narses and John
D = Roman archers
E = 1,500 Roman cavalry
F = Gothic cavalry on left wing
G = Gothic infantry
H = Gothic cavalry on right wing

Phases
1 = Gothic cavalry charges
2 = Narses advances Roman archers to attack
      Goths from sides
3 = Roman cavalry advances to enclose Goths
4 = Gothic cavalry eventually flees in chaos,
      trampling infantry en route

them, but then delayed battle, since he was still awaiting the arrival of the last 2,000 soldiers from the northern army, first by a single combat that one of Narses' *bucellarii* won, then by a war dance that he performed and finally by asking for talks.

On hearing that the 2,000 had arrived, Totila retired to his tent with the Goths following; after a rapid lunch he returned in the hope of catching the Romans at their meal, but Narses had ordered his men to eat in their ranks. Totila now placed his infantry behind the cavalry while Narses advanced the two contingents of Roman archers on his wings so as to form a crescent. Totila apparently ordered his men to use only their spears, relying on their speed to reduce the impact of Roman superiority in archery and on the weight of their charge to disrupt the Romans, but as his cavalry advanced they found themselves raked by archery fire from either side and suffered heavily even before they reached the Roman positions. Towards evening the Gothic horsemen eventually retreated after a hard fight and in their disorderly flight they trampled their infantry, which had not opened its ranks to let them through. The Romans pressed the chaotic rout, killing 6,000 and capturing many more prisoners, who were subsequently executed; many of the victims were Roman soldiers who had switched allegiance. Totila himself perished, whether killed during the pursuit or shot in battle by an arrow was uncertain, since he had equipped himself as an ordinary soldier to avoid being a focus of attention. The battle was probably fought towards the end of June.[79]

Narses now dismissed the Lombard contingent, whose unruly behaviour had extended to indiscriminate arson and raping women in sanctuaries. Valerian escorted them out of Italy and then approached Verona where the garrison was prepared to agree terms, but the Franks in Venetia intervened to insist that the city belonged to them and Valerian was not prepared to confront them. The Goths who had fled Busta Gallorum assembled at Ticinum, where they elected Theia as leader; he exploited the valuables stored there to rebuild his army and contemplated drawing the Franks into alliance. Narses ordered Valerian to keep watch on Theia while he proceeded to Rome. En route he accepted the surrender of Narni and left a garrison at Spoleto with orders to rebuild the defences. At Perugia the two Roman deserters in command of the garrison disagreed about surrender, but the advocate of resistance was killed and the city gave in. At Rome the

---

79. Proc., *Wars* 8.29–32.

Gothic garrison prepared to resist by constructing a small fortress based on Hadrian's Mausoleum as a safe refuge but still attempted to defend the whole circuit. Neither side had enough troops to deploy all around the walls, but Narses, after launching fierce attacks at specific points, detached Dagistheus to use ladders to assault a section that was currently quiet; the Romans broke into the city and opened the gates, while the Goths fled to Portus or to Hadrian's Mausoleum, which soon surrendered. The loss of Rome led the Goths to kill numerous Roman senators and patricians whom they had been holding elsewhere in Italy, as well as their children.

In the south the Romans defeated the defenders of Taranto and blockaded the city closely, while the Goths remained at Acherontida. Narses extended his hold on central Italy, capturing Centumcellae, Nepi, and Petra Pertusa. His next target was the coastal city of Cumae in Campania, where the main Gothic treasure was stored, and this threat forced Theia to move south with his army. In Campania the two armies faced each other across the steep ravine of the river Draco. The Goths defending the south bank had seized the bridge across the river and fortified it with wooden towers equipped with *ballistae*, with the result that the stand-off lasted for two months until the Romans captured the ships that had been resupplying Theia. Being short of provisions the Goths retreated to Mons Lactarius, the rugged Amalfi peninsula, but there they were even more hard-pressed and so decided that battle was preferable to starvation.[80]

The Goths charged in the early morning, catching the Romans by surprise before they could form up with their usual officers in their regular units, so that they had to fight where they stood. The Goths soon dismounted, followed by the Romans, and Theia led the Gothic phalanx, displaying conspicuous bravery as he attracted Roman fire. Each time that his shield became too heavy from all the missiles lodged in it, he exchanged it with one of his guards, until towards midday he was mortally wounded by a javelin when changing his shield, which had twelve missiles in it. The Romans secured his corpse and cut off his head to display to the enemy in the hope of discouraging them, but the Goths fought with determination until nightfall and the battle resumed on the next day with equal intensity and heavy casualties on both sides. The Gothic leaders

---

80. The battle is dated to 1 October 552 by Agnellus 79, although this might seem to be too early if the armies had confronted each other for two months at the river Draco, as Procopius records; accordingly Stein, *Bas-Empire* 604, proposed emending Agnellus to give the date of 30 October.

then appealed to Narses, framing their request in religious terms that they knew would appeal to this devout man; to avoid continuing the fight against desperate men he agreed to let them withdraw from Italy with the possessions they had stored in different fortresses. A body of 1,000 Goths under Indulf left before the end of discussions and retired to Ticinum. This defeat marked the end of the Ostrogothic kingdom in Italy while Procopius concludes his narrative with the brief comment that the Romans captured Cumae although this did not in fact happen until the winter of 553/4.[81]

Narses and the Franks, 553–554

The narrative is taken up by Agathias, who provides a somewhat different version of the terms agreed by Narses: the Goths were permitted to retain possession of their own properties provided that they became loyal subjects of the empire. Goths living south of the Po in Liguria and Tuscany observed the agreement whereas those north of the river approached the Franks for help.[82] The Goths' appeal to Theodebald resulted in two of the chief men at his court, the Alamann brothers Butilinus and Leutharis, leading an army of Franks and Alamanns into Italy in 553 while the king continued to profess neutrality. After Mons Lactarius Narses' next target was Cumae, whose defenders were led by Theia's young brother Aligern, but its steep site and Aligern's energetic resistance thwarted assaults, so that Narses resorted to undermining one corner of the defences. Even the collapse of a section of the wall and gate did not allow the Romans to penetrate the defences. Narses decided to tighten his blockade by building a mound to encircle the city while moving his troops north to Tuscany to consolidate Roman control there before the Franks arrived. He detached part of his army under John, Valerian, and Artabanes, along with the Heruls under Fulcaris, to cross the Appennines into the Po valley in the hope of holding the Franks there. While in Tuscany he secured the surrender of Centumcellae, Volterra, Luna, and Pisa.[83]

The only place to hold out was Lucca, whose citizens and garrison agreed to surrender in thirty days if the Franks did not arrive. In the

---

81. Proc., *Wars* 8.33–5.
82. Agathias, *Hist.* 1.1.
83. Agathias, *Hist* 1.7–11.

Po valley the Romans had camped near Parma, which the Franks had already occupied. When Fulcaris with his Heruls and some Roman troops rashly approached the walls, Butilinus had advance warning and laid an ambush in the extramural amphitheatre; this routed most of the attackers, but Fulcaris and his bodyguard stood their ground to avoid the shame of defeat and were all slain. This success prompted the Goths in Emilia and Liguria to open their cities to the Franks while John and Artabanes retired to Faventia (Faenza) to be closer to Ravenna. On learning of this retreat, Narses at once sent Stephanus to order them back to Parma to monitor the Franks; in response to excuses that they lacked supplies because Antiochus the praetorian prefect had not appeared and that pay was in arrears, Stephanus sent to Ravenna and brought Antiochus to resolve the problems, with the result that the army returned to Parma. At Lucca, when the thirty days had expired and the city declined to surrender, Narses pretended to hold a public execution of the hostages he had taken but then revealed the ruse in the hope that this act of mercy would bring about surrender. The garrison was determined not to give in and, when Narses tightened the siege by bringing up siege equipment and maintaining a heavy bombardment of missiles, they led a sally along with the local militia. This was beaten back with heavy losses, since the locals no longer wanted to fight, and at last, after three months of siege, terms of surrender were agreed. Narses left Bonus, the *quaestor exercitus* responsible for defending the lower Danube frontier, in charge at Lucca while he proceeded to Ravenna to supervise the move of the army into winter quarters.[84]

Over the winter of 553/4 Aligern decided to surrender Cumae, reckoning that the Franks had not invaded Italy to assist the Goths but to further their own interests. With the agreement of the besiegers he travelled to Ravenna, where he presented the city's keys to Narses, who arranged for a Roman garrison to enter the city while the remainder of the besieging army retired to its winter quarters. Narses sent Aligern to Cesena to inform the Franks that he had surrendered the whole Gothic treasure to Narses, so that there was no longer the prospect of great wealth for the invaders. He then moved to Rimini with his entourage, from where he marched out to confront 2,000 marauding Franks. His initial attacks were ineffectual, since the Franks formed a solid shield wall that warded off missiles, but Narses lured them out of position with a feigned flight

---

84. Agathias, *Hist* 1.11–19.

in the Hunnic manner; as soon as the Franks had scattered in pursuit, the Romans massacred the infantry who could not escape like the cavalry.[85]

For the 554 campaign Narses gathered his troops at Rome and subjected them to some rigorous training. Meanwhile the Franks had moved south into Samnium, where they split into two groups, Butilinus taking the larger part south through Campania, Lucania, and Bruttium as far as the straits of Messina while Leutharis ravaged Apulia and Calabria as far as Dryus. By mid-summer Leutharis had satisfied his desire for booty and so sent to Butilinus to urge him to withdraw; the latter declined, citing his oath to help the Goths who were encouraging him with the promise of making him king. When Leutharis had reached Fano as he retired up the Adriatic, his advance guard of 3,000 was surprised by the Roman commanders at Pesaro, Artabanes and Uldach. The survivors fled in panic to their camp, where Leutharis deployed his men, but this allowed their prisoners to escape to nearby forts, taking with them much of the booty. The Franks retired as far as Ceneda in Venetia, where most of the army was stricken by fever and perished.

Butilinus had been hurrying back through Campania, with his army also affected by disease since Narses had commandeered food supplies along their line of march. He camped between Capua and Casilinum by the banks of the Casulinus (Volturno), in a strong position with the river on one side and earthworks elsewhere built up from wagon wheels placed at an angle and covered with earth as far as their axle hubs. He also took control of the bridge and secured it with a wooden tower filled with his best soldiers. Narses had marched south from Rome to confront him, but Butilinus was confident that he could determine the timing of any engagement; he still commanded about 30,000 men whereas Narses had 18,000, a large army by Roman standards but still outnumbered.

Narses first acted to prevent the Franks from foraging at will and a captured hay wagon was used to set fire to the Franks' tower so that the Romans secured possession of the bridge. This setback spurred the Franks to action and both sides deployed for battle. Narses commanded the cavalry on the right wing, on the left Valerian and Artabanes were placed in an ambush, while the armoured infantry formed a shield wall in the centre with archers, slingers and javelin-men behind. In the middle of the

---

85. Agathias, *Hist* 1.19–22.

phalanx a space was kept open for the Heruls, whose participation in the battle was in doubt after Narses had executed one of their leaders for killing a servant for no proper reason. The rank and file Heruls were disaffected, but Sindual, the Herul leader, told Narses that he believed they would not miss the fight. This uncertainty over the Heruls in fact helped the Romans, since it was reported to Butilinus that their absence had left the Roman line in disarray. Butilinus formed the Franks into a large wedge-shaped formation, solid at the apex and then gradually opening up a void as its two wings fanned out. The Frankish charge broke through the Roman line where the Heruls would have stood, pushing back the Romans without inflicting significant losses and continuing towards the Roman camp, at which point Narses ordered the cavalry on both wings to turn inwards and shoot arrows into the backs of the Frankish infantry, who had to concentrate on the men in front of them and made easy targets for mounted archers. The Franks also now had to confront the Heruls, who rushed up to join the fray, so that the Franks found themselves surrounded and the majority were slain for the loss of only eighty Romans. Narses returned to Rome after his army had plundered the enemy camp and recovered substantial booty.[86]

Mopping Up and Reorganization

The destruction of both Frankish armies heartened the Romans but there was still fighting to be done, as Narses reminded his army. The fort of Campsa to the east of Naples was held by the Hun Ragnaris with 7,000 Gothic troops and over the winter of 554/5 Narses blockaded it since the site was too strong for an assault. Early in 555 Ragnaris met Narses to discuss terms, but after an inconclusive meeting he attempted to shoot Narses, only to be mortally wounded by one of Narses' *bucellarii*. The Goths now agreed terms and Narses sent them to Constantinople.[87] The capture of Campsa left Narses in control of Italy south of the Po, but north of the river numerous cities and forts remained in Gothic or Frankish hands and imperial authority was clearly weak.

Verona was captured on 20 July 561 and its keys, as well as those of Brixia, were delivered to Justinian in November.[88] Probably in the context

---

86. Agathias, *Hist* 2.1–10.
87. Agathias, *Hist* 2.11–14.
88. Agnellus 79; Malalas 18.140.

of the capture of Verona, Narses had asked the permission of Amingus, leader of the Franks with whom he was at peace, to cross the river Adige in pursuit of the Goth Widin; Amingus, however, came to help Widin but the two were defeated by Narses, with Amingus being killed and Widin dispatched to the east.[89] The Heruls led by Sinduald, who had served with Narses from the start of his Italian campaign, were stationed in the north, probably near Tridentum, to serve as a buffer against incursions from the north, much as they had operated in the Balkans when settled around Singidunum. Shortly after Justinian's death, these Heruls revolted and proclaimed Sindual king, another indication of the limits to Roman control in this area, but he was soon defeated and executed by Narses.[90]

Justinian had legislated to organize the imperial administration of Italy after the long Gothic interregnum, first through the Pragmatic Sanction of 13 August 554 and then a law on debtors issued after the end of the Frankish invasion.[91] Under these laws Narses was put in charge of overseeing the return of Italy to normal Roman government. The acts of Totila were annulled, as being those of an illegitimate ruler, and anyone who had been forced to sell their property during his reign could recover it for the price they had received. Exiles and prisoners had their property returned, owners their slaves, and landlords their tied peasants. Tax arrears were halved and there was to be a delay of five years in their collection. Tax collection was entrusted to provincial governors rather than the praetorian prefect, with the governors nominated by the local bishops and leading men. Supplies for troops were to be purchased at market prices; legal cases involving a civilian were not to be tried by military courts. The city of Rome again received its free grain rations, salaries for professors and doctors, and the funds for repairing public buildings and aqueducts.[92]

The laws established the principles on which Italy was to be administered but any return to normality would have been slow.[93] The majority of Italy's most fertile regions – Tuscany, Campania, Apulia, Emilia – had been ravaged more than once and their major cities subjected to siege or even sacked, so that the basis for provincial administration was weak. There

---

89. Paul the Deacon 2.2.
90. Paul the Deacon 2.3.
91. Justinian, *Novels Appendix* 7, 8.
92. Wickham, *Italy* 27.
93. See Wickham, *Italy* ch.1, pp.25–7.

had been starvation in the countryside and reports of cannibalism may not be exaggerated. Many of the large landowners, Gothic nobles as well as Roman senators and patricians, had been killed or had migrated to the East from where they did not return, to be replaced by the heterogeneous leaders and soldiers of the eastern armies. For several years military might had been the basis for decisions and the impact of the praetorian prefects at Ravenna had been limited; Bessas and Conon at Rome will not have been the only commanders to profit from their positions of power.

Although Narses, as supreme commander until his death in 568, does not seem to have shared their greed, power did remain in military hands and his local subordinates may have had greater needs or fewer scruples. It was bound to take Italy much longer than the African provinces to adjust to the shock of rejoining the Roman world and it is likely that there was only gradual progress during the last decade of Justinian's reign, after which the migration of the Lombards in 568 soon disrupted life in the Po valley and the central provinces. The civil administration was already overshadowed by the military, and the Lombard presence simply accentuated that process in the territories that remained under Roman control. Cassiodorus undoubtedly presents us with a rosy-tinted view of Italy under Ostrogothic control, but it was certainly much more prosperous than the ravaged landscape and sacked cities that Justinian's campaigns had secured for the empire. Only in the south, and especially on Sicily which had suffered only one year of ravaging in 550, was there likely to have been any return to reasonable prosperity. It is unsurprising that papal correspondence demonstrates the importance of its estates on Sicily for its economic health.

Chapter 8

The Balkans

O
ur knowledge of military events in the Balkans during Justinian's reign is fragmentary, since Procopius did not devote a specific book to the region. This might be because Belisarius never campaigned there, at least until several years after Procopius had finished work on the *Wars*, so that there was no personal focus to launch the narrative. More probably the discrete, episodic nature of tribal invasions and Roman responses militated against a coherent, continuous narrative.[1] As a result, Procopius inserted major events as and when they related to activity in the East and especially Italy. For the Heruls, Franks, and Lombards he does provide some of the sort of introductory material with which he begins his Persian, African, and Italian narratives, but this information is dispersed.[2] Most of Procopius' accounts of Balkan events emphasize the gloomy predicament of the region as it endured repeated tribal assaults with numerous captives being led north of the Danube, but by the time he composed these accounts his agenda was to criticize Justinian's management of events and so his information may be distorted. His successor Agathias, however, did have the extensive Kutrigur invasion of 559 to report and he devoted to it the final chapters of his work.[3]

This apparent lack of attention in contemporary historiography cannot be taken to suggest that the region was of limited importance. In Procopius' *Buildings* Justinian's activities, especially military constructions, across the Balkan provinces were celebrated at considerable length and improving regional administration attracted the emperor's legislative attention between 535 and 537.[4] The provinces mattered greatly for a number of reasons. Justinian himself was a native of the Balkans and

---

1. For speculation on Procopius' motives, see Sarantis, *Balkan Wars* 229–40.
2. Proc., *Wars* 5.12.13–13.13; 6.14, 25.1–4; 7.33–4; 8.20.
3. Agathias, *Hist.* 5.11–25.
4. Justinian, *Novels* 26, 41, 50.

acted to elevate his modest place of birth by transforming it into the city of Justiniana Prima.[5] The prefect of Illyricum was relocated there from Thessalonica and its archbishop was given authority over the provinces of northern Illyricum, again at the expense of Thessalonica. The provinces also continued to provide significant numbers of troops for Roman armies throughout Justinian's reign, with many of his leading generals coming from the region, and it was the location for imperial stud farms. Finally, the provinces were Constantinople's hinterland, a barrier between trans-Danubian threats and the riches of the capital and its suburbs, the region that provided most of its water supply and a certain amount of its food in the form of grain and livestock.[6]

In contrast to the campaign theatres treated in the preceding three chapters, in the Balkans there was no single main enemy that the Romans had to confront, but rather three different major types of enemy in distinct geographical locations. In the northwest on the middle Danube the former provinces of Pannonia were fought over by the Ostrogothic kingdom in Italy and the Gepids and Lombards, Germanic tribal groups organized under kings. These had re-emerged in their own right as the Hunnic federation of Attila disintegrated in the 450s and 460s, when the Gepids took the lead in throwing off Hunnic control.

Along the lower Danube the region between the Carpathians and the river was occupied by the Sklavenes, or Slavs, whose social and political structures above village level were rudimentary, while the Antes, similar in most respects to the Slavs but with a clearer leadership structure, held the land up the Black Sea coast to the east of the mountains. Both Slavs and Antes were recent arrivals on the Danube, having moved down from the north to settle territory that had been depopulated during the Hunnic ascendancy in the mid-fifth century. The Slavs in particular tended to operate in relatively small groups under an individual leader rather than banded together into bigger units. They were adept at surviving in difficult terrain, whether marshes or wooded uplands, and so were difficult to target and also were capable of moving beyond the reach of Roman forces.[7]

Finally the plains to the north of the Black Sea were held by Hunnic groups; these are referred to as Bulgars when they raided during Anastasius'

---

5. Proc., *Buildings* 4.1.17–27.
6. For detailed discussion of all aspects of the Balkans during Justinian's reign, see the excellent work of Sarantis, *Balkan Wars*.
7. See Whitby, *Emperor Maurice* 80–3.

reign but by Justinian's reign separate units of Kutrigurs and Utigurs, who were based respectively to the west and east of the river Don, had emerged. The location of the Utigurs to the north-east of the Sea of Azov brought them into the scope of Roman policy in Transcaucasia, since they were neighbours to the Sabir Huns, who both served in Roman and Persian armies and raided across the Caucasus. There were also tribal units settled within the empire, in particular the Heruls, who had been granted lands in Upper Moesia centred on the Morava valley in return for military service. All of these groups, especially the more highly organized Germanic and Hunnic ones, incorporated people of different ethnic backgrounds whose identity was usually submerged by that of the dominant element.[8]

The traditional Roman frontier for the Balkans had run along the Danube, following the withdrawal from the trans-Danubian province of Dacia in the 270s. The defences had survived the incursions of the Goths in the later fourth century, but the onslaught of Attila's Huns in the 440s and early 450s had destroyed many of the key cities and devastated the countryside.[9] The chaos created by the sudden collapse of Hunnic power by 460 led to decades of turmoil within the Balkans as different elements of his federation fought for survival and territory. The two main groups to trouble the Romans were the Gothic bands led by Theoderic Strabo and Theoderic the Amal, who competed both with the Romans for recognition and payments and with each other for followers and prestige, until the death of Theoderic Strabo in 481 allowed his rival to consolidate the war-bands. The departure of the Amals to Italy in 488 eventually gave the provinces some breathing space, and under Anastasius, Roman authority was gradually advanced northwards up the Black Sea and then inland up the Danube, although the three revolts of Vitalian between 513 and 515 will have caused new disruption.

From the Roman perspective the provinces in the northern and central Balkans were impoverished when compared to much of Anatolia or the Levant, but for tribal groups fighting for their survival north of the Danube they offered fertile lands, rich booty, and safety.[10] Although population

8. For example, Mundo a member of the Gepid royal family served Theoderic the Ostrogoth with his followers until Theoderic's death, while the Rugian Eraric had a sufficiently strong reputation to be chosen Gothic king in 541, although his ethnicity soon told against him.
9. For an overview of developments, see Whitby, 'Balkans'.
10. Sarantis, 'Military Provisioning', argues that agriculture in the Balkans was less disrupted than has often been assumed. Certainly, to outsiders it would have appeared a land of plenty.

levels appear to have remained sufficiently high through to the mid-sixth century and beyond, to judge from the ability of Justinian's generals to recruit successfully, there were also emptier areas where emperors could attempt to settle tribal groups in return for military service: in 479 Zeno offered Theoderic the Amal territory for settlement near Pautalia in the spacious, beautiful but deserted region of Dardania.[11] The Heruls were allocated land by Anastasius in the vicinity of Singidunum, although by 562 this could be offered to the Avars, while in Lower Moesia and Scythia there were probably substantial settlements of federates, possibly remnants of Theoderic's warband who had preferred to remain in the Balkans in imperial service rather than risk the move west.

Religion was one factor that could be used to strengthen links between tribal groups and the empire. In 528 Grepes, king of the Heruls, came to Constantinople where he was baptized on the Feast of the Epiphany, 6 January 528, with Justinian standing as sponsor; leading Heruls and twelve of his relatives were also baptized.[12] Since these Heruls had been settled within the empire for the past generation, as Procopius records in his excursus on their origins, the conversion is not surprising.[13] Later in the year Justinian sponsored the baptism of another tribal leader, this time Grod, king of Huns who lived near the city of Bosporus, on the Kerch peninsula at the western end of Crimea.[14] This initiative was less successful since, after Grod returned home and had melted down his people's silver and electrum idols, the traditional priests engineered his overthrow and replacement by his brother Mougel. In fear of Roman reprisals these Huns captured Bosporus and killed the Roman garrison, prompting Justinian to appoint John as the *comes* of the straits of the Black Sea based at Hieron with some Gothic troops, send a naval expedition under an exarch, and dispatch Baduarius with an army to march overland to Crimea. The Huns withdrew and the Romans recovered the city of Bosporus.

It is unclear whether these events at the northern end of the Black Sea contributed to the first tribal incursion into the Balkans under Justinian.[15]

---

11. Malchus fr.20.201–4.
12. Malalas 18.6.
13. Proc., *Wars* 6.14–15.
14. Malalas 18.14.
15. Malalas 18.21. The surviving abridged version of Malalas has to be supplemented with the additional information preserved in Theophanes (*A.M.* 6031, pp. 217.26–218.17). Theophanes

Malalas does not make a connection between the events, but it would not be surprising if the repulse of Huns in the Crimea led that group, or others affected by their expulsion, to invade the empire in search of wealth. At any rate, in 528 an army of Bulgars under two leaders crossed the Danube into Scythia and Lower Moesia.[16] They were met by Justin, *dux* of Moesia, and Baduarius, *dux* of Scythia, though they are referred to as *stratelates* and so also held the senior rank of general, *magister militum vacans*. The Romans were defeated with the loss of Justin. He was succeeded by Constantiolus, who together with the generals Ascum, a Hun, and Godilas, the former perhaps *MM per Illyricum* and the latter *MM per Thracias*, confronted the invaders in Thrace, to the south of the Haemus mountains, where they surrounded them, killed the two leaders, and recovered the booty. While they were returning from the victory, presumably northwards to their provincial commands, the generals were surprised by other Huns who lassoed them; Godilas managed to cut his way free, but Constantiolus and Ascum were led into captivity. The former was eventually ransomed for 10,000 *solidi*, but nothing more is heard of Ascum. Considering that Justinian had sponsored his baptism, he was clearly a Hun of some importance and might have been eliminated by his captors, just as Attila had executed royal Hunnic rivals who had sought refuge with, or taken service in, the empire. The incursion was substantial, since the raiders had overcome the provincial forces at the disposal of the two frontier *duces*, but deployment of the regional armies of Illyricum and Thrace along with other elements was able to overcome them.

Ascum's successor as *MM per Illyricum*, either directly or after an interval, was the Gepid warlord Mundo, who had served Theoderic in Italy with his followers for several years but decided to return to the Balkans after the king's death.[17] He approached Justinian in 529, possibly as a result of an invitation, to offer his services and the emperor appointed him *MM*, which meant that he and his followers received Roman salaries. On reaching Illyricum he was attacked by an army of Huns and disparate other tribes, but defeated these, sending the booty and one of the Hun leaders to Constantinople. In 530 Mundo was again in action, first attacking and expelling from Illyricum the Getae, quite

placed the invasion 10 years too late, in the *annus mundi* equivalent of 538/9, but his information is entirely derived from Malalas where the chronological sequence is secure.
16. Discussion in Sarantis, *Balkan Wars* 21–32.
17. Malalas 18.46.

possibly Gepids, and then killing 500 Bulgars who had been plundering Thrace.[18] There is inevitably a temptation to amalgamate these events placed in adjacent years by different sources, but that should be resisted:[19] Marcellinus Comes was a native of the Balkans living and writing in Constantinople with a keen interest in his homeland, while Malalas at Antioch will have received official reports of events in the capital.

Mundo took over from Belisarius as *MM per Orientem* after the latter's defeat at Callinicum in 531 and his successor in the Balkans was Chilbuldius, a member of Justinian's entourage; his ethnic identity is unknown, but the 'Chil' element of his name was common among the Franks. We only know of his actions thanks to a digression in Procopius, where he is explaining the background to the appearance among the Antes in 546 of an imposter claiming to be the Roman general Chilbuldius.[20] Chilbuldius was appointed in Justinian's fourth year, i.e. 530/31, with the task of preventing the Huns, Antes, and Slavs from crossing the Danube. These targets indicate that Chilbuldius was operating along the lower Danube, in provinces that pertained to the *MM per Thracias*, but this was not the first time that the military resources of the western Balkans had been used to support operations in Thrace. For three years Chilbuldius performed this task with great success, to the extent that the Romans took the fight to the tribes north of the river, but on one of his ventures beyond the Danube his small band was caught by a large force of Slavs and he perished, with the result that the frontier again became easy to cross. Marcellinus records under the year 535 an engagement in which the patrician Sittas, *MM praesentalis*, defeated a group of Bulgars near the Danube. The deployment north of the Haemus of the capital's defenders indicates that the incursion was a major problem that exceeded the abilities of the forces available in Thrace.

Justinian's early years witnessed considerable activity in the Balkans and the insecurity can be pushed back into Justin's reign, since an invasion of Antes was annihilated at some point in the early 520s by Germanus, who had recently been appointed *MM per Thracias*. We only hear of this since Procopius wanted much later to explain why Slav raiders in 550 were terrified to learn that Germanus was leading an army in the Balkans.[21]

---

18. Marc.Com. *s.a.* 530.
19. Discussion in Sarantis, *Balkan Wars* 51–60.
20. Proc., *Wars* 7.14.
21. Proc., *Wars* 7.40.5–6.

It is clear that Roman control relied heavily on the recruitment of different ethnic leaders – men like Ascum, Mundo, and Chilbuldius – who probably brought a certain number of followers with them, that defences in the Balkans were insufficient to deter incursions, and that in particular the troops available to defend the eastern Balkans, the diocese of Thrace, could only cope if supported from either Illyricum or the praesental armies.

One particular problem was that the city of Sirmium and much of the northern and western Balkans were occupied by the Goths: Theoderic's general Pitzias had captured Sirmium from the Gepids in 504 and then moved south to support the Goths' ally Mundo in defeating an army led by the *MM per Illyricum* at Horreum Margi in Dacia. The establishment of the Heruls near Singidunum created a buffer, but the Goths were still in a position to exert pressure eastwards and southwards and ensure that groups raiding to the west of the Carpathians continued into Roman territory rather than pillaging Gothic lands. In 530 or shortly afterwards Gothic troops had attacked the Roman city of Gratiana, in the context of a conflict with the Gepids in the region of Sirmium;[22] granted that the Gepids were allies of the Romans, in receipt of imperial subsidies, it is not impossible that they had been encouraged to probe the strength of Gothic control of the region.

The move from diplomatic dialogue between Justinian and the Gothic king Theodahad to open conflict created an opportunity to recover lost territory. Justinian's first move was against the coastal province of Dalmatia, whose control would provide additional lines of communication with an army in Italy, especially through Salona. Mundo, who had returned as *MM per Illyricum* after the conclusion of peace with Persia, led the attack in 535, presumably taking with him much of his regional army, and captured Salona.[23] Theodahad committed what is described as a 'great army' under Asinarius and Gripa to deal with this threat, which suggests that he viewed this as a greater danger than Belisarius, who had spent much of 535 in occupying Sicily. The Goths surprised Mundo's son, Maurice, while on a scouting mission and his death spurred Mundo to attack. Although the Romans routed the Goths, Mundo perished in a reckless pursuit with

---

22. The attack was raised as a grievance in Justinian's negotiations with Amalasuentha and mentioned in a communication to the Senate in 534 (Cass. *Var.* 11.1.10–11); how much earlier it had occurred is not known.
23. Proc., *Wars* 5.5.11.

the result that the Romans withdrew from Dalmatia, including Salona. The Goths too were leaderless but occupied many forts in the province.[24]

Justinian's Measures to Strengthen Balkans

In 535 Justinian embarked on a series of administrative changes in the Balkans, the first of which related to his birthplace, the village of Tauresium, which he had re-established as the city of Justiniana Prima.[25] The city's bishop was elevated from metropolitan to archbishop and given authority over provinces in the northwest; these had once been controlled from Sirmium, when the praetorian prefect of Illyricum had been based there, but were then administered from Thessalonica after Attila's depredations forced the prefect to move south to a safer location. Now Roman authority was expanding again to re-occupy Viminacium and two forts north of the Danube.[26] In the same year Justinian legislated to consolidate military and civil authority over the Long Walls of Constantinople in the new post of Praetor of Thrace, to improve the security of the capital's rich suburbs along the Bosporus and its water supply but also to engage in military activity beyond the Walls if necessary.[27]

A third major change related to the Lower Danube, whose defences had been breached more than once in Justinian's early years. The new position of *quaestor exercitus* was created with authority over the frontier provinces of Lower Moesia and Scythia Minor that stretched from Novae to the Black Sea, together with Cyprus, Caria, and the Aegean islands. The arrangement might seem cumbersome, but the provinces of the *quaestura exercitus* were linked by sea and this did ensure that safer and more productive regions in the Mediterranean could support the impoverished frontier zone.[28] Justinian had to legislate about the hearing of legal appeals from the provinces and set out the process for the *quaestor* to distribute their *annonae* to his troops, a duty which he had taken over from the praetorian prefect.[29] The date of this law, 18 May 536, provides a

---

24. Proc., *Wars* 5.7.1–10.
25. Discussion in Sarantis, *Balkan Wars* 139–55.
26. Justinian, *Novel* 11; 14 April 535.
27. Justinian, *Novel*; 18 May 535.
28. Lee, 'Warfare' 408–9. Sarantis. 'Military Provisioning', argues that the Balkans were more self-sufficient, but the situation along the Danube probably remained difficult, hence the need for a unit based on links by ship.
29. Justinian, *Novel*. 41.

terminus ante for the new provincial arrangement, although it probably did not take long for clarification to be requested on such important matters as judicial decisions and military remuneration. The judicial provision was soon adapted in a law of 1 September 537, which limited the volume of cases that had to come before the *quaestor*, by stipulating that appeals from the Mediterranean provinces would be heard at Constantinople by the praetorian prefect and a representative of the *quaestor*.[30]

The elevated archbishop of Justiniana Prima was based in the new fortified city, whose construction by the emperor is celebrated as the first item in *Buildings* 4, the book devoted to the Balkans.[31] Procopius' reference to churches, colonnades, fountains, official residences, markets, streets, and shops basically corresponds to the ruins excavated at the site of Tsaricin Grad in Serbia, provided that his hyperbole about their magnificence is discounted. The new city was small, originally no more than eight hectares in area even after the defences were extended, and was crammed in behind strong walls on a narrow plateau along one main street with one major crossing. Most space was taken up by buildings for the praetorian prefect and archbishop, while the civilian population would have been quite small.[32] The chronology of Justinian's numerous other constructions in the Balkans, both described and listed in *Buildings* 4, is unknown and cannot be established from what archaeological evidence is available, but work must have started at many sites in the 530s, since the emperor will have wanted to locate his new administrative capital in a reasonably secure region.

It used to be fashionable to dismiss Procopius' evidence for these constructions on the basis that this panegyrical account was based on little solid information, with the result that he had recourse to long lists of names and generic eulogy.[33] The ability of tribal invaders to range across the Balkans in the 550s was thought to prove that there had not been any significant defensive work, while Procopius stood accused of transferring credit to Justinian for work commissioned by Anastasius. Panegyric does have to be handled with caution, but this scepticism is excessive[34] and the current trend is to accept that Justinian oversaw widespread reconstruction

---

30. Justinian, *Novel* 50.
31. Proc., *Buildings* 4.1.17–27.
32. Evidence summarized in Sarantis, *Balkan Wars* 155–61.
33. E.g. Cameron, *Procopius* 85, 94.
34. Whitby, *Maurice* 71–8.

during his reign, continuing the work that Anastasius had begun along the Black Sea and the Lower Danube.[35]

Justinian's overall intention was to refurbish the centres of Roman authority throughout the Balkan provinces, shore up the frontier defences along the Danube, strengthen other sites where regional and praesental troops were based, safeguard the main communication routes leading from the Danube across the Stara Planina (Haemus) to Constantinople and Thessalonica along with their logistical underpinning, and provide refuges for the rural population. Although Procopius praised the new security of the Danube frontier, the distribution of construction work indicates that the reality was recognized that it was not possible to halt all incursions, so that precautions had to be taken internally. The only places where an attempt was made to check hostile movement were at Thermopylae, the gateway to central and southern Greece which was walled and garrisoned, the Isthmus of Corinth which connected the Peloponnese with the north, the Chersonese peninsula (Gallipoli) whose narrow neck was walled off, and the vicinity of Constantinople protected by the refurbished Long Walls. Justinian's aim was to ensure the survival of the Balkan population, which was important for the sustenance of provincial cities, military recruitment, and imperial administration. Although raids did continue throughout his reign, it is possible to interpret the depth that many of the later raids had to penetrate in search of booty as a sign that easy pickings were not available further north. The building works were probably carried out throughout his reign, since defences needed constant attention to repair natural and enemy damage and new refuge sites were identified.

530s and 540s

In 536 Justinian again tried to secure Salona and neighbouring territory, sending Constantianus to collect troops in Illyricum. After assembling his army at Dyrrachium, at the Adriatic end of the Via Egnatia, Constantianus sailed up the Adriatic coast to Epidaurus, where his advance was observed by Gripa's spies who reported back that several 'myriads' of men were approaching. As a result Gripa withdrew from Salona, since he did not trust the defences or the inhabitants' loyalty. Constantianus sailed to the island of

---

35. See Sarantis, *Balkan Wars* 161–98 for an overview.

Lesina (modern Hvar), where he learned of Gripa's retreat so that he advanced to the mainland and approached Salona after taking necessary precautions to secure the route. There he energetically repaired the defences, while Gripa withdrew his army to Ravenna; as a result, Constantianus was able to take over Dalmatia and Liburnia, securing the allegiance of the Goths settled there.[36]

The departure of the Goths left a gap in Pannonia that was rapidly filled by the Gepids, who took control of 'Sirmium and practically all of Dacia'.[37] It is likely that the Lombards also took this opportunity to seize territory vacated by the Goths in the former Roman provinces of Noricum.[38] An imperial optimist could present these developments as the allocation of territories to allied groups for settlement,[39] but the reality was that Justinian had no authority over what happened in the northwest Balkans. The Gepid occupation of Sirmium in particular rankled: its location was now relevant not just to north-south movement across the Danube and its tributaries, but to communications between Constantinople and Italy, since traditionally the main route between Constantinople and the West, especially for armies on the march, had been the military highway that led through Serdica to Sirmium and then over the Julian Alps into northern Italy. At some point Justinian stopped his annual subsidies for the Gepids, who were raiding the empire, and in 538 he sent the *magister militum* Calluc,[40] perhaps the successor to Mundo in Illyricum, against them. As often the Romans were initially successful but were then defeated in battle with the loss of Calluc.[41]

In 539 Huns crossed the Danube and plundered everything from the Adriatic to the suburbs of Constantinople, in the process capturing the city of Cassandreia at the neck of the Pallene peninsula in northern Greece and thirty-two forts and leading off 'twelve myriads' of prisoners.[42] Procopius reports this in a brief digression from the build-up to the resumption of war in the East; there is no mention of intervention by Roman forces and it is probably relevant to the success of this incursion that the reinforcements recently sent to Italy included several units from

---

36. Proc., *Wars* 5.7.26–37.
37. Proc., Proc., *Wars* 7.33.8.
38. Sarantis, *Balkan Wars* 89–94, noting that Procopius was mistaken about the location of Sirmium, which was in the diocese of Pannonia whereas Dacia remained in Roman hands.
39. Proc., *Wars* 7.33.10.
40. Proc., *Wars* 7.33.9. The name suggests he was another non-Roman, but his ethnicity is unknown.
41. Marc.Com. *s.a.* 538.
42. Proc., *Wars* 2.4.4–6.

the Balkan field armies. Procopius describes this as the most damaging raid ever, an impression he underlines by noting the number of forts captured and the vague reference to the enormous number of 120,000 captives. The brief account immediately follows his notice of a comet, which was another warning of the impending misfortunes of the renewed war with Persia. If it were possible to rely on Procopius' precise wording, it would appear that the raiders had begun their rampage on the Adriatic coast and so would have crossed the middle Danube near Sirmium, quite possibly with the acquiescence of the Gepids, who would want to divert the Huns from themselves and inflict further harm on the empire after Calluc's recent attack. The Huns then moved east to the capital, where the reference to 'suburbs' might indicate that the raiders had penetrated Constantinople's Long Walls. It was, however, Procopius' intention at this point to paint as gloomy a picture of the situation as possible, as he reprised in the *Secret History*,[43] so the geographical indications may well not be exact; the one specific detail is the city of Cassandreia.[44] The information is a reminder of the fragility of our knowledge of Balkan affairs, since Procopius only mentions the incursion because it contributes to the gloomy prospect of war with Persia.

As part of this pessimistic scene, Procopius also refers to subsequent Hunnic incursions. One overpowered the defenders of the Chersonese, where the invaders scaled the wall after wading through the sea and even crossed the Hellespont at Sestos to ravage the Asiatic coast. Another was repulsed by the guards at Thermopylae but then circumvented them by using paths through the mountains to ravage the lands north of the Peloponnese. In each case the Huns pillaged the regions normally protected by these walls.[45] These events are undated, nor is it clear whether Procopius is describing two distinct incursions or one raid that split to attack different targets, as Zabergan's did in 559. In 540 Alexander 'Scissors', while en route to Italy to oversee the restoration of Roman administration, stopped at Thermopylae to reorganize its garrison, perhaps

---

43. Proc., *SH* 18.20.
44. Sarantis, *Balkan Wars* 101–78, argues that the raid was less serious than Procopius made out, on the basis that Cassandreia was already in ruins (Proc., *Build*. 4.3.21–2) and that 32 small rural forts was not a large number out of the hundreds that existed across the Balkans. That said, Procopius may well have exaggerated the dilapidation of Cassandreia in *Buildings*, even 32 forts will have represented several thousand inhabitants and their possessions, and there will have been extensive ravaging of the countryside along the invasion route.
45. Proc., *Wars* 2.4.7–11.

in response to this recent circumvention of the barrier. The former guards are said to have been local farmers, who stood to arms when needed, i.e. presumably *limitanei* who normally supported themselves from their land allotments. In their place Alexander stationed 2,000 troops on the basis that this was in the interests of the inhabitants of the Peloponnese. Procopius only records this information in the *Secret History* because it offers an opportunity to criticize Alexander's financial parsimony: Alexander stipulated that these troops would not be an additional charge on the public treasury, to which end he annexed the civic revenues of the cities of Greece, removing the funds that supported public entertainments and buildings.[46] A less jaundiced interpretation of the change would view it as a way of strengthening the defences of Thermopylae after their recent failure,[47] without imposing extra costs on the state.

From the early 540s Procopius was probably based in Constantinople for most of the time, since he does not seem to have accompanied Belisarius on his second, unsuccessful command in Italy (544–8). His overall perspective on these years was grim, as the East was devastated by Khusro's invasion of 540, the African provinces plagued by repeated Berber raids, Italy increasingly controlled by Totila's restoration of Gothic fortunes, and the empire debilitated by plague. He was, however, now better placed to secure information about events in the Balkans, especially raids that penetrated towards the capital, and the travails of the region supported his agenda of highlighting the empire's problems and Justinian's failings. The scope for exaggeration in his accounts, especially when referring to 'myriads' of captives, should not be forgotten.

It is possible that there was further ravaging in 544, which triggered the return to the Balkans of troops serving in Italy under Vitalius, *MM per Illyricum*. These units had probably accompanied their commander to the west in 539, but, quite apart from arrears of pay and a shortage of provisions, the soldiers had now heard that their families at home had been captured by unspecified Huns.[48] Our next information on Balkan events comes in the context of Narses' recruitment for service in Italy of

---

46. Proc., *SH* 26.31–4. Discussion in Curta, *Edinburgh History* 13–15, although he accepts Procopius' biased representation of the funding change, which he describes as outrageous, and does not recognize the soldier-farmers as *limitanei*.
47. The change must be subsequent to the Hunnic raid, since Procopius would otherwise have criticized Alexander's interference as useless as well as costly to provincials.
48. See Sarantis, *Balkan Wars* 240–7.

Heruls, whom he was leading to Thrace to spend winter 545/6 there. En route they encountered and defeated a larger raiding band of Slavs, which had crossed the Danube and secured numerous captives, who were now liberated. Narses also came across a member of the Antes who was claiming to be the Roman general Chilbuldius, who was believed to have died in 535. Procopius then narrates the story of the fake Chilbuldius, which provides further information: that neighbouring Slavs and Antes fought at some point, probably in the late 530s, with the Slavs securing various prisoners, that the Antes raided Thrace and made off with captives, and that Justinian sent an envoy to the Antes to offer them the city of Turris on the north bank of the Danube and regular payments to keep the peace.[49]

Granted that Roman authority north of the Danube was very limited, it is likely that the offer of Turris recognized that the Antes already occupied the site. Only the diplomacy can be dated, since the Antes had stipulated that their 'Chilbuldius' should be restored to his position as general and Narses encountered him while they were travelling to Constantinople for this to be enacted. Although Narses exposed the imposter, it would appear that the agreement with the Antes survived since there is no mention of any attack by them during the second half of Justinian's reign.[50] Over the next few years, incursions into the Balkans seem to have crossed the middle Danube, which might mean that the Antes were preventing movement through their territory into Scythia. In late 547 or early 548 a group of Slavs ravaged south as far as Dyrrachium on the Adriatic, capturing a number of forts in the area in spite of being shadowed by 15,000 troops under the Roman commanders in Illyria.[51]

The next Balkan events that we know about concern the Heruls. These need to be pieced together from a digression in Procopius about Herul origins and rulers, which is attached to the notice of their departure from Italy with Narses in 538, and a later passage in the context of Justinian's dealings with the Gepids and Lombards.[52] The Heruls feature frequently in Procopius' accounts of Justinian's various campaigns and had given good service under native leaders such as Pharas and Philemuth, troops that were provided under the agreement that had given them their territory near Singidunum. Problems emerged when in about 548 the Heruls

49. Proc., *Wars* 7.14.
50. Sarantis, *Balkan Wars* 257–53.
51. Proc., *Wars* 7.29.1–3.
52. Proc., *Wars* 6.14–15; 7.34.42–5.

murdered their king, Ochus, presumably successor to Grepes whose baptism Justinian had supported. There were doubts about whether he should be replaced, but eventually envoys were sent to those Heruls who had migrated north when the people fragmented after their defeat by the Lombards in the early sixth century. This mission, to the remote island of Thule, a land of the midnight sun, was absent for a long time during which the Heruls at Singidunum decided that they should not bring in a leader without Justinian's consent and so sent to Constantinople. In response Justinian dispatched to them as king, Suartua, a Herul who had been in the capital for a considerable time. Initially he was accepted, but when the envoys at last returned from Thule with the brothers Datius and Aordus and 200 warriors, Suartua was ousted; back in the capital he was given the signal honour of being appointed *MM praesentalis*. The Herul supporters of Datius realized that Justinian was not going to accept their choice of ruler and so 3,000 warriors attached themselves to the Gepids. An army sent in 549 by Justinian to confront the Gepids contained 1,500 Heruls under Philemuth, and part of this army encountered the Herul contingent in the Gepid army and defeated it.

The easiest explanation of these events is that the Heruls, as many of the empire's other tribal neighbours, were split between leaders who favoured accommodation with Rome, undoubtedly in return for the lavish rewards that collaboration brought, and those who preferred hostility, whether because they valued freedom or because they were not benefitting from Roman munificence cannot be known. Religion too may have been a factor since Grepes will have been baptized as orthodox, but Herul soldiers in Africa had been affected by imperial legislation against 'Arians' and so were Homoians, as were the Gepids.[53] On this occasion it would appear that a majority of the Heruls opposed the Roman connection, although the ability of Narses soon afterwards to recruit 3,000 Heruls to lead to Italy suggests that the split was fairly even.

The conflict with the Gepids mentioned above had come about as a result of hostility between the Gepids under King Thorisin and their Lombard neighbours under King Audouin; the latter had recently taken the throne on the death of the young Waltari, whose regent he had been. Audouin appealed to Justinian for assistance and the Gepids also sent envoys, for whom Procopius created a debate, in which the Lombards

---

53. Proc., *Wars* 4.14.14.

accused the Gepids of bad faith, expressed incredulity that Justinian should be their allies and pay them subsidies, and mentioned their Arian beliefs in contrast to Lombard orthodoxy; in response the Gepids pointed to their superior strength and long-standing links with Rome.[54] Justinian sent 10,000 cavalry under John, as well as Philemuth's 1,500 Heruls, to support the Lombards before proceeding to Italy, but at news of their approach the Gepids promptly made peace with the Lombards. This did not last long, perhaps because during the earlier disagreement each side had given refuge to a disappointed claimant to their rival's throne: the Lombard Ildigisal had brought his Lombard and Slav followers over to the Gepids, whereas the young Ustrigoth, whose right to the Gepid throne Thorisin had usurped, fled to the Lombards.[55] Ildigisal commanded quite a significant following since, when Audouin demanded his surrender, he took 6,000 Slav troops – the largest single force of Slavs known from Justinian's reign – with him to Italy in 549 where he defeated Lazarus, a Roman commander in Venetia, before withdrawing east to live among the Slavs.[56]

Conflicts in 550s

At the same time as these conflicts between rival Germanic kingdoms, the Balkans continued to be ravaged by Slavs and others. In early 550 a large band of up to 3,000 Slavs crossed the Danube unopposed and then moved south to cross the Hebrus, namely advancing over the Stara Planina and into the Thracian plain. There they split into two groups of 1,800 and 1,200 with one heading west into Illyricum while the other remained in Thrace. Both achieved successes against local Roman commanders and the group in Thrace then routed the cavalry based at Tzurullum (Çorlu), only 35km from the Long Walls. They captured the commander, the *candidatus* Asbadus, one of Justinian's forty personal bodyguards, and then burned him alive after first flaying strips of skin off his back. Numerous forts were taken by siege, with the most important casualty being the coastal city of Topirus in Thrace: there the Slavs lured the garrison outside the walls, where they were annihilated in an ambush. They then overcame

---

54. Proc., *Wars* 7.34.
55. Proc., *Wars* 7.35.19; 8.27.20.
56. Proc., *Wars* 7.35.20–2.

the desperate resistance of the inhabitants, who poured down boiling oil and pitch on the attackers while everyone threw stones; 15,000 men were killed while women and children were taken prisoner, contrary to the standard Slav practice of killing captives in various gruesome ways.[57]

In summer 550, while Germanus was gathering troops for his Italian expedition at Serdica (Sofia), he learned that a large Slav band had crossed the Danube and advanced to Naissus (Nis); these had clearly crossed the middle Danube and were moving up the Morava valley. Captives revealed that their intention was to besiege Thessalonica and capture it and nearby cities, but, when news of Germanus' presence reached their main force, the Slavs fled to Dalmatia in awe of his reputation.[58] Later that year, with Germanus now dead, these Slavs returned and joined others who had recently crossed the Danube, some suspected in response to encouragement from Totila to distract the Romans from gathering their planned reinforcements for Italy. The Slavs split into three groups and ravaged widely, before spending the winter in Roman territory.

In 551 Justinian sent a substantial army under the eunuch Scholasticus, which confronted the Slavs near Adrianople (Edirne). The Slavs were hampered by all their booty and the Roman commanders intended to blockade them on a hill, but their troops lost patience and insisted on an engagement in which they were defeated with heavy losses. The Slavs then devastated the region of Astike up to the Long Walls, but as they withdrew they were caught by a Roman army, which defeated them and recovered large numbers of captives.[59]

The same year the Gepids ferried over the Danube 12,000 Kutrigurs under Chinialon, whom they had summoned to support them in their conflict with the Lombards; these had arrived too late for that action and so had to be diverted to alternative sources of plunder. Justinian's response was to send gifts to the Utigurs to the east of the Sea of Azov to encourage them to attack Kutrigur territory; the Utigurs secured the support of 2,000 Tetraxitae Goths, their neighbours, crossed the Don, and defeated the Kutrigurs after a hard fight. The Utigurs returned home with numerous prisoners, while Roman captives who had been taken back to Kutrigur territory managed to escape and ultimately return to reach their

57. Proc., *Wars* 7.38.
58. Proc., *Wars* 7.40.1–7.
59. Proc., *Wars* 7.40.31–45.

homelands. Justinian ensured that this misfortune was communicated to Chinialon; he was persuaded to withdraw without causing further damage, with a payment and a promise that his men would be given lands to settle in Thrace if they found it impossible to re-establish themselves north of the Black Sea. It so happened that 2,000 warriors with their households under the leadership of Sinnion had fled from the Utigur attack and now approached the empire. In response to their pleas they received lands in Thrace, much to the displeasure of the Utigur leader, Sandil.[60]

Although Procopius does not record the extent of destruction caused by this raid, Chinialon led a large army and the mere effort of keeping it supplied will have consumed provincial resources, let alone the booty that was collected. We do not know if any of Chinialon's followers decided to take up Justinian's offer of land in Thrace, but the example of Sinnion, who had been one of the commanders of Huns in Africa, indicates the fluidity of allegiances across the Danube frontier: war leaders had to provide for their followers and this would probably take them in different directions at different times as it did for Ildigisal the Lombard.[61]

Separately we hear of another Hunnic incursion into the Balkans in early 551. When Narses set out from Constantinople to march to Salona to join the troops gathered there for the expedition to Italy, his progress was halted at Philippopolis in Thrace since his route was blocked by Hun raiders; only when these continued south towards Thessalonica, apparently without intervention, was Narses able to continue.[62] It is unlikely that these Huns formed part of Chinialon's force – at least Procopius does not make the connection or refer to them as Kutrigurs – and it is more than likely that the pressures that pushed Chinialon and Sinnion to seek their fortunes in the empire were operating on other leaders as well. Invaders did not only come from the north in 551: as part of his efforts to disrupt Roman preparations in the Balkans, Totila sent 300 raiding ships across the Adriatic which ravaged Corfu and the mainland to the south near Nicopolis.[63]

Trouble continued into 552 when a large group of Slavs invaded Illyricum, where the army sent by Justinian under the two sons of Germanus, Justin and Justinian, could do no more than shadow their movements, cutting off stragglers when possible. In the absence of firm

---

60. Proc., *Wars* 8.19.13–19.22.
61. Proc., *Wars* 3.11.12; discussion in Sarantis, *Balkan Wars* 288–92.
62. Proc., *Wars* 8.21.20–2.
63. Proc., *Wars* 8.22.17, 30–2.

opposition the Slavs secured considerable booty, which they were able to take back home since the Gepids had agreed to convey them over the Danube at the cost of one gold coin per head, thereby thwarting the Romans from using their naval strength to attack them.[64] This was not the first time that the Gepids had helped invaders across the Danube, since they must have conveyed Chinialon's Kutrigurs over the river and quite possibly others before that. The danger to the empire's Balkan defences was clear and so Justinian was responsive when both Gepids and Lombards approached him with a request for friendship. The agreement between Gepids and Lombards soon foundered and the Lombards requested imperial help, which was arranged in the form of an expedition commanded by the Romans Justin and Justinian, the Persarmenian Aratius, the Herul Sindual who was now *MM praesentalis*, and the Goth Amalafrida. This heterogeneous army proceeded to Ulpiana, where Justininan instructed it to halt since the city was wracked by religious dissension. Most commanders obeyed, but Amalafrida, who may have been more independent as a leader of allied troops, continued and helped the Lombards achieve a crushing victory; the incident ends with King Audouin reproaching Justinian for not sending the promised support.[65]

The last Balkan activity to be reported by Procopius is the fate of the Lombard Ildigisal. After returning from Italy in late 549 to rejoin the Slavs, Ildigisal was recruited into imperial service and given command of a unit of palace guards, presumably as *comes scholae*; whether he brought with him his large Slav following is unknown. His prominent presence in Constantinople angered Audouin, who demanded his surrender. Although Justinian flatly refused, Ildigisal became discontented with his situation, which was observed by Goar, a Gothic leader who had been captured in Dalmatia in the late 530s and had already rebelled once against Justinian. Goar persuaded Ildigisal to flee and together they reached Apri in Thrace, where they joined the Lombard troops stationed nearby; these may have been among the followers who had accompanied Ildigisal into the empire. After seizing horses from an imperial stud farm, they were confronted by the Kutrigurs who had recently been settled in Thrace. The Kutrigurs were defeated and did nothing more to halt the Lombards' progress into Illyricum where an army under Aratius, Rhecithangus, Leonianus, and Arimuth had rushed to

---

64. Proc., *Wars* 8.25.1–5.
65. Proc., *Wars* 8.25.6–15.

oppose them. Lombard scouts surprised these commanders while drinking from a stream, killing all of them and leaving their leaderless troops unable to oppose them. Ildigisal sought refuge with the Gepids and Thorisin, who refused to surrender him to the Lombards but instead demanded the return of the Gepid royal, Ustrigoth. Both kings declined to surrender their refugee, but the two royal fugitives were soon eliminated by their hosts.[66]

The frequent raids of the years 548 to 552 are then followed by a period of apparent quiet. There are various ways in which this contrast can be explained. One is that these five years really had been a period of heightened activity in the Balkans, whether because Totila had been trying to stir up trouble for the empire to delay Justinian's preparations to send an army to Italy, or because bad relations with the Gepids prompted them to encourage other groups to invade, helping them to cross the Danube. The fracture of the Heruls into pro- and anti-Roman groups, with the latter joining the Gepids, undermined Roman authority in the region of Singidunum, which was effectively the empire's front line against the Gepids. In this case the stabilization of the situation on the middle Danube after Audouin defeated the Gepids could have led to a period of greater peace. Also Narses' defeat of the Goths and Franks in Italy might have permitted the return of some of the troops that had been siphoned off to support his efforts, for example the men from the *quaestura exercitus* on the lower Danube who will have accompanied their commander Bonus to Italy.

On the other hand, the apparent contrast between 548–52 and the next six years might just be a historiographical illusion. Procopius devotes much more attention to Balkan events between 548 and 552 than usual, because in these years successive Roman commanders were busy in the Balkans preparing forces to be led to Italy against Totila. He naturally reported occasions when their activities were hampered by tribal incursions and took the opportunity to point to the failings of Justinian's policies. Procopius brought his narrative to a close in 553, the continuation of Marcellinus Comes concluded in 548, and very little information at all is recorded in Malalas between 533 and 556, so that lack of evidence in the sources does not prove there was peace after 553. Procopius' continuator Agathias did not have any incursions worthy of note to report until the extensive Kutrigur invasion of 559 threatened the capital and could not be ignored. His silence does not mean that there were not constant lower-level raids

---

66. Proc., *Wars* 8.27.

across the Danube that may not have penetrated beyond the frontier provinces. It is probable that there is some truth in both explanations.

The arrival at Constantinople of an embassy from the Avars in 557/8, probably during the winter, is recorded by Theophanes in a notice that preserves much more information than the brief statement in Malalas.[67] Their hair, which was long at the back and braided with ribbons, attracted attention. The Avars had had some contact with the empire in the fifth century, but this embassy followed their flight from the Turks in central Asia to the vicinity of the Black Sea, which had brought them within Roman horizons. In less than two decades they were to become the dominant power on the Danube, Rome's most dangerous opponent since the death of Attila. More information about their approach is provided by Menander, who says that their wanderings led them into contact with the Alans, whose leader Saroes informed Justin, the current *MM* in Lazica to the south of the Caucasus; Justin secured Justinian's approval for the visit of an embassy, for which the Avars selected Candich. At Constantinople Candich boasted of Avar strength and advised Justinian to secure their alliance with rich gifts, annual payments, and fertile territory to settle. In response Justinian sent golden couches, golden cords, and other objects along with Valentinus as ambassador to discuss an alliance and action against Roman enemies.[68]

In winter 559 Kutrigur Huns under Zabergan crossed the frozen Danube. The raid was noted by Malalas,[69] not surprisingly since it affected the capital, and he recorded a number of specific details, but the longest account is in Agathias, who attributes the attack to jealousy of the benefits that the Utigurs derived from their alliance with the Romans.[70] Granted that the Avars were already threatening Hunnic groups around the Black Sea, with the Unigurs, Zali, and Sabirs being the first to succumb,[71] it is possible that Zabergan was both building up resources to confront them and reconnoitering possible new territories. The Kutrigurs entered Thrace in March 559, where Zabergan split his forces into three groups, sending one to raid Greece, a second to attack the Chersonese, and the

---

67. Theophanes 232.6–14; Malalas 18.125; for early contacts, see Pohl, *Avars* ch.2.
68. Menander fr.5.1–2.
69. Malalas 18.129, although most of his account is lost in the textual lacuna that covers the years 558 to 562 and has to be reconstructed from Theophanes 233.11–234.12.
70. Agathias, *Hist.* 5.11–25; 12.6–7.
71. Menander fr.5.2.11.13.

third to approach Constantinople; this last group under Zabergan himself comprised 7,000 horsemen. Agathias set out to highlight Justinian's neglect of the empire, using this account to air his views on the decline in Roman military numbers, and he presented the Kutrigur advance on the capital as meeting no opposition. Malalas, however, refers to an engagement in Thrace in which the general Sergius and Edermas, a senior official, were captured and then to the defeat of a conscript force at the Long Walls. According to Agathias these walls had long been neglected and were in a state of disrepair, whereas Malalas more plausibly attributes their damage to the massive earthquakes that rocked the capital in 557 and 558.

Inside the Long Walls Zabergan plundered the rich suburbs and camped at Melantias on the Sea of Marmara, less then 30km from the Theodosian walls, so that Justinian had valuables removed from all extramural churches and conveyed into the city or ferried across the Bosporus. The *scholae*, *protectores*, unspecified *numeri*, and senators were posted at the Golden Gate in the Theodosian walls and at Sycae across the Golden Horn. Raiding extended as far as the district of S. Stratonikos at Decaton, i.e. the tenth milestone from the centre of Constantinople and only three of four kilometres from the walls. Eventually Justinian summoned Belisarius from retirement, who together with other senators led out a scratch force, of which the core comprised 300 of his veterans but the majority were untrained. He had to commandeer all available horses in the capital, including those belonging to religious institutions or used for chariot racing. At the village of Chiton he encamped and had a trench dug, after which he began to pick off Kutrigur stragglers and impress on the enemy the size of his army by having felled trees dragged around to raise clouds of dust. Zabergan led 2,000 men against the Roman position, but Belisarius had prepared an ambush that resulted in the flight of the Kutrigurs with the loss of 400 men. After this the raiders withdrew via Tzurullon, Arcadiopolis, and the shrine of S. Alexander at Drizipera, though Malalas does not record if these were sacked or just bypassed. Agathias alleges that jealous comments about Belisarius' victory dissuaded him from pursuing their retreat.

The force sent south into Greece failed to penetrate the defences at Thermopylae and retired north,[72] while those attacking the Chersonese were

---

72. Curta, *Edinburgh History* 15, asserts that this group bypassed the defences at Thermopylae to ravage as far as the Isthmus of Corinth, but this contradicts what Agathias states.

repulsed with heavy losses by the local commander, Germanus, who came from Justiniana Prima and was related to the emperor. An attempt to pass around the seaward end of the walls, as the Huns had achieved in the early 540s, failed, since Justinian had subsequently strengthened their moles, as celebrated in *Buildings*,[73] so that the raiders had to construct reed boats capable of holding three or four men each. They launched about 150 of these, in response to which Germanus concealed twenty light boats filled with soldiers behind the sea wall, until they pounced after the attackers had rounded the end of the wall; as a result all the reed boats were destroyed and their occupants killed. A few days later Germanus led a sally against the demoralized enemy and inflicted considerable losses, though he was wounded in the thigh. These two reverses persuaded the Kutrigurs to rejoin Zabergan in Thrace. He declined to withdraw from there until he had received rewards from the emperor comparable to those given to the Utigurs and, by threatening to kill his captives if they were not ransomed, he forced Justinian to send him money.

The Kutrigurs' departure from the empire is reported differently in Malalas and Agathias. The former says that the invaders remained in the empire until August; Justinian sent warships to the Danube to impede their crossing, as a result of which they asked to be allowed to withdraw and were escorted north by Justin, the future emperor. By contrast Agathias reports that Justinian wrote to the Utigur leader Sandil, reproaching him for allowing his rivals to enjoy such success and encouraging him to attack their territory while they were still absent. The strategy worked, with the result that the two groups weakened each other through their mutual ravaging and fighting.[74] The fact that the Utigur actions resembled those of 551 does not mean that the account has been fabricated on the basis of Procopius' earlier narrative, since the opportunity was the same and hence the response. After Easter Justinian made a very rare excursion from the capital to Selymbria (Silivri) on the Sea of Marmara, where he remained until August to supervise the reconstruction of the Long Walls.

Before long both Kutrigurs and Utigurs had been subjugated by the Avars. This may have been followed by attacks on the Antes, since the Avar Chagan was advised by a Kutrigur in his entourage to kill an envoy sent by the Antes after their first defeat by the Avars. The murder of the envoy was followed up with further ravaging of the property of the Antes.

---

73. Proc., *Buildings* 4.10.10–19.
74. Agathias, *Hist* 5.24–5.

The dates of these events are not specified, but in a speech attributed to the Chagan in 569 he referred to his conquest of both Hunnic groups.[75] Thereafter they constituted subordinate elements within the Avar federation. Justinian took a hard line in further negotiations with the Avars, offering them the territory near Singidunum that the Heruls had previously occupied and rejecting their demand to be allowed to settle south of the Danube in Scythia. The general Justin discovered that the Avars were feigning friendship but planned to attack the empire once they had managed to ferry their army across the Danube, and he advised Justinian to prolong discussions in Constantinople. When the envoys were eventually released without achieving their demands, they used some of their gifts to purchase weapons, which Justin confiscated when they reached the Danube.[76] This brought the Avars and Romans into conflict, though without immediate consequences since the Avars moved west to attack the Franks. In 562 a Hun incursion captured Obaisipolis, in response to which Justinian dispatched the *magister militum* Marcellus to recover the city, and then in April the same Huns captured Anastasiopolis in Thrace.[77]

The overall impression from the narratives of Procopius and Agathias is that Justinian's policies for defending the Balkans were ineffective and left these provinces open to frequent debilitating raids. Procopius makes his disapproval of Justinian's treatment of tribes beyond the Danube frontier clear in a number of ways. He used a speech composed for Lombard envoys and a message from the Utigur Sandil to place his own criticisms in the mouths of foreigners.[78] The Lombards rehearsed the outrageous behaviour of the Gepids over the years after their appropriation of Sirmium, and asked what they had ever done in return for all the Roman gifts they had received, while Sandil complained that the Kutrigurs were being rewarded with land south of the Danube after

---

75. Menander fr.5.3; fr. 12.6.20–5.
76. Menander fr.5.4.
77. Theophanes p.236.25–30, but derived from Malalas. Obaisipolis is otherwise unknown and the text is regarded as corrupt. The editor of Theophanes, de Boor, suggested Novae (losing its first letter), whereas the translators of Malalas (p.299 note) speculate that it might be Odessus (via Odyssopolis). Sarantis, *Balkan Wars* 354–5, believed that the Malalas translators were correcting de Boor, but they merely offer an alternative guess. The capture of a major trading port and garrison base on the Black Sea would have been a significant achievement and Odessus seems an unlikely success.
78. Proc., *Wars* 7.34.6–24; 8.19.8–22.

ravaging the empire and carrying off numerous Roman captives whereas the Utigurs were left in their current homeland. The impact of tribal raids is also underlined by reference to the unprecedented nature of the destruction, the innumerable captives removed beyond the Danube, and the inability of Roman forces to do more than shadow the movements of raiders without confronting them. On occasion Roman forces even appear to wave raiders on to southern destinations, provided that they moved out of their way.

This criticism is not, however, universal. Agathias ended his history with a paragraph that noted how the mutually destructive fighting of the Kutrigurs and Utigurs benefited the empire and led people to recognize the wisdom of Justinian's approach to handling the tribes.[79] Menander, while expressing a preference for the energetic action that the vigorous younger Justinian might have undertaken, states that even in his enfeebled age the emperor would have crushed the Avars 'if not by war, at least by wisdom', if he had not died, and compliments his use of the Avars to destroy Rome's other enemies.[80] Both authors reflect the context of composition. Agathias wrote after Justinian's death, when Justin II manifested a new and more belligerent approach to international dealings that did, in the short run, bring benefits since the Avars, after being summarily refused the gifts they had been receiving from Justinian, focused their energies on their western borders for a decade. Menander was writing under Maurice, whose attempts to confront the Avars were for long thwarted by a lack of troops in the Balkans, so that diplomacy was the only way to buy time. Procopius was working on *Wars* 7 at the same time as he was creating the *Secret History*, and there are overlaps in the emotive rhetoric deployed about the magnitude of destruction.[81]

An assessment of the effectiveness of Justinian's policies in the Balkans is difficult. The standard view is to follow the lead of the narrative historians and conclude that for much of his reign the Balkans were left with inadequate defences, since campaigns in the East and Italy took precedence: for example in 538 reinforcements for Belisarius were largely drawn from the Balkan armies, while in 553 the *quaestor exercitus*, Bonus,

---

79. Agathias, *Hist.* 5.25.6.
80. Menander fr. 5.1.17–26; 5.2.8–10.
81. Proc., *SH* 18.20–1.

was given charge of Lucca with a substantial force that presumably included his provincial soldiers from the lower Danube. As a result, invading groups ranged widely over the northern and central Balkans, occasionally penetrating as far as the Long Walls of Constantinople and Thermopylae. Granted the shortage of troops, Justinian had to do his best with gifts and payments, grants of land, and setting tribes against each other. A much more optimistic interpretation is advocated by Alexander Sarantis,[82] who argues that rhetorical accounts of unprecedented ravaging have to be scaled back and gives Justinian considerable credit for mastering the Gepid threat and providing protection for most of the region.

As ever the truth is probably somewhere in between. Procopius in particular wanted to criticize Justinian, which in the public text of the *Wars* had to be done indirectly, and so he has magnified problems. On the other hand, minimizing the impact of raids entails discounting most of our evidence as exaggerated and ignoring the human cost of even a relatively minor incursion. The redeployment of troops from the Balkans to other theatres certainly left the provinces more open to invasion than they would otherwise have been, and this seems to have continued through until Justinian's final years and the achievement of some sort of peace in Italy. What is clear is that, despite this shortage of troops, Justinian pursued an active policy in the Balkans, one that embraced improved defensive works across the region, establishment of buffer zones within and beyond the Danube through settlement of Heruls and alliance with Antes, and the cultivation of rivalries between neighbouring northern peoples. Although the Balkan provinces were repeatedly ravaged, the disruption was probably not as bad as it had been under Leo and Zeno in the latter part of the fifth century, when large warbands were based there for year after year. A robust skeleton for imperial control survived the repeated incursions, and the Danube fleet continued to patrol the frontier – at least when the river was not frozen – to deter incursions.

---

82. Conveniently summarised at *Balkan Wars* 393–7.

Chapter 9

Internal Challenges

The previous four chapters have treated the major campaign theatres of Justinian's world. We now focus internally, on events in the major cities of the empire and at Constantinople in particular, whose inclusion in a volume on Justinian's wars is justified by the scale of violence that was sometimes involved. Maintaining law and order in the capital often required the deployment of troops under senior commanders, and the death toll of 30,000 or more, on the final day of the Nika Riot in January 532, was the largest single recorded violent loss of life in the eastern empire throughout Justinian's reign, far surpassing the casualties in even the bloodiest of battles. It is also relevant to Justinian's wars since, during the reign of his uncle, he orchestrated a campaign of intimidation against potential rivals and people of influence in order to secure the succession for himself, and then the crisis of the Nika Riot made the acquisition of external victory more pressing. In addition to urban rioting, the opportunity is taken to consider briefly two major plots that threatened Justinian's hold on power, and in particular how he responded to these threats. For someone who reigned for thirty-eight years, two plots are not a lot and the overall stability of his regime reflects his success in establishing its foundations.

Urban violence in the sixth and seventh centuries is inextricably linked with the Hippodrome and the groups who organized the racing and other entertainments and led the supporters in their chants. There were four racing teams, known by their colours – Blues, Greens, Whites and Reds – of which the Blues and Greens were the leaders or senior groups while the Whites and Reds were junior partners (to Blues and Greens respectively). In the sources these groups are often referred to as *meros* (pl. *mere*), 'part', or sometimes as *demos* (pl. *demoi*), 'people', though the standard term in modern scholarship is 'factions', which goes back to the Latin word for the professional performers who participated in games.[1] The formally

---

1. For the origin of this less than ideal term, which was not used in antiquity for the circus partisans, see Alan Cameron, *Factions* ch.1.

registered members of the factions were relatively small,[2] but these highly organized groups of supporters regularly coordinated wider responses in the Hippodrome and elsewhere, ideally in support of the emperor but obviously with the capacity to register dissent. Their ability to direct the expression of popular views was important at imperial accessions, as in 518 for Justin, and was exploited in the developing ceremonial calendar at Constantinople.

Our understanding of the factions of late antiquity was revolutionized by the publication in 1976 of Alan Cameron's *Circus Factions*, whose greatest service was to dispose of a number of highly inventive and influential theories about the factions and the opposition between Blues and Greens. In an effective demolition job Cameron demonstrated that the factions were not split on religious lines between orthodox Blues and anti-Chalcedonian Greens,[3] that they did not constitute an urban militia from the fourth century onwards, although there were occasions when they were called upon to defend the city walls, and that they did not divide between them the residential districts of Constantinople, although there were specific areas that had connections with a particular faction, for example through the location of stables. The presumption that all faction members were drawn from the lower classes because they were involved in popular entertainment and public violence is unjustified: quite possibly the majority were men of the people, but their public influence ensured them the patronage of prominent individuals and their activities drew in individuals of education and wealth, for example Menander the historian who abandoned his legal studies to pursue the excitements of faction involvement.[4]

Where Cameron's analysis is weaker is with regard to the political significance of the factions. He rightly disproved the thesis that they were quasi-political parties with distinctive programmes, or agents of popular sovereignty to place in the balance against imperial domination, but then struggled to explain the importance they clearly had at moments of extreme crisis, such as the Nika Riot or in the civil war between Phocas and Heraclius in 610. He also did not have a convincing explanation for the rise to prominence of the circus factions in the mid-fifth century,

2. The only figures that we have relate to 602, when there were 1,500 registered Greens and 900 Blues: Theophylact, *Hist.* 8.7.11.
3. For the factions as the joint champions of orthodoxy, see Potter, 'Anatomies'.
4. Menander fr.1; see Bell, *Social Conflicts* 146–7.

when, after centuries during which the most significant violent events were connected with theatres and the claques that operated there, the hippodromes became the focus for triggering urban violence.

Two things appear to have happened in the fifth century. First, at an unknown date the organizations responsible for theatrical entertainments were merged with those which underpinned races in the hippodromes. Second, Emperor Theodosius II, probably at some point in the 440s, demonstrated the importance of the factions in the Hippodrome for the propagation of his image throughout the cities of the empire, which reinforced the existing provision that chants in provincial cities should be conveyed to the capital by the *cursus publicus*.[5] The Hippodrome was the place of victory, where the emperor could regularly associate himself with the successful charioteers, provided he was accorded the appropriate chants.[6] If the emperor valued the contribution of the factions, then they became significant actors in the empire's public life and other leading figures could see advantages in being connected with a faction as patron or benefactor. From the perspective of the factions, if chants in favour of an emperor mattered, then so too did hostile chanting.[7]

The majority of our information on the factions comes from the chronicle tradition of John Malalas, in part through his extant abridged manuscript, in part through later chronicles that used his work. This evidence is supplemented by the historical excerpts made for Constantine Porphyrogennitus in the tenth century: the collection entitled *de Insidiis*, 'On Plots', contains material from both John Malalas and the early seventh century chronicler John of Antioch, whose work is otherwise lost. Popular violence was not an issue that normally attracted the attention of the tradition of classicizing historians, who tended not to report on internal or urban affairs, although Procopius made an exception for the massive Nika Riot, which he reported in a pair of chapters devoted to plots against the rulers of Persia and Rome.[8]

---

5. For discussion and the suggestion that the trigger was an empire-wide change in seating arrangements instituted by Emperor Theodosius, see Whitby, 'Violence', and 'Factions'; this was to ensure that his favoured Green Faction directly faced him, but resulted in them sitting next to rather than opposite the Blues, with a consequent increase in opportunities for violent interaction.
6. For the emperor presenting the rewards of victory, see Plate 5.
7. Cf. Bell, *Social Conflict* 142–5, for the need to correct Cameron on the political aspect of factions.
8. Proc., *Wars* 1.23–4.

The reign of Anastasius had witnessed numerous instances of serious urban violence in both Antioch, which John Malalas recorded as an eye-witness, and Constantinople. Anastasius wanted to treat the two main factions equally and to that end had proclaimed his allegiance to the Reds, a rare example of an emperor supporting one of the minor colours. It is not clear that this policy was particularly successful. Some of the recorded violence related to the prominent charioteer Porphyrius, about whom we know a certain amount thanks to the dedicatory epigrams that accompanied a sequence of honorific statues erected to him by the Blues and Greens;[9] among other achievements, Porphyrius claimed credit for contributing to the defeat of the rebel Vitalian.

The most serious rioting of Anastasius' reign was triggered by his religious innovations, in particular the addition to the Trisaghion of the phrase, 'He who was crucified for us', which was associated with Miaphysite opponents of Chalcedon. In November 512 the unrest was exceptionally severe and included an attempt to proclaim as emperor Areobindus, the husband of Anicia Juliana whose father had briefly been western emperor in 472 and whose mother was daughter of Valentinian III. This was only foiled by the fact that Areobindus had ensured he was not at home when the rioters came to his house. The rioting eventually died down when Anastasius entered the Hippodrome without wearing his imperial crown and accepted full responsibility for the disturbances.[10] Although the factions are not mentioned as being involved in the disturbances, the failed proclamation and the final performance in the Hippodrome strongly suggest that they were contributing and that Anastasius saw them as agents who could ensure a positive response to his offer of forgiveness.

The reign of Justin is also known for widespread disturbances, even if not of this focused ferocity. Malalas or his derivatives say that the Blues began to cause trouble in Antioch, but this then spread to other cities and lasted for five years, until in 522/3 Justin appointed the former *comes Orientis*, Theodotus, city prefect at Constantinople, with specific orders to sort out the violence. Theodotus proceeded energetically, even ordering the execution of the *illustris* Theodosius for his involvement in unrest. It was believed that Justinian had contributed to encouraging the disruption and in his *Secret History* Procopius makes the most of this

---

9. On his fascinating career, see Alan Cameron, *Porphyrius*.
10. Malalas 16.19; Evagrius 3.44.

link, accusing him of protecting the malefactors and so increasing their lawlessness.[11] Theodotus' crackdown came close to ensnaring Justinian, though there is disagreement over the details. According to John of Nikiu, Theodotus announced that, after Theodosius, the patrician Justinian was going to be his next target, at which point Justinian conveniently fell ill and Justin dismissed Theodotus. Procopius placed Justinian's illness earlier in the sequence of events, with his absence from affairs giving scope to rivals to pursue his misdeeds, but as soon as Justinian recovered he acted to denigrate Theodotus and had him removed from office.[12] Whatever the truth, Theodotus had made powerful enemies and after his dismissal he withdrew to Jerusalem in 524, where he sought sanctuary in a church to escape the assassins who had been sent after him.

The full story behind these events will never be known for certain, but a plausible interpretation is that the parvenu Justinian, who was far from sure of succeeding his uncle, patronized the Blue Faction from 518, providing them with immunity for their misdeeds as they assisted him by intimidating his potential rivals amongst the aristocracy.[13] Procopius alleged that the Blues robbed, and on occasions killed, men of distinction with impunity to the extent that some took to flight or even switched factional allegiance. The ensuing mayhem was exploited to settle private scores, legal process was subverted, women were coerced, and one rich woman even jumped into the Bosporus to drown herself rather than submit to the wishes of her factional captors.[14] Even if some of the allegations are urban myths, or even Procopius' own invention, the incidents had plausibility. One probable result of these activities is that it was the Senate that urged Justin, against the emperor's wishes, to elevate Justinian, perhaps first to the rank of *nobilissimus* and then to Caesar in 527:[15] individual senators were keen to curry favour with the man believed to be behind the factions' crimes. As soon as he was proclaimed co-emperor on 1 April 527, Justinian sent orders throughout the empire that rioters and murderers, regardless of their faction, were to be punished for their misdeeds, a move that brought a period of quiet.[16]

---

11. Proc., *SH* 7.15–42; 9.32–38.
12. Discussion in Potter, *Theodora* 96–7.
13. Bell, *Social Conflicts* 158–60.
14. Proc., *SH* 7.15–39.
15. Zonaras 15.5.37; Victor of Tununa 11.109.
16. Malalas 17.18.

Nika Riot

These events from the reigns of Anastasius and Justin provide a necessary background for the most violent event of Justinian's reign, the Nika Riot. In 527 the *carte blanche* enjoyed by the Blues for their misdeeds had been terminated, so that, although they continued to be supported by the emperor, they no longer dared to behave as they had done in the early 520s. This is the plausible context for the assertion in Procopius' *Secret History* that Theodora attempted to protect the Blues from her husband's efforts to punish their misdeeds.[17] At the same time the Greens continued to be at a disadvantage, and served as the vehicle for those wishing to voice protests. Pseudo-Zachariah reports that a large number of people from across the empire, who wished to register complaints against the administration of John the Cappadocian as praetorian prefect, came to Constantinople where they were supported by one of the factions, so that there were constant chants against the emperor. Although the faction is not named, this can only have been the Greens.[18]

The intensity of Green hostility to Justinian is illustrated in a remarkable dialogue that preserves a series of exchanges in the Hippodrome of Constantinople between the Greens and Justinian's spokesman. This dialogue, which is known as the *Acta dia Kalopodion*, is preserved in fullest form by Theophanes, with a small section of the opening also appearing in the *Chronicon Paschale*;[19] its presence in two independent branches of the chronicle tradition indicates that the record originated in Malalas, even though there is no trace of it in our abbreviated manuscript.[20] The precise date of the exchanges is not recorded, but probably took place in the first few days of January.[21] The Greens began by protesting against

---

17. Proc., *SH* 10.16–18.
18. Ps.-Zach., *HE* 9.14a.
19. Cameron, *Factions* App. C, pp. 317–33, provides a translation and extended discussion of the exchanges, but his argument that the dialogue is not relevant to the Nika Riot is flawed since he does not accurately analyze the preservation of the information in *Chronicon Paschale*: see Whitby, *Chronicon* 113–14; Meier, 'Inszenierung' 278–86; Potter, *Theodora* 246 n.9.
20. The length of the dialogue made it an easy element to exclude from what was already a very long account of the riot.
21. Cameron, *Factions* 327, favoured a date early in Justinian's reign, arguing against the preference of Maas for a date at the very end of the reign; other views are summarized by Greatrex, 'Riot' 68 n.41. Greatrex's own position is unclear, but he regards the hostility between Blues and Greens as surprising in the context of 532 and so presumably supports a different date; he is another scholar not to consder the implications of the layout of the manuscript of the *Chronicon Paschale*.

one of Justinian's eunuch bodyguards, the *spatharius* Calopodius, whom they accused of wronging them, but after Justinian's herald responded by calling the Greens 'Jews, Manichees, and Samaritans', escalated their complaints by introducing the unpunished murders of twenty-six Greens and then exclaiming, 'Would that Sabbatius had never been born, so that he would not have had a son who is a murderer.' This extremely insulting reference to Justinian's peasant father prompted the Blues to intervene to accuse the Greens of being the real murderers. Further exchanges ended with the Greens agreeing to keep quiet, against their will, but observing this by walking out of the Hippodrome after the final taunts, 'Better to be a pagan than a Blue, God knows', and 'May the bones of the spectators be dug up', the latter a curse that the spectators be killed.

These extracts from the dialogue give an indication of the mood in the Hippodrome in the days immediately before the Nika Riot broke out. The traditional hostility between Blues and Greens persisted, the Greens felt that they were being harshly treated by powerful individuals close to Justinian and were prepared to combine the standard chants wishing victory for the emperor with pointed insults, and Justinian offered no concessions to assuage Green anger. Popular moods, however, could change quickly, given the right stimulus. On 10 January the city prefect Eudaemon arranged the execution of seven faction members, who had been found guilty of violent crimes including murder.[22] Although four were to be beheaded and the other three impaled, after being paraded through the city and taken over the Golden Horn, some of them were hanged. Two of these survived since the scaffold broke, and they perhaps also survived a second attempt at execution, at which point the watching crowds acclaimed the emperor while monks from S. Conon's took the pair to sanctuary in S. Laurence's, where the prefect put them under guard. By chance the survivors were one Blue and one Green and so the factions found themselves united in their chants: for them the escape of the pair from the death sentence was clearly a divine reprieve, and the emperor

22. The detailed events of the subsequent rioting need to be pieced together from the representatives of the chronicle tradition; the account in Procopius, *Wars* 1.24, presents a different, more imperial perspective, that he probably obtained from Belisarius, who could have reported on the view of events from inside the palace. For reconstructions of events, see Bury, 'Nika Riot', and *HLRE* II.39–48; Greatrex, 'Riot' 67–80.

as the embodiment of law should give effect to God's will through an imperial decree.[23]

The Ides, 13th January, was a traditional date for chariot races and in the Hippodrome the Blues and Greens chanted for their common request, the liberation of the prisoners who had escaped execution. Seated in the imperial Kathisma, Justinian declined to give in,[24] with the result that the chanting continued for twenty-two out of the scheduled twenty-four races for several hours, at which point the mood of the crowds changed and the chanting switched to 'Long live the merciful Blues and Greens'. When the race meeting finished, Justinian retired into the palace while the factions jointly set off for the *praetorium* of the city prefect, after agreeing for themselves the password 'Nika', 'Victory'; this was to prevent them from being infiltrated by the *excubitores*, the imperial bodyguards who would normally have had responsibility for quelling unrest. When the prefect declined to remove the guards watching the two faction members at S. Laurence's, the rioters broke into the *praetorium*, freed the prisoners being held there, killed some officials, and set fire to the building, with the conflagration spreading to buildings lining the Mese, Constantinople's main street.

So far the disturbance was a purely factional affair, triggered by the chance event that had brought the Blues, hitherto loyal to the emperor, into alignment with the Greens. Justinian's first response was to order the flag to be raised at the Hippodrome to signal that there would be further racing on Tuesday the 14th. He wished to conciliate the factions without going so far as to cave in to their demands for the prisoners and, since cancellation of entertainments could provoke rioting, the offer of further races might calm the situation.[25] This, however, did not appease the rioters, who set fire to seating in the Hippodrome, from where the blaze spread to the baths of Zeuxippus.

On the 15th, or possibly the 16th, the mood became more serious and political. Outside the palace the city was in the hands of the rioters and the crowds continued to chant, but when Justinian sent the two *magistri militum* Mundus and Constantiolus with the acting *magister officiorum* Basilides from the palace to discover the current demands, the rioters

---

23. Greatrex, 'Riot' 61.
24. For its appearance, see the images of Theodosius from his obelisk on the Hippodrome spina (Plates 5, 10, 12).
25. Cameron, *Factions* 275–6 with 276 n.6; Greatrex, 'Riot' 70 n.53.

insisted that the praetorian prefect, John the Cappadocian, the *quaestor* Tribonian, and Eudaemon the city prefect must be dismissed. It is easy to see why the factions wanted the removal of Eudaemon and John, since the former was responsible for order in the city and was presumably still guarding the reprieved faction members, while opposition to the latter had drawn complainants from across the empire.[26] Tribonian, however, is different since his role in organizing Justinian's legal reforms might appear to be relevant primarily to those most closely involved in using the law, namely upper class people with education and money, especially since his reputation for accepting bribes must have resulted in many being upset by his legal decisions.[27] On the other hand, while his perceived closeness to Justinian may have been enough to make him a target, it is also important to remember that the factions had members from all levels of society and that Procopius alleges that the factions had corrupted legal processes, dictated the decisions of judges, and taken sides in law suits.[28] Although Justinian promptly dismissed these senior officials, the crowds did not disperse, so that Justinian sent Belisarius with a force of Goths from the palace to remove them. Fighting continued until the evening and the Goths killed many, in response to which the rioters set fire to the Chalke, the main entrance to the palace, which was burnt down along with the adjacent accommodation for the *scholae* and other imperial guards, the Senate building, and the Great Church of S. Sophia.

A significant development that evening was that the rioters proceeded from the palace towards the Harbour of Julian, to the house of Probus, nephew of Emperor Anastasius, where they chanted: 'Another emperor for the city', 'Probus, emperor for Romania.' Probus was not at home, just as Areobindus had not been in 512, and so the initiative for this attempt to elevate a new emperor must have come from the factions rather than senatorial opponents of Justinian, who would have known where to find their candidate. After more than three days of rioting, during which Justinian had displayed a combination of stubbornness in resisting

---

26. *Contra* Cameron, *Factions* 186, who ascribes the hostility to the two prefects as the work of senatorial agents. Greatrex, 'Nika' 61 n.5, argues that John's tax policies could not have aroused widespread opposition yet, since he had only been in post for one year, but, to my mind, even the proposal of significant changes that would make local elites pay higher taxes would have generated complaints and missions to Constantinople.
27. Proc., *Wars* 1.24.16.
28. Proc., *SH* 7.30–2, 10.19; Honoré, *Tribonian* 53–5, accepts the hostility of the factions to Tribonian without question.

demands to release the prisoners and weakness in immediately dismissing his most senior officials, conditions for change seemed favourable and so the factions took matters into their own hands. It has been suggested that this proclamation could not have been a serious attempt to elevate an alternative emperor, since Probus, as an opponent of Chalcedon, would have been unacceptable to the orthodox factions; therefore the factions were just attempting to apply more pressure on Justinian to extract further concessions.[29] This line of argument is flawed: many senators, including Anastasius' other two nephews, were known to be inside the palace with Justinian and so unavailable, whereas it might have been hoped that Probus could be found.

At some point in proceedings, probably on the 15th, Justinian had ordered the troops attached to the *MM praesentalis* that were stationed in the vicinity of the capital to enter the city to help to restore order. These entered the walls on Saturday 17th and so had presumably arrived outside the city on Friday 16th; in some cases they had marched over 30km, so that the latest the summons could have been sent is Thursday 15th. The decision to call on these troops probably came after a tense discussion inside the palace at which Justinian contemplated flight by ship, probably to Heraclea where some praesental troops were based, perhaps because the destruction of the Chalke and guards' quarters had made the palace vulnerable. After his departure, the palace was to be guarded by Mundo and his son with 3,000 unspecified troops and the *cubicularii*;[30] in this context the lack of mention of the *scholarii* and *excubitores* is striking and their loyalty may already have been in question. He was, however, persuaded that it was better to stay in the palace and fight, a key advocate being the empress Theodora, to whom Procopius attributed a rousing speech that concluded with the aphorism, 'Kingship is a good winding sheet'. Although Procopius placed this debate on the final day of the Riot, immediately before the massacre in the Hippodrome, he probably did this for dramatic effect. As the situation worsened, Justinian had two options, to abandon the city to join loyal troops and make his return or to hold out in the palace until the troops could reach him, and on the 15th he chose the latter course.[31]

---

29. Greatrex, 'Riot' 75.
30. Theophanes 184.27–30.
31. Proc., *Wars* 1.24.32–7. Greatrex, 'Riot' 78, defends the placing of the discussion on Sunday 18th on the basis that Justinian did not want to be present in the city during the anticipated massacre, but such an explanation is not credible: emperors were held responsible for events

On Friday the 16th further parts of the centre of Constantinople were burned and the destruction continued on Saturday 17th as the troops summoned by Justinian began to fight their way towards the city centre. They would have waited for daylight to enter the city, to reduce the difficulties of fighting on terrain that was much more familiar to their opponents than to them. Casualties among the rioters were significant and included women. Both sides set fire to buildings when they found themselves coming under pressure and the resulting blazes extended the destruction across further parts of the city. That afternoon Justinian dismissed those senators sheltering with him in the palace with instructions to guard their own homes. Those who were sent out included two of Emperor Anastasius' nephews, Hypatius and Pompeius. According to Procopius, they were suspected by Justinian of plotting against him,[32] but this is an obvious inference from what happened on the next day: if Justinian really had suspicions about them, he is more likely to have kept them under close watch inside the palace. The arrival of loyal troops was at last enabling Justinian to reassert his authority across the city, and as part of that process it would be helpful if every senator could ensure that his substantial residence could not be commandeered by the rioters as a defensive base.

Early on Sunday the 18th Justinian went into the Kathisma, the imperial box, in the Hippodrome carrying the Gospels; he promised that there would be no punishment for anyone, since he took full responsibility for everything that had happened. This action was similar to Anastasius' bare-headed appearance in the Hippodrome in 512, but Justinian was less successful: there was some chanting in his favour, the traditional 'May you be victorious', but others chanted 'You are foresworn, ass.' The willingness of some of the crowd to chant for Justinian indicates that there were already cracks in the opposition to the emperor, or more precisely that members of the Blue faction were already reverting, perhaps with financial inducements, to their normal allegiance. Other rioters now came upon Hypatius and Pompeius, acclaimed the former as emperor, and found for him elements of imperial regalia that were stored in the palace of Placillianae, including a gold torque that had to substitute for a

---

whether or not they were present, for example Theodosius I for the massacre at Thessalonica in 390, so that absence would not absolve Justinian. Theophanes (derived from Malalas) correctly placed imperial thoughts of flight earlier in the rioting.
32. Proc., *Wars* 1.24.19–21.

crown, after which they led him to the Hippodrome and installed him in the Kathisma.

There is no way of knowing what Hypatius' intentions were and opinions vary: he may have seen the chaos of five days of rioting, Justinian's willingness to abandon senior officials, and the factions' interest in proclaiming an alternative emperor as the opportunity to claim the throne that he had been denied at his uncle's death in 518, or he may have been the reluctant victim of the factions' current hostility to Justinian, or he was even acting as an *agent provocateur*. Marcellinus Comes alleged that the whole riot was the product of a senatorial plot to proclaim Hypatius and Pompeius, but this account, written in the immediate aftermath of the riot, has rightly been dismissed as the first official version of events.[33] Procopius' narrative suggests that Hypatius' senatorial associates wanted him to take the throne, since he records a discussion about whether they should develop their coup from the Placillianae palace or move to the Hippodrome.[34] Procopius does refer to the belief that Hypatius was really on the emperor's side and was playing a double game, which is supported by the *Chronicon Paschale*. This records that from the Kathisma he dispatched the *candidatus* Ephrem to inform Justinian that he had managed to assemble all his enemies in the Hippodrome for the emperor to dispose of as he wished. This message was never delivered, since Ephrem was told that the emperor had left the palace, after which Hypatius continued with greater confidence. Among Hypatius' supporters were 250 young Greens wearing body armour, which suggests a degree of forward planning by some of those involved in the proclamation.

Justinian, with an entourage that included Constantiolus, Mundo, Basilides, and Belisarius, attempted to reach the Kathisma via the passage leading directly from the palace, but found that the bronze doors were locked; their guards refused to open them since they preferred to await the outcome of events, a worrying sign of divided loyalties. Meanwhile the *cubicularius* Narses had taken the initiative by distributing money among the Blues, so that they began to chant in favour of Justinian and Theodora, thereby causing chaos in the Hippodrome since the Greens turned to stoning their erstwhile allies. This permitted Narses, Mundo,

33. Bury, 'Nika Riot' 92–3; the fact that the confiscated property of executed senators was soon restored to their families suggests that the need for such a diversionary explanation quickly faded.
34. Proc., *Wars* 1.24.22–31.

and Belisarius to enter the Hippodrome with the troops at their disposal, including some of the *excubitores* and *scholarii* who had been won back to their proper allegiance. They began to kill all those found inside, both inhabitants of Constantinople and visitors, while Justinian's cousins, Boraides and Justus, went to the Kathisma to apprehend Hypatius.

The lowest figure for the final death toll is 30,000 while the highest is 80,000; the difference may be explained by whether the tally covers the whole week of rioting or just the final massacre, but even the lowest figure indicates a very high loss of life in a city with a population of 400–500,000. On Monday the 19th Hypatius and Pompeius were executed, despite pleading innocence on the grounds that they had been helping Justinian identify his real enemies; according to Pseudo-Zachariah, Justinian wanted to spare them, but Theodora insisted they be killed.[35] The corpses were dumped in the sea and their property confiscated, while a number of other senators, perhaps eighteen in total, were also punished with confiscation and in some cases exile. The emperor sent messages throughout the empire to announce his victory over the rebels, just as if it had been over external enemies.

Interpretations of these violent events have varied. Was there a genuine senatorial plot to overthrow Justinian that took advantage of a sustained display of public hostility to launch a coup, or was the devious Justinian orchestrating events in such a way that he had an excuse to eliminate his opponents and seize their property, or was this simply a sequence of fierce rioting that acquired its own dynamics and gradually evolved into something very different from its starting point? It is difficult to sustain an argument that senators – or more particularly the nephews of Anastasius – had been plotting to overthrow Justinian in the early days of the riot, since otherwise they might have ensured that Probus was at home to receive his acclamation as emperor, or directed the factions to a more enthusiastic candidate. That said, when Hypatius was presented with the opportunity to seize the throne, he did not demur but acted as a potential emperor and had an armed guard to support his claim. The message that he sent to Justinian about assembling his enemies in the Hippodrome does not prove that Justinian had masterminded the denouement to destroy his enemies:[36] there were easier ways to achieve this than by facilitating

---

35. Ps.–Zach., *HE* 9.14b.
36. The basis for Greatrex's argument at 'Riot' 76ff.

the proclamation as emperor of a potential rival, since that could easily have backfired. The most plausible analysis is that major riots have their own dynamic and can shift from one objective to another as their internal momentum takes over. What began as an unusual display of solidarity between the rival Blues and Greens, created by the specific circumstances of the two prisoners who had survived their executions, morphed into a wider protest against some of Justinian's most senior officials, whose actions had already been provoking complaints, before finally the inability of the imperial authorities to restore order in the capital suggested to others that there might be an opportunity to change ruler.

A key factor in this unrest was Justinian's inability to control the violence through normal mechanisms. Part of the problem was that he had to deal with the combined factions, whereas emperors could usually, though not always, rely on the support of one to oppose the other.[37] Popular superstition may also have played a part, since the escape from execution of the two prisoners – especially if this happened twice or was reported to have happened twice – would have suggested that they had received divine pardon.

It appears that Justinian could not rely entirely on the loyalty of all the palace guards. During the early days of the riot, it is not specified what troops were deployed from the palace to restore order, and the first specific indication is that Belisarius was accompanied by a force of Goths when he unsuccessfully tried to impose calm after the dismissal of Justinian's ministers. When Justinian contemplated flight, the normal imperial guards, the *scholarii* and *excubitores*, are not mentioned as remaining to defend the palace. On Sunday the 18th the guards behind the Kathisma declined to allow Justinian into the royal box, Hypatius had at least one of the forty *candidati* in his entourage, and there had been defections among both the *excubitores* and the *scholarii* since Justinian is said to have managed to win back the loyalty of some of them before the final massacre. Since the troops within the city could not suppress the unrest, Justinian had to call on the units under the *MM praesentalis* that were stationed in Europe, many on the road leading from the Golden Gate to Heraclea and beyond the Long Walls, but it inevitably took some time for these to

---

37. United action by Blues and Greens in opposition to an emperor was not unknown, but when it occurred the situation was bound to be serious.

arrive, and then it could not have been easy for them to enter a city that was substantially in the hands of rioters familiar with local conditions.

Rioting in 550s and 560s

It is not surprising that the Nika Riot was followed by several years of quiet in the capital. Quite apart from the massive death toll, the destruction of much of the city centre entailed a sustained campaign of building work that would have provided employment for the urban population. The fact that the detailed version of Malalas terminates in 533, with only very brief information for the next twenty-five years or so, does not explain the lack of reports. Although his coverage of the first six years of Justinian's reign is exceptionally detailed, it is unlikely that even his sparse record of subsequent years would have overlooked major public disorders. From 547 the chronicle tradition reports a dozen riots that continued through until Justinian's final years and it is likely that the Nika Riot ushered in fifteen years of relative quiet. In these later years the majority of riots had a close connection with the Hippodrome and, where we have information, imperial guards were involved in suppressing the violence.[38]

On the other hand, other factors did trigger unrest, a debasement of the coinage in March 553 that provoked outrage among the poor and a bread shortage in May 556; the latter protest did occur in the Hippodrome and certainly involved the factions, since Justinian subsequently punished some prominent Blues because they had dared to insult him in the presence of a Persian ambassador.[39] Justinian's final years witnessed considerable unrest, with the Greens in particular being singled out as responsible for murders and other violent crimes, for which harsh punishments were imposed by Julian, the city prefect. He had been appointed to succeed Zemarchus in 565 after fighting at the Strategion between the Greens and *excubitores* and soldiers had left several dead on both sides, clearly in the expectation that he would prove more effective in stopping the trouble.[40] It is possible that Justinian's advancing years, awareness of plots against him, financial pressures, or just general uncertainties about who was now in charge inside the palace contributed to destabilizing matters in the city.

---

38. E.g. Malalas 18.99 *excubitores*; 18.135 *comes excubitorum*.
39. Malalas 18.117, 121.
40. Malalas 18.151.

Justinian's record in managing popular violence is mixed, but then so too was that of Anastasius, whereas Justin appears to have turned a blind eye to what was happening, with the brief exception of the appointment of Theodotus as city prefect in 523. The fact that Justinian had been involved in condoning the considerable factional violence of Justin's reign placed him at a disadvantage, when as emperor he tried to distance himself from the tactics that had displaced all potential rivals. The Blues were accustomed to imperial indulgence and Justinian's attempt to clamp down equally on both factions at the start of his reign would have caused unease, even if Theodora intervened to protect the Blues on occasions. The equal treatment of both factions at the start of the Nika Riot lost Justinian the support of the Blues for a few very difficult days. Thereafter it appears that his preference for the Blues was constant and they normally enjoyed better treatment. In 540 when Khusro held races at Apamea, he favoured the Greens and intervened to prevent the Blue chariot from winning since he knew that the Blues were identified with Justinian, while in 556 leading Blues were singled out for punishment after becoming involved in the chants about bread precisely because they were expected, unlike the Greens, to support the emperor and see that he was not embarrassed in front of foreign dignitaries.

Three years after Justinian's death, his successor Justin II reacted to rioting in the Hippodrome by sending messages to both factions, reminding the Blues that Justinian was dead but telling the Greens that he was still living with them.[41] Justinian, however, may have found a way to prevent the Greens from becoming completely divorced from his regime, even though they routinely received severe punishment,[42] since John the Cappadocian is recorded as a patron of the Greens.[43] Justinian's signal failure was the Nika Riot, when his understandable attempt to steer a mid-course between harsh suppression and capitulation failed because it did not send clear messages to the rioters. Since condoning crime was something that the emperor, who was in the midst of his project to overhaul Roman law, could

---

41. Theophanes 243.4–9.
42. Proc., *SH* 11.36.
43. John Lydus, *de mag.* 3.62. This presumably began after his discomfiture during the Nika Riot and was designed to ensure that he was not exposed to such collective hatred again, but it also benefitted Justinian by demonstrating that the Greens had the support of such a powerful individual.

not contemplate, the commitment of troops at the start of the unrest might have avoided the carnage of the final day.

The Nika Riot was the most spectacular internal threat to Justinian's rule, but not the only one. There were two serious conspiracies during the reign and on the first occasion at least Justinian displayed a surprising degree of leniency in the face of treason, but this mercy might be compared with his attempts to avoid bloodshed at the start of the Nika Riot: magnanimity and mercy were desirable imperial qualities. The first conspiracy, in the latter part of 548, was triggered by the resentment of two Persarmenians, members of the royal Arsacid house, and is only reported by Procopius.[44] The instigator, Arsaces, was angry with Justinian because the emperor had had him scourged briefly and then paraded through the capital on a camel after he had been caught in treasonable correspondence with Khusro. His relative Artabanes had switched loyalties from Persia to Rome in the early 540s and, as a member of a royal family, had planned to marry Justinian's niece, Praeiecta, but was thwarted in this by Theodora, who insisted that he stay with the Armenian wife to whom he was already married. By the time Theodora died on 28 June 548, Praeiecta had married one of Anastasius' relatives, and Arsaces stoked Artabanes' resentment over this by recalling the death of his father, John, during negotiations with Buzes about rebel Armenians in 539.

He also held out the prospect of support from Germanus, who had recently been at odds with Justinian over the estate of his brother Boraïdes, since Justinian had overturned Boraïdes' will in favour of Germanus and his sons to give more of the property to the daughter. Arsaces enrolled a third Persarmenian, Chanaranges, but when he revealed matters to Germanus' elder son, Justin, in spite of trying to arouse his jealousy at the prospect of the imminent return of Belisarius, whose fame would eclipse that of their family, the plot began to unravel. Justin reported the plans to his father, who in turn told the *comes excubitorum*, Marcellus. Marcellus proceeded cautiously, even after receiving confirmation of the plot from the reputable Leontius, and as a precaution Germanus also revealed matters to Buzes and Constantianus, who, like Germanus, were former generals. When eventually Marcellus informed Justinian, he ordered the conspirators to be tortured to confirm the truth but was also angry with Germanus for not telling him sooner. Germanus did manage

---

44. Proc., *Wars* 7.32.

to clear his name by clarifying how he had proceeded and also thanks to the honesty of Marcellus in accepting the blame for all delays. Within two years Artabanes had been appointed *MM per Thracias* despite his plotting, while Germanus was married to the Ostrogothic princess, Matasuentha, and put in supreme command of the war against Totila.

The central figures in the second conspiracy in November 562, were much less exalted, the leaders being Ablabius the former *melistes*, namely a musician associated with one of the factions, the banker Marcellus, and Sergius, a relative of Aetherius, the *curator* of part of the imperial estates (the *domus* of Antiochus).[45] Aetherius had been accused two years earlier of plotting against the emperor but then acquitted, and in 566 would be executed for plotting to poison Justin II. Ablabius had shared the details with the *comes foederatorum* Eusebius, with the result that he was arrested when entering the palace armed with a sword, while Marcellus, who was caught with a dagger, killed himself. Sergius sought refuge in the church to the Virgin at Blachernae, but the accusation of treason meant that he was driven out, to be interrogated by the city prefect, Procopius. Sergius implicated two financiers, one of them, Isaac, attached to the household of Belisarius, as well as Belisarius' *suboptio* or deputy quartermaster, Paul, who implicated his master under interrogation.

The elderly Belisarius was required to dismiss all his followers and remained under a cloud until being restored to favour in July 563. It is probably correct to connect this conspiracy with the financial pressures that are evident at the end of Justinian's reign: money had to be found to pay seven annual instalments of peace payments to Persia in a lump sum, the rebuilding of S. Sophia and other buildings damaged in the earthquakes of 557 and 558 will have been very costly, and much of the Balkans had been ravaged in 559. When Justin II ascended the throne he moved fast to repay his predecessor's debts, celebrating this with a bonfire of the relevant documents in the Hippodrome,[46] and also remitted taxes in spite of the acknowledged pressures on the treasury.[47] The conspirators must have had an alternative candidate for the throne in mind; although Belisarius fell under suspicion, both his age and his long record of loyalty to

---

45. Malalas 18.141.
46. Corippus, *In laudem Iustini* 2.360–404; probably the same event credited by Theophanes, 242.22–7, to the Augusta Sophia in 567/8.
47. Justinian, *Novel* 148.

Justinian make him an implausible proposition, and it is more likely to have been Justin, son of Germanus, or his cousin the future emperor Justin II.

Justinian's management of internal affairs has to be judged a success overall. Under his uncle's reign, his campaign to secure the succession for himself produced the desired result and the one challenge, from the prefect Theodotus, was quickly snuffed out in such a way that others were unlikely to attempt to copy his behaviour. Once installed as emperor, he attempted to be more even-handed in his treatment of the factions, on the model of Anastasius, perhaps mitigating the impact of the sudden change on the Blues by exploiting Theodora's attachment to them. The Nika Riot was his worst failure, and a very large one at that, on a par with the rioting of 512 that came close to costing Anastasius his throne, but he did eventually sanction the decisive action that quelled the unrest. The next three decades of his reign were no more troubled than those of most emperors, and he certainly never had to face the serious challenges that Zeno had from Illus and other Isaurians or Anastasius did during the three revolts of Vitalian. This internal stability was important for Justinian's ability to fight external enemies, since the distractions and costs of civil strife had always created major problems for the empire.

Conclusion

Justinian's grand ambitions, the arrogance of some of the claims in his legislation and the extravagance of the eulogies of his achievements in panegyrics such as Procopius' *Buildings* make it tempting to want to cut him down to size by pointing to his various failures and the transience of many of his achievements. Furthermore, it can be argued that he was responsible for the empire's numerous problems in the half century after his death. Here the case for the prosecution is that Justinian's unreasonable attempt to resurrect the western empire overstretched imperial resources, so that his successors had to confront an increased set of challenges without having the money or the troops to do so successfully, while his theological meddling created and solidified fault lines in the eastern provinces that made it easier for invaders to succeed in the seventh century.

For his legacy to be assessed, a balance needs to be struck between the positives and negatives. On the plus side of the ledger the legal reforms clarified and ordered the massive body of Roman Law, presenting its legacy in a format that could easily be exploited as the basis for much European Law. In terms of architecture and literature, his reign left permanent memorials in the form of S. Sophia, the historical works of Procopius of Caesarea, or the religious hymns of Romanus the Melodist. One undoubted failure was in the religious field, where the Church was no more unified at the end of this reign than at its start. Granted that this was the arena in which Justinian took the keenest personal interest and to which his own intellectual formation made a significant contribution, this is a heavy indictment.

Somewhat on the plus side might be placed the sheer survival of his reign for almost four decades and the ability of his nephew to succeed to the throne. Granted that at the start of the sixth century Justinian and his family were still outsiders, parvenus from the backward central Balkans, this is an achievement. In contrast to the patrician nephews of Emperor Anastasius and the imperial pedigree that Anicia Juliana bestowed on her husband Areobindus, the competent military officer Justin was a man of little personal significance, someone who could be entrusted with important tasks precisely because his background ensured that he could never be a real threat to those ambitious for imperial office. Justinian's contribution to the success of the family was crucial, since his patronage of the Blue circus faction provided him with loyal supporters in the capital and in all the major cities of the empire, people who could be relied upon to watch out for his interests since their own positions were intricately bound up with those of the emperor. If the Nika Riot came close to destroying this stability, Justinian weathered that storm and learned the necessary lessons.

On the military front the evidence is far from clear-cut. As far as the East is concerned, he inherited a state of high tension close to full-blown war, but he brought the ensuing conflict to a conclusion in 532 at a significant but not outrageous cost. When his hopes of a permanent agreement with Persia were dashed by the catastrophic invasion of 540, he managed to stabilize the frontier in Upper Mesopotamia relatively quickly and after 544 confine further hostilities to Lazica, until such time as Khusro accepted that continued fighting would produce fewer benefits than a peace agreement. Again there was a cost in 561/2, but this was lower than what had been demanded from Anastasius by Kavadh as the Roman contribution to defending the Caucasus passes, and the staggering of payments meant that there was a greater incentive for the Persians to maintain the agreement than after 532.

In comparison with the 520s, the empire in the 560s had strengthened its grip on the north-eastern sector of the frontier, where the Laz, along with their dependencies in the Caucasus, and the Tzani were under tighter control, and the frontier in Armenia was protected more strongly with additional fortifications. This secured for the empire areas that were important in terms of military recruitment. Further south in Upper Mesopotamia and Syria it is likely that after two decades of peace the cities and countryside had substantially recovered from Khusro's invasions, although Antioch after two destructive earthquakes as well as the 540 sack will not have fully returned to its fifth-century prosperity in spite of considerable imperial investment. Palestine had suffered from the two Samaritan revolts, but not from foreign incursions, and continued to flourish, as did Egypt. The elevation of the Jafnid Harith as supreme phylarch had brought reasonable stability to the desert frontiers.

In the Balkans, too, Justinian inherited a difficult situation: the provinces were slowly recovering from the extensive destruction of Attila, the depredations of the war-bands that emerged from the fragmentation of his confederation, and the disruption of Vitalian's revolts. Justinian certainly continued Anastasius' policy of pushing Roman influence upstream along the Danube, and his construction of fortifications stabilized the population in wider swathes of the provinces. Along the Adriatic the defeat of the Ostrogoths allowed the Romans to recover Dalmatia, but on the middle Danube the Gepids took over the strategic site of Sirmium from the Goths, enabling them to pose a significant threat to the empire by regulating movement across the Danube and its tributaries. To contain the Gepids, Justinian first settled allied Heruls near Singidunum and then supported the Lombards as a counterbalance. Overall his policy of setting tribal groups against each other was reasonably successful, in spite of the ability of Zabergan's Kutrigurs to penetrate deep into Roman territory after crossing the frozen Danube in 559.

The key issue throughout his reign was the extent to which units of the Balkan armies had been dispatched for service elsewhere in the empire. At his death the next critical challenge was only just emerging, as the Avars were embarking on the construction of a super-federation that would rival that of Attila. Whether Justinian could really have managed their threat, as the historian Menander suggested, is impossible to prove, but most probably he would have avoided the unnecessary insults that Justin II conveyed when he received the Avar ambassadors at the start of his reign; also he might not have relied so trustingly on the oaths that convinced Tiberius not to attend to the Danube defences in the late 570s.

The re-conquest of Vandal Africa was very much Justinian's project, undertaken at his insistence in the face of opposition from senior officials. The strategy of exploiting, and possibly even helping to create, diversions in Libya and Sardinia certainly made Belisarius' task much easier by removing some of the best Vandal troops from Carthage at the crucial time. Procopius does, however, make clear that luck played a significant part in Belisarius' rapid success. Following Gelimer's surrender, Justinian's contribution was mixed. Good governors such as Solomon, Germanus, and John Troglita were appointed, but so too was the ineffectual Areobindus. The rapid imposition of Nicene orthodoxy delivered one of the reasons for the expedition, but also caused resentment among Roman troops, and the failure to ensure that soldiers were paid on time contributed to the mutiny that destabilized the provinces and encouraged Berbers to raid. The demands of the war in Italy meant that it was not possible to allocate troops to restore order quickly or completely in the 530s, and then the resurgence of war with Persia continued the problem. It was not until the first of the five-year truces in the East that John Troglita could be provided with sufficient resources to bring peace, by which time the provincial population will have suffered severely from years of ravaging, even if the overall losses were nothing like the '500 myriads' that Procopius claimed in his *Secret History*.[1] Following the re-conquest it must have taken time for the re-imposition of Roman taxation to generate the revenues required to support the local garrison, hence probably the problems with military pay in the 530s, but in the last fifteen years of Justinian's reign the provinces had a good chance of being profitable for the empire and even the disruption caused by the Three Chapters dispute eventually died down.

Italy was a different matter. Justinian's diplomacy contributed to the instability of the Amal dynasty after Theoderic's death, thereby creating the opportunity for a move into Italy with the possibility of annexing much of the peninsula under an agreement with one of its rulers. Once it became clear that serious fighting would be required, he reinforced Belisarius' small initial expeditionary force with sufficient troops to create the conditions for an end to hostilities. So far, so good. It is possible that a relatively quick victory, with damage limited to a few key cities such as Naples and Rome and to forts along the Via Flaminia that led north from Rome to Ravenna, might have enabled the East to draw some tangible benefit from the recovery of Italy, but that was not to be. By the end of 539 Milan in Liguria and several sites in Picenum had suffered considerably, and there was worse to come when Totila sparked the Gothic revival. Furthermore, success in Italy could only be achieved by the redeployment of significant numbers of troops from the East and Balkans, denuding the defences of those areas so that their devastation in the 540s was an indirect consequence of the Italian adventure.

Whether the offer to partition Italy along the line of the Po, which Justinian negotiated with Witigis in 540 but which Belisarius insubordinately and deviously evaded in the hope of securing the whole peninsula, could have been sustained is unknowable. On the basis of the failure of other power-sharing deals in antiquity, I doubt it would have done more than postpone a further reckoning when either distractions

---

1. Proc., SH 18.8; this claim is made in the context of Procopius' attack on Justinian's destruction of humanity, which allegedly inflicted a 'myriad myriad of myriads' casualties, namely 1,000,000,000,000 deaths (*SH* 18.4), somewhat greater than the present-day population of the world, let alone that in the sixth century.

in the East offered the Goths the chance to recover lost possessions or turmoil within the Gothic kingdom enticed the Romans to finish the job they had started. After the Lombard invasion, the peninsula was divided between the empire and a tribal kingdom, admittedly one that held the central duchies of Spoleto and Beneventum in addition to the northern territories that Witigis would have retained. That situation left successive popes complaining about threats to Rome, which the East could do little to resolve in the later sixth century. The deal with Witigis would have saved parts of Italy from repeated ravaging, but Justinian has to take responsibility for the decisions of his representative on the ground. His attempts to balance Belisarius' power by the dispatch of the *cubicularius* Narses had caused more harm than good and he had to accept that his local commander would make his own decisions in the light of current circumstances. Justinian did not punish Belisarius for his disregard for imperial orders, and, although he did not grant Belisarius a triumph, he was pleased with the receipt of the Gothic treasure.

The combination of the apparent completion of the conquest and the return of war on the eastern front meant that Justinian redeployed from the West the troops that might just have quashed the Gothic revival in its early stages. As a result Italy had to endure a further fourteen years of fighting, sieges, hungry armies moving across the landscape, and Frankish invasions, during which the whole peninsula was devastated and even Sicily was ravaged once. Towns and cities were wrecked, famine gripped the countryside as a result of ravaging and the displacement of farming communities, the population plummeted, as apart from a lucky few who could relocate to the East, the inhabitants perished from hunger, were killed, or led off into captivity. Italy in 555 was a very pale shadow of its prosperous state only twenty years before, Rome had been reduced from a sizable city to a modest town in terms of population, and its senatorial aristocracy had been killed or left impoverished to struggle until it disappeared in the early seventh century.[2] There was now no local counter-balance to the papacy, whose economic and political power dominated affairs and became the main object of competition. Whatever improvements might have occurred in Justinian's final decade as Narses restored stability

---

2. O'Donnell, *Ruin*, views the elimination of Theoderic's golden age through the lens of 21st-century western wars on Afghanistan and Iraq, with Justinian as an agent of destruction no more capable of rebuilding Italy than George W. Bush could Iraq.

could not have made much progress before the arrival of the Lombards in 568 ensured that any recovery in northern and central Italy was halted.[3]

The acquisition of Africa and Italy represented a considerable expansion of the empire in terms of territory, but with regard to resources there could have been only a limited increase. North Africa had always been one of the richest parts of the empire, and there is every reason to believe that a reasonable element of this prosperity was restored well before the end of Justinian's reign. Italy, by contrast, had for centuries benefited from flows of resources from the provinces to support the imperial court, lavish senatorial lifestyles, and the megalopolis of Rome. Much of this expenditure will have ceased during the reconquest, but at the same time the devastated peninsula lacked the resources to underpin its defence and administration. Only in the south and on Sicily did circumstances permit a return to prosperity, but even the wealth of Sicily would scarcely have offset the on-going costs of holding territories further north. The main benefit of the westward expansion was that this had enabled Justinian to exercise authority over the western churches and most importantly the Pope. If Constantinople had not been in control of Rome and Carthage, Justinian's Theopaschite and Three Chapters initiatives would have been received no more favourably than Zeno's Henoticon had been.[4] As it was, Justinian could apply pressure to bring reluctant communities into line with his latest thinking. The problem was that such adjustments in the West did not lead to reconciliation in the East between Miaphysites and Chalcedonians. If the Roman positions in the Balkans and along the frontier with Persia were marginally better at the end of Justinian's reign than at the start, there was limited advantage overall and a massive human cost to show for almost four decades of conflict.

Apart from the destruction of warfare in all these arenas, there is also the factor of the plague to be considered when assessing the resilience of the empire. Its initial impact was a hammer blow whose apocalyptic effects, especially in Constantinople, were graphically described by the contemporary witnesses, Procopius and John of Ephesus. By contrast, when Evagrius came to compose his chapter on the plague in the early 590s, his account is more measured.[5] He had caught and survived the plague

---

3. Cf. Cameron, *Procopius* 193–4.
4. As can be seen from the continued opposition in the 590s of Milan and Aquileia, now under Lombard control, to the condemnation of the Three Chapters.
5. Evagrius 4.29.

in 542, when aged about six, and then had lost relatives and dependants in its subsequent visitations, including a daughter and grandson only two years previously, but he recognized that the impact of the plague was patchy, with some places escaping relatively lightly whereas others were hit hard. It is difficult to identify how it affected military campaigns, since, apart from the report that Khusro's army near Lake Urmiah was being affected in 543, with the result that he moved to the Tigris valley where the plague had not yet taken full hold,[6] we do not have information on how the movements and actions of armies in the East or in Italy were determined by fear of its approach or impact. Nor is there evidence for how its mortality might have reduced the capacities of both the empire and its enemies to prosecute war: Khusro clearly assembled a very large army, accompanied by even more non-combatants, to mount the siege of Edessa in 544. It is best to assume that there was considerable short-term disruption and massive fear, as in any pandemic, but that the empire was sufficiently resilient to rebound from the first few occurrences of the plague.

Italy is central to the argument that the Justinianic expansion over-stretched imperial resources, with the plague as a factor that contributed to constraining these, and so left his successors with impossible challenges. Italy constituted a new commitment that for its protection required troops from outside who had to be funded by the transfer of tax resources. To my mind, this need not have prevented Justin II from managing his affairs successfully, but for the fact that his desire to do things differently from his predecessor – an urge that continues to infect modern leaders – led him to make poor choices. He believed that Justinian's policy of paying foreigners to keep the peace was demeaning for the might of Rome. He would have endorsed 'Make Rome Great Again' as a slogan, and so at the first possible opportunity he snubbed an embassy from the Avars that had come to the capital for their normal gifts. This did not immediately cause problems, since the Avars retired to extend their authority around the Black Sea and then over the middle Danube and west towards the Frankish kingdoms, but a decade later they had become a force to rival that of Attila and had not forgotten the earlier snub.

The same arrogance convinced Justin in 572 to refuse to make the payment agreed under the terms of Justinian's Fifty-Year Peace with

---

6. Proc., *Wars* 2.24.8, 12.

Persia,[7] especially since he believed that his negotiations with the central Asian Turks would lead to a two-pronged attack on Persia and that a revolt in Persarmenia would cause further problems for Khusro. Just as Julian the Apostate had invaded Persia in 363 to demonstrate his superiority in all respects to his predecessor Constantius, who had conducted dogged defensive campaigns on his eastern frontier, so Justin expected to overshadow Justinian by recovering the city of Nisibis that the Romans had been forced to surrender two centuries before. In the event his confidence was misplaced and the war he provoked soon produced the loss of Dara in 573, a disaster that turned Justin insane. The conflict with Persia rumbled on until 591, meaning that there were never enough troops available to defend the Balkans or limit the Lombards' move into central Italy. Although the situation in the Balkans was being re-established by Maurice in the 590s, the sustained strenuous efforts required proved too much for his troops to endure. The resultant mutiny that placed Phocas on the throne ushered in a decade of internal strife and provided Khusro II with an excuse to attack. Although the Romans eventually won this 'last great war of antiquity' after twenty-five years,[8] they were left in a much weaker position to confront the Arab invasions of the 630s.

An alternative thesis does not just allocate Justinian some responsibility for the troubles of his successors but asserts that his western conquests were decisive in the creation of the new threats that would in due course undermine his successes.[9] According to this analysis, Justinian's need for increasing numbers of non-Roman soldiers to prosecute his western wars created a taste for salaries and especially booty that could not be sustained in the generation after his death when the main enemies were the less wealthy tribes beyond the Danube. As a result the Lombards chose to invade Italy on their own account in 568 after winning their conflict with their neighbouring Gepids. Undoubtedly the Lombards were attracted to Italy by the fact that they had seen the territory during their service in Roman armies, most recently that of Narses in 552 when they had been dismissed for their unruly behaviour. But there was a much more pressing reason for their move west, namely the shadow cast by the Avars whose assistance

---

7. Justinian had made the first payment covering the seven years to 569, and Justin must have accepted the need to send the money for the next three years as agreed, but the transition to annual payments was a different matter.
8. See Howard-Johnston, 'Persian Campaigns'.
9. Pohl, 'Justinian' 272–3.

had been decisive in securing victory over the Gepids. By 567 the Avars had demonstrated their ambition and might in subduing the powerful Hunnic groups around the Black Sea, such as the Kutrigurs and Utigurs, and it would have been obvious to the Lombards that the new presence of Avars on the Danube would not be comfortable for those located closest to them. The Lombards were pushed west primarily by the threat posed by the Avars, not because Justinian had accustomed them to Roman wealth; their rapid success in taking over northern Italy was undoubtedly helped by Justin's decision to remove Narses from his position in Italy. If Justinian was not responsible for the Lombard encroachment, he certainly can take none of the blame for the rise of the Avars. He had treated them with cautious respect and it was Justin whose disregard left them unchallenged to become a ferocious power. In truth, it was Justinian's towering reputation that Justin felt obliged to match, which was more damaging to the empire in the late sixth century than the extension of commitments generated by western conquests or their impact on participants.

Overall, if the balance sheet for Justinian's various campaigns is, at best, scarcely positive, it is still unreasonable to blame him for the empire's problems over the next fifty years.[10] Resources were found in 550–2 for the pacification of Italy and, even if Justinian was borrowing heavily in the later years, Justin had the money to redeem the pledges at the start of his reign and to bequeath some money in the treasury to be spent by his generous successor, Tiberius (578–82). The problems were caused by Justin's temperament, for which Justinian cannot be held responsible: in spite of Berber incursions into the African provinces in 569–71 and the contemporary Lombard advance into Italy, Justin chose to provoke Khusro in 572 by withholding the payment agreed under the terms of the peace treaty. He thereby courted the risk of campaigns in three separate regions at a time when the expansion of Avar power beyond the Danube had already frightened the Lombards. It is unknowable whether the empire could have assimilated the Lombards and resisted the Avars, if it had not had to channel military resources to the eastern frontier, but the ability of Maurice to contain the Avar threat in the 590s suggests it might have been possible.

---

10. Cf Jones, *LRE* 300–2 for a broadly similar conclusion.

It is worth considering the extent to which Justinian deserves credit or blame for the military results achieved by the generals whom he appointed. He was fortunate in having available a significant number of capable commanders. Pride of place inevitably goes to Belisarius, but in no small part that is because of the way in which Procopius represents his actions and narrates those of others from his standpoint, so it is worth considering quite how successful he was. A negative assessment would point to his failure at Minduos in 529, give most credit for the victory at Dara to the *magister officiorum* Hermogenes as the senior commander, and highlight the problems in controlling his troops before Callinicum and his questionable behaviour during the battle that led to his dismissal from office; his second command in the East stabilized the frontier, but with only limited benefits. In the West, victory at Ad Decimum was the fortunate result of Gelimer's distraction and luck played a part in his overall success. In Italy he was able to outmanoeuvre Witigis, who proved to be a poor leader, but could not cope with Totila's tactics. Belisarius had two signal advantages: first, unswerving loyalty to Justinian from his early service as a bodyguard through the crisis of the Nika Riot and the triumphs in Carthage and Ravenna that might have turned the head of a different man, to his death and, second, a favourable treatment in the historical sources.

It is certainly arguable that the eunuch Narses was a superior commander, especially in his deployment of infantry as well as mastery of cavalry tactics, and others such as Sittas, Mundo, and Chilbuldius all proved effective, although in each case these commanders met their deaths through energetic and perhaps incautious behaviour. Loyalty was a key factor for Justinian when making senior appointments and that explains his continued use of leaders such as Bessas, Martin, and John the nephew of Vitalian, whose records were mixed. It also explains the problems that some leaders, Belisarius in particular, had in securing the co-operation of other commanders, some of whom were subordinates, since Justinian was reluctant to give absolute authority unequivocally to any single leader. In 538 John disobeyed Belisarius' instruction to remove his horsemen from Rimini, in 539 John and Justin declined to obey his order to relieve Mundila at Milan, thereby contributing to the subsequent massacre, and in 546 Bessas in Rome refused to collaborate with Belisarius at Portus to lift the Gothic siege. Success at Carthage in 534 and Ravenna in 540 led on each occasion to reports going back to Constantinople about Belisarius' dangerous ambitions.

Justinian may not have had experience of leading troops in the field but that did not stop him from intervening in campaigns to give instructions about what should be done. In general he favoured action: in 537 he ordered Martin and Valerian to proceed immediately to Rome rather than wait on the Adriatic, in 539 he acted to resolve the stand-off between Belisarius and Narses by recalling the latter from Italy, in 542 he reproached his commanders in Italy for their inaction in the face of Totila's energy, and in 551 he instructed the garrison at Thermopylae to sail to Italy to relieve Croton. Even the emperor's orders were not always obeyed: thus in 551 John had been instructed by Justinian to remain at Salona for Narses to arrive, but he responded to the urgent request from Valerian to sail to the relief of Ancona, deciding that this crisis meant he could not wait to request fresh instructions from the capital. The speed of communications in the ancient world meant that there was no way that the centre could control every last action at the periphery: the man on the ground inevitably had a certain amount of independence, which elevated the importance of ensuring the loyalty of these individuals. The murder of Gubazes in 555 illustrates the problem. Rusticus had managed to secure Justinian's agreement to Gubazes' death if he resisted arrest, which unsurprisingly is what transpired, and Justinian could only respond after the event with a formal investigation and the execution of two of the guilty parties. Whether he would have punished them if they had not also been defeated by the Persians is unknowable.

Another aspect of Justinian's involvement in military campaigns was the allocation of resources through the praetorian prefect and *magister officiorum*. Even in peacetime the army consumed the bulk of imperial revenues and so there was always a balance to be struck when it came to action, especially if more than one campaign theatre was clamouring for attention. Procopius provides evidence for problems on all fronts, discontent among troops in Africa, Sicily, Italy, and Beroea over the failure to provide pay on time and increasingly desperate requests from commanders for more troops, for example from Belisarius in Italy in 537 or again in 544–8. It does appear that Justinian hoped that his western expeditions could succeed without the commitment of substantial numbers of troops. In the case of Africa the shadow of Basiliscus' catastrophe made this a sensible initial approach, and with regard to Italy the possibility that the peninsula might have been surrendered by its rulers may also have suggested that a limited expedition was appropriate at first. Difficulties multiplied rapidly when the preservation of the riches of the east came into competition with the protection of the African provinces from Berber raids and the suppression of the Gothic resurgence in Italy under Totila.

However, the fact that, when conditions in the East and Africa permitted, Justinian took time to allocate ample resources first to Germanus and then to Narses to crush Gothic opposition does indicate that he understood that penny-pinching would not achieve results. His problem was that the empire could only sustain the considerable costs of campaigning energetically on one frontier at a time, with the result that troops had constantly to be switched between theatres, with the Balkans usually suffering the consequences of the absence of local troops.

Justinian's ambition was to be remembered and, whatever verdict one reaches on him as an individual ruler, whether that he was the greatest of Byzantine emperors or a destructive proto-Hitler or Stalin, there is no doubt that he succeeded.[11] He dominated his century, which can be referred to as the Age or Epoch of Justinian. Just as his Great Church towered over Christian Constantinople for nine centuries, so the imperial reputation that was enshrined in the Acts of the Council of Constantinople, codified in his *Corpus Iuris Civilis*, and recorded by Procopius overshadowed his successors. The campaigns conducted by his generals have not been forgotten.

---

11. See Cameron, *Procopius* 21 for reference to such autocratic parallels.

Glossary of Terms

acheiropoietos 'not made by human hands'. A term for a number of miraculous images that appeared in the sixth century

agentes in rebus imperial officers, who reported to the *magister officiorum*, used for wide range of public business

ala unit of cavalry

annona ration allocation for Roman soldiers

Anti-Nicene. Christians who did not accept the Trinitarian formula of the Council of Nicaea, which had upheld the full equality of all three members of the Trinity

Aphthartodocete heresy. Doctrine promoted by some Miaphysites that Christ's body did not experience corruption

arithmos literally 'number', unit of infantry soldiers

ballista / ae standard Roman artillery for firing missiles

bucellarii guardsmen in the service of generals and other senior military officers, whose name derived from *bucellatum*

bucellatum double-baked bread or biscuit that formed part of soldiers' rations when on campaign

candidatus / i the emperor's 40 personal bodyguard(s)

Chalcedonians. Christians who accepted the doctrinal formulation of the Council of Chalcedon that emphasized the composite dual nature of Christ as man and God

city prefect (*praefectus Urbis*). Officer responsible for administration in Constantinople and Rome

comes count, generic term for senior officer, in most cases with civilian responsibilities

comes excubitorum commander of the elite palace guards, the *excubitores*

comes Orientis administrative head of the diocese of Oriens (The East) based at Antioch

comes rei privatae official in charge of emperor's private estates and revenues

comes sacrarum largitionum financial official in charge of customs dues, mining revenues, and minting coins

comes sacri stabuli officer with specific responsibility for imperial horses

comitatenses literally 'companions', mobile soldiers who in the fourth century accompanied emperors on campaign, but who by the sixth century formed part of provincial garrisons

curialis/es leading member(s) of provincial cities, involved in running local affairs

curopalatus official responsible for the palace at Constantinople

cursus publicus the system supporting the movement of public business along the main highways

domesticus/i personal attendant(s), including personal guard

dromon. Standard Roman warship

dux commander of military forces at provincial level

excubitores elite unit of palace guards

foederati/federates. Originally non-Roman troops serving under a formal agreement (*foedus*, 'treaty'), although by the sixth century their numbers did include some inhabitants of the empire

Homoians. Anti-Nicene Christians who held that the persons of the Trinity were similar (*homoios*) to each other, rather than the same and equal as in the Nicene formula

katalogoi literally 'registers', hence applied to soldiers recruited on the basis of such registers

limitanei troops stationed near or along frontiers (*limites*)

magister militum (*MM*) general in charge of one of the emperor's main armies (Africa, Armenia, East, Italy, Illyricum, praesental, Thrace)

magister officiorum powerful official responsible for much of the running of the court, including access to the emperor and the palace guards, as well as billeting of soldiers, arms factories, and the *cursus publicus*

medimnos the standard measure for grain, usually about 52 litres in volume

Miaphysites. Christians who rejected the compromise formulation of the Council of Chalcedon and insisted on the single nature of God the Word in Christ.

Patrician. Normally the highest rank for members of the imperial court

praepositus sacri cubiculi powerful eunuch in charge of imperial bedchamber

praetorian prefect of the Orient. The empire's chief financial official, responsible for collecting taxes and financing armies

quaestor exercitus official in charge of the *quaestura exercitus quaestor sacri palatii* the empire's senior legal officer

quaestura exercitus administrative unit created by Justinian that linked Danubian and Aegean provinces

rhetor lawyer

schola / ae unit(s) of the palace guard

scholarii members of the *scholae*, palace guards

solidus / i standard Roman gold coins struck at rate of 72 to the (Roman) pound

Theopaschite formula. Doctrinal wording intended to reconcile Chalcedonians and Miaphysites that emphasized that God the Word (Christ) suffered on the Cross

Tome of Leo. Doctrinal letter of Pope Leo I which underpinned the doctrinal formula of Chalcedon

Three Chapters. Justinian's initiative of the 540s and 550s that was intended to persuade Miaphysites to drop their hostility to the Council of Chalcedon by condemning three leading clergy whose orthodoxy had been accepted by the Council

Bibliography

Abbreviations

BAR	*British Archaeological Reports*
BMGS	*Byzantine and Modern Greek Studies*
Byz.	*Byzantion*
BZ	*Byzantinische Zeitschrift*
CAH	*Cambridge Ancient History*
DOP	*Dumbarton Oaks Papers*
GRBS	*Greek, Roman and Byzantine Studies*
PLRE	*Prosopography of the Later Roman Empire*
JHS	*Journal of Hellenic Studies*
JLA	*Journal of Late Antiquity*
JÖB	*Jahrbuch der Österreichischen Byzantinistik*
JRA	*Journal of Roman Archaeology*
JRS	*Journal of Roman Studies*
TTH	Translated Texts for Historians

Sources

The Acts of the Council of Chalcedon, trans. with introduction and notes Richard Price and Michael Gaddis (TTH 45; Liverpool, 2005).

The Acts of the Council of Constantinople of 553, with related texts on the Three Chapters Controversy, trans. with introduction and notes Richard Price (TTH 51; Liverpool 2009).

Agapius, *Kitab al-'Unvan*, part 2.2, ed. and trans. A.A. Vasiliev, *Patrologia Orientalis* 8 (1912) 399–547.

Agathias, *The Histories*, translated with an introduction and notes J.D.C. Frendo (Corpus Fontium Historiae Byzantinae 2A; Berlin, 1975).

Ammianus Marcellinus, 3 vols., trans. J.C. Rolfe (Loeb; Cambridge, MA., 1935–9).

318 The Wars of Justinian

Anonymous Valesianus, in Ammianus Loeb vol.3 (Loeb; Cambridge, MA., 1939).

Anthologia Palatina, see *Greek Anthology*.

Boethius, *Consolation of Philosophy*, in Boethius, *The Theological Tractates* trans. H.F. Stewart, E.K. Rand and S.J. Tester (Loeb; Cambridge, MA., 1973).

Cassiodorus, *Variae* trans. (selection) S.J.B. Barnish (TTH 12; Liverpool, 1992).

Chronicon Paschale, 284–628 AD, trans. Michael Whitby and Mary Whitby (TTH 7; Liverpool, 1989).

Collectio Avellana (imperatorum pontificum aliorum inde ac. A. XVII usque ad A. DLII), ed. O. Guenther (*Corpus Scriptorum Ecclesiasticorum Latinorum* 35.1–2; Prague, 1895).

Constantine VII Porphyrogenitus, *De Caerimoniis aulae Byzantinae*, ed. J.J. Reiske (Bonn, 1829).

Constantine Porphyrogenitus, *Three Treatises on Imperial Military Expeditions*, introduction, ed. trans. and comm. John F. Haldon (Corpus Fontium Historiae Byzantinae, series Vindobonensis 28; Vienna, 1990).

Corippus, *Iohannid*, trans. George W. Shea (Lewiston, 1998).

Corippus, *In Laudem Iustini Augusti Minoris Libri IV*, ed. trans. and comm. Averil Cameron (London, 1976).

Cyril of Scythopolis, *Life of Saba*, trans. R.M. Price and J. Binns, *The Lives of the Monks of Palestine* (Cistercian Studies 114; Kalamazoo, 1991).

Dialogue on Political Science, see *Three Political Voices*.

Dracontius, ed. and trans. (French) Étienne Wolff, *Dracontius* vols 3–4 (Paris, 1995–6).

Ennodius, ed. with comm. W. Hartel (Vienna, 1882).

Epistulae Austrasiacae, ed. W. Gundlach, *Monumenta Germaniae Historica*, *Epist.* III (Berlin, 1892).

Evagrius Scholasticus, trans. and comm. Michael Whitby (TTH 33; Liverpool, 2000).

Greek Anthology, Anthologia Graeca, trans. W. Paton, 5 vols. (Loeb; Cambridge, MA., 1916–18).

John of Ephesus, *Lives of the Eastern Saints*, ed. and Latin trans. E.W. Brooks (*Patrologia Orientalis* vols 17.1, 18.4, 19.2; Paris, 1923–5).

John Lydus, *De magistratibus, On the Magistracies of the Roman State* trans. Thomas F. Carney, *Bureaucracy in Traditional Society: Romano-Byzantine Bureaucracies Viewed from Within* (Lawrence, 1971).

———, *De Mensibus*, ed. R. Wünsch (Leipzig, 1898).

John of Nikiu, *The Chronicle of John, Bishop of Nikiou*, trans. R.H. Charles (London, 1916).

Jordanes, *Getica*, trans. Peterr Van Nuffelen and Lieve Van Hoof, *Jordanes, Romana and Getica* (TTH 75; Liverpool, 2020).

Julian, *Letters*, trans. W.C. Wright (Loeb; Cambridge, MA., 1923).

Justinian, *The Codex of Justinian, a new annotated translation, with parallel Latin and Greek text*, ed. Bruce W. Freier, (Cambridge, 2016).

Justinian, *Novels*, ed. R. Schöll and G. Kroll (Berlin, 1928).

Letter of Tansar, trans. Mary Boyce (Rome, 1968).

Liberatus, *Breviarium causae Nestorianorum et Eutychianorum*, ed. J.-P. Migne, (*Patrologia Latina*; Paris, 1866).

Liber Pontificalis = The Book of the Pontiffs (Liber Pontificalis). The ancient biographies of the first ninety Roman bishops to AD 715, rev. ed. and trans. Raymond Davis (TTH 6; Liverpool, 2000).

Life of Theodore of Sykeon, trans. Dawes & Baynes, *Three Byzantine Saints*.

Luxorius, trans. in Morris Rosenblum, *Luxorius: a Latin Poet among the Vandals* (New York, 1961).

Malalas, *The Chronicle of John Malalas*, trans. Elizabeth Jeffreys, Michael Jeffreys and Roger Scott (Byzantina Australiensia 4; Melbourne 1986).

Malchus, fragments ed. and trans. in R.C. Blockley, *The Fragmentary Classicising Historians of the Later Roman Empire* (Liverpool, 1983).

Marcellinus Comes, *The Chronicle*, trans. Brian Croke (Byzantina Australiensia 7; Sydney, 1995).

Maurice, *Strategicon*, trans. George T. Dennis (Philadelphia, 1984).

Menander Protector, *The History of Menander the Guardsman*, trans. Roger C. Blockley (ARCA 17; Liverpool, 1985).

Narratio de Aedificatione Templi S. Sophiae, trans. Cyril Mango, *The Art of the Byzantine Empire 312–1453: sources and documents* (Englewood Cliffs, 1972).

Paul the Deacon, *History of the Lombards*, trans. William Dudley Foulke (New York, 1907).

Paul the Silentiary, *Ecphrasis*; see *Three Political Voices*.

Priscian, *Panegyricus Anastasii*, trans. P. Coyne, *Priscian of Caesarea's De laude Anastasii imperatoris* (Lewiston, 1991).

Priscus, fragments ed. and trans. in R.C. Blockley, *The Fragmentary Classicising Historians of the Later Roman Empire* (Liverpool, 1983).

Procopius, *Buildings*, ed. and trans. H.B. Dewing (Loeb; Cambridge, MA., 1940).

Priscus, fragments ed. and trans. in R.C. Blockley, The Fragmentary Classicising Historians of the Later Roman Empire (Liverpool, 1983).

Procopius, *Secret History*, ed. and trans. H.B. Dewing (Loeb; Cambridge, MA., 1935).

Procopius, *Wars*, ed. and trans. H.B. Dewing (Loeb; Cambridge, MA, 1914–28); rev. trans. Anthony Kaldellis, *Prokopios, The Wars of Justinian* (Indianapolis, 2014).

Pseudo-Dionysius of Tel-Mahre, *Chronicle* Part III, trans. W. Witakowski (TTH 22; Liverpool, 1995).

Pseudo-Zachariah, *The Chronicle of Pseudo-Zachariah Rhetor: Church and War in Late Antiquity*, trans. G. Greatrex, R. Phenix, and C. Horn (TTH 55; Liverpool, 2011).

Syrianus, *De Re Strategica*, trans. G.T. Dennis, *Three Byzantine Military Treatises* (Corpus Fontium Historiae Byzantinae 25; Washington DC., 1985).

Theophanes, *Chronographia, The Chronicle of Theophanes Confessor*, trans. Cyril Mango and Roger Scott (Oxford, 1997).

Theophylact Simocatta, *History*, trans. M. and M. Whitby (Oxford, 1986).

Three Byzantine Saints, trans. E. Dawes and N. Baynes (London, 1948).

Three Political Voices from the Age of Justinian: Agapetus, Advice to the Emperor, Dialogue on Political Science, Paul the Silentiary, Description of Hagia Sophia, trans. P.N. Bell (TTH 52; Liverpool, 2009)

Vegetius, *Epitome Rei Militaris*, trans. N.P. Milner (2.ed., TTH 16, Liverpool, 1996).

Victor of Tunnuna, *Chronica*, ed. and trans. (Italian) Antonio Placanica, *Chiesa e impero nell'età di Giustiniano* (Florence, 1997).

Victor of Vita, *Victor of Vita. History of the Vandal Persecution*, trans. John Moorhead (TTH 10; Liverpool, 1982).

Zonaras, *Epitome Historiarum*, ed. L. Dindorf (Leipzig, 1870).

Modern Scholarship

Joseph D. Alchermes, 'Art and Architecture in the Age of Justinian', in Maas, *Age* 343–75.

S.E. Alcock, 'Roman Imperialism in the Greek Landscape', *JRA* 2 (1985) 5–34.

Pauline Allen, 'The Definition and Enforcement of Orthodoxy', in Averil Cameron et al., *CAH XIV* 811–34.

J.J. Arnold, *Theoderic and the Roman Imperial Restoration* (Cambridge, 2014).

Susan Ashbrook Harvey, *Asceticism and Society in Crisis. John of Ephesus and the Lives of the Eastern Saints* (Berkeley, 1990).

Jean Ch. Balty, 'Apamée au VIe siècle. Témoignages archéologiques de la richesse d'une ville', in J. Lefort and C. Morrisson (edd), *Hommes et richesses dans l'Empire byzantine IV-VI siècle* (Paris, 1989) I. 79–92.

Jonathan Bardill, 'The Date, Dedication, and Design of Sts. Sergius and Bacchus in Constantinople', *JLA* 10 (2017) 62–130.

Sam Barnish, A.D. Lee, and Michael Whitby, 'Government and Administration', in Averil Cameron et al., *CAH XIV* 164–206.

Franco Basso and Geoffrey Greatrex, 'How to Interpret Procopius' Preface to the *Wars*', in Lillington-Martin and Turquois, *Procopius* 59–72.

Peter N. Bell, *Social Conflict in the Age of Justinian. Its Nature, Management, & Mediation* (Oxford, 2013).

Peter Birks and Grant Mcleod, *Justinian's Institutes, translated with an Introduction and the Latin Text of Paul Krueger* (London 1987).

Sylvie Blétry, 'Guerre et paix sur l'Euphrate entre Perse et Byzance au temps de Justinien: *si vis pacem, para bellum*. Les apports de l'étude du cas historique et archéologique de Zenobia', in Eugenio Amato (ed.), *En Kalois Koinopragia. Hommages à la mémoire de Pierre-Louis Malosse et Jean Bouffartigue* (*Revue des Études Tardo-Antiques*, Suppl.3, 2014) 73–102.

R.C. Blockley, *East Roman Foreign Policy: Formation and Conduct From Diocletian to Anastasius* (Leeds, 1992).

———, 'Subsidies and Diplomacy: Rome and Persia in Late Antiquity', *Phoenix* 39 (1985) 62–74.

———, *Menander*, see Sources, Menander.

H. Börm *Prokop und die Perser: Untersuchungen zu den römischen-sasanidischen Kontakten in der ausgehenden Spätantike. Oriens et Occidens* 16 (Stuttgart, 2007).

———, '"Es war allerdings nicht so, das sie es im Sinne eines Tributes erheilten, wie viele meinten…" Anlässe und Funktion der persischen Geldforderungen an die Römer (3. bis 6. Jh.)', *Historia* 57 (2008) 327–46.

———, 'Justinians Triumph und Belisars Erniedrigung. Überlegungen zum Verhältnis zwischen Kaiser und Militär im späten Römischen Reich', *Chiron* 42 (2013) 63–88.

———, 'Procopius, His Predecessors, and the Genesis of the Anecdota: Antimonarchic Discourse in Late Antique Historiography', in H. Börm (ed.), *Antimonarchic Discourse in Antiquity* (Stuttgart, 2015) 305–45.

Glen Bowersock, *The Throne of Adulis: Red Sea Wars on the Eve of Islam* (Oxford, 2013).

David Braund, *Georgia in Antiquity: A History of Colchis and Transcaucasian Iberia, 550 BC–AD 562* (Oxford, 1994).

Sebastian Brock, 'The Orthodox-Oriental Conversations of 532', *Apostolo Barnaba* 41 (1980) 219–28.

———, 'The Conversations with the Syrian Orthodox under Justinian (532)', *Orientalia Christiana Periodica* 47 (1981) 87–121.

D. Brodka, 'Die geschischtsmächtigen Faktoren in den Historiae des Agathias von Myrina', *JÖB* 52 (2002) 161–76.

———, *Die Geschichtsphilosophie in der spätantiken Historiographie: Studien zu Prokopios von Kaisareia, Agathias von Myrina und Theophylaktos Simokattes.* (Studien und Texte zur Byzantinistik 5; Frankfurt, 2004).

Peter Brown, *The World of Late Antiquity* (London, 1971)

Robert Browning, *Justinian and Theodora* (London, 1971).

———, 'Education in the Roman Empire', in Averil Cameron et al., *CAH XIV* 855–83.

Timothy Bruce Mitford, *East of Asia Minor. Rome's Hidden Frontier* (Oxford, 2018).

J.B. Bury, 'The Nika Riot' *JHS* 17 (1897) 92–119.

———, *A History of the Later Roman Empire from the Death of Theodosius to the Death of Justinian* (London, 1923).

Alan Cameron, *Porphyrius the Charioteer* (Oxford, 1973).

———, *Circus Factions: Blues and Greens at Rome and Byzantium* (Oxford, 1976).

———, 'The House of Anastasius', *GRBS* 19 (1978) 259–76.

———, and A.M. Cameron, 'Christianity and Tradition in the Historiography of the Late Empire', *CQ* 14 (1964) 316–28.

Averil Cameron, 'The "Scepticism" of Procopius', *Historia* 15 (1966) 466–82.

———, 'Agathias on the Early Merovingians', *Annali della Scuola Normale Superiore di Pisa* ser.2.37 (1968) 95–140.

———, 'Agathias on the Sassanians', *DOP* 23–4 (1969–70) 67–183.

———, *Agathias* (Oxford, 1970).

———, *Procopius and the Sixth Century* (London, 1985).

———, 'Models of the Past in the late Sixth Century: The Life of the Patriarch Eutychius', in G. Clarke (ed.) *Reading the Past in Late Antiquity* (Canberra, 1990), 205–23; reprinted in ead., *Changing Cultures in Early Byzantium* (Aldershot, 1996) II.

———, (ed.), *The Early Byzantine and Islamic Near East III. States, Resources, Armies* (Princeton, 1995).

Averil Cameron, Bryan Ward-Perkins and Michael Whitby (edd.), *The Cambridge Ancient History XIV. Late Antiquity. The Empire and Successors, 425–600* (Cambridge, 2000).

Averil Cameron and Peter Garnsey (edd.), *The Cambridge Ancient History XIII. The Late Empire, AD 337–425* (Cambridge, 1997).

A. Christensen, *L'Iran sous les Sassanides* (Copenhagen, 1944).

Frank M. Clover, 'Felix Karthago', in F.M. Clover and R.S. Humphreys (edd.), *Tradition and Innovation in Late Antiquity* (Madison, 1989) 129-69.

Roger Collins, 'The Western Kingdoms', in Averil Cameron et al., *CAH XIV* 112–34.

I. Colvin, 'Reporting battles and understanding campaigns in Procopius and Agathias: classicising historians' use of archived documents as sources', in A. Sarantis and N. Christie (edd.), *War and Warfare in Late Antiquity* (Leiden, 2013) 571–97.

———, 'Comparing Procopius and Malalas', in Lillington-Martin and Turquois, *Procopius* 201–14.

Lawrence I. Conrad, 'The Arabs', in Averil Cameron et al., *CAH XIV* 678–700.

Salvatore Cosentino, 'Naval Warfare: Military, Institutional and Economic Aspects' in Yannis Stouraitis (ed.), *A Companion to the Byzantine Culture of War* (Leiden, 2018) 308–55.

Florin Curta, *The Edinburgh History of the Greeks, c. 500 to 1050. The Early Middle Ages* (Edinburgh, 2011).

Brian Croke, *Count Marcellinus and his Chronicle* (Oxford, 2001).

———, 'Justinian, Theodora and the Church of Saints Sergius and Bacchus', *DOP* 60 (2006) 25–63.

Brian Croke and J. Crow, 'Procopius and Dara', *JRS* 73 (1983) 143–59.

James Crow, Jonathan Bardill and Richard Bayliss, *The Water Supply of Constantinople* (London, 2008).

J.W. Crowfoot, 'Notes upon Late Anatolian Art', *Annals of the British School at Athens* 4 (1897/8) 79–94.

C. Dauphin, 'Mosaic Pavements as an Index of Economic Prosperity and Fashion', *Levant* 12 (1980) 112–34.

Beate Dignas and E. Winter, *Rome and Persia in Late Antiquity: Neighbours and Rivals* (Cambridge, 2007).

Jistre H.F. Dijkstra and Greg Fisher (edd.), *Inside and Out: Interactions between Rome and the Peoples on the Arabian and Egyptian Frontiers in Late Antiquity* (Leuven, 2014).

Hazel Dodge and Bryan Ward-Perkins (edd.), *Marble in Antiquity. Collected Papers of J.B. Ward-Perkins* (London, 1992).

J. Durliat, *Les Dédicaces d'ouvrages de défense dans l'Afrique byzantin* (Coll. de l'École Française de Rome 49; Rome, 1981).

Jas Elsner, 'The Rhetoric of Buildings in the *De Aedificiis* of Procopius', in Liz James (ed.), *Art and Text in Byzantine Culture* (Cambridge, 2007) 33–57.

Hugh Elton, 'Military Forces', in Sabin et al., *Cambridge History* 270–309.

J.A.S. Evans, 'Christianity and Paganism in Procopius of Caesarea', *GRBS* 12 (1971) 81–100.

———, 'The Attitudes of the Secular Historians of the Age of Justinian towards the Classical Past', *Traditio* 32 (1976) 353–58.

———, *The Age of Justinian. The Circumstances of Imperial Power* (London, 1996).

———, 'The Date of Procopius' Works: A Recapitulation of the Evidence', *GRBS* 37 (1996) 301–13.

Kaveh Farrokh, *The Armies of Ancient Persia. The Sassanians* (Barnsley, 2017).

Arther Ferrill, *The Fall of the Roman Empire. The Military Explanation* (London, 1986).

Moses Finley, *The Ancient Economy* (new ed., Berkeley, 1999).

Greg Fisher, 'The Political Development of Ghassan between Rome and Iran', *JLA* 2 (2008) 311–34.

Clive Foss, *Byzantine and Turkish Sardis* (Cambridge, MA., 1976).

———, *Ephesus after Antiquity. A Late Antique, Byzantine and Turkish City* (Cambridge, 1979).

———, 'The Near Eastern Countryside in late antiquity: a review article', in J. Humphrey (ed.), *The Roman and Byzantine near East: Some Recent Archaeological Research* (*JRA* suppl.14; Ann Arbor, 1995) 218–23.

———, 'The Lycian Coast in the Byzantine Age', *DOP* 48, 1994, 1–52.

W.H.C. Frend, *The Rise of the Monophysite Movement* (Cambridge, 1972).

Patrick Gray, 'The Legacy of Chalcedon. Christological Problems and their Significance', in Maas, *Age* 215–38.

Geoffrey Greatrex, 'The Dates of Procopius' Works', *BMGS* 18 (1994) 101–15.

———, 'The Nika Riot. A Reassessment', *JHS* 117 (1997) 60–86.

———, *Rome and Persia at War, 502–532* (ARCA 37; Leeds, 1998).

———, 'Lawyers and Historians in Late Antiquity', in R. Mathisen (ed.), *Law, Society, and Authority in Late Antiquity* (Oxford, 2001) 148–61.

———, 'Recent Work on Procopius and the Composition of Book VIII', *BMGS* 27 (2003) 45–67.

————, 'Malalas and Procopius', in M. Meier (ed.) *Die Weltchronik des Johannes Malalas* (Stuttgart, 2016) 169-85.

————, 'Life and Works', in M. Meier and F. Montinaro (edd.), *Companion to Procopius* (Leiden/Boston, forthcoming).

————, Richard Burgess, and Hugh Elton, 'Urbicius' Epitedeuma. An Edition, Translation, and Commentary', *BZ* 98 (2005) 35–74.

Geoffrey Greatrex and Samuel N. C. Lieu, *The Roman Eastern Frontier and the Persian Wars II, AD 363–630. A Narrative Sourcebook* (London, 2002).

A. Guillaumont, 'Justinien et l'église de Perse', *DOP* 23/4 (1969/70) 41–66.

John F. Haldon, *Recruitment and Conscription in the Byzantine Army c.550–950: a Study of the stratiotike ktemata* (Sitzungsberichte der Österreichischen Akademie, phil.-hist. Kl. 357; Vienna, 1979).

————, *The Byzantine Wars* (Stroud, 2001).

John Haldon, Hugh Elton, Sabine R. Huebner, Adam Izdebski, Lee Mordechai and Timothy P. Newfield, 'Plagues, Climate Change, and the End of an Empire: a Response to Kyle Harper's The Fate of Rome (1): Climate', *History Compass* 16.12 (2018).

John Haldon, Hugh Elton, Sabine R. Huebner, Adam Izdebski, Lee Mordechai and Timothy P. Newfield, 'Plagues, Climate Change, and the End of an Empire: a Response to Kyle Harper's The Fate of Rome (3): Disease, Agency, and Collapse, *History Compass* 16.12 (2018).

K. Hannestad, 'Les forces militaires d'après la guerre gothique de Procope', *Classica et Medievalia* 21 (1961) 136–83.

Jill Harries, *Law and Empire in Late Antiquity* (Cambridge, 1999).

Martin Harrison, *A Temple for Byzantium. The Discovery of Anicia Juliana's Palace-Church in Istanbul* (Austin, 1989).

Kyle Harper, *The Fate of Rome: Climate, Disease, and the End of an Empire* (Princeton, 2017).

Peter Heather, 'Cassiodorus and the Rise of the Amals: Genealogy and the Goths under Hun Domination', *JRS* 79 (1989) 103–28.

————, *Goths and Romans 332–489* (Oxford, 1991).

————, 'The Huns and the End of the Roman Empire in Western Europe', *English Historical Review* 110 (1995) 4–41.

————, *The Goths* (Oxford, 1996).

————, 'The Western Empire, 425–76' in Averil Cameron et al., *CAH* XIV 1–32.

————, *The Fall of Rome. A New History* (London, 2005).

————, *Empires and Barbarians. Migration, Development and the Birth of Europe* (London, 2009).

———, *Rome Resurgent. War and Empire in the Age of Justinian* (Oxford, 2018).

Michael Hendy, *Studies in the Byzantine Monetary Economy c.300–1450* (Cambridge, 1985).

Peregrine Hordern, 'The Justinianic Plague' in Maas, *Age* 134–60.

A.M. Honoré, 'Some Constitutions Composed by Justinian', *JRS* 65 (1975) 107–23.

———, *Tribonian* (London, 1978).

James Howard-Johnston, 'Procopius, Roman Defences North of the Taurus and the New Fortress of Citharizon', in D.H. French & C.S. Lightfoot (edd.) *The Eastern Frontier of the Roman Empire* (*BAR* Int. Series 553; Oxford, 1989) 203–28.

———, 'The Two Great Powers in Late Antiquity. A Comparison', in Averil Cameron, *States* 157–226.

———, 'Heraclius' Persian Campaigns and the Revival of the East Roman Empire, 622–630', *War in History* 6 (1999) 1–44.

Robert G. Hoyland, *Theophilus of Edessa's Chronicle and the Circulation of Historical Knowledge in Late Antiquity and Early Islam* (TTH 57, Liverpool, 2011)

———, *The 'History of the Kings of the Persians' in Three Arabic Chronicles. The Transmission of the Iranian Past from Late Antiquity to Early Islam* (TTH 69, Liverpool, 2018).

Caroline Humfress, 'Law and Legal Practice in the Age of Justinian' in Maas, *Age* 161–84.

S. James, 'The Fabricae: State Arms Factories of the Later Roman Empire', in J.C.N. Coulston (ed.), *Military Equipment and the Identity of Roman Soldiers* (Proceedings of the Fourth Roman Military Equipment Conference; Oxford, 1988) 257–331.

Elizabeth Jeffreys (ed.), *Studies in John Malalas* (Byzantina Australiensia 6; Sydney, 1990).

A. H. M. Jones, *The Later Roman Empire 284–602: A Social, Economic, and Administrative Survey* (Oxford, 1964).

Walter Kaegi, *Byzantine Military Unrest 471–873* (Amsterdam, 1981).

Kimberley Kagan, 'Redefining Roman Grand Strategy', *The Journal of Military History* 40 (2006) 333–62.

Anthony Kaldellis, 'The Historical and Religious Views of Agathias: a Reinterpretation', *Byz.* 69 (1999) 206–52.

———, *Procopius of Caesarea: Tyranny, History, and Philosophy at the End of Antiquity* (Philadelphia, 2004).

————, 'Procopius' *Persian War*: a thematic and literary analysis', in Ruth Macrides (ed.), *History as literature in Byzantium: papers from the Fortieth Spring Symposium of Byzantine Studies, University of Birmingham, April 2007* (Farnham, 2010) 253–273.

————, 'Byzantine historical writing, 500–920', in S. Foot and C.F. Robinson, with I. Hesketh (edd.), *The Oxford History of Historical Writing*, vol. 2 (Oxford, 2011–12) 201–17.

James Keenan, 'Egypt', in Averil Cameron et al., *CAH XIV* 621–37.

Chris Kelly, 'Emperors, Government and Bureaucracy', in Cameron and Garnsey, *CAH XIII* 138–83.

Elizabeth Key Fowden, *The Barbarian Plain, Saint Sergius between Rome and Iran* (Berkeley, 1999).

E. Kislinger and D. Stathakopoulos, 'Pest und Perserkriege bei Prokop. Chronologische Überlegungen zum Gesehen 540–545' *Byz.* 69 (1999) 76–98.

Derek Krueger, *Symeon the Holy Fool. Leontius' Life and the Late Antique City* (Berkeley, 1996).

Dan Lawrence and Tony J. Wilkinson, 'The Northern and Western Borderlands of the Sasanian Empire: Contextualising the Roman/Byzantine and Sasanian Frontier', in Sauer, *Sasanian Persia* 99–125.

A. D. Lee, *Information and Frontiers: Roman Foreign Relations in Late Antiquity* (Cambridge, 1993).

————, 'Evagrius, Paul of Nisibis and the Problem of Loyalties in the Mid-Sixth Century', *Journal of Ecclesiastical History* 44 (1993) 569–85.

————, 'Warfare and the State', in Sabin et al., *Cambridge History* 379–423.

————, *From Rome to Byzantium. The Transformation of Ancient Rome* (Edinburgh, 2013).

————, 'Food Supply and Military Mutiny in the Late Roman Empire', *JLA* 12 (2019) 276–94.

————, *Warfare in the Roman World* (Cambridge, 2020).

Paul Lemerle, *Byzantine Humanism: the First Phase. Notes and Remarks on Education and Culture in Byzantium from its Origins to the 10ᵗʰ Century*, trans. Helen Lindsay and Ann Moffat (Byzantina Australiensia 3; Canberra, 1986).

E. Leone, *Changing Townscapes in North Africa from Late Antiquity to the Arab Conquest* (Bari, 2007).

J.H.W.G. Liebeschuetz, *Barbarians and Bishops. Army, Church, and State in the Age of Arcadius and John Chrysostom* (Oxford, 1990).

————, *Decline and Fall of the Roman City* (Oxford, 2001).

————, 'Arab Tribesmen and Desert Frontiers in Late Antiquity', *JLA* 8 (2015) 62–96.

Detlef Liebs, 'Roman Law', in Averil Cameron et al, *CAH XIV* 238–59.

Christopher Lillington-Martin, 'Procopius on the Struggle for Dara in 530 and Rome in 537–38: Reconciling Texts and Landscapes', in Sarantis and Christie, *War* 599–630.

———, 'Procopius, *paredros/quaestor*, *Codex Justinianus*, 1.27 and Belisarius' Strategy in the Mediterranean', in Lillington-Martin and Turquois, *Procopius* 157–85.

Christopher Lillington-Martin and Elodie Turquois, *Procopius of Caesarea: Literary and Historical Interpretations* (Abingdon, 2018).

Lester K. Little (ed.), *Plague and the End of Antiquity: the Pandemic of 541–750* (Cambridge, 2007).

E.N. Luttwak, *The Grand Strategy of the Roman Empire* (Baltimore, 1976).

———, *The Grand Strategy of the Byzantine Empire* (Cambridge, MA., 2009).

Michael Maas, 'Roman History and Christian Ideology in Justinianic Reform Legislation', *DOP* 40 (1986) 17–31.

———, *John Lydus and the Roman Past. Antiquarianism and Politics in the Age of Justinian* (London, 1992).

———, (ed.), *The Cambridge Companion to the Age of Justinian* (Cambridge, 2005).

———, 'Roman Questions, Byzantine Answers: Contours of the Age of Justinian', in Maas, *Companion* 3–27.

R. MacMullen, *Corruption and the Decline of Rome* (New Haven, 1988).

Harry J. Magoulias, 'The Lives of Saints as Sources for Byzantine Agrarian Life in the Sixth and Seventh Centuries', *Greek Orthodox Theological Review* 35 (1990) 59–70.

Rowland Mainstone, *Hagia Sophia. Architecture, Structure and Liturgy of Justinian's Great Church* (London, 1988).

K. Maksymiuk, 'A New Proposal for the Identification of the Sasanian Commander Mermeroes of Byzantine Sources: Sapur of Ray from Mehran', in M.B. Panov (ed.), *The Byzantine Missionary Activity and its Legacy in Europe* (Skopje, 2017) 93–8.

———, 'The Two Eyes of the Earth: the Problem of Respect in Sasanid-Roman Relations', *GRBS* 58 (2018) 592–606.

Cyril Mango, *Byzantium: the Empire of New Rome* (London, 1980).

———, *Le développement urbain de Constantinople (IVe-VIIe siècles)* (Paris, 1985).

———, 'The Triumphal Way of Constantinople and the Golden Gate', *DOP* 54 (2000) 173–88.

Cyril Mango and Gilbert Dagron, *Constantinople and its Hinterland: Papers from the 27th Spring Symposium of Byzantine Studies* (Aldershot, 1995).

E.W. Marsden, *Greek and Roman Artillery, Historical Development* (Oxford, 1969).

J.R. Martindale, *The Prosopography of the Later Roman Empire II, A.D. 395–527* (Cambridge, 1980).

———, *The Prosopography of the Later Roman Empire III, A.D. 527–641* 2 vols. (Cambridge, 1992).

John Matthews, *The Roman Empire of Ammianus* (London, 1989).

———, *Constantinople* (forthcoming; Oxford, 2021)

D.J. Mattingly, *Tripolitania* (London, 1995).

Michael McCormick, *Eternal Victory. Triumphal Rulership in Late Antiquity, Byzantium and the Early Medieval West* (Cambridge, 1986).

———, 'Emperor and Court', in Averil Cameron et al., *CAH XIV* 135–63.

Otto Mazal, *Justinian I und seine Zeit. Geschichte und Kultur des Byzantinischen Reiches im 6. Jahrhundert* (Cologne, 2001),

Mischa Meier, *Das andere Zeitalter Justinians* (Göttingen, 2003).

———, 'Die Inszenierung einer Katastrophe: Justinian und die Nika-Aufstand', *Zeitschrift für Papyrologie und Epigraphik* 142 (2003) 273–300.

———, *Justinian. Herrschaft, Reich und Religion* (Munich, 2004).

M. Meier and F. Montinaro (edd.) Brill's *Companion to Procopius* (Leiden, forthcoming).

Volker Menze, *Justinian and the Making of the Syrian Orthodox Church* (Oxford, 2008).

Andy Merrills and Richard Miles, *The Vandals* (Chichester, 2010).

Fergus Millar, 'Rome, Constantinople and the Near Eastern Church under Justinian: Two Synods of C. E. 536', *JRS* 98 (2008) 62–82.

Stephen Mitchell, *Anatolia, Land, Men and Gods in Asia Minor II. The Rise of the Church* (Oxford, 1993).

Yves Moderan, 'L'Afrique reconquise et les Trois Chapitres', in C. Chazelle and C. Cubitt (edd.), *The Crisis of the Oikoumene: the Three Chapters and the Failed Quest for Unity in the Sixth-Century Mediterranean* (Turnhout, 2007) 39–83.

John Moorhead, *Justinian* (London, 1994).

———, *Theoderic in Italy* (Oxford, 1992).

James Murray, 'Procopius and Boethius: Christian Philosophy in the *Persian Wars*', in Lillington-Martin and Turquois, *Procopius* 104–19.

James J. O'Donnell, *The Ruin of the Roman Empire* (New York, 2008).

Fatih Onur, 'The Anastasian Military Decree from Perge in Pamphylia: revised 2nd edition', *Gephyra* 14 (2017) 133–212.

David A Parnell, 'The Social Networks of Justinian's Generals', *JLA* 8 (2015) 113–35.

———, *Justinian's Men: Careers and Relationships of Byzantine Army Officers, 518–610* (London, 2017).

Richard Payne, 'Cosmology and the Expansion of the Iranian Empire, 502–628 CE', *Past & Present* 220 (2018) 3–33.

Charles Pazdernik, 'War and empire in Procopius' *Wars*', forthcoming in Meier and Montinaro, *Companion*.

———, 'Justinianic ideology and the power of the past', in Maas, *Age* 185–214.

———, 'Reinventing Theoderic in Procopius' *Gothic War*', in Lillington-Martin and Turquois, *Procopius* 137–53.

Maxime Petitjean, 'Classicisme, barbarie et guerre romaine: l'image du cavalier dans le monde roman tardif', *Antiquité Tardive* 22 (1914) 255–62.

Walter Pohl, 'Justinian and the Barbarian Kingdoms' in Maas, *Age* 448–76.

———, *The Avars: A Steppe Empire in Central Europe, 567–822* (Ithaca, 2018).

David Potter, 'Anatomies of Violence: Entertainment and Violence in the Eastern Roman Empire from Theodosius I to Heraclius', *Studia Patristica* 60 (2011) 61–72.

———, *Theodora. Actress, Empress, Saint* (Oxford, 2015).

Andrew Poulter, *The Transition to Late Antiquity on the Lower Danube. Excavations and Survey at Dichin, a Late Roman to Early Byzantine Fort and Aqueduct* (Oxford, 2019).

Price, *Acts*: see Sources, *Acts of the Council of Constantinople*.

Richard Price, *The Council of Ephesus of 431, Documents and Proceedings* (TTH 72, Liverpool, 2020).

Price and Gaddis, *Acts*: see Sources, *Acts of the Council of Chalcedon*.

Denys Pringle, *The Defence of Byzantine Africa from Justinian to the Arab Conquest: an Account of the Military History and Archeology of the African Provinces in the Sixth and Seventh Centuries* (BAR Int. series 99.i; Oxford, 1981).

John H. Pryor and Elizabeth Jeffreys, *The Age of the DROMON: the Byzantine Navy ca. 500–1204* (Leiden, 2006).

Avner Raban and Kenneth G. Holum, *Caesarea Maritima. A Retrospective after Two Millenia* (New York, 1996).

Philip Rance, 'Drungus, *drouggos*, and *drouggisti*: A Gallicism and Continuity in Late Roman Cavalry Tactics', *Phoenix* 58 (2004) 96–130.

———, 'Narses and the Battle of Taginae (Busta Gallorum) 552: Procopius and Sixth-century Warfare', *Historia* 54 (2005) 424–72.

———, 'Battle', in P. Sabin et al., *Cambridge History* 342–78.

———, 'The Date of the Military Compendium of Syrianus Magister (formerly the Sixth-century Anonymous Byzantinus)', *BZ* 100 (2008) 701–37.

———, 'Maurice's *Strategicon* and the 'Ancients': the Late Antique Reception of Aelian and Arrian', in Philip Rance and Nicholas V. Sekunda (edd.), *Greek Taktika: Ancient Military Writing and its Heritage* (Gdansk, 2017) 217–55.

Giorgio Ravegnani, *Soldati di Bisanzio in età giustinianea* (Rome, 1988).

———, *Soldati e guerre a Bisanzio* (Rome, 2009).

Ian A. Richmond, *The City Wall of Imperial Rome* (Oxford, 1930).

C. Robin, 'Arabia and Ethiopia', in Scott Johnson (ed.), *The Oxford Handbook of Late Antiquity* (Oxford, 2012).

Alan J. Ross, 'Narrator and Participant in Procopius' *Wars*', in Lillington-Martin and Turquois, *Procopius* 73–90.

Charlotte Roueché, *Aphrodisias in Late Antiquity* (*JRS* Monographs 5; London, 1989).

Ze'ev Rubin, 'The Reforms of Khusro Anushirwan', in Averil Cameron, *States* 227–97.

———, 'The Sasanid Monarchy', in Averil Cameron et al., *CAH XIV* 638–61.

Philip Sabin, Hans van Wees and Michael Whitby (edd.), *The Cambridge History of Greek and Roman Warfare II. Rome from the Late Republic to the Late Empire* (Cambridge, 2007).

G.E.M. de Ste. Croix, 'The Council of Chalcedon' in Michael Whitby and Joseph Streeter (edd.), *Christian Persecution, Martyrdom, and Orthodoxy* (Oxford 2006) 259–319.

Alexander Sarantis, 'Tactics: a bibliographic essay', in Sarantis and Christie, *War* 177–207.

———, *Justinian's Balkan Wars. Campaigning, Diplomacy and Development in Illyricum, Thrace and the Northern World, A.D. 527–65* (ARCA 53; Leeds, 2016).

———, 'Romans or Barbarians? Ethnic Identities and Political Loyalties in the Balkans According to Procopius', in Lillington-Martin and Turquois, *Procopius* 217–37.

———, 'Military Provisioning in the Sixth-Century Balkans', *JLA* 12 (2019) 328–65.

Alexander Sarantis and Neil Christie (edd.), *War and Warfare in Late Antiquity. Current Perspectives* (Leiden, 2013).

Peter Sarris, 'The Justinianic plague: origins and effects', *Continuity and Change* 17 (2002) 169–82.

———, *Economy and Society in the Age of Justinian* (Cambridge, 2006).

Eberhard W. Sauer (ed.), *Sasanian Persia: Between Rome and the Steppes of Eurasia* (Edinburgh, 2017).

Eberhard Sauer, Hamid Omrani Rekavandi, Tony J. Wilkinson and Jebrael Nokandeh, *Persia's Imperial Power in Late Antiquity: the Great Wall of Gorgan and the Frontier Landscapes of Sasanian Iran* (British Institute of Persian Studies, Archaeological Monographs 2; Oxford, 2013).

Eberhard Sauer, Jebrael Nokandeh, Konstantin Pitskhelauri and Hamid Omrani Rekavandi, 'Innovation and Stagnation: Military Infrastructure and the Shifting Balance of Power between Rome and Persia', in Sauer, *Sasanian Persia* 241–67.

Roger Scott, ''The Classical Tradition in Byzantine Historiography', in Margaret Mullett and Roger Scott (edd.), *Byzantium and the Classical Tradition* (Birmingham, 1981) 61–74.

Irfan Shahîd, *Byzantium and the Arabs in the Sixth Century* (Washington, 1995).

Brent D. Shaw, 'War and Violence', in G.W. Bowersock, Peter Brown and Oleg Grabar (edd.), *Interpreting Late Antiquity. Essays on the Postclassical World* (Cambridge, MA., 2001) 130–69.

Anne Sheppard, 'Philosophy and Philosophical Schools', in Averil Cameron et al. *CAH XIV* 835–54.

J.-P. Sodini et al., 'Déhès (Syrie du Nord): campagnes I-III (1976–1978). Recherches sur l'habitat rural', *Syria* 57 (1980) 1–304.

Claire Sotinel, 'Emperors and Popes in the Sixth Century, the Western View', in Maas, *Age* 269–90.

Pat Southern and Karen R. Dixon, *The Late Roman Army* (London, 1996).

C.J. Stallman-Pacitti, *Cyril of Scythopolis: a Study in Hagiography as Apology* (Brookline, MA., 1990).

Ernst Stein, *Histoire du Bas-Empire* vol.2 (Paris, 1949).

Dionysios Stathakopoulos, *Famine and Plague in the Late Roman and Early Byzantine Empire: a Systematic Survey of Subsistence Crises and Epidemics* (Aldershot, 2004).

I. Syvänne, *The Age of Hippotoxotai* (Tampere, 2004).

J.L. Teall, 'The Barbarians in Justinian's Armies', *Speculum* 40 (1985) 294–322.

E.A. Thompson, *A History of Attila and the Huns* (Oxford, 1948).

R.W. Thomson, 'Armenia in the Fifth and Sixth Century', in Averil Cameron et al., *CAH XIV* 661–77.

W. Treadgold, *Byzantium and its Army* (Stanford, 1995).

Bryon C.P. Tsangadas, *The Fortifications and Defense of Constantinople* (New York, 1980).

J.J. van Ginkel, *John of Ephesus, A Monophysite Historian in Sixth-Century Byzantium* (D.Litt. dissertation, Rijksuniversiteit Groningen, 1995).

Peter van Nuffelen, 'The Wor(l)ds of Procopius', in Lillington-Martin and Turquois, *Procopius* 40–55.

Lucas van Rompay, 'Society and Community in the Christian East', in Maas, *Age* 239–66.

A.A. Vasiliev, *Justin the First. An Introduction to the Epoch of Justinian* (Cambridge, MA, 1950).

K.A. Ward, M. Crapper, K. Altüg and J. Crow, 'The Byzantine Cisterns of Constantinople', *Water Supply* 17 (2017) 1499–1506.

Bryan Ward-Perkins, 'Land, Labour and Settlement' in Averil Cameron et al., *CAH XIV* 315–45.

———, 'Specialized Production and Exchange' in Averil Cameron et al., *CAH XIV* 346–91.

Connor Whately, 'The Genre and Purpose of Military Manuals in Late Antiquity', in G. Greatrex and H. Elton (edd.), *Shifting Genres in Late Antiquity* (Farnham, 2015) 249–261.

———, *Battles and Generals. Combat, Culture, and Didacticism in Procopius' Wars* (Leiden, 2016).

———, 'Procopius and the Characterization of Bessas: Where History Meets Historiography", in Lillington-Martin and Turquois, *Procopius*, 123–136.

———, 'Procopius on the Siege of Rome in AD 537/538', in Jeremy Armstrong & Matthew Trundle (edd.), *Brill's Companion to Sieges in the Ancient Mediterranean* (Leiden, 2019) 265–84.

Robin Whelan, *Being Christian in Vandal Africa: the Politics of Orthodoxy in the Post-Imperial West* (Oakland, 2018).

Mary Whitby, 'On the Occasion of a Ceremony in mid-sixth century Constantinople: *candidati, curopalatus, silentiarii, excubitores* and others', *Historia* 36 (1987) 462–88.

Michael Whitby, 'Procopius' Description of Martyropolis', *Byzantinoslavica* 45 (1984) 177–82.

———, 'Justinian's Bridge over the Sangarius and the Date of Procopius' *de Aedificiis*', *JHS* 105 (1985) 129–48.

———, 'The Long Walls of Constantinople', *Byz.* 55 (1985) 560–83.

———, 'Procopius and the Development of Roman Defences in Upper Mesopotamia', (*BAR* Int. Ser. 297; Oxford, 1986) 717–35.

———, 'Procopius' Description of Dara (*Buildings* II.1–3)', *ibid.* 737–83.

———, 'Notes on some Justinianic Constructions', *Byzantinisch-Neugriechischen Jahrbücher* 23 (1987) 89–112.

———, *The Emperor Maurice and his Historian. Theophylact Simocatta on Persian and Balkan Warfare* (Oxford, 1988).

———, 'Procopius and Antioch', (BAR Int. Ser.553; Oxford, 1989) 537–53.

———, 'Recruitment in Roman Armies from Justinian to Heraclius (*ca.* 565–615), in Averil Cameron, *States* 61–124.

———, '*Deus nobiscum*: Christianity, Warfare and Morale in Late Antiquity', in M.M. Austin, J.D. Harries & C.J. Smith (edd.), *Modus Operandi, essays in honour of Geoffrey Rickman* (London, 1998) 191–208.

———, 'The Violence of the Circus Factions', in K. Hopwood (ed.), *Organised Crime in Antiquity* (London 1999) 229–53.

———, 'The Army, *c.* 420–602' in Averil Cameron et al., *CAH XIV* 288–314.

———, 'The Balkans and Greece, 420–602', in Averil Cameron et al., *CAH XIV* 701–30.

———, *Rome at war AD 229–696* (London, 2003).

———, 'The Church Historians and Chalcedon' in G. Marasco (ed.), *Greek and Latin Historiography in Late Antiquity* (Leiden, 2003) 447–93.

———, 'Emperors and Armies, A.D. 235–395' in Simon Swain and Mark Edwards (edd.), *Approaching Late Antiquity. The Transformation from Early to Late Empire* (Oxford, 2004) 156–86.

———, 'War and State in Late Antiquity; some economic and political connections' in B. Meissner, O. Schmitt, & M. Sommer (edd.), *Krieg – Gesellschaft – Institutionen. Beitraäge zu einer vergleichenden Kriegsgeschichte* (Stuttgart, 2005) 355–85.

———, 'Factions, Bishops, Violence and Urban Decline', in J.-U. Krause & C. Witschel (edd.), *Die Stadt in der Spätantike – Niedergang oder Wandel?* (*Historia Einzelschrift* 190; Stuttgart, 2006) 441–61.

———, 'Religious Views of Procopius and Agathias', in Darius Brodka and Michal Stachura (edd.), *Continuity and Change. Studies in Late Antique Historiography. Electrum* 13 (Krakow, 2007) 73–93.

————, 'The Role of the Roman Army in the Defence of the Balkans' in A. Poulter (ed.), *The Transition to Late Antiquity*, (*Proceedings of the British Academy* 41; London, 2007) 135–61.

————, 'Army and Society in the Late Roman World: a Context for Decline?', in Paul Erdkamp (ed.), *A Companion to the Roman Army* (Chichester, 2011) 515–31.

————, 'Procopius' Missing Year', forthcoming in *Byzantion* 91 (2021).

————, 'Ancient Rome: Principate to Late Antiquity (27 BCE-AD 630)', in Beatrice Heuser and Isabelle Duyvesteyn (edd.), *The Cambridge History of Strategy* (Cambridge, 2021) vol. 1 ch. 10.

Mark Whittow, 'Ruling the Late Roman and Early Byzantine City: a Continuous History', *Past and Present* 129 (1990) 3–29.

————, 'Rome and the Jafnids: Writing the History of a 6th-c. Tribal Dynasty', in J. Humphrey (ed.), *The Roman and Byzantine Near East: some Recent Archaeological Research* (*JRA* suppl. 31; 1999) 207–24.

Chris Wickham, *Early Medieval Italy. Central Power and Local Society 400–1000* (London, 1981).

Index